Handbook
for Storytellers

"I Know an Old Lady" told with an automotive drip pan used as a magnetic board

Handbook for Storytellers

CAROLINE FELLER BAUER

AMERICAN LIBRARY ASSOCIATION
Chicago, 1977

Design by Vladimir Reichl

Pen-and-ink drawings by Kevin Royt

Library of Congress Cataloging in Publication Data

Bauer, Caroline Feller.
    Handbook for storytellers.

    Includes bibliographies and index.
    1. Story-telling—Handbooks, manuals, etc.
I. Title.
LB1042.B38   372.6'4   76-56385
ISBN 0-8389-0225-1

For
P E T E R
who made
"... and they lived happily ever after"
a reality

Contents

Figures

Preface

When I was in the third grade my best friend and I would walk to the local library each Wednesday afternoon to hear stories. I don't remember the library or even the storyteller, but I do remember the stories and how we laughed at the ridiculous, cried at the sad, or shuddered in terror over the fearful. I too wanted to tell stories when I grew up. Now that I am an adult, I do tell stories, but I find that my ambitions have expanded; I want others to tell stories too.

Storytelling today is an increasingly organized activity. In my own family two of my grandparents were superb storytellers and two were excellent listeners. Oral narration in my grandparents' world, as it was in Homer's, was something like a cottage industry—a storyteller was trained at home and passed the art on to the next generation. However, just because we now train storytellers in organized courses and volunteer programs doesn't mean that the art no longer exists. When I was taking a course at the Cordon Bleu Cooking School in Paris, many of my French friends were astonished that such a formal cooking school existed in their country. They had learned to cook at home. Here, in the United States, despite the availability of packaged cake mixes and frozen food, much meal preparation still involves cooking. Cooking is still taught in some homes; in homes where it is not, those who want to learn must go out and take lessons somewhere else. The same is true of the art of storytelling. If you don't get at-home training, then you have to find training elsewhere. This handbook will not only start you in your schooling, it also will introduce you to some of the techniques and resources you need to develop and extend your storytelling skills.

Innovation and change characterize our way of life. Even the basic definition of storytelling is constantly changing. The oral interpretation of literature and folklore can now be only part of the definition, because oral narration by a single storyteller to an individual listener or group is merely one way of telling a story. Puppets, records, television, creative drama are among the ways the storyteller reaches out and tells a story. The sources we use usually come from printed material. Nevertheless, the origin of most of the tales we tell lies in the oral tradition.

The purpose of this handbook is to help you learn how to present literature to children, young adults, and adults through storytelling. It explores, in an introductory fashion, the many different ways you can use supportive media to tell a story. I hope it will be useful to beginning as well as advanced storytellers, to parents and to professionals. As you read through this book for the first time, jot down the ideas you think you might like to try. Then start planning your first storytime program.

visiting storyteller at the New York Public Library. Since 1972, she has had her own weekly storytelling program, *Caroline's Corner,* on KOAC/KOAP-TV in Portland, Oregon, sponsored in part with a grant from the Oregon Library Association. Before that, she was a storyteller on television and radio in both Portland and Aspen, Colorado.

The range of Dr. Bauer's interests and activities is almost phenomenal. She is a member of such diverse professional organizations as the Puppeteers of America, the Society of American Magicians, the American Folklore Association, the National Council of Teachers of English, and the American Library Association.

Dr. Bauer lives in Tigard, Oregon, with her husband, Peter, her daughter, and a Bedlington terrier named Susie. Her "leisure time" activities include skiing (as a member of the National Ski Patrol), tennis, horseback riding, kayaking, drawing, and cooking.

Photograph by Anthony Capone

Jacket design by Kevin Royt
Photography by Sidney Pivecka

Thank you,

DON BRODIE, *friend fantastic*
MARY NORMAN, *colleague extraordinary*
SYLVIA ROYT, *editor supreme*

PART ONE

Getting Started

There is no point in learning a story if you are not going to get a chance to tell it to someone, somewhere. This section introduces you to some of the procedures involved in finding an audience and provides locations for the story program. If you have already been involved with story programming you might feel that this part of the book is unnecessary for you, but perhaps you should just browse through it anyway. Maybe you could use it as a checklist to refresh your memory. Remember the last time you took a vacation and you forgot to take your tooth brush? This section reminds you to take your tooth brush and toothpaste, too!

1 / Some Suggestions on Planning

You'd like to try storytelling. How do you start? By learning a story? By finding an audience to hear the story? One of the problems with modern storytelling is that we tend to get excited about program content, leaving little time for the less interesting but important details of planning.

Planning could begin with the location of the program, remembering that the potential audience may range from preschool children to senior citizens. A book program can be held in many different locations and for a variety of different occasions, wherever people gather. Here are just a few possibilities:

Libraries
Hospitals
County fairs
Classrooms
Little League practice
Neighborhood garage sales
Playgrounds
Birthday parties
Detention centers
Senior citizens' clubs
Backyards
Shopping center malls
Your own home
Churches
Child-care centers
Firehouses

Craft fairs
Police stations
Boy Scout, Girl Scout,
    Campfire Girl meetings
Opening of a new building
Christmas tree lighting
    ceremony
Moonlight sales
Art festivals
Adult club meetings
Book fairs
Saturday markets
School buses during field trips
A community outing:
    the 4th of July breakfast?
    the water carnival?

Sometimes it pays to use your imagination to find a location for a planned or spur-of-the-moment storytime. There you are at the ball field with your Little League team, waiting for last year's champions to arrive to play this season's Big Game. The members of your team are nervous and excited. What do you do? *Tell a story!*

Choosing the site and the occasion for your storyhour is only the beginning. You must also determine the age of your target audience, for you may want to divide the program by age groupings or combinations of groups. And, finally, you must decide whether a single program or a series of programs aimed at a specific audience is your goal. You may plan a single story session and find that it develops into a weekly or monthly event. On the other hand, you may miscalculate the needs of the community and find that a series is simply not needed. Often the location itself will dictate the type of program to present.

Age Groups

Preschool and Primary Programs

The preschool storytime is for children, aged three to five, who enjoy simple stories, songs, and books. Many of these children, if attending school at all, do not attend full time and are an eager audience for any organized entertainment. Programming for this age group is usually strongly supported by parents who are looking for activities outside the home—especially if these are book-oriented. If you are a teacher of preschool or primary children, storytime is undoubtedly a daily activity in your classroom. It is through stories, poems, and songs that children acquire information as well as an appreciation for the written word and fine illustration.

Children in the primary grades, the five- to eight-year-olds, are also active listeners. The classroom is a perfect place to hold storyhours for these youngsters. If you are a public librarian or church-group leader you may be tempted to include both preschool and primary children for one storyhour, especially if the groups can be kept small. Keep in mind, however, that most primary-grade children are able to listen longer and understand on a higher level than preschool children. One of the objectives of the programs will be to teach the audience to listen to more complicated stories. This comes about as children become more accustomed to listening.

The Middle Grades

The children who are in grades four through seven also enjoy book- and story-oriented programs and are old enough to appreciate longer folktales and myths. Members of this age group like to belong to organized clubs (Boy Scouts, Girl Scouts, Camp Fire Girls, etc.) and provide a ready-made audience. Approached by means of good publicity, a loyal storytelling following can be built in the library or other designated location.

Programs for middle-graders may be of a traditional and formal nature, but they may also afford an opportunity for experimentation with media as well as with group participation.

Young Adult Programming

Stories from traditional literature, poetry, and excerpts from contemporary books will probably be the most popular program offerings for teen-agers and young adult groups. Another exciting aspect of the oral presentation of literature may be employed by introducing this group to the book-talk technique which uses storytelling as well as reading aloud in a planned program. Young adults may be reached in the classroom, in the library, or through special interest clubs.

Adult Programming

The idea of holding storyhours for adults seems almost revolutionary in today's world. It is hard to imagine that a few generations ago stories were told almost exclusively for the enjoyment of adults; the presence of children, if allowed at all, was merely tolerated. Adults today enjoy stories just as much as they once did and just as much as children. Men's and women's clubs might welcome oral presentations of literature. Retirement homes will be delighted to hear the old familiar stories in a modern setting. Parents, as a group, present a particular challenge since they may want to attend adult storytelling festivals, but will also welcome special children's programs, because they are parents.

Family Storyhours

If you have a professional interest in storytelling because you are a teacher or librarian, or a volunteer in a hospital, club, or day-care center, use your art and perfect your skills with your own family. Start a family storytelling tradition. Choose a night to relax and enjoy stories or read aloud as a family affair. Don't limit these sessions to the preschoolers at home either. The entire family can enjoy a good story well told. As the children grow up they can tell stories of their own or take turns at reading alternate chapters aloud. If Mom is home with the children most of the time, ask Dad to read aloud. Don't reserve those creative multimedia storytelling projects for your work at the day-care center. Treat your own family to an evening of production stories too.

Now think in terms of families where you work. Would it be feasible to plan some family programs at your school or library? Our local public library has well-attended family evenings featuring a film, a guest artist, or a story-teller. The families come to enjoy the program, punch and cookies, and some casual get-together conversation. At the end of one recent program there even was a flurry of activity at the reference desk when one of the business-men present suddenly remembered that he had been meaning to get to the library to look up some facts. An entertaining program, some socializing and simple refreshments, and the availability of useful information and refer-ence sources add up to an enthusiastic library patron and supporter.

Program Techniques

Single Program or Series Planning

The division of groups by age is just one possibility of programming. If you are a public librarian, for instance, you may want to simply schedule an event and welcome whoever comes. Obviously, a program scheduled for 10 AM Wednesday morning during the school term will attract mainly pre-schoolers, their mothers or sitters. On the other hand, a 9 PM program will almost certainly exclude the preschoolers. Keep in mind that planning a young adult program on the eve of a championship basketball game is a sure way to reduce the attendance at your program, unless you advertise it as a "Down-with-Basketball" event for the antiathletes.

In a way, it is easier to plan for an entire series of programs than a single program. Promotion for a single evening of poetry takes the same amount of time and effort as promotion for an entire series of guest artist appearances. If you decide on a series of after-school children's programs, I suggest that you plan a set session of storyhours for a limited period, perhaps once a week for six weeks. This will enable you to plan six outstanding programs without feeling the pressure of "putting on a show" every week forever. Series plan-ning also enables you to begin with simple stories and poems at the outset of the series and advance to more sophisticated and longer stories at the end. Such planning also enables you to estimate the number of children that may attend each program in the series.

Should the demand and your energy seem to warrant another series, you can begin a new series almost immediately. Probably many of the same chil-dren will continue to come to the next series, but since your earlier series was a great success, the new one will attract some new faces. If too many chil-dren sign up for a given session or series, they can be placed on a waiting list for the next time. Don't be tempted to serve too many children at once. It is far better to serve a small group well than a large group inadequately.

You will probably find that participation tends to be more constant with a series. Signing up for a series is rather like signing up for a course and implies a certain obligation on the part of those children and parents who come. If you are a classroom teacher or school librarian with a captive audience you might also consider scheduling in terms of a series. A series not only provides you with the opportunity for progressively teaching your audience to listen and participate, it also forces you to plan your material well in advance.

Before you schedule your program series, find out what other offerings there are in the community. Autumn, when school reopens, may be a good time for beginning a new storyhour series, but the children and their parents may be overwhelmed with choices then. Sometimes there is a restless period after Christmas. That might be the perfect time for book programs. Spring could be a poor time for indoor activities in your area because then children may be eager for more physical activity out of doors. On the other hand, in some communities regularly organized activities come to an end in the spring, and this could be just the right time for a new storyhour series. In some situations, such as in the suburban community where I now live, the summer months are among the library's busiest. The children are anxious for organized activities and attend the summer library programs with great enthusiasm. In other places library attendance may slacken off in the summer because the children are away at camp or vacationing with their parents.

Special Events

Occasionally you will want to schedule a special program to honor a particular group, to celebrate a holiday, to commemorate an anniversary or some other event. Traditional holidays such as Christmas, Thanksgiving, or Halloween often inspire such a storyhour. There are also minor holidays such as Arbor Day, birthdays of favorite authors or artists, as well as intriguing holidays of your own invention, perhaps Magic Day (when you may tell stories featuring magicians), Haiti Day (the day you will tell stories from Haiti or the Caribbean), or any other special "day" you decide to celebrate with stories.

Dial-A-Story

Preschoolers delight in playing with the telephone, but ordinarily have no one to call. Capitalizing on this preoccupation and introducing the children to stories and the library can be accomplished with a Dial-A-Story program.

The San Francisco Public Library as part of the Library's Early Childhood Education Project successfully planned a weekly program for two- to five-year-olds. In this program young children are encouraged to call a designated telephone number to hear a three-minute story that is changed each week.

To begin such a project contact the local telephone business office. A knowledgeable service representative will explain the various methods of providing this popular service. Careful planning is necessary. You also must have the storytelling personnel capable of recording the stories and sufficient phone lines to handle the incoming calls.

One small Oregon county library used county recreational funds to rent two recording playback machines to play into two telephone lines. The Dial-A-Story program seemed such a good idea that the plan was covered by the neighboring big city newspapers and television stations. The county library was thrilled that they were being noticed until the city children began calling in to hear stories, overloading and tying up project and home phones so that no one was properly served. The moral is if you have limited equipment, keep the audience small. It is better to serve a smaller population with quality service than a large metropolitan region with mediocre to poor service.

Storytelling Festival

Another special event to consider is a Storytelling Festival planned for adults only, for children only, or for a mixed age group. The festival can feature stories from a particular country or region or stories centered around a single theme or subject. The program can be put on by a lone storyteller or by a group of storytellers, and concurrent sessions may be held to keep the groups small.

A special springtime festival is held for the children's librarians at New York Public Library. Stories are told to the librarians by selected storytellers new to the system as well as by a few oldtimers. In schools throughout the State of Oregon an Arts Day held each spring features short sessions with talented local artists and storytellers. Plan a festival for your school, staff, or community.

The Activity Program

Yet another type of storytelling program features the formal telling of stories, followed by a period in which the audience participates by playing games or making things that are related to the stories. This kind of program with specific examples is more fully described elsewhere in this handbook.

Preplanning

Once you've decided to whom, when, and where you will tell your stories, you must concentrate on working out all the other details of your program.

Physical Location

Give careful consideration to the physical location of the program in your planning. If the storyhour will take place in a park, try to select a shady area, or at least a quiet one. Obviously it is less desirable to try to compete with the noise of traffic or the cheer and whoops of the playground or a baseball game. This means that you should select a story site during the same time of day that the program will take place, not on a romantic moonlit night when the park is devoid of children.

A hospital storytime may present additional considerations. It might mean telling tales to a bedridden audience which would eliminate some of the usually desirable eye contact, but would nevertheless be gratefully received.

In a library or school the program takes on an added dimension when it is given in a completely separate room, which should be nearby the main room if at all possible. However, be adaptable. Sometimes, particularly as a visiting storyteller, your heart may drop as you enter a proposed storytelling site, but it could and often does turn out to be a good experience for you and your audience. Once I drove in a dreadful rainstorm to a campsite to put on a program. I was the first one to arrive. There I found only a bare bulb hanging from a ceiling in a leaking, chairless barn and I said to myself, "What a good place to tell a ghost story." Yet, when the campers arrived, the whole atmosphere changed. They were wet but attentive and receptive, and the gloom I had anticipated never materialized.

My first stories were told when the New York Public Library's Central Children's Room was located at 42nd Street. The storyhour was held in another room, two flights up. Led by an assistant, the children would slowly make their way up the stairs and down a long corridor to the storyhour room. There the storyteller was waiting behind closed doors for the magic signal. A child was chosen to knock three times on the door. The storyteller slowly opened the door, invited the children in, and the storyhour began. It must have been a real adventure, even for sophisticated New York children, to be led through marble halls up stairs to this special room, and added something to the storyhour, even though it seemed inconvenient to the library staff.

When I was a branch librarian in the same system, storyhours were held in a dusty attic piled high with broken, unused furniture. At first, from my adult point of view, it seemed an entirely unattractive place; but when I saw the children's reactions of awe and wonder, I realized what a splendid story room it really was. Not many of the apartment-dwelling children who came to my storyhour had ever seen a real attic let alone spent time in one. I'm certain that those stories were long remembered in part because of the magical atmosphere in which they were told.

Equipment Checklist

If you plan to do any multimedia storytelling you will surely need equipment of some kind. After you decide on your program, be sure to arrange for the equipment you will need—an easel, a felt board, a slide projector and screen—to carry it out successfully. Although it seems obvious to suggest that you will have to use the proper projector to show a film, filmstrip, or slides, don't forget to check whether the room can be adequately darkened. Of course you also must know how to run the projector or find someone else who can before the program. Make sure you know where the electrical outlets are and whether an extension cord will be needed. Set up chairs, exhibits, and equipment well before the audience arrives.

Favors and Treats

A souvenir passed out to each member of the audience to take home will transform a storyhour program into a truly memorable event. Obviously it is not feasible or even advisable to provide a memento at each program; however, I personally love to give gifts. When I find something appropriate and timely, I like to hand it out after the program.

Bookmarks make useful favors. They can be used to impart information about the books available in the library, announce a future story session, or serve as a written program. Almost any object, however simple or ordinary, can take on significance in association with a story. Once, after I had told the Japanese story "Momotaro" about the little boy who came out of a peach pit, I gave everyone a peach pit saved from summer and sprayed with gold. A local printer provided the small paper pads I handed out after telling "The Nuremburg Stove," a story about an aspiring artist. A suitable favor need not even cost anything more than some creative effort on your part. The French story *Stone Soup,* adapted and illustrated by Marcia Brown (Scribner, 1947), suggests that each child in the audience go home with a pretty stone you collected on your last trip to the beach.

Holidays naturally lend themselves to gift giving and also avail children an opportunity to make and give gifts. A birthday candle to celebrate Hans Christian Andersen's birthday or dried pumpkin seeds to handcraft a Halloween necklace could be given as holiday favors. Origami, the age-old Japanese art of paperfolding, can be used in conjunction with storytelling to create a variety of animals and interesting objects that make lovely presents. Why wait for a traditional holiday? Originate a special event of your own to celebrate. Teach the children step by step how to make a frog after you tell them "The Frog Prince" to observe Kindness Day, a holiday you invented to remind everyone about the Golden Rule.

Sometimes something to eat is the magic ingredient needed to round out a program. Obviously you cannot feed a hundred or so children at an assembly, nor should you consider providing an edible treat for every program in a series, even if you could afford to do so. It just seems very appropriate, even irresistible, on occasion. Fortune cookies to accompany a Chinese New Year celebration or cheese slices to nibble on after you tell Adelaide Holl's *Moon Mouse* (Random, 1969) are only two of many possible treats suggested by the stories you tell.

Decorations and Exhibits

Recall a bygone era—the wind whistling around the eaves of a stone house built on the heath, light from a peat fire flickering on the storyteller; Granny in her rocking chair, and all the listeners crowded close. This nostalgic and picturesque scene exists mostly in our imaginations. What we are really seeing or reacting to is the ambience evoked by the storyhour, more often than not presented in the somewhat humdrum environment of a classroom or library. It is up to the storyteller to create a particular mood or feeling and convey it to an audience. Sometimes a change to a natural setting such as a backyard or a court, the library steps, even a different arrangement of the chairs will provide the right background or generate the feeling of anticipation we want for our stories. The use of exhibits and decoration is yet another way to conjure up a desired mood or produce a different frame of reference.

Table Exhibit

A table placed behind the storyteller makes a handy "shelf" for the storyhour exhibit. A solid colored tablecloth on the table will add a festive air and a welcome touch of color to the room. Now you have a place to display the storyhour "wishing candle" in its special candleholder, a vase of cut flowers

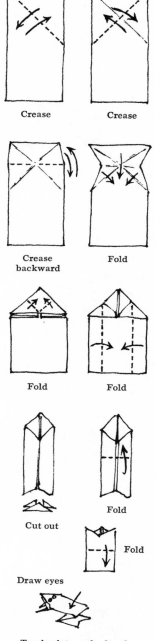

Crease   Crease

Crease backward   Fold

Fold   Fold

Cut out   Fold

Draw eyes

Tap back to make frog hop

or a growing plant, and the books that the stories you will tell come from. Use well-arranged fresh cut flowers whenever possible. They not only add a gracious tone to the program, but also provide an esthetic experience for those children who rarely see cut fresh flower arrangements in their homes.

If you have just one object to represent a particular story (an old-fashioned iron cooking pot representing "The Wonderful Pot" or an hourglass as a symbol for the "Lost Half Hour"), it can be effectively displayed on the storytime table. This symbolic artifact should not, however, be so intriguing that everyone's attention is drawn to the table instead of the storyteller. This kind of exhibit is more decorative than informational, rather like the flower borders or illuminated letters in a book. There is no need to mention the fact that the object relates to the stories you are telling, for your listeners should make the connection on their own. A few may come up after the stories to examine the item at a closer range. If you do have a story-related object which you feel would be too distracting, share it with your group at the end of the session. At one time I kept a fully furnished doll house on permanent display in the storyhour room. One day as I was giving a book talk on stories about dolls, eyes started turning to look at the doll house in the corner of the room. I suppose the children were looking to see if the doll family were walking around inside the house. Now I've learned to bring the doll house to the front of the room as a display, but only when I want it to be the focus of attention.

A Storytelling Symbol

Create an individual symbol that instantly proclaims "Storytime!" and use it to decorate the corner or room in which you tell stories. Consider making a standing screen ornamented with book covers or character cutouts to symbolize the storyhour and also serve as a backdrop to your stories. A wall hanging or felt banner complete with your storytelling logo that can be brought out from a closet and hung on the wall or fastened to a stand is another way to personalize your classroom or club program (*see* fig. 1). Encourage the children to design a storyhour logo for the banner you or the "Friends of the Library" will sew. A large black spider on a field of red could represent Anansi, the African spider that "owns all the stories"; a felt cutout of a candle representing the storytime wishing candle might be another choice of program symbol.

An almost life-sized book character, a clown, or an animal cut from plywood or constructed from papier mâché to stand at the entrance to the storyhour area could become a permanent storyhour symbol. This special figure

Figure 1. Handmade appliquéd banner used as the storytime symbol

Figure 2. *Sylvester and the Magic Pebble* displayed on a plywood model of the book's hero

Figure 3. Handmade character dolls for the storytime corner: Raggedy Ann, Tweedledee and Tweedledum, Peter Rabbit, and Babar

Laura, heroine of the *Little House* series

might hold the book or books you are going to use in your next story program or it could be used to hold a sign announcing an upcoming storyhour special (*see* fig. 2).

Even a stuffed doll can serve as a storyhour symbol. One of my students made a four-foot-high Laura Ingalls Wilder doll to use in her storyhour. Raggedy Ann, Tweedledum and Tweedledee, Peter Rabbit, and Babar are other student-made storybook character dolls that children will recognize, identify with, and enjoy.

If you use cushions instead of chairs for storytelling you may want to have a permanent collection of cushions (each individually decorated by the children in your school or by the "Friends of the Library" group). These could be embroidered, painted with textile paints, or appliqued with storybook characters and used exclusively for storytime. Examples are shown in figure 4.

Figure 4. Cushions for the storyhour. Represented here is the heroine of *Harriet the Spy*. Cushions represent *A Natural History of Giraffes*, *Little Red Riding Hood*, and *There's a Nightmare in My Closet*

For Special Storyhours

It's Christmas! Valentine's Day! Halloween! Or the day you've planned to tell stories from China or Spain, about dogs or the circus. It's a special storyhour. Why not make it even more special by decorating the room with student-made murals, artifacts, posters, or seasonal decorations? If you are lucky enough to have a separate room for your storyhours you can really be creative in your decorations. Make your room cozier by stringing figured or patterned bed sheets around the walls of the room, changing the room's character entirely. Caution! Don't attempt to use this total decoration idea too often, and try to steer away from those trite, commercially produced items available at card shops and party-goods counters.

The Exhibit as Part of the Storyhour

Occasionally you will find that you or a friend own a particular collection relevant to the story you are telling. Decide on the best way to display these artifacts. If they are to be displayed on a table, put them behind the children so that they are not tempted to look instead of listen. If the things are valuable, or fragile, and therefore not touchable, make sure that you can exhibit them in locked glass cases to protect them. Perhaps you may choose first to tell the story and then show an artifact or collection. For instance, I collect anything and everything that has to do with Little Red Riding Hood: antique mugs, lantern slides, dolls, miniatures, wall hangings, advertising cards, whatever. Naturally, if I tell Little Red Riding Hood or a variant of the story I like to show some of the things in my collection as part of the storyhour. Since the "story is the thing," I try not to let the exhibit overpower the telling of the story, but use it only to increase an awareness of the different ways that artists and artisans interpret a traditional tale.

Bulletin Boards

Don't overlook the potential of the permanent bulletin board that may be hanging in the story room. Often a permanent bulletin board is an unsightly mess covered with notices of events long since over. Use the bulletin board to your advantage. It can publicize the next story session or be used as a display area to decorate for the book program. Don't permit displays or announcements on the bulletin board to become a permanent part of the room's decoration. It should be changed periodically and completely or you are not using it effectively. Even if you are announcing the same event, use the same information with a different arrangement and vary your materials from one time to another—fabrics, felt, tissue paper, construction paper, cut-out letters, small objects are all suitable and potentially eye-catching.

If you want your bulletin board display to be effective:

> Keep it simple; the crowded configuration placed among the usual bulletin board clutter is asking to be ignored.
>
> Keep it bright; happy colors gladden the passerby's eye.
>
> Use three-dimensional objects; the unexpected captures attention.
>
> Be sure your lettering is neat and professional; don't ruin artwork and displays with amateurish lettering.
>
> Don't keep the same display up too long; too long is when you no longer look at it admiringly.

And after you take down a display or exhibit, store its salvageable parts for future reuse. Experience will prove that recycling the reusable saves effort as well as time.

Picture Sources for Exhibits and Craft Projects

Many of the exhibits and craft ideas mentioned in this handbook need pictures. Naturally you will want such pictures to be associated with the books you use in your storyhour programs. Either draw your own or look for what you need in one of the picture sources that follow.

It is important to start collecting potentially useful pictures and other things because you never know when a really exciting idea for a program will come to mind. Then when it does, you can go to the "goodies" drawer or cabinet and pull out what you need to make that idea a reality, rather than begin the long, tedious, and often fruitless search for the right items. Who knows, perhaps your collection, as it grows, will suggest what your next program will be. These collections are also useful for creating exhibits, favors, and treats.

Rule One. Do NOT throw away any usable picture source, for you may find that you have just tossed out a potential program idea. Set aside a spare drawer or box to save pictures for later use; better still, keep an organized picture file by subject. Don't wait till you need a picture. You won't find it then.

Junk mail. Are you inundated with unwanted junk mail at your house? An advertisement for a forthcoming travel book or a land development corporation often yields some lovely color photographs. Mail-order catalogs also contain pictures of almost anything you might need.

Publishers' catalogs. Catalogs from publishers often contain small reproductions of their books and are an excellent source of book-oriented material.

Conference pickups. If you attend library or education conferences and walk around the exhibits, you will return home with an armful of handouts—bookmarks, prints, advertisements, and posters—materials often illustrated with pictures of and from your favorite books.

Discarded books. Are your picture books becoming tattered and torn? When you replace them, be sure to save any potentially useful pictures.

Stamps. Foreign and domestic stamps often have outstanding pictures on them. Ask your friends to save their stamps for you.

Greeting cards. Stationery is becoming so attractive that it's a shame to use it only once—to send a message. Save all the tasteful greeting cards you receive. Christmas cards, valentines, or friendly notes all are potential sources of colorful pictures.

Magazines. Those of us who grew with *Life* magazine can only mourn its passing since it was a major pictorial resource. However, there are still many fine magazines published. Before you throw away a magazine, clip and file interesting pictures.

Photographs. Did you take pictures of your last book week activities, summer book activities, book fair? Photographs are pictures, too, although we sometimes think of them as something to store separately.

Original drawings. Pictures drawn by you, by a talented staff member, or by children are the most personal illustrations of all and provide a magnificent contrast to the commercialism of some of today's advertising art.

Sale books. In your browsing around the sale tables of the local bookstore, take the opportunity to flip through a beautifully illustrated book of animals, art, travel, or a specialized subject. You know that you'll never actually read such a book, but it could contain a wealth of pictorial source material. Don't let your upbringing (*never* destroy a book) keep you from cutting up a book for a much better use.

Garage sale books. Your next-door neighbors may provide you with an excellent choice of titles in good condition. Look over the weekend ads listing garage sales and stop at the houses that are having garage and moving sales. You will often find available at nominal cost among the items for sale books that children feel they have outgrown. Those that you don't add to your collection can be cut up for crafts and exhibit projects.

Wrapping paper. If you received a beautifully wrapped gift for your birthday, save the paper. Don't throw it away or put it in your wrapping paper drawer. (Is anyone that organized?) Think of it as a potential picture source.

Stickers. These are usually imported and available at gift counters in animal, flower, and abstract designs. Stay away from the "cute" or the obvious. No use putting your energy into something that won't be artistically superior to the slap-dash, prosaic art of the commercial.

Postcards. When you receive a lovely postcard from a traveling friend, don't be envious, be thankful. Then save the card for future use in your story-hour program.

Wallpaper samples. Ask your local paint and wallpaper dealers to save their discontinued wallpaper samples for you. These discards are a valuable source of materials for storyhour projects.

Antique advertising cards. As you browse through the thrift shops, antique shows, and garage sales in your area, keep your eyes open for old advertising and merit cards. Some are considered collector's items and may be fairly expensive. Others are real bargains and make charming pictures for storytime projects.

Coloring books. Today there are published a great variety of story-related coloring books that will provide you with quality outline drawings for your art projects.

Photocopied pictures. The copy machine can be used to reproduce your favorite storybook illustrations. Color these with felt pens or watercolors if you prefer color to black and white.

Lettering Aids for Exhibits and Bulletin Boards

After you have expended a considerable amount of time and energy planning and assembling an exhibit, it really is a pity to spoil it with crude, amateurish lettering. Unless you are skilled at lettering, your posters, bulletin board displays, and exhibit signs will look better and more professional if you use a lettering device, precut letters and numbers, or transfer letters and numbers to get your message across. Ask your local art supply dealer, school supply dealer, or stationer for suggestions on how to make your lettering jobs easier and more professional-looking. Following is a partial listing of lettering aids that are available through your local stationer or art supply store or write directly to the manufacturer to find the address of a supplier in your area. Check the catalog of your library or school supplies dealer for lettering aids you can order by mail.

LIBRARY/SCHOOL SUPPLIERS
(refer to catalog of supplier)

Beckley-Cardy Co.
1900 N. Narragansett Ave.
Chicago, IL 60639

Demco Educational Corp.
Box 1488
Madison, WI 53701

Dick Blick Co.
P.O. Box 1267
Galesburg, IL 61401

The Highsmith Co., Inc.
P.O. Box 25, Highway 106 East
Fort Atkinson, WI 53538

Josten's
Library Services Div.
1301 Cliff Rd.
Burnsville, MN 55337

Macmillan Arts and Crafts
9520 Baltimore Ave.
College Park, MD 20740

STENCILS, LETTERING KITS,
TEMPLATES

Dennison (Lettering Guides)
Framingham, MA 01701

Duro Decal Co. (Stencils)
1832 Juneway Terrace
Chicago, IL 60626

E-Z Letter Stencil Co.
P.O. Box 829
Westminster, MD 21157

Pickett Industries (Templates)
17621 Von Karmen Ave.
Irvine, CA 92705

Rapid Design (Templates)
Box 6039
Burbank, CA 91510

WRICO Kits and Supplies
Wood-Regan Instrument Co.
Nutley, NJ 07110

PLASTIC LETTERS

Western Specialty Mfg.
Cheyenne, WY 82001

MAGNETIC LETTERS

American Guidance Service
Publisher's Bldg.
Circle Pines, MN 55014

Fisher-Price
East Aurora, NY 14052

Weber-Costello Co.
1900 N. Narragansett Ave.
Chicago, IL 60639

VINYL LETTERS

Dennison
Framingham, MA 01701

PRESSURE-SENSITIVE, DRY TRANSFER,
AND RUB-ON LETTERS

Artype, Inc.
343 E. Terra Cotta Ave.
Crystal Lake, IL 60014

Chartpak
Leeds, MA 01053

E-Z Letter-Quik Stik Co.
P.O. Box 829
Westminster, MD 21157

Letraset U.S.A., Inc.
33 New Bridge Rd.
Bergenfield, NJ 07621

Prestype, Inc.
194 Veteran's Blvd.
Carlstadt, NJ 07072

CUTOUT POSTERBOARD LETTERS

Duro Decal Co.
1832 Juneway Terrace
Chicago, IL 60626

Almost everyone enjoys a story, whether it is told or read, but not every story will appeal equally to everyone who hears it. For that reason, keep in mind that there are going to be occasions when you will be unable to please or capture the attention of someone in the audience. Remember that tastes do vary and that no two children are or ever will be impressed with the same things at the same time. In fact, you may never know what has impressed a child. It could be your voice, the language of the story you've just told, its characters, its plot, your gestures or lack of them, the flowers on the table, the doll that represents the story's central character, or the special story-related activity you provided afterward.

Your enthusiasm for the stories you share, your evident enjoyment of the books from which you select those stories, and the rapport you establish with an audience and each of its members may stimulate some of the nonreaders among them to read a book or two themselves. And this could be habit-forming, which makes all the planning you do and all the effort you expend on your program worthwhile.

2 / The Storyteller

Assume you are organizing a storytime program. Who will you find to actually tell the stories or give the book talks? You, first of all. Anyone can learn to tell a story, but, like any other worthwhile endeavor, to do this well takes effort and time. This handbook can only give you hints and suggestions for preparing and you are the one who must implement its ideas. Although you will probably enjoy being part of your own programs, there will be times when you will want or need to involve others.

The Guest Storyteller

A guest storyteller may make a storyhour special by providing a welcome change of pace as well as briefly relieving you of your storytelling responsibilities. Look for storytelling talent at your local college theater department and amateur theater group or among the retired teachers and librarians in your community. Many professional people really enjoy participating in an ongoing program, and the busier they are the better. Some may not have time to spare for your group and probably will tell you so when you ask. Still, if you establish contact but are turned down with a "maybe some other time," be sure to call again.

Of course, the "proper" way of approaching an outside speaker is to write a letter, but the efficient and personal way is to visit or use the telephone. In my experience, it is more difficult to turn down a telephoned or person-to-person request than a letter. A letter is much too easily answered with a "no."

Incidentally, you should be aware that prominent professionals often charge for their services. If you don't have enough money for a fee or expenses, don't be discouraged. A speaker might want to reach your group for his or her own reasons—to become better known in your community, to publicize an event of his or her own, for public service, or the best reason of all, for enjoyment.

In your initial contact with a potential guest be explicit about what you want. Give complete details of what is involved: where the program will take place, who the audience is, how much time is involved, and whether you expect the guest to attend a dinner or autograph party. Make certain that you are clear about any financial arrangements. Will you pay for transportation, arrange for a room, pay a speaker's fee or honorarium? All these facts will help the potential guest decide whether to accept or reject the invitation and to plan his or her involvement in the subsequent program.

Don't expect all potential performers in the storyhour program to be professionals. You may find possible guests almost anywhere—the browser in the children's area at the bookstore or the person sitting next to you at a dinner party may provide you with a lead to just the program guest you have been looking for. If the banjo player, the radio announcer, or the amateur magician you meet casually has never before performed for children but finds the prospect intriguing, she or he may spend extra time and effort to prepare for your audience. How do you determine whether a guest will be a smash hit or a flop? Before you delegate the responsibility of an entire program to an untried performer, "audition" him or her first in a segment of one of your programs. However, it is really better to take a chance and risk being disappointed than to lose a volunteer talent by default.

An incidental benefit of having a guest storyteller is that he or she may invite you to do a return program. A reciprocal invitation enables both of you to tell the stories you have learned to new audiences. If you have been meaning to take time to learn some new stories but just haven't gotten around to it, you may find that an invitation as a guest to another group is just the incentive you need to prepare a new story or finish that scratch film you started months ago.

Guestmanship

Before the program. After your guest has agreed to come, make certain that you follow up with a written reminder of the date, time, and place well before the day of the event. By doing this you not only inform your guest when and where he or she is expected, you also avoid disappointing your audience and yourself because of a possible misunderstanding.

Some speakers appreciate being told exactly what you want them to do. Others want to be told only the time, the place, the size of the group, and its composition (ages, interests). Try as much as possible to cater to a guest's desires and needs. However, sometimes you, the program organizer, have more suitable ideas than the guest. Some time ago I was asked to take part in a week-long arts festival. The organizer wanted all the performers to meet together to plan how they would relate to each other. It was a very ambitious and probably valid idea, but I was simply too busy to take part in the planning. We never did get together, which may have been a mistake. The festival attracted many children and with more preplanning, could have been even better than it was. Another time I was asked to be a dinner speaker at a banquet. It seemed to me that a committee member called daily about my talk. I even had a visit from the banquet chairman inquiring if I had composed my speech yet. At first I was annoyed but in the end was delighted, for he had many ideas geared to make the evening a grand success. He encouraged me to duplicate a handout for the guests. We jointly decorated the tables with ceramic figures of characters from children's books. The door prize was the book I featured in my talk. Without continued communication we wouldn't have been able to coordinate our efforts.

If a guest comes from out of town and must stay overnight or for a meal, be hospitable and make sure he or she feels at home and at ease. Try to have someone meet the guest at the airport or bus station, and, if possible, arrange for meals at private homes. However, always check with the guest beforehand. He or she may prefer a quick meal at the hotel coffee shop and an early-to-bed evening.

Once, during a week's lecture tour far from home, I arrived at the airport of the first of my scheduled stops with three large trunks of exhibit materials. No one was on hand to meet me and there were no messages. Worrying and uncertain about whether I was in the right town on the right date, I took a taxi to the hotel. Eventually someone did contact me there, but with this unsettling experience my trip started off on the wrong note.

After the program. Be sure to send a follow-up thank you to the guest. It may be appropriate to mention some of the favorable comments that you heard. This is always appreciated. It also reestablishes contact in the event you want to invite your guest back.

Volunteers

A Storytelling Guild

A successful storytelling program doesn't just happen, as the Storytelling Guild of Medford, Oregon, proves. It takes organization and hard work. The program began some years ago when Myra Getchell, the children's librarian at the public library in Medford, gathered together five interested women to help plan and contribute to the library storyhours. Originally the volunteers limited their efforts to the central county library and a school or two. When they discovered that there were neighborhood children playing in the streets who were unaware of the library's storyhours, they recruited and trained other volunteers and organized mobile storytelling units to go to the children.

Today, several years later, in addition to the library and school storyhours, mobile story units make forty scheduled stops in a once-a-week, ten-week spring storytelling program series that reaches 7,000 children. Not only do the decorated storymobiles (privately owned cars, by the way) carry books and, occasionally, live animals, their programs include puppet shows and group singing in addition to traditional storytelling. Each week storytellers go to the Head Start Center, and at Christmastime every Head Start child receives a book of his or her own as a present. One or two storytellers also will go to local birthday parties in return for a small donation to the Storytelling Guild.

As if all this was not enough activity for one group, the guild also holds an annual children's festival. The first year the festival was financed as a joint project by the Jackson County Library System and the Medford American Association of University Women. The $50 it cost to put on that first festival was repaid from the 25¢ admission fee. Although the guild had planned for 50 to 100 children a day for the three days, a total of 1,500 actually came. Several years later the attendance had swelled to 11,000! A thousand volunteers helped put on a recent festival which now includes ballet, mime, puppetry, storytelling, an animal fair, arts and crafts, Pageant Wagon Theater plays, and a poetry tree.

In the arts and crafts section of the festival there are separate booths where children can create do-it-yourself projects from materials donated by local merchants. My daughter came home with a batik hanging, a sandcasting, stitchery, a carpentry project, a dried plant arrangement, macaroni jewelry, and a clay sculpture. She had danced Greek dances and eaten Greek food (each year another country is featured), seen a puppet show, participated in a creative dramatic presentation of *The Wizard of Oz*, and listened and listened to stories under a storytelling tree.

The Storytelling Guild of Medford is headed by a board of directors that includes the editor of its newsletter, *The Satchel* (donation, $2), a consultant from the public library, a director of party storytelling, a director of storymobiles, a director of school storytelling, Head Start storytelling, and the children's festival director. Every other year a storytelling forum featuring workshops and a guest speaker is held for the member-volunteers and potential guild members.

Obviously, the activities of such an ambitious group take an enormous amount of planning. Potential members of the guild are put through a training session in order to determine individual talents, and each member is encouraged to contribute in her own way: driving storymobiles, baking cookies, sewing costumes, making puppets, or telling stories. Why not try this in your own community? At least three other towns in Oregon have profited from Medford's example with festivals of their own.

Remember that training is an essential element in any volunteer program. Take the time to properly educate for quality programming. Good leadership and the reactions of delighted children should attract volunteers who will take their job seriously. It is unnecessary to begin your volunteer program with something as ambitious as a storytelling guild. Start with a few friends or colleagues. Organizations such as "Friends of the Library," the PTA, or the professional women's club could well be excellent sources of "storytelling power." Don't be discouraged if some of your recruits are not good storytellers. They may have other talents you need. Perhaps they can help with publicity, arrange for transportation, or make props. The National Story League, an organization dedicated to the art of storytelling, could be another source of volunteers. Write to Hazel G. Krouse, 414 Fifty-eighth St., Altoona, PA 16602, to find out if there is a local chapter in your community.

Plan the volunteer program with care and creativity and you will be rewarded with smoothly run storytimes.

Student Storytellers

You may discover that some of the older children and young adults who have been coming to your storyhours at the library, school, church, or club are as interested in learning and telling stories as you are. Since these young people are potential volunteers, consider organizing a storytelling class for them. Keep the class small. If you limit your learner's group to as few as three to no more than ten children, its members will be assured of your personal attention and guidance. It is important for members of the group to feel at ease with one another and this is best accomplished when the group is small.

Begin their training by letting them perform informally by telling jokes, describing their families, or relating school experiences. Tell them a story or anecdote yourself or perhaps invite a guest. You may want to begin with a discussion of what makes a good story or what makes a good storyteller (I don't do this myself; I go right to work). Explain that there are different types of stories (i.e., folktales, fables, myths, epics, and modern short stories) that are suitable. Show the student books that will provide story ideas and encourage them to browse and read through these, and decide which stories they would like to learn, beginning, as you did, with something short and simple. Make sure you have the time to devote to helping each child individually from the beginning. Give them each a chance to be heard and encourage them to practice on each other to develop their proficiency and gain self-confidence. To help your students select appropriate stories, provide them with a list of stories particularly suited to the beginner.

Permit the student who is ready to perform to tell his or her story all the way through. Don't interrupt to make suggestions. Take notes as you listen. Be responsive. Don't frighten a novice performer with a frozen or disdainful expression on your face. Be sure to say something positive about each performance when it is over. Point out any common faults, those shared by other student performers, but do not permit a situation to develop in which everyone acrimoniously criticizes everyone else. To pinpoint and correct particular faults, talk privately to each child.

If you have access to a videotape machine, this is a good time to put it to use, for the students can each tell a story and see themselves as others see them. Although videotaping may be a frightening experience, it can also be a great deal of fun and makes performing in front of a live audience seem easy.

Working one story over and over again to perfection can be boring. Let each student try a variety of stories in the shelter of the group. When an individual seems comfortable in front of his or her friends, then you might begin to work more seriously with the idea of performance. Try to work individually with each student to build confidence.

To whom can the students tell stories? Fifth graders can tell them to third graders, seventh graders to fourth graders, and second graders can entertain high school seniors. Wherever an adult can tell stories, your student group should be welcome too: hospital wards, the public library, day-care centers, and playgrounds.

If administrators and teachers are reluctant to take time away from other activities to permit your group to tell stories, approach and convince them personally. After the initial storyhour success make plans for another, for by then the administrator will have heard that the program was enthusiastically received. Don't let success go to your head. Be cautious about performing in front of an assembly or other large group. Storytelling is for small intimate groups, not mobs. Even the most experienced storyteller finds it difficult to effectively show his or her art to a group of a hundred or more people.

Keep the program brief. Twenty minutes is more than enough. It is not necessary to coordinate the program around a theme, for each storyteller can tell his or her story in turn. However, opening and closing with a song might help to give cohesiveness to the program. Let your students travel together. They can take comfort in each other's presence, and half the fun is discussing the experience later. A storytelling class can be a useful elective in a junior high or high school curriculum. After all, the students actually are studying literature, folklore, theater, and a child-care activity, all in one class.

3 / Promotion

What if you planned a storyhour and nobody came? If it was your first storyhour you might even feel relieved for a moment or two. But of course the real purpose of the book program, reaching the children, would have been lost. Part of planning and producing an event is thinking and doing something about publicity. How many children can your storyhour room comfortably accommodate? Is it better to have a small, interested group of the same age or a larger group of children of mixed ages in the audience? Is it better to publicize a single, special event or an entire series? What is the purpose of the publicity? Is it a public relations campaign for your organization or is it an invitation to the public to come and enjoy a particular event? These are all questions which deserve careful consideration.

For instance, I once put on a very special storyhour in a branch of the New York Public Library, a Winnie the Pooh program. I arranged for a soprano from the Juilliard School of Music, who happened to be a clerk in the library, to sing the Fraser-Simson *Songs of Pooh* and I was to recite A. A. Milne's poems between her selections. Obviously I wanted a good attendance for this special occasion. My publicity, although crude, drew 150 children, in contrast to our regular storyhours which usually attracted an audience of 20 or so! Everyone in the entire branch ran about borrowing chairs to accommodate the overflow crowd. The program was worth every bit of effort. Afterward, I heard a little boy say to his sister, "I'll remember that my whole life." Without publicity, these two children might not have been there at all.

Another time, when I was teaching at the university, I planned an evening storytelling festival for adults, for which I invited five former students and two talented professors to perform. Naturally, I wanted people to come. The room assigned to us held 150 but thanks to the publicity, 300 people jammed the room while another 100 or so sat on the steps outside! The university's resourceful audiovisual technician set up a loudspeaker so that the stepsitters could at least hear what was going on inside. Surely this evening can be considered a huge success. Weren't all those people who came exposed to the art of storytelling? In retrospect, this program probably was overpublicized and undoubtedly frustrated some adults who weren't able to really experience the flavor of storytelling at all.

Undeniably, publicity for an event is almost as important as planning the program itself, but keep in mind that whatever you choose to do will involve spending some money. Your expenditures need not be high, for there are many ways of achieving effective, low-cost publicity. Your promotional efforts can range from informal notices posted on bulletin boards to paid commercial advertising. Planning and budgeting for publicity gives you an opportunity to exercise your imagination and involve all of your staff (if you have one) or your friends and family. Unfortunately, only experience can tell you which method of publicity will reach your potential audience. And although at the time all those people squeezing into that university room seemed a disaster, it was thrilling to think that all those people wanted to hear folk stories. How did we do it? This chapter is filled with ideas for you.

Posters

It may seem obvious, but be sure that the posters you make clearly spell out the *name* of the event, the *time*, the *date*, and the *place!* You may also want to include such information as names of performers, or a phone number for additional details.

Always keep in mind that posters are advertisements on which the information you want to disseminate should be clearly presented by means of eye-catching graphics. At the same time, beware of the prevailing trend to make poster art so "mod," so unconventional that the message it is supposed to convey becomes lost in the design. The problem is to make your poster both different *and* clear. Try a new shape. Make it three-dimensional by attaching objects to it—boxes, fabric dolls, dried flowers, feathers. Look at signs around your town and take especial note of any that you have been ignoring and ask yourself why. Have they been in the same spot too long? Do they contain too much information? Are their colors drab? Are they in the wrong place? Analyze each problem to avoid making a similar mistake.

The most important element in poster composition is good lettering. Your best friend (whom you may have cajoled into "creating" for you) may be a wonderful artist; but if he or she cannot letter well by hand, then you do it. Today there are available a number of quick and easy ways to do a professional job of lettering—with stencils, cutout wood, plastic, or cardboard letters, stick-on letters, and transfers. There really is no excuse for crude or illegible lettering on your posters or displays.

After all the work you've put in on your poster, you will want to find exactly the right place to hang it. If you are working in an institution—a school, church, or clubhouse—you should certainly place your posters around your building. But be sure to look beyond that conventional bulletin board where others usually tack their announcements. Discover a new place—perhaps a telephone booth, the ceiling of a classroom, the stairwell wall, the entrance door to the building—all are potential exhibit spaces for your eye-catching graphics.

Outside the building, ask shopkeepers for window space, but consider where you are most likely to attract the audience you are aiming for: the ice cream store, variety shop, toy shop, local bar, hardware store, or garden shop? No use wasting posters. And don't forget to go back and remove your signs after the event is over.

Minisigns

Even in our literate society there are numerous people who automatically ignore any printed matter that is put in front of them. To capture this otherwise oblivious audience, try placing tiny signs, 1 inch by 2 inches or smaller, in obvious places. Make your minisigns on some easily *removable* material, such as masking tape or small peel-off labels and attach to doorknobs, the top step, locker doors, milk cartons, toothpick holders, salt shakers, or on the library checkout counter. Use your imagination and these tiny advertisements for a blitz minicampaign.

Souvenirs and Bookmarks

Give something away. People wonder why you're doing it, which is why they read any attached advertising copy. A souvenir need not be expensive; it can be a cut flower, a peanut in a shell, a pine cone, or a sea shell. Hanging on the "present" is a small announcement of the upcoming event. Be imaginative and make the giveaway appropriate to the program theme. Are you having a pet show or a storyhour featuring dogs? Give away a dog biscuit. Are animal stories on the program? Animal crackers make fine souvenirs. Indian stories today? A small colorful bead may well end up a cherished gift. Any small present, especially if unexpected, is endowed with a certain magic. Children especially enjoy getting something, no matter how trivial and adults at least will be curious about why they are being handed a present. Keep in mind that because it is an adult who drives or brings a child to the storyhour, or reminds him or her that "today is the day," your efforts to reach adults are worthwhile.

Bookmarks are eminently suitable giveaways, especially so since your programs are book-oriented. Of course, bookmarks can be printed, but those you make yourself can be very effective. Save used greeting cards. All those Christmas cards, valentines, birthday cards, and pretty little everyday cards that your friends send can be of practical use. All you need to do to turn them into bookmarks is to cut off the greeting and print your message on the back, perhaps while you're watching the late movie on TV. That way you can recycle and spread the word.

Don't just slip a bookmark, announcement, or memo into a package or book. Hand it directly to the child or adult with a simple oral greeting and reminder such as "Don't forget our storyhour Wednesday." This implies a personal invitation, which is more effective than an inanimate notice, even one printed on the back of a pretty picture.

Chalkboards

A chalkboard hanging on the wall of your library or classroom or resting on a checkout counter or desk is a good place to write a "Daily Reminder."

When you arrive at work each morning make it a habit to write a new message on the chalkboard. Changing the message daily will build up a chalkboard following who automatically look for each day's bulletin on your board. To publicize your storyhour that will be held a week from Wednesday, begin the week before with reminders or quotes from the stories you'll be telling. Keep changing the message daily to alert your potential audience that the time for the program is at hand.

Although the chalkboard message is most often encountered in schools, there is no reason why this practical gimmick should not be utilized elsewhere. Instead of a poster, hang a blackboard in your clubhouse, church, or even the window of a much frequented grocery store. Drop in on your way about town and change the message on the board daily.

Chalkwalk

Chalk, particularly the colored kind, not only is fun to use, but it also washes away easily. The day before your event, make a drawing on the sidewalk outside your meeting hall to remind the public of your program, or perhaps enlist some of your regular storyhour children who enjoy drawing pictures to do so for advertising purposes. A drawing contest may even help bring newcomers to the storyhour. Do, however, be a good citizen and wash the sidewalk down to remove your artwork after it has served its purpose.

Sandwich Boards

The old-fashioned sandwich board still catches people's attention, especially if the person wearing it is attractively costumed. Use cardboard that is not too heavy and wear the sandwich as you walk around a shopping center or other places where the people are.

Badges, Buttons, Balloons, and Bumper Stickers

Make your own name tag or button with your mininotice attractively printed on it. Stationery stores usually sell blank name tags and some also stock blank buttons for you to transform. Pin on your badge whenever you will be out in public.

Balloons, because of their great appeal, can also serve as publicity, especially if you are trying to reach children. Use permanent ink felt markers to letter a notice or reminder on the inflated balloons. If you think you will be using this idea more than once, buy an inexpensive pump, for the idea begins to lose its charm after you've blown up the tenth balloon!

For a special event or to publicize your organization, you might want to buy some professionally printed balloons or bumper stickers. Look in the yellow pages under "Advertising Specialties" for names of those specializing in personalized souvenirs. Wouldn't it be grand to have the whole town driving around with bumper stickers advertising the library storytime?

Tickets

There is something about having a ticket to an event that makes the holder feel obliged to go. You may want to send out tickets on request, which provides you with a way to estimate how many children to expect. Also, you might encourage an audience by leaving tickets to be distributed in classrooms, Sunday schools, and other appropriate agencies. The tickets need not be printed. They can be mimeographed, photocopied, or even handwritten.

I like to use tickets in other ways. While the children are assembling for the storyhour, tickets are handed out. These are then collected as the children enter the room. Somehow this gives the storyhour a more festive feeling and heightens anticipation. Because I collect the tickets at the door, I can reuse them over and over again. This also enables me to count attendance without taking time from the session itself. Because I reuse my tickets, I've tried to make them attractive and durable. One way to do this is to silkscreen them on heavy paper stock. Once in a while, usually for a holiday storyhour, I create a special ticket that can also be used as a bookmark or souvenir. Of course, these special tickets are not collected. Some storytellers prefer to put each child's name on a ticket and give it to him or her before every storyhour. No doubt this welcomes and involves the child, but I personally find this awkward for a variety of reasons: my memory for names is atrocious, and it is not polite to ask a child his or her name for the fifteenth time. Furthermore, children often mumble their names which can complicate the distribution of the tickets. Yet, if you can remember names easily because the group is small enough and stable, try using personalized tickets. Children do like them.

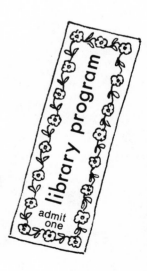

Special Invitations

The best way to draw an audience is to invite people personally. It is generally impractical to address and send individual invitations to a number of children, but you can invite particular groups such as Ms. Jensen's fourth grade class, Brownie troop 614, or the Little League team. Other children come, of course, but even so, make it a practice to invite a new group to each session.

Minispeeches

Attending a meeting? Ask for a few minutes to announce your project. Keep it short! Try to sound enthusiastic. If you know in advance that you will be given some time, you might arrange a "visual" to gain your audience's full attention. Use the overhead slide projector that might be set up already. Bring a poster or related artifact to hold up. If you don't have a captive audience, try to capture one by an announcement in a crowded place. However, if a gathering does not present itself, go on a walking campaign, visiting classrooms or groups to make your announcement.

Telephoning

Telephoning is another way to make personal contact. Call the children in your area (class lists or registration materials will give you current telephone numbers). When you reach a child or his parents, suggest the child bring a friend along.

Mailers

A mimeograph machine can help you produce announcements in quantity for mailing. Keep your message simple and print it on eye-catching, colored paper. Because we are all inundated with "throw away mail," design your flyer so that it will be opened and, more important, read.

Try to send mailers to people who you know might be interested. You don't want to waste time and money sending announcements of a preschool story-hour to a retirement home unless it happens to have a volunteer grandmother program.

Doorknob Hangers

When you are attempting to introduce a new program in your community, don't hesitate to borrow ideas from the commercial advertisers. For example, give something away in a door-to-door canvass, perhaps a package of a few seeds for the garden along with a notice describing the forthcoming event; hang the surprise on the doorknobs in the neighborhood you would most like to reach. Even in the city where no one has a yard? All the more reason to cheer up the residents with seeds, but choose some that will grow and thrive indoors. Ask your local wholesale florist what seeds are available and suitable to your purpose. Would he be a prospective contributor to the project? Consult your local garden club or horticultural society—either may be intrigued with an idea that promotes their interests at the same time.

Newspapers

Many adults are somewhat hesitant about approaching a newspaper for publicity, but announcements of upcoming events are news too. Editors need to be told what is being planned, or they can't possibly publish any news about it. Write a publicity release with all the names and places spelled correctly and drop it off at the newspaper office yourself. You may even be able to suggest a time for taking pictures. Is your announcement an item for the society section, the sports page, or the general news section? Ask the receptionist to help you contact the appropriate editor or reporter.

A follow-up news story or picture after the event is over creates a good image for the future. However, if there is a superabundance of activity at the same time—Christmas, for instance, usually crowds the community calendar —you may want to consider whether publicity before or after the event would be most helpful to your program in the long run.

Don't forget to write a thank-you note to the paper if it did a good job of covering your event. Reporters are human, too, and appreciate a kind word. Many libraries establish contact with a particular reporter or editor on a newspaper so that they can always speak to the same person when they have news. Remember that your news about a program of stories about Spain might just possibly be the most exciting item in the paper for the reader who is planning a trip to that country.

Radio and Television

Radio and television stations are licensed by the Federal Communications Commission, and, as part of their obligation to the public, they are required to offer a certain amount of public affairs programming. This includes announcements for nonprofit organizations which should encourage you to establish contact with your local radio and TV stations. Well in advance of your event, find your way to the right office and ask the receptionist who to contact. Be prepared to supply written copy for the announcements, for the less work a station has to do, the more likely it will be inclined to help you.

Paid Advertisements

If you find it impossible to get an article in the newspaper or an announcement on the air, consider buying an ad. This may be much less expensive than you think. By all means, try to get someone to donate the price of the ad but if that fails, try for a discount at least.

Summing It Up

You're probably saying to yourself, "You mean I have to plan the story-hour, learn the stories, and do all this to publicize it?" The answer, of course, is that you may not need to do all of the foregoing to publicize your program, but you may have to do some. In many communities, if you whisper, a crowd appears. In others, the first few story sessions have to be advertised, and after that you may not need to do another thing.

Furthermore, no one says that *you* personally have to handle the promotion by yourself. Perhaps you have people on your staff who would enjoy doing the publicity. Allow on-the-job time to create materials or suggest that they go home early in order to make posters at home. If you are part of a school system, ask the graphic arts department to help you. Solicit help—a high school art class project to make posters for your event may be just what the teacher was looking for.

There are always people who volunteer their time to worthwhile projects, if they are asked. Whether you enlist their aid formally through the "Friends of the Library" or informally by asking your own friends and contacts, be sure you tell your volunteers exactly what you would like done and when you expect it to be finished. Also, be sure that you send a thank-you note when the project is over, even if the volunteer is your sister.

One of my former students, now head of a library, reported to me that she had tried all of my publicity ideas except dressing up as a witch and walking through the community to advertise a Halloween program. I have, therefore, left that particular idea off this list. You may find some of these publicity ideas more useful or easier to use than others. Fine! Whatever works for you is best. The point is: SPREAD THE WORD!

4 / Introducing and Closing the Program

Many factors influence choice of material and technique of presentation: the age and interests of the audience, the time allotted for the session, and the experience and personality of the leader. Although the main content may be traditional storytelling, the recitation of poetry, the offering of non-narrative folklore, a multimedia presentation, a puppet show, a magic show, or a story-related activity, the entire program, however, also includes other necessary elements. These are the initial introduction, the transitions between stories or activities, and the closing of the program. In order to present a truly effective storyhour, you must plan for the entire program, including these moments surrounding the main content.

Setting the Mood

The introduction to a single story or to the program as a whole often sets the mood for the entire period. A question such as "How many of you like to laugh, raise your hands?" suggests that the story will be funny, and in effect, you have set the mood that will elicit a humorous response to whatever you tell. On the other hand, if you want to create an atmosphere of romance or suspense, you might use only a candle for lighting and introduce the story at a slower, more reserved tempo.

The Storyhour Symbol

A traditional storyhour opening is the lighting of a candle. When the candle is burning the children learn that the time has come to settle down and listen. After the last story is told, the storyteller or a child from the audience blows out the candle and everyone silently makes a wish. If you don't want to use the storyhour candle, substitute your own trademark. Perhaps you have a banner that you unfurl at the beginning of each program or a bell that rings to summon your audience. If you play the guitar, harmonica, or some other portable instrument, you may want to begin and end each program with your own theme song. Whatever you choose, it is pleasant in this era of sudden change to build and maintain a tradition in the storyhour, something that automatically means "It's time for stories."

Introducing the Story or Program

If you have planned the program around a theme, you may want to make some sort of general introduction before announcing each story. Suit the introduction to the group and to yourself, but keep it brief, being careful not to overwhelm the story itself.

One way to introduce the individual story is with a personal comment, perhaps to tell where you learned it, why you like it, or how it relates to a personal incident of your own. For instance, you might tell about the time

Figure 5.
A storyhour symbol

that you forgot to bring the salt on a camping trip. Everything tasted so flat that you were reminded of the English story "Cap O'Rushes," the story you are going to tell.

Another style of introduction is more academic. Look up some background information beforehand. Briefly discuss the author, country, or type of story you have chosen, but try not to make your introduction sound like a lecture. Choose information that is of interest to you so you will sound enthusiastic when you present it. Such material frequently is found in the preface or introduction to a collection. Mira Ginsburg prefaces her collections of Russian stories with factual information about the lands and the peoples from whom the stories were collected. Books such as Georgess McHargue's *The Impossible People* (Holt, 1972) offer a wealth of speculations on the origins and characteristics of giants, dwarfs, dragons, and fairy folk. Don't overlook the encyclopedia as a source of pertinent information for a lively, informative introduction.

The book itself can provide yet another introductory approach. You are, after all, telling stories to children to make them aware of the fact that stories come from books and to encourage them to read stories on their own. A good introduction, then, might be simply to display the book and tell your listeners that in it is the story they are about to hear. Nearby, you might also exhibit several books containing similar stories, either variants of the one you are about to tell or with related themes.

Still another way of introducing material, related to the theater program, is to borrow a useful device from vaudeville: an easel holding large cards, on each of which is printed the title of the story you will tell and the title of the book it comes from, if they differ. Display the appropriate title card immediately before you tell the story. The lettering on the cards must look professional and be large enough to be read easily. If you have access to a mechanical sign printer or to paste-on letters, this may be a useful idea for you.

Artifacts and Crafts

An artifact or exhibit, when you include it as part of the storyhour, may serve to focus attention, aid the listener to recall the story, or arouse curiosity and assuredly helps make the storyhour an exciting, special time. Experience will bear out that a variety of objects used in different ways really does make the program visually as well as aurally interesting. Besides, looking for, selecting, or making just the right item to introduce a story is a fascinating as well as very satisfying part of the storyteller's preparation.

If you do sometimes use an artifact in the storyhour, make sure it is an item of quality. Mass-produced gimmickry which passes for art abounds in our country and we need not make a special effort to show it to children. At the same time, before you go on to the sections with ideas for buying or making objects relating to storytelling, let me caution you about becoming too involved with the visual at the expense of the proper learning and telling of your story. For those who delight in "little things"—antiques and crafted objects—this can be a danger. On the other hand, if you think of yourself as all thumbs, incapable of making anything, I encourage you to try some of these projects, since most not only are simple to do but also are fun and otherwise rewarding. Then too, consider the possibility of trading your time. For example, if you can't sew and a friend or colleague is an excellent seamstress, trade her a freshly baked pie or some babysitting time for the storytelling apron you've been yearning to have.

Although many of the ideas I suggest may seem more appropriate for the preschool or primary program, almost all of them can be adapted for use with audiences of older children.

Things to Buy or Bring from Home

A music box. You may have one with a tune that lends itself to a program theme, e.g., "Raindrops Keep Falling on My Head" (rain stories) or "Who's Afraid of the Big Bad Wolf?" (*The Three Little Pigs*). If you don't have a music box, perhaps you can borrow one that plays an appropriate tune for that special storyhour you've been wanting to present.

Stack boxes or nesting dolls. Although these articles are usually imported, they are not necessarily expensive. They come from Scandinavia, Russia, Poland, East Germany, and Japan and are generally available at Christmas. Introduce the first story, tell it, then open the outer doll. Introduce a finger play and open the next doll. Tell a story and open the third, continuing in this manner until there is only one doll left to say goodbye to the children. Use the stacking boxes in the same way.

A box. Find something pretty, perhaps antique silver or carved wood. When you open it, the magic of storyland flies out. Keep the lid open until the storyhour is finished. Let the children help you catch the magic and close the box for another day.

A puppet. A handmade or purchased monkey puppet for the Curious George stories (by H. A. and Margaret Rey, published by Houghton, 1941-66) or a favorite puppet, named by the children, who becomes your constant storyhour friend and assistant may help identify your storyhour program. (*see also* Puppetry chapter.)

Figurines. You may find some at your local bookstore or gift shop; others can be ordered. Ceramic figures of Winnie the Pooh, Piglet, Eeyore, and Owl are available from Martha Maier, 1974 Buck St., Eugene, OR 97405.

Miniature English porcelain nursery rhyme characters such as Little

Figure 6. Storytelling apron

Figure 7. Story bag and its book-related contents

Miss Muffet and Humpty Dumpty are available from George Wade, Burslem Stoke-on-Trent, England, ST6 4AE.

Figurines of Beatrix Potter's book characters can be ordered from Frederick Warne & Co., 101 Fifth Ave., New York, NY 10003 (a discount is available to libraries).

Pewter figurines, among them characters from *Alice's Adventures in Wonderland* and *The Wonderful Wizard of Oz*, as well as Sherlock Holmes and Dr. Watson and Don Quixote and Sancho Panza may be purchased from the Sales Shop of the New York Public Library, Fifth Avenue at 42d St., New York, NY 10018. You may request a pamphlet which describes these.

Bronze or silver miniature figures, one of a kind book characters, cast by the lost wax process—Alice in Wonderland, Little Red Riding Hood, one of the Pooh characters, whomever you fancy—may be obtained by special order from Mary Ann Dabritz, 5408 SE 99th St., Portland, OR 97266.

Finger puppets. Knitted finger puppets to use with nursery rhymes and other children's poetry are easily made, if you knit. If you don't, you may buy such characters as the Owl and the Pussycat and the Laura Ingalls Wilder family from Dorothy Tharpe, 201 W. 26th St., Scottsbluff, NE 69361.

Felt finger puppets are somewhat easier to make. If you have neither time nor talented volunteers to make them for you, felt finger puppets for such familiar fairy tales as *Little Red Riding Hood, The Three Little Pigs, The Three Billy Goats Gruff* may be purchased from Shirley Tingey, 110 Hardy Ave., Eugene, OR 97403. Arts and crafts shops and senior citizens' bazaars often are good sources of ready-made or made-to-order puppets.

Stuffed animals or dolls. Use an old favorite such as a worn stuffed rabbit to represent Margery Bianco's *The Velveteen Rabbit* (Doubleday, 1958) or a fuzzy teddy bear when you tell about Winnie the Pooh and Christopher Robin. Be aware that the Walt Disney Pooh characters are not modeled after the original illustrations by Ernest H. Shepard. However, Mattel does produce a respectable *Cat in the Hat* doll that young children easily recognize. Try to find handmade, quality stuffed animals and dolls to use in your storyhours. The children already see too many shoddily made stuffed animals and dolls with fixed plastic smiles everywhere else.

Recordings or tapes. Music at the beginning or the end of the storyhour helps give the program a feeling of continuity. Choose something to fit the mood of your stories.

Storytelling apron. You can make a muslin apron with removable pockets in primary colors. The storyteller's apron (*see* fig. 6) enables you to put objects representing each of the stories in a pocket. As a child calls out a color you extract the object representing a story you are going to tell.

Mugs and plates. Wedgwood puts out a set of children's dishes decorated with scenes from Beatrix Potter's *Peter Rabbit.* This English firm also produces a children's Christmas plate with a scene from a different fairy tale each year. Six dessert plates, each with a reproduction of an original Kate Greenaway lithograph, are available from Invento, 145 E. 57th St., New York, NY 10022. Children's plates and mugs decorated with pictures or the alphabet are occasionally available at antique shows and thrift shops. You may even have a mug or plate at home that you can use in one of your story sessions.

Live animals. Bring a rabbit, a bird, a dog, or a cat from home to show the children, then read books or tell stories about that animal. Caution: Be aware that this does not always work out and that a live animal can be incredibly distracting. One of my students once brought a real bear cub to the university for a storyhour. Although the cub was very young, the situation got completely out of hand when he began clawing, growling, and knocking over the furniture in the receptionist's office. The uproar attracted a crowd outside the library door before the animal finally calmed down. It was fortunate that our spectators were college students rather than impressionable three-year-olds.

Interesting and unusual containers. Often something is packaged in such an imaginative way it seems as though there must be a storytelling use for it. The plastic "eggs" which contain pantyhose, film cans, and other attractive packages can be decorated and filled with objects or book titles and opened before you tell each story.

Holiday decorations. Of course you will want to have appropriate decorations and maybe even a special storyhour on the major holidays. A Halloween jack-o-lantern, a Christmas tree or gingerbread house, an Easter bunny, and so on. Write the Children's Book Council, 67 Irving Place, New York, NY 10003, for their publication called *The Calendar.* It gives the usual important dates as well as little known dates such as "the first use of the 'forward pass' in football" (West Point vs. Notre Dame, 1913). *The Calendar* also suggests book titles that celebrate each date.

Treasure trunk. Use a trunk, suitcase, or specially decorated cardboard box to hold the books of the day. If your trunk is pretty and small enough, it can become the permanent surprise box in your library.

Draw a shirt. You'd like to wear an illustration from your favorite book on a tee shirt? Or the wildly imaginative drawing made by a child in your storytelling program? Deco Dence, 718 Lexington Ave., New York, NY 10022, is one firm that will reproduce any artwork or photograph on a tee shirt for you to wear at your next storyhour special. Other firms that do this often advertise in the shopper's sections of magazines and the Sunday newspapers.

Plastic plates. Draw a picture of your favorite book or story character and have it reproduced on a plastic plate. Two manufacturers that produce plate-making kits are: Small Fry Originals Plastics Manufacturing Co., 2700 S. Westmoreland Ave., Dallas, TX 75224; and Make-A-Plate, 460 Totten Pond Rd., Waltham, MA 02154.

Coloring books. Kate Greenaway's *Mother Goose* rendered for coloring by Nancy Perkins and published by Dover; *A Mother Goose Coloring Book,* available from Bellerophon Books, 153 Stewart St., San Francisco, CA 94105; *Winnie the Pooh, Peter Rabbit, Babar,* and *Raggedy Ann,* available from Determined Productions, Box 2150, San Francisco, CA 94126; Kate Greenaway's *Miniature Coloring Book,* available from Merrimack Publishing Corp., 85 Fifth Ave., New York, NY 10003, are all potentially useful to the resourceful storyteller.

Antique book and game replicas. Merrimack Publishing Corp., 85 Fifth Ave., New York, NY 10003, in a recent catalog indicates that *Alice in Wonderland* card games, Kate Greenaway puzzles and mugs, books illustrated by Randolph Caldecott and Walter Crane, among others, are available.

Postcards and greeting cards. Reproductions of Arthur Rackham and Kay Nielsen illustrations may be purchased from Green Tiger Press, 7458 La Jolla Blvd., La Jolla, CA 92037.

The Medici Society, Ltd., London, prints greeting cards and postcards from the books of Racey Helps and Molly Breet, available at Medici Society, Ltd., 225 Fifth Ave., New York, NY 10010.

Marcel Schurman & Co., 1355 Market St., San Francisco, CA 94103, imports wrapping paper, greeting cards, and toys from foreign countries. The cards illustrated by the Swedish artist Carl Larrson are especially delightful.

Miniature furniture. Swedish Modern dollhouse furniture made by Lundy is available from the American distributor, Block House, Inc., 1107 Broadway Toy Center North, New York, NY 10010.

The catalog of Federal Smallwares Corp., 85 Fifth Ave., New York, NY 10003, includes replicas of antique dolls and furniture that may be just what you need for the storyhour dollhouse.

Another catalog, that of Enchanted Doll House, Manchester Center, VT 05255, also includes miniatures of all kinds for that special display.

Things to Make or Do

Following are some suggestions for things to make for introducing the books in a program or for exhibits. If you enjoy arts and crafts you won't mind the time it takes to complete these projects. Remember too, that once you make something it may be used many times in many different ways.

Miniature books. Children like small things. Try making a miniature posterboard folder that looks like a book. Decorate it with a drawing representing a specific title and place inside a quote that will serve as an introduction. To finish your book, cover it with clear contact paper or laminate it if you have access to a laminating press.

Giant books. Use poster board or plywood to make giant book covers. Such a "book" can serve as a permanent beginning to your storyhour. Inside the covers you can list the program of today's storyhour, changing the listing for each storyhour.

Story bag. Draw the figures of animals and characters, as well as other identifiable objects from your favorite picture books on stiff paper or tagboard. Cut out and place in a special large bag or envelope (*see* fig. 7). Let a child reach into the bag and pick out a figure. Whichever one he or she chooses represents the book you read. Be sure you always have on hand the represented books, ready to read or show. Small animals, other book-related figurines, and objects carved of wood or made of other materials also are suitable for the story bag.

Knitted, crocheted, and sewn dolls. Knit or crochet a doll or a puppet; patterns are available from Spadea Syndicate, Inc., Dept. PM-7, 2 Bridge St., Milford, NJ 08848. To sew dolls and toys à la Beatrix Potter, patterns that really work may be found in Margaret Hutchings's *Toys from the Tales of Beatrix Potter*, photographs by Eve Legg (Warne, 1973). *The Pooh Craft Book* by Carol Friedrichsen, illustrated by Ernest H.

Shepard (Dutton, 1976), provides patterns and instructions for sewing the much-loved characters from the Milne books.

Painted rocks. What do you do with those pretty rocks you brought home from your vacation? Paint them with a book title on one side, a picture representing the book on the other.

Puzzles. Make use of the illustrations from a discarded book or book jackets. Mount them on cardboard, laminate or cover them with clear contact paper, and cut out pieces for a puzzle. Make sure you identify the pieces by a number or symbol on the back so that you can gather them back together. You may have enough puzzles for each child or two children working as a team; when all the puzzles are together, it's book time. You can make your own puzzles from scratch by drawing freehand or tracing a picture from a book and proceeding as above.

Go Fish game. Cut several 2″ fish from posterboard and attach a paper clip to the mouth of each. Then print the title of a story or program theme on the back of every fish. Removable labels (available at the stationery store as mailing labels) make the fish reusable. Next, make a fishing rod with a stick, a length of string, and a magnet for bait (small inexpensive magnets can be bought at toy shops and hardware stores). The fishpond can be a sturdy corrugated box with high sides (hand-decorated, of course) so that the fisherman doesn't see what he or she is fishing for. Choose a child from the group to fish for the stories and as each fish is caught, be prepared to tell the story it represents. Change the titles for each session.

Character map. On a mounted map of the world mark with tacks or small flags the origin of the stories you will tell. Point out to the group where the story you are going to tell, or have told, comes from.

Clothespin dolls. Search through the stores in your town until you find some old-fashioned wooden clothespins. Dress these with felt and fabric to represent the characters in the stories you tell.

Handmade blocks. Cut a length of 4″x4″ lumber into equal sections to make 4″x4″ blocks. For smaller blocks cut 1″x1″ lumber in a similar manner. Sand the wood and apply a coat of shellac or polyurethane varnish as a sealant. Paint the blocks if you prefer them to be more colorful. Cut out and paste pictures from discarded books on the sides of the blocks. Some examples are shown in figure 8. I think Beatrix Potter's pictures perfectly suit these storytime blocks. Cover the pictures with several coats (the more the better) of polyurethane varnish. Let each coat dry overnight for a smooth finish. If you hate cleanup jobs as much as I do, wrap your varnish brush in aluminum foil and store it in the freezer after each use.

Figure 8. Storytime blocks

Between Stories

Some storytellers find the transition between two formal story presentations somewhat awkward. The atmosphere or mood you wish to maintain should dictate your handling of the time between stories. If your preference is for the more formal mood, such as that suggesting a theater presentation, you might simply pause briefly between stories, then launch into an introduction for the next story. Or, if time permits, you might give a brief booktalk to introduce a new addition to the library or to promote an old favorite. In this more formal, dignified atmosphere the children will remain seated and participate by listening only.

If you prefer a more relaxed atmosphere, you may want to use your transition period for participation activities: games, responsive songs, riddles, or creative dramatics. Maybe someone in the group has a question to ask you or wishes to tell about a similar story he or she has read or heard. I prefer the more formal or dignified presentation, for the storyhour is a prepared program, not a discussion period or class session; however, do what is most comfortable for you.

Closing the Program

Some storytellers sing a song or recite the same rhyme to begin and end the storyhour. Do what you find works for you. A simple "Thank you for listening" might be sufficient. If the storyhour opens with a ritual, perhaps you will want to close it with a similar ritual, such as blowing out the storyhour candle.

Is there something you'd like your listeners to do at the close of the storyhour? Instead of sending them straight home, perhaps you will invite them to look at, touch, or play with exhibit material. When the program is held in a library, you'll want to suggest that the audience might want to check out a book. Don't forget to remind the group about the next program.

Something to Take Home

The book you featured in the storyhour might just lend itself to inexpensive or virtually free souvenirs. Of course you can't give something away every time, but for that special occasion, keep your imagination open. Here are a few ideas about what to give *after* the story:

Apple seeds. (It won't take long to save enough to hand out) To remember Nonny Hogrogian's *Apples* (Macmillan, 1972) or Julian Scheer's *Rain Makes Applesauce* (Holiday, 1964).

Balloons. (Do not have to be blown up) To remember "In which Eeyore has a birthday and gets two presents" in A. A. Milne's *Winnie the Pooh;* il. by Ernest H. Shepard. Colored by Hilda Scott. (Dutton, 1974).

Cheerios. To remember the doughnuts in Robert McCloskey's *Homer Price* (Viking, 1943).

Chocolate chip cookies. To remember James Marshall's *George and Martha* (Houghton, 1972).

4-inch nails. (From the hardware store) To remember "The old woman and the tramp" in Ellin Greene's *Clever Cooks* (Lothrop, 1973).

Peach pits. (Paint them gold) To remember Nathan Zimelman's *I Will Tell You of Peach Stone;* il. by Haru Wells (Lothrop, 1976).

Pebbles. (Available free on the beach and purchased inexpensively at the aquarium or garden shop) To remember William Steig's *Sylvester and the Magic Pebble* (Windmill, 1969).

Pumpkin seeds. (Save them from the jack-o-lantern) To remember Gloria Skurzynski's *The Magic Pumpkin;* il. by Rocco Negri (Four Winds, 1971), or Lennart Hellsin's *The Wonderful Pumpkin;* il. by Svend Otto (Atheneum, 1976).

Raisins. To remember Russel Hoban's *A Baby Sister for Frances;* il. by Lillian Hoban (Harper, 1964).

Vegetable seeds. (Buy at less than half price at the end of the growing season from seed wholesalers) To remember Ruth Krauss's *The Carrot Seed;* il. by Crockett Johnson (Harper, 1945).

Walnut shells. (Save them till you have enough) To remember Jean B. Hardendorff's *A Bed Just So;* il. by Lisl Weil (Four Winds, 1975).

Discipline or Holding Your Own

I like to pretend that there is no such thing as having a discipline problem in the storyhour. How could anyone not want to hear a story, I think to myself. However, a former student of mine called me up recently in great distress, complaining about the vandalism in her inner-city library and the disruptions in her storyhour. Each person must react to these situations as they see best, but here are a few general thoughts:

Not every disruption is a destructive disruption. You should not necessarily consider it to be a problem because children articulate their reactions:

"Look at that elephant!" "Oh, no, she better watch out!" Such verbal reactions reflect interest and attention. You do not always have a problem if one child hits another—that too is also natural and can be taken care of by calmly and quietly separating them. You may be able to minimize problems of discipline if the storyhour is an elective activity. It may help if you are fortunate enough to have separate facilities for programs. If someone wants to come to the storyhour, which is a special treat, he or she must behave or not be allowed to come the next time.

It is well to remember that not everyone is interested in books; indeed, some may have had bad book experiences. Once during my career as a high school librarian, I was reduced to tears when the students refused to listen to a carefully chosen short story I had prepared for them. My first reaction was to forget the whole thing. Then I slowly realized that part of the problem was my own shortsightedness. The school was attended by "difficult" students. They had very little interest in literature, but loved magazines and books with pictures. To them the library was a place to play cards, to listen to music, and to exchange gossip with friends. These young adults had never heard a story meant for adults or a book talk. I'd simply gone about the whole matter too fast, deciding suddenly one day, "Today I'm going to tell you something about a book you'd enjoy." No wonder they thought I'd lost my senses.

After I had swallowed my pride and reconsidered, I started over again. I had been writing little notes on a blackboard near my desk each day suggesting books or articles to read. Now I began writing "Next drop-out soon" or "Have you been invited to drop-out?" Since the students were always talking about leaving school I thought my programs should be times to "drop out." I asked, by written invitation, only five people to the first program which I held in the book stacks, no other secluded place being available. The kids I chose I hoped were the leaders of the rebellion and one very pretty girl. They all came, out of curiosity I suppose, and I kept them less than ten minutes with a phonograph playing two "in" recordings and showing them two books: the *Encyclopedia of Sports* (I also could have used *The Guinness Book of World Records*) and a new book on sports car racing.

The next time I invited three of the same boys back and invited four new ones. By the tenth week I was back in the library proper, talking to everyone. Many were still ignoring me, listening to the radio and playing cards while I talked, but at least they weren't throwing things, and I had reached a few.

5 / Preparing and Telling the Story

For the purist, the ultimate in storytelling is to tell a story without props or pictures—just YOU and the story. However, whether you tell a story simply standing or sitting in front of an audience or with a stage full of production items, your storytelling techniques will be the same.

What is this mysterious art? Is there really a magical secret to learning and telling a story that only a few can discover? I think not. In my experience with several hundred storytelling students, I've found that nearly everyone can tell an acceptable story. As for being an outstanding storyteller, that is a different matter, for storytelling is like other arts: in order to be truly great, you almost have to be born with that inner talent. How do you know whether or not you have it? Only by working on some stories and telling them to an audience. But, to repeat, almost everyone who takes the time to learn can become a competent storyteller. I've noticed, for example, that Oriental students are all so much more advanced in drawing than my American students. I was curious about this phenomenon and when I visited the Orient I inquired about art training in the schools. It turned out that my students' art talent did not spring from nothing. The simple fact is that instead of being a sometimes-taught elective, art is part of the curriculum. The moral which applies here is: what you are exposed to, you can learn. It holds true of storytelling. Please try. Those of us who are telling stories need you out there to carry on an age-old tradition.

Perhaps the most important element in good storytelling is finding the right story for you. Each of us has a distinct personality which should be capitalized upon. Are you someone who speaks softly and slowly? Or do you have a deep booming voice and a bawdy nature? Maybe you are "the life of the party," always the first with a new joke which you tell with vigorous, flamboyant movements. What is your taste in literature? Do you like to cuddle up with long philosophical treatises, or do you prefer gothic novels? You don't have to actually sit down and analyze yourself. As you read through story collections, myths, epics, short stories, and other materials suitable for storytelling use, you will find something that appeals to, and is usually suitable for, you.

We are always reading about professional actors and actresses who don't want to have a reputation for doing only one role. We hear of the comedian who would like to play serious roles or the character actor who wants to attempt a role as a musical comedy hero. You too may wish that you had a genuine Appalachian accent so you could tell a Jack Tale with authenticity. But for now, start at the beginning: choose something that suits you. I find, for instance, that I'm mostly attracted to humorous folktales, especially those based on Jewish lore, but now that I've told stories to a variety of groups for a number of years, I am discovering that I don't want to have a one-sided repertoire. As I learn new stories I try to add new types to my list so that I can end up with a Russian fable, a Greek myth, a story by Oscar Wilde, or any other kind of story a program requires.

Choosing the story to tell is important, so take it seriously. Read as much as you can and make sure that you like your final selection; you'll be spending a lot of time with it.

Learning a Story

After you have chosen a story that you feel is worth your time, the actual learning begins. No one can tell you how to learn a story, for each of us has a method of his or her own. You will find, as with all endeavors, that the key lies in practice. Your first attempt may take a great deal of time, but after you learn how to learn, the whole process will become much easier. You will probably want to begin with a simple folktale. A story someone has written, one which relies heavily on the flavor of the language, has to be learned almost word for word. This is a more difficult project and can be tackled later.

You may want to adapt my way of learning a story to suit your needs. First, I find that I want to own the story that I'm going to learn; this usually means actually buying a copy of the book. My interest in storytelling has resulted in a large personal library. I bought the book that contained the first story I ever learned and I have been buying books ever since. Owning the book means that I can at any time go back to a story to refresh my memory, and I am always certain of having a copy of the book to exhibit on my story-hour table. If I don't want to carry a book around with me, I take along a copy of the story (three cheers for the invention of the copy machine!). Whenever I get the chance I read the story over. You'll be amazed at the number of spare moments you can find in your day: standing in line to get into a movie, the waiting room at the dentist, waiting for a bus, in the bathtub, waiting for a meal to cook, and coffee breaks at the office. How wonderful to put all that waiting time to real use! I read a new story all the way through at least three times. Then I begin telling it to myself. If I forget a section I stop for that session. The next time I start from the beginning again and try to learn a little more. Much of my learning process entails other people. I like to practice on people. Some storytellers look in a mirror to practice. I find this absolutely terrifying, but you should try it; it may be the right thing for you. Whom do I practice on? On everyone, the family first. Children are critical and appreciative, roommates are amused, husbands are sometimes bored. Friends are willing, at least the first time. But I find strangers the best listeners of all. They can be caught completely unaware. Try this: You're out for a day of skiing and find yourself on a ski lift with a man you don't know in the opposite chair, a 15-minute ride with no escape. Simply ask "Want to hear a story?" He has to say "yes," so tell your story. Imagine how he'll describe this experience when he returns from his ski trip. Or this: You are at a dinner party. Someone asks what you do, and you answer, "I'm a librarian." "I'm a teacher." or "I'm a volunteer storyteller at the local library." Of course, then someone else will say, "Tell a story." Do it. It's good practice. The more you actually tell the story the better storyteller you will be.

When you feel you really know the words of the story, you can begin working on what the words mean and how to express that meaning. Beginners often make the mistake of thinking they are ready for the children when they have learned the words of the story. You also must feel so comfortable with the words that you will not panic if you forget where you are in the story. You must be able to give thought to "feeling" the events of the story. It is helpful to keep a file of stories that you have learned or want to learn for easy availability.

Your next question will probably be, "Should I memorize the story?" The answer is that all-encompassing: "That depends." Some storytellers feel that, except in the case of a literary tale or a story someone has written, memorization should be kept at a minimum or that it should not be a part of learning a story at all. They feel that you make a story more personally your own if you tell it in your own words. I do not agree. In nearly every instance, the stories you tell will have been selected from books. No matter that originally the story existed in the unwritten province of folklore. The source you are using was adapted by someone. If you choose your material carefully, your author will be competent as a collector *and* as a writer. Unless you feel that your phrasing is better, why not lean heavily upon the printed word? This does not mean that you will sit down and learn word for word what is in a book. It means that you will memorize some key phrases, or that you will memorize only the beginning and ending of a work, or that you will memorize a particularly enchanting passage or two.

One suggestion that I hope you will take is to list the events of each story in your mind. After all, you can't kill the dragon until the hero has met that fearsome beast. Think logically and you will learn logically. After you tell the story to an audience you will find yourself making subtle changes; you are making it your own. When I first began taping a children's television story-telling series, my director asked me for a script. I gave him a copy of a folk-tale taken from a book. Halfway through rehearsal I could see him in the director's glass booth jumping around and literally tearing his hair. He stopped the show and started ranting through the loudspeaker, "What king? There's no king here!" Indeed, I had added a character without even realizing it and thought that I was telling the story exactly as printed. But I did not remove the king from the story; I liked him. Eventually the director and I decided not to use a script at all, since I changed the stories with each telling.

What needs to be emphasized is that there is no right, or wrong way to go about learning a story. In my university storytelling classes, as well as my adult classes, I spend little time discussing the actual learning process. Any-one who has gone through an organized educational system in the United States or abroad has found his or her own way of learning material. The only encouragement I can really give is to those who have been out of a formal learning situation for some time. At first, learning a story will take some time, but after a short period it will be easier.

This is a good place to mention the art of relearning a story. Obviously, you are not going to all the trouble of learning a story to tell it only once. Or at least, I hope you're not. It would be a pity not to tell your stories on many different occasions. However, there are stories that are only used once a year, or on special holidays, such as Christmas stories. You may be actively en-gaged in storytelling activities one year, but then be away doing other things for a time. What do you do when you want to reuse a story that's been dor-mant in your mind? Take it out, dust it off, shine it up a bit, and you're ready to go. The second time around is much easier, especially if you learned the story well initially. It is now that your copy of the story comes in handy. Simply take it out, read it through a time or two, practice a little, and you're all set. Sometimes you will be astonished to discover that when you tell the story the next time you do it even better than before. Somewhere, somehow, the story has jelled and truly become your own. Don't take a chance, though, on dredging a story back up through your memory; always look at the story again before telling it.

At times you will find a story that is too long to learn, or one that has a good plot but is written in stilted or unsuitable language. It's tempting to try to cut or rewrite the story to suit your own purposes. My advice in this situation depends on your own storytelling experience. What I strongly sug-gest is that you look for another story to learn, because adapting a story can be a difficult procedure. If you are a late-night TV-movie viewer, you have seen that even professional editors often make mistakes, often sacrificing the more poignant and important scenes for spectacle. You might well find yourself doing something similar. This is not to say that you should never cut a story; it just means that you should be extra careful when you do it. You may be able to find another version of the story that better fits your needs. A popular picture-book version of a nonsense story is Arlene Mosel's *Tikki Tikki Tembo* (Holt, 1968). However, I prefer a much shorter, more compact version collected by Jeanette Perkins Brown in *The Storyteller in Religious Education* (Pilgrim, 1951).

If you work at an institution, school, library, or church telling stories on a regular basis, or if you run a birthday party storytelling business, you will want to keep records of your storytelling activities. Your records will include information on what stories were told, on what date, and to whom. You might even want to include comments on the proceedings and on the success or failure of the programs.

Wherever you tell stories, you will want to keep your own personal file. Even a simple list of the stories in your repertoire is better than nothing at all. At first it will seem silly to write down the one story that you know. How could you ever forget that you learned it? Doubtless you will learn many stories, and, as your general knowledge increases, your memory for details may decrease. The story file is somewhat like a recipe file. If you own the actual books you may not need to keep a copy of the story in another location, but at least make a notation of which book the story is from. I am merely trying to spare you some of the agonizing moments I've spent searching for a lost story. I've been known to run all around the library, school, and my own home screaming, "Thief! Thief!" only to find out that the robber is my own sloppiness. But, I do have a list of stories I tell carefully tucked into my wallet. One never knows when one will be asked to tell a story. So, when I am asked, I just whip out my little list and decide what to tell. The list is especially useful as an indicator that you need to broaden your horizons. One glance will tell you that it's time to look for a suitable Greek myth because you already know so many stories about witches.

Telling the Story

Now you are ready to tell your story. The most important advice I can give you is this: Do not "act out" the story. You are not an actress, but a storyteller. Don't use your voice to convey characterization, unless you have had voice training. Portraying Father Bear with a big powerful voice, and a squeaky voice for Baby Bear turns out to be a disaster for most people. Characterization emerges through descriptive language: "a little wisp of a girl . . ." or "he was so thin that he could only eat noodles." Let the language tell the story.

I once had a very competent acting student in my storytelling class who insisted on using dialects in her telling of Joseph Jacobs's *Tom Tit Tot,* an English variant of *Rumpelstiltskin.* Her plan was to have the girl speak with a cockney accent and the prince with an educated Oxford accent. She did it the first time so charmingly that I invited her to tell the story to another class. In the middle of the story, the characters switched roles. The girl became the Oxford graduate; the prince, the cockney. This experience heightened my resolve to caution novices on the use of dialects. On the other hand, a regional story is very much improved with an authentic dialect. A good Irish brogue improves an Irish story 100 percent. However, be aware that some dialects can be offensive to their respective folk groups if they are used incorrectly. I personally try to stay away from most accented stories, although I feel that I don't do a bad job with a French or a Jewish accent. If you come from an ethnic or national background and have heard a particular accent for a number of years, you might want to try a story using that accent.

Difficult or unpronounceable words are another problem. If you don't know what a word means, look it up. Don't guess. It is not only embarrassing, it's unprofessional to say a word sweetly and gently that turns out to be an insult that should be said harshly and with a certain amount of venom in the voice. You don't want to be caught without a correct answer when someone asks you what is a "calabash," a "billet" of wood, or a "dreidel." I don't think it is necessary to give another meaning to the word while you tell the story, either. Nor do I advise simply removing the word and substituting something easier. It ruins the original spirit of the story. I am appalled by the number of books in the library that have been mutilated by teachers, who, in rewriting a book to read aloud, have gone through it, deleting words, replacing them with simpler words. An edition of a children's biography of Abraham Lincoln is an extreme example of this. An unknown hand had gone through changing words, even in direct quotations from letters written by Lincoln. It may sometimes be advisable to explain, before you begin your telling, a word or phrase which is central to the understanding of the story. One of my favorite stories is Isaac Bashevis Singer's "The First Shlemiel" in his *Zlateh the Goat* (Harper, 1966). In New York I told the story many times and to everyone's great amusement. The first time that I told it in Oregon it didn't get the same reaction. Much to my dismay I discovered that many Oregonians didn't know the meaning of the word "shlemiel." I puzzled about how to introduce the story in the future. At last I found a way that involved teaching the audience two Yiddish terms instead of one. "The difference," I now explain, "between a shlemiel and a shlimazl is that a shlemiel is the kind of a guy who is always spilling the soup and a shlimazl is the guy he spills it on."

If you are wondering what to wear, wear whatever you feel comfortable in, but I suggest that you wear something a little special, not just the clothes you wear to rake leaves. However, keep in mind that no one is coming to look at you. They are coming to *hear* you tell a story. Don't wear anything that might be particularly distracting or that you might play with. Beware of the locket or chain around your neck that you unconsciously twist and untwist as you speak. I usually don't recommend a costume, a witch or whatever, unless the occasion is a dressing-up day and you are portraying a favorite character. Some people choose to wear the same distinctive article of clothing for each storyhour; this may be a storytelling apron or they may copy the African custom of wearing a story hat.

I like to stand while I'm telling a story for two reasons. The first is that I like to be able to express myself somewhat with body movements. The other reason is that I want to create a more formal atmosphere when I am telling a story in the traditional manner. Standing separates the storyteller from the audience and creates the more formal feeling of the theater.

A case for sitting can be made for exactly the opposite reasons. Sitting in a chair or on a stool confines your movements so that the audience must get most of the impact of the story aurally. If you and your audience are sitting, a more intimate atmosphere is established. Choose whichever suits *you* best.

It happens to the inexperienced and the experienced. It happens at the worst of times. You forget. You suddenly go quite blank. What should you do? Stop, and think. That is the only way out. A friend of mine was telling *Prince Sneeze* when she suddenly forgot what happened on the third sneeze, a very important part to the conclusion of the story. After a moment, she simply told her audience, "Remember that third sneeze and later I'll tell you what happened." When finally the phrase came to her, she stopped and said, "Remember that third sneeze? Now I'll tell you what happened," did just that, and continued her story.

You won't always come up with such presence of mind. Sometimes you have to just quietly stand there until the story comes back to you. Maybe forgetting is one reason that we exhibit the book the story comes from. You can always pick up the book and glance at the story. Sometimes merely looking at the book will help you recover. Just don't panic.

Stagefright is a malady which strikes with various symptoms, including nausea, hot flashes, quavering voice, and frequent trips to the restroom. Some of us never have it, some of us always have it. I used to suffer dreadfully as a child from this peculiar sickness. Now it rarely strikes me. The reason for this is that I have much more self-confidence and feel sure of my material. One reaches this stage through experience. I do occasionally suffer various degrees of stagefright when I conjure up thoughts of an unseen audience. Suddenly my stomach will drop a foot or two at the thought of facing a possibly hostile group of colleagues at a conference. My fears have always been unjustified. Once I was asked to give a paper before the Philological Association of the West. Naturally, I pictured the association as being peopled with serious, grave gentlemen all contemplating the comma in Shakespeare. My subject was "Violence in Children's Folklore." I planned to show transparencies and sing (off-key) as part of my speech. After my introduction, I wobbled to my feet and croaked out the first sentence of two. When I recited the first bit of folklore,

> Mary had a little lamb
> Her father shot it dead
> And now it goes to school with her
> Between two chunks of bread.

the audience of dark-suited men laughed—gaily, happily, joyously. They liked it! I had conjured up dire reactions for nothing. From this experience I learned the first rule to dispel stagefright: the audience is for you, they want you to succeed. They are so much on your side that they are afraid to react and sometimes you don't know what their reactions really are. This is, of course, one of the problems with adult groups. Children are easier to work with, and you probably will not suffer as much stagefright working with them (except at first) as you will with adults. Children react! They laugh and cry out loud.

My favorite story regarding stagefright is one purported to be a statement by Dwight D. Eisenhower: "I never feel stagefright anymore, I just imagine that the whole audience is naked, but I, the speaker, am fully clothed."

Common Faults

Ask your friends to tell you if you do any of these things:

Speak too fast. In an effort to "get it all over with" we sometimes race through material. As a first-year storyteller at the New York Public Library, my storytelling supervisor came to observe me giving a storyhour. I told Harold Courlander's "The Goat Well." Afterwards she took me to lunch. Her remarks are stamped permanently into my memory. "Miss Feller, you have good expression. Someday you might be a good storyteller, but that story usually takes 15 minutes to tell and you told it in four minutes and 38 seconds."

Speak too slowly. Sometimes the whole pace of a story drops. We tend to talk too deliberately, almost caressing each word. This sometimes happens if you tell the story too often. You are actually a victim of boredom. I recall a Festival of Arts at a school. A student and I were asked to attend. We went to at least 12 classes separately. My repertoire, at the time, was varied enough so that I could tell a different story to each class. The poor student only knew one story, which she told over and over. The pace of the story became slower and slower. She confessed afterward that near the end of the day she was no longer thinking about the story she was telling, but instead was planning an entire menu in her head for the guests that would be at her home that night.

Speak too softly. Remember that everyone has to hear you. Speak up and out. Don't be afraid to be heard. I was amused recently at a meeting in which the dean of a college had been asked to introduce a children's poet. He mumbled a few words, all the while looking at his feet. When the audience in the back complained of not being able to hear, he murmured that maybe a microphone was needed. "I don't think we'll need one," boomed the poet from the opposite side of the room. The dean shuffled off the platform and a tiny woman walked on to dominate the entire room with her resonant voice, without any mechanical aid.

You may find yourself in a situation where a microphone is needed. If this happens I suspect that you are telling stories to too many people, a sometimes unavoidable circumstance such as a banquet or large meeting. Be aware that using a microphone takes some experience. The most common pitfall is to stand too closely to the microphone, thereby obstructing the audience's view of the speaker as well as distorting the sound. Because I like to move when I speak, I try to use microphones as little as possible. Once at a large library meeting I was making an announcement while standing at my seat; before I had finished, someone suggested that I use the microphone on the stage. I ran up on stage and spoke into the microphone in the same loud voice. It was like the "Surprise Symphony"; the audience jumped halfway out of their seats. So, speak naturally when using a mechanical device.

Speak with too high a voice. A common fault with many women is that their voices are just naturally too high to be pleasant sounding. If you have this problem, and many women do, consciously practice dropping your voice when you speak publicly. It was interesting to me to hear tapes of the time I spent as a disc jockey. Between records, when I spoke extemporaneously, my voice was unpleasantly high; however, when I read the news my voice perceptibly dropped. That's when I made a conscious attempt to get my voice into a lower register.

Lack of eye contact. When you are talking to a group, you must make its members feel as though you are talking to each one individually. This is the great advantage of traditional storytelling. Freed from props and books, you are able to establish direct eye contact with every single member of your audience. Glance at a selected few in a random pattern. You will find yourself gratefully looking at someone who seems constantly nodding her or his head with approval and smiles. There is one of these in nearly every group. That person may be thinking about something else, but she or he seems to be hanging onto your every word. Contrasted to this person is the listener whose face is stone-blank. I sometimes find myself directing my entire storyhour to what seems like a hostile face until that person reacts in some way. Try not to lose hope if someone in the audience actually falls asleep. Perhaps you've done it yourself when you were very tired and relaxed. Just remember that most of the audience is attentively listening.

Use distracting gestures. To gesture or not to gesture? I hope that I don't sound like a broken robot, but the answer is: it's up to you. My grandmother, who could recite poetry in nine different languages, had taken what she called "elocution." In elocution you were taught exactly when and which gesture to use. To a modern audience such mechanical gesturing may be comical, but I don't ever remember laughing at my Grandma, so all that arm waving, head hanging, and body turning must have been effective.

One of my students used to tell stories as if he were tied to a post and told not to move a muscle, not even to blink; yet his voice was mesmerizing and we fell completely under his spell. I know that I move around quite a bit when I tell a story, making particular use of hand gestures. If the question of what to do with your hands is at first a problem for you, my advice is to lightly clasp them behind you. When you feel that you must demonstrate the smallest or the tallest, show the size with your hands and again put them behind your back.

You may be unaware of aimless, distracting movements such as swaying or biting your lip; it helps to have a friend critique you to discover such faults.

One of the torturous but effective devices I use in my storytelling classes is the videotape machine. If you have access to such a machine, through the school system or library, use it to practice telling a story. It only takes a few minutes of watching a rerun of yourself to spot any outstanding shortcomings. Microphones are usually sensitive enough to pick up the sound of your voice, even if it is hoarse with fright. After an artificial situation such as this, you will find telling a story to a real live audience easy and enjoyable.

Bibliography: Stories by Subject

After you have learned a story or two, you might find that the stories you know have common elements: the same theme, a similar background, or characters with the same desires. After you become aware of these categories you are ready to create a storyhour around a particular theme. Advertise the storyhour by announcing the subject: "Wishes" or "Tales from Japan." You might mix and match too. A story that fits into a wishes theme one week might be used in a storyhour featuring magic another time. The stories in the following list are among my personal favorites. If some intrigue you, look them up, read them through, and learn them to tell. The stories listed under a subject heading are not necessarily all to be used in the same storyhour. And of course, you don't always need to have a theme to make a good story-telling program—just good stories.

The authors and book titles listed in this bibliography refer to books that may be included in the two following bibliographies of collections and single tales.

Anansi

Anansi is a folk character who figures in African and Jamaican lore. A trickster, he is half man, half spider. Many stories about Anansi are included in *The Hat-Shaking Dance and Other Ashanti Tales from Ghana* by Harold Courlander with Albert Kofi Prempeh (Harcourt, 1957). *A Story, A Story* by Gail E. Haley (Atheneum, 1970) is a picture-book version of an Anansi story.

FROM AFRICA
"The Hat Shaking Dance," title story in Courlander's *The Hat Shaking Dance*. This story explains why spiders are bald. The dance itself can be acted out. Start out slowly building up to a zany movement in climax.

FROM JAMAICA
"Bandalee" in Philip M. Sherlock's *Anansi, the Spider Man* (Crowell, 1954). Land Turtle races Anansi and almost outwits him.

"Kisander," also in Sherlock's *Anansi, the Spider Man*. Anansi and Mouse steal from Cat in this tale.

Hans Christian Andersen

Andersen was born April 2, 1805. Celebrate the birthday of this great storyteller by telling some of his stories. These should be almost memorized, so use an accepted translation. A few favorites are:

"The Tinderbox" in Andersen's *It's Perfectly True* (Harcourt, 1938). Three huge dogs, gold, and a witch are the exciting elements in this popular Andersen story.

"The Swineherd," also in Andersen's *It's Perfectly True*. An ungrateful princess realizes her mistakes too late to marry a prince turned swineherd. All the ironic humor of Hans Christian Andersen.

"The Nightingale," in Andersen's *It's Perfectly True*. Also a picture book version, translated by Eva Le Gallienne and illustrated by Nancy Ekholm Burkert (Harper, 1965).

Artists and Stories for Art Lovers

"The Boy Who Drew Cats" by Lafcadio Hearn in Bryna and Louis Untermeyer's *Unfamiliar Marvels* (Golden Pr., 1962). A goblin rat is killed by the cats the boy draws. A scary Japanese story.

"The Nuremberg Stove" by Louise de la Ramée in Margaret Hodges's *Tell It Again* (Dial, 1963). A young aspiring artist hides in a beautiful stove and meets a king.

Authors

"The Peterkins Try to Become Wise" in Lucretia Hale's *Peterkin Papers* (Osgood, 1880). The foolish Peterkins attempt to write a book.

Birds

Tico and the Golden Wings by Leo Lionni (Pantheon, 1964). Tico is rewarded for his kindness with golden feathers.

Jorinda and Joringel by the Grimm Brothers (World, 1964). A witch turns children into birds.

"The Steadfast Tin Soldier" in Andersen's *It's Perfectly True*. A brave toy soldier adventures in a nursery. A touching ending brings tears to the eyes of the listeners.

Illustrations to show at the end of the storyhour:

Andersen, Hans Christian. *Fairytales;* il. by children from 18 nations. Orion, 1958.

———— *Seven Tales;* tr. by Eva Le Gallienne; il. by Maurice Sendak. Harper, 1959.

And a biography:

Godden, Rumer. *Hans Christian Andersen.* Knopf, 1954.

"A Chinese Fairy Tale" by Laurence Housman in Eileen Colwell's *A Storyteller's Choice* (Walck, 1964). A long and beautiful story in which an artist's apprentice becomes a great artist under unusual circumstances. To be told with quiet dignity. Also in Mary Davis's *A Baker's Dozen* (Harcourt, 1930).

"The Two Painters" in Louis Untermeyer's *The World's Greatest Stories* (Evans, 1964). The rivalry of two great artists, Zeuxis and Parrhasius.

"Rhyming Ink" by Margaret Baker in Sidonie M. Gruenberg's *Favorite Stories* (Doubleday, 1942). Simon Smug's wife buys ink that helps him become a poet. A nonsense story.

"The Seven Lazy Sisters" in Helen Olson's *Stupid Peter* (Random, 1970). The sisters are turned into crows for lying.

"The Tongue-Cut Sparrow" in Yoshiko Uchida's *The Dancing Kettle* (Harcourt, 1949). Be kind to birds.

Camels

"How the Camel Got His Hump" in Rudyard Kipling's *Just So Stories* (Doubleday, 1946). Kipling's stories should be told in *his* language. This one is short.

"How the Camel Got His Proud Look" in Eulalie Ross's *Buried Treasure* (Lippincott, 1958). This Chinese story is much kinder to the camel than Kipling's story.

The Dancing Camel by Betsy Byars (Viking, 1965). This modern story can be shortened for a lively storyhour.

"Ali and the Camels" in Robert Gilstrap's *The Sultan's Fool* (Holt, 1958). Ali can't manage to count the correct number of camels.

Cats

Puss in Boots by Charles Perrault (Harcourt, 1959). A cat finds a princess for his master.

"King of the Cats" in Edna Johnson's *Anthology of Children's Literature* (4th rev. ed.; Houghton, 1970). A short, scary story.

"Mr. Samson Cat" by Valerian Karrick in Johnson's *Anthology*. Also in Eulalie Steinmetz Ross's *The Buried Treasure and Other Picture Tales* (Lippincott, 1958). A Russian story about a "dreadful animal."

"The Priceless Cats" in Johnson's *Anthology*. An Italian cat tale.

The Clever Three

"Clever Manka" in Parker Fillmore's *The Shepherd's Nosegay* (Harcourt, 1958). Manka outwits her husband.

"Clever Grethel" in Mary Bleecker's *Big Music* (Viking, 1946). Grethel wears red

rosettes on her shoes and eats her master's chicken.

"Clever Elsie" in *Tales From Grimm* tr. by Wanda Gág (Coward, 1936). Elsie isn't clever at all, but neither is her family.

Cooks

"The Woman Who Flummoxed the Fairies" in Leclaire Alger's *Heather and Broom* by Sorche Nic Leodhas, pseud. (Holt, 1960). The fairies are happy to send a master baker back to her own home in this Scottish story.

"The Baker's Daughter" in Margery Bianco's *A Street of Little Shops* (Doubleday, 1932). Also in Bleecker's *Big Music* and in Phyllis Fenner's *Fools and Funny Fellows* (Knopf, 1961). The beautiful baker's daughter has her own ideas about which cake to bring to a friend's birthday party. A tongue-in-cheek satire.

The Funny Little Woman by Arlene Mosel (Dutton, 1972). A laughing woman is captured by underground monsters. A Japanese story.

"The Lady Who Put Salt in Her Coffee" in Hale's *Peterkin Papers*. The Peterkins try to change salt to sugar.

Dancing

These stories are for the storyteller who would like a little movement in storytelling.

"Wee Meg Barnileg and the Fairies" in Ruth Sawyer's *The Way of the Storyteller* (Viking, 1962). This story should be told in Sawyer's language and, if possible, with a slight Irish brogue. Meg dances with the fairies after a year of penance for naughty manners.

"Murdoch's Rath" by Juliana H. Ewing in Johnson's *Anthology*. Pat dances with the fairies on the Rath and becomes a rich man.

The Twelve Dancing Princesses by Andrew Lang (Holt, 1966). A soldier outwits twelve princesses who dance each night.

"Cinderella" in Andrew Lang's *The Blue Fairy Book* (Longmans, 1948) or Arthur Rackham's *The Arthur Rackham Fairy Book* (Lippincott, 1950). The English version is "Cap O'Rushes," in Joseph Jacobs's *English Fairy Tales* (Dover, 1967). This traditional French tale also appears in a picture book by Marcia Brown (Scribner, 1954). Also in Charles Perrault's *Perrault's Fairy Tales* (Doubleday, 1972).

"Nella's Dancing Shoes" by Eleanor Farjeon in Eulalie Steinmetz Ross's *Blue Rose* (Harcourt, 1966). Nella loses her dancing shoes and finds them in a jungle.

"The Goat Well" in Harold Courlander's *Fire on the Mountain* (Holt, 1950). A trader dances with joy in the marketplace.

The Devil

Oté by Pura Belpré (Pantheon, 1969). A near-sighted devil brings bad luck to a Puerto Rican family.

"The Devil's Hide" by Parker Fillmore in Phyllis Fenner's *Time To Laugh* (Knopf, 1942). A long funny story about a Finnish boy who outwits the devil.

"Perfection" in Natalie Babbitt's *The Devil's Storybook* (Farrar, 1974). The devil finally outwits an all too perfect little girl.

Dogs

"Jean Labadie's Big Black Dog" in Natalie Carlson's *The Talking Cat* (Harper, 1952). Also in Eileen Colwell's *A Second Storyteller's Choice* (Walck, 1964). An imaginary dog is the main culprit in this amusing French-Canadian story.

"The Tinderbox" in Andersen's *It's Perfectly True*. Three huge dogs run errands for a young soldier. Tell this story with as many of Andersen's original words as possible.

Dolls

The Velveteen Rabbit by Margery Bianco (Doubleday, 1926). A long sensitive story about a stuffed animal who is loved by a small boy.

"The Magic Glass" in Richard Hughes's *The Spider's Palace* (Looking Glass Library, 1960). The real people become toys.

"The Steadfast Tin Soldier" in Hans Christian Andersen's *It's Perfectly True*. A tin soldier is in love with a ballet dancer.

Foolish Fellows Who Made Good

"The Lost Half Hour" by Henry Beston in Eulalie Steinmetz Ross's *The Lost Half Hour* (Harcourt, 1963). Also in Child Study Association's *Castles and Dragons* (Crowell, 1958). Bobo appears to be quite stupid, but wins a Princess in this longer imaginative story.

"How Boots Befooled the King" in Howard Pyle's *The Wonder Clock* (Dover, 1965).

A foolish boy is able to fool a king. A long story by a master storyteller.

"Doctor Know It All" in Gág's translation of *Tales from Grimm*. Peasant Fish makes observations that turn out to be well-kept secrets and becomes a wealthy man. A variant is "Doctor and Detective Too" in Mary Hatch's *13 Danish Tales* (Harcourt, 1947).

Forgetfulness

"Poor Mr. Fingle" in Bianco's *Street of Little Shops*. Also in Gruenberg's *More Favorite Stories* (Doubleday, 1948). Mr. Fingle spends years wandering about the hardware store, because he's forgotten what he came to buy.

"Soap, Soap, Soap" in Richard Chase's *Grandfather Tales* (Houghton, 1948).

Another story about a boy who can't remember what he's shopping for.

"Icarus and Daedalus" by Josephine Preston Peabody in Johnson's *Anthology*. Also in Untermeyer's *The World's Greatest Stories*. Icarus forgets that his wings are made of wax in this Greek legend.

Foxes

"El Enamo" in Charles Finger's *Tales of Silver Lands* (Doubleday, 1924). The terrible El Enamo is outwitted by the fox.

"Mighty Mikko" in Fillmore's *The Shepherd's Nosegay*. A lovable fox finds a princess and a suitable castle for his

master. Similar to *Puss in Boots*.

"The Fox and the Bear" in Yoshiko Uchida's *The Magic Listening Cap* (Harcourt, 1955). A Japanese story in which the bear finally outwits the fox.

Gifts and Presents

"Rocking Horse Land" in Association for Childhood Education International's *Told Under the Magic Umbrella* (Macmillan, 1962). Also in Laurence Housman's *The Rat Catcher's Daughter* (Atheneum, 1974). Housman's story about the magic horse that Prince Freedling receives for his birthday.

The Swineherd by Hans Christian Andersen (Harcourt, 1958). A princess refuses

a prince's thoughtful gifts.

"How the Good Gifts Were Used by Two" in Pyle's *The Wonder Clock*. Also in Fenner's *Fools and Funny Fellows*. A rich brother and a poor one encounter St. Nicholas.

The Third Gift by Jan Carew (Little, 1974). Work, beauty, and imagination are the three gifts.

Goats

The first two are for older children, the last three for preschoolers.

"The Goat Well" in Courlander's *Fire On the Mountain*. An African trader is tricked into believing that a well produces goats.

"A Horned Goat" in Lucia Borski's *The Jolly Tailor* (Longmans, 1957). A Polish story about a fierce horned goat.

"Ticky-Picky Boom-Boom" in Sherlock's *Anansi, the Spider Man*. The goat butts the ghostlike yams into many pieces.

The Three Billy Goats Gruff by Peter C. Asbjørnsen and Jorgen E. Moe (Harcourt, 1957). "Who's that tripping over my bridge?"

The Wolf and the Seven Little Kids by the Grimm Brothers (Harcourt, 1959). Never open the door to strangers, is the moral of this popular story.

Greed

"The Rat Catcher's Daughter" in Housman, *The Rat Catcher's Daughter*. A father insists that his daughter be turned into gold. A beautiful story that should be told in Housman's own words.

"Shrewd Todie and Lyzer the Miser" in Isaac Bashevis Singer's *When Shlemiel Went to Warsaw* (Farrar, 1969). Todie tricks Lyzer into believing that his silver spoons give birth to teaspoons.

Once a Mouse by Marcia Brown (Scribner, 1961). An Indian fable pictured in woodcuts by a distinguished artist.

"The Fisherman and His Wife" in Gág's translation of *Tales from Grimm*. The discontented wife of a fisherman finally wishes for too much. A similar story is "The Golden Fish" in Arthur Ransome's *Old Peter's Russian Tales* (Dover, 1969), and also "The Beautiful Birch" in Mirra Ginsburg's *How Wilka Went to Sea* (Crown, 1975).

Hats

"How Boots Befooled the King" in Pyle's *The Wonder Clock*. The youngest brother tricks the king and marries the princess.

"The Magic Listening Cap" in Uchida's *The Magic Listening Cap*. A poor man finds luck with a magic cap.

"The Magic Cap" by Johan Hart in Ross's *The Buried Treasure*. In this Dutch story a farmer uses a cap to get revenge on some scoundrels.

"Hats to Disappear With" by Tanya Lee in I. K. Junne's *Floating Clouds, Floating Dreams* (Doubleday, 1974). A bandit tries to play a goblin's game.

Heroines

Famous folktale heroines who don't just sit back and wait to be rescued.

"Clever Manka" in Fillmore's *The Shepherd's Nosegay*. The Burgomaster marries a girl who turns out to be cleverer than he.

"The Barber's Clever Wife" by Flora A. Steele in Fenner's *Fools and Funny Fellows*. An "exceedingly clever person" sets her wits to work.

"Molly Whuppie" in Joseph Jacobs's *English Fairy Tales*. A girl outwits a giant.

"Elsie Piddock Skips in Her Sleep" in Association for Childhood Education International's *Told Under the Magic Umbrella*. Also in Colwell's *A Storyteller's Choice*. A long and beautiful story by Eleanor Farjeon featuring a skipping contest.

Holidays

A holiday storyhour might feature stories that are applicable to that holiday, but a good story is a treat on any day.

Christmas

"The Christmas Apple" by Ruth Sawyer in Ross's *The Lost Half Hour*. A touching story similar to Raymond M. Alden's *Why the Chimes Rang* (Bobbs, 1945). Try to tell it in Sawyer's own words.

"The Silver Hen" by Mary E. Wilkins in Ross's *The Lost Half Hour*. The children search for a silver hen and meet the Snowman in a very cold story.

"The Peterkins' Christmas Tree" in Hale's *The Peterkins*. Also in Fenner's *Fools and Funny Fellows*. As usual, the Peterkins have an amusing solution to an unusual problem.

Halloween and Thanksgiving

"The Pumpkin Giant" by Mary E. Wilkins in Mary Gould Davis's collection, *A Baker's Dozen* (Harcourt, 1930). Also in Ross's *The Lost Half Hour* and in a picture-book version retold by Ellin Greene (Lothrop, 1970). The origin of pumpkin pies is amusingly related. A long story.

"Rapunzel" in Gág's translation of *Tales from Grimm*. Also a picture-book version illustrated by Felix Hoffmann (Harcourt, 1961). A young girl locked in a doorless tower uses her long hair as a ladder for visitors.

"The Golden Arm" by Mark Twain in Benjamin A. Botkin's *Treasury of American Folklore* (Crown, 1944). Or the English version in Jacobs's *English Fairy Tales*. A short, scary story. Try also "Teeny Tiny" in Jacobs's *English Fairy Tales*, which has a similar surprise ending.

"The Huckabuck Family" in Carl Sandburg's *Sandburg Treasury* (Harcourt, 1970). A tall-tale nonsense story for Thanksgiving.

"Baba Yaga and the Little Girl with a Kind Heart" in Ransome's *Old Peter's Russian Tales*. Baba Yaga is the Russian witch; take care.

Mother's Day

"My Mother Is the Most Beautiful Woman in the World" by Becky Reyher in Hodges's *Tell It Again*. A sensitive Russian story that demonstrates that "We do not love people because they are beautiful, but they seem beautiful to us because we love them."

The Importance of Trees

Use these for Arbor Day or spring or any time, of course.

"The Apple of Contentment" in Gruenberg's *Favorite Stories*. A magic tree brings good luck to a younger sister. A Howard Pyle story.

"The Selfish Giant" in Oscar Wilde's *The Happy Prince* (Penguin, 1962). Also in

Ross's *The Lost Half Hour.* A beautiful story for spring with religious overtones.

Valentine's Day

"The Forest Bride" in Fillmore's *The Shepherd's Nosegay.* The mouse bride turns out to be the most talented wife of all.

The Importance of Clothes

"A Guest for Halil" in Alice Kelsey's *Once the Hodja* (Longmans, 1943). A short story in which a suit of clothes is invited to a banquet. A variant appears as "King Clothes" by M. A. Jagendorf in *The Arbuthnot Anthology of Children's Literature* by May Hill Arbuthnot and others; 4th ed., revised by Zena Sutherland (Scott, Foresman, 1976).

"The Emperor's New Clothes" in Andersen's *It's Perfectly True.* Also in Fenner's *Time to Laugh.* "But he has nothing on!"

Interesting Families

Anansi the Spider by Gerald McDermott (Holt, 1972). Each of Anansi's six sons has a particular talent.

Five Chinese Brothers by Claire Bishop (Coward, 1938). Four brothers display their particular physical traits to save a fifth from an undeserved hanging.

"The Three Brothers and the Giant" in Beatrice Schenk de Regniers's *The Giant Book* (Atheneum, 1966). Three French

Laziness

"Fool's Paradise" in Isaac Bashevis Singer's *Zlateh the Goat* (Harper, 1966). Atzel wishes to die because he hears that there is no work in Paradise.

"Lazy Heinz" in Gág's translation of *Tales from Grimm.* Lazy Heinz and his wife

"Princess and the Vagabond" in Ruth Sawyer's *Way of the Storyteller.* A variant of the "Taming of the Shrew" to be told in Sawyer's own words. Also good if you can sing since a song is important to the story. For older children. Adults like this too.

said a little child. Andersen's favorite story of a town's pride.

New Patches for Old by Barbara Walker and A. E. Vysal (Parents, 1974). Hasan alters some trousers, but his wife, daughter, and mother-in-law work on the same trousers with hilarious results.

"The Obsession with Clothes" in I. L. Peretz's *The Case Against the Wind* (Macmillan, 1975). The Devil tempts Basia Gittel into spending her money for finery.

boys outwit a giant and marry the king's daughters.

"Long, Broad and Sharpsight" in Ruth Manning-Saunders's *A Book of Wizards* (Dutton, 1967). Three comrades with unusual traits help a prince.

Tuck Everlasting by Natalie Babbitt (Farrar, 1975). The Tucks live forever, but is that enviable? A thought-provoking fantasy.

rationalize so that they never have to get out of bed.

"Ah Tcha the Sleeper" by Arthur Bowie Chrisman in Johnson's *Anthology.* Ah Tcha can't seem to stay awake in this story of the origin of tea.

Marriage

"Mary, Mary So Contrary" in Fillmore's *The Shepherd's Nosegay*. A farmer's wife is so contrary that she floats upstream.

"Gone Is Gone" in Wanda Gág's *Gone Is Gone* (Coward, 1935) or in Fenner's *Fools and Funny Fellows*. A man changes places with his wife with disastrous results.

"Gudbrand-on-the-Hillside" by Peter C. Asbjørnsen in Fenner's *Time to Laugh*. A Norwegian wife constantly forgives her foolish husband.

"Bluebeard" in Lang's *The Blue Fairy Book*. Or his Finnish counterpart of "The Three Chests" in Fillmore's *The Shepherd's Nosegay*. Curiosity gets a young wife into trouble.

"The First Shlemiel" in Singer's *Zlateh the Goat*. Shlemiel tries to end his life with a pot of poison that is really a pot of jam.

Even the Devil Is Afraid of a Shrew by Valerie Stadler (Addison, 1972). A man married to a shrew outwits her and the Devil in a folktale from Lapland. Picturebook version.

Mosquitoes

"The Conceited Elephant and the Very Lively Mosquito" by Lobagola in Bleecker's *Big Music*. The small wins over the big. A shorter story.

"Brother Rabbit and the Mosquitoes" in Bleecker's *Big Music*. One of Joel Chandler Harris's Brer Rabbit stories. Use gestures to "act out" this dialect story.

"The Flea" by Ruth Sawyer in Bleecker's *Big Music*. Also in Ross's *The Buried Treasure*. This is a story about a flea rather than a mosquito, but they're a bit similar, don't you think? The story is a long one, with Spanish words in it, and funny. Learn Sawyer's own words to tell this most effectively.

Multiplication

These stories all feature the multiplication of objects or people.

"The Doughnuts" in Robert McCloskey's *Homer Price* (Viking, 1943). This is a single chapter in a book of episodic small-town adventures. A doughnut machine continues to produce doughnuts until an entire luncheonette is crowded with them. A long story, that is easily shortened and not difficult to learn.

Millions of Cats by Wanda Gág (Coward, 1928). The classic picture book in which a man finds "hundreds of cats, thousands of cats, millions and billions and trillions of cats."

"Palace on the Rock" by Richard Hughes in Fenner's *Time to Laugh*. A king has so many children they must be hung outside the palace on a rock.

"Sorcerer's Apprentice" in Roger L. Green's *A Cavalcade of Magicians* (Walck, 1973). A student of the greatest magician in all of ancient Egypt misuses his power and gets into trouble.

"Two of Everything" in Alice Ritchie's *The Treasure of Li Po* (Harcourt, 1949). Also in Child Study Association International's *Castles and Dragons*. A magic pot produces two of everything, even people.

"Uncle Bouqui Rents A Horse" in Courlander's *Piece of Fire*. An action-packed story from Haiti. Ti Malice keeps adding imaginary people and animals to the back of a rented horse.

Music

"The Nightingale" in Andersen's *It's Perfectly True*. A long and beautiful story about the beauties of nature.

"The Musicians of Bremen" in Gág's translation of *Tales from Grimm*. Four animals make "music" and frighten a group of robbers.

"Orpheus" by Padraic Colum in Johnson's *Anthology*. In this Greek legend the music of Orpheus drowns out the voices of the sirens that beckon ships to disaster.

Night

"The Sack of Diamonds" in Olson's *Stupid Peter*. A little woman uses a slingshot to send diamonds up to the sky.

Hildilid's Night by Cheli Ryan (Macmillan, 1971). An old woman tries to destroy the night.

"The Milky Way" in Adet Lin's *The Milky Way and Other Chinese Tales* (Harcourt, 1961). A popular Chinese story about the origin of the Milky Way.

"Juan Bobo" by Rafael Ramírez de Arrellano in Dorothy Carter's *Greedy Mariani* (Atheneum, 1974). Juan thinks a pot is lazy and challenges it to a race.

"A Pot of Gold" in Ellen Margolis's *Idy the Fox-chasing Cow and Other Stories* (World, 1962). To claim the gold one must work in complete silence.

Nonsense Words

These stories feature silly nonsense words and phrases. Be prepared to have the children chant them back to you endlessly.

"Master of All Masters" in Jacobs's *English Fairy Tales*. A short funny story in which a master insists on calling things by names he has invented.

"The China Spaniel" in Hughes's *The Spider's Palace*. A school, a town, and finally the world chant a nonsense sentence.

"Cheese, Peas and Chocolate Pudding" by Betty Van Witsen in Elizabeth Sechrist's *It's Time for Story-hour* (Macrae Smith, 1964). A young boy's diet is rather limited in an easy-to-tell story for younger children.

"Crab and the Jaguar" in Valerian Karrick's *Picture Folktales* by Valery Carrick, pseud. (Dover, 1967). "Eyes, little eyes of mine! Fly back to me from the blue sea, from the blue sea, quick, quick, quick, quick!"

"Ticky-Picky Boom-Boom" in Sherlock's *Anansi*. The yams chant while chasing a tiger.

"How Bozo the Button Buster Busted All His Buttons When a Mouse Came" in Sandburg's *Sandburg Treasury*. One of Sandburg's Rootabaga stories.

Odd Names

These stories are variants of Rumpelstiltskin.

Duffy and the Devil by Harve Zemach. "All my work! Gone up in smoke! I swear I'll never knit another thing ever again!"

"Tom Tit Tot" in Jacobs's *English Fairy Tales*. Also a picture-book version by Evaline Ness (Scribner, 1965). "Nimmy nimmy not, My name's Tom Tit Tot."

"Yung-Kyung-Pyung" in Sherlock's *Anansi*. The names of the king's three daughters are discovered by Anansi and his friends.

"The Ogre Who Built a Bridge" in Yoshiko Uchida's *The Sea of Gold* (Scribner, 1965). A Japanese variant of Rumpelstiltskin.

Pots and Kettles

"The Talking Pot" in Hatch's *13 Danish Tales*. "Take me, take me," cried the pot, "and you'll never cause to rue it."

"The Dancing Kettle" in Uchida's *The Dancing Kettle*. A kettle sprouts a badger head and legs and dances around the room.

"Two of Everything" in Ritchie's *The Treasure of Li-Po*. A magic pot produces double of anything put into it.

Rain

"The Jolly Tailor Who Became King" in Borski's *The Jolly Tailor*. Also in Bleecker's *Big Music*. A merry little tailor repairs a hole in the sky.

"When the Rain Came Up from China" in Dell McCormick's *Tall Timber Tales* (Caxton, 1939). A Paul Bunyan tall tale of Oregon's Douglas fir country.

Riddles

These stories incorporate riddles in the stories. Use a few of the riddles you know between stories (also see Non-narrative Folklore).

"Princess and Jose" in Anita Brenner's *The Boy Who Could Do Anything* (W. R. Scott, 1942). The riddle of the sphinx is featured in this Mexican story.

"The Riddlemaster" by Catherine Storr in Kathleen Lines's *The Faber Storybook* (Faber, 1961). Polly solves riddles to keep from being eaten by a wolf. A modern story.

"The Flea" in Ross's *The Buried Treasure*. Also in Bleecker's *Big Music*. An ant, a rat, and a beetle help a shepherd boy solve a riddle.

"Riddle in the Dark" in J. R. R. Tolkien's *The Hobbit* (Houghton, 1938). This section of *The Hobbit* makes a good introduction to Tolkien's writings.

"Clever Manka" in Fillmore's *The Shepherd's Nosegay*. Come "neither by day nor by night, neither riding nor walking, neither dressed nor undressed."

"The Riddling Youngster" in Vivian Thompson's *Hawaiian Legends of Tricksters and Riddlers* (Holiday House, 1969). A young boy has a riddle contest with a high chief in old Hawaii.

"How to Become a Witch" in Maria Leach's *Whistle in the Graveyard* (Viking, 1974).

Just one of the short ghost stories in a good collection.

Salt

"Salt" in Ransome's *Old Peter's Russian Tales*. Also Harve Zemach's *Salt*, a picture book illustrated by Margot Zemach (Follett, 1965). How Ivan the Ninny became a rich man.

"Cap O'Rushes" in Jacobs's *English Fairy Tales*. A daughter loves her father "as much as fresh meat loves salt."

"Why the Sea is Salt" in Peter C. Asbjørnsen's *East O' the Sun and West O' the Moon* (Doran, 1922). "Grind salt, and grind both good and fast."

Short, Short Stories

Sometimes you need a short story at the beginning or the end of a storyhour, especially if you are doing radio or television work where timing is critical.

"The Storyteller" in Courlander's *Fire on the Mountain*. Similar to the endless story in the Arabian Nights.

"The Princess on the Pea" in Andersen's *It's Perfectly True*. The Princess felt a pea under 35 mattresses and featherbeds.

"The Snooks Family" in Virginia Tashjian's *Juba This and Juba That* (Little, 1969). No one can blow out the candle.

"The Tail" by Joseph Jacobs in Fenner's *Fools and Funny Fellows*. "If it had not been for that this tale would have been a great deal longer." A really short story.

"The Three Fridays" in Kelsey's *Once the Hodja*. The Hodja can't decide what to preach on Friday. See also the other stories in this book.

"The Gunniwolf" in Wilhelmina Harper's *The Gunniwolf* (Dutton, 1967). An amusing variant of Little Red Riding Hood with lots of action.

Sneezes

"The Three Sneezes" by Roger Duvoisin in Fenner's *Fools and Funny Fellows*. "You will die when your donkey has sneezed three times." A Swiss droll.

"Ebenezer-Never-Could-Sneezer" by Gilbert Patillo in Fenner's *Time to Laugh*. "Ah-ah-ah-Choo."

"Prince Sneeze" in Henry Beston's *Henry Beston's Fairy Tales* (Aladdin, 1958). "Everytime the Prince sneezes, something shall change." An original and amusing story.

"The Stolen Turnips, the Magic Tablecloth, the Sneezing Goat, and the Wooden Whistle" by Arthur Ransome in Effie L. Power's *Bag O' Tales* (Dover, 1969). "And as it sneezed, good gold pieces flew from it in all directions, till the ground was thick with them."

Tricksters Who Get Tricked

"How the Clever Doctor Tricked Death" by Manuel J. Andrade in Sharp's *Greedy Mariani*. The Doctor saves his own life and those of his patients through trickery. A story from the Dominican Republic to learn and tell.

"Nuts" in Babbitt's *The Devil's Storybook*. A not-so-greedy farm wife tricks the Devil, giving him a stomach-ache as well.

The Parrot and the Thief by Richard Kennedy (Little, 1974). A caged parrot outwits a sly thief.

Come Again in the Spring by Richard Kennedy (Harper, 1976). Old Hark wins a wager with Death.

Unwanted Guests

"Leave Well Enough Alone" in Rose Dobbs's *More Once-Upon-A-Time Stories* (Random, 1961). A young wife takes her husband's directions literally with unhappy results. A short funny story.

"The Old Woman and the Tramp" by G. Djurkla in Sechrist's *It's Time for Storyhour*. Also in May Hill Arbuthnot's *Time for Old Magic* (Scott, Foresman, 1970). A tramp makes soup from a 4-inch nail. Parallel stories appear as the Russian *Nail Soup* by Harve Zemach (Follett, 1964) and Marcia Brown's picture-book version of the French story *Stone Soup* (Scribner, 1947).

"Go Close the Door" in Solomon Simon's *More Wise Men of Helm* (Behrman House, 1965). Jewish version of the ballad story "Get Up and Bar the Door" in Johnson's *Anthology*.

"Winnie the Pooh Goes Visiting" in A. A. Milne's *Winnie the Pooh* (Dutton, 1926). One chapter in which Pooh gets stuck in Rabbit's hole and must stay for a week.

Wishes

"The Three Wishes" in Jacobs's *More English Folk and Fairy Tales* (Putnam, 1922). A man gets his wishes, but with ridiculous results. A similar story in Dobbs's *Once Upon a Time* and Gruenberg's *Favorite Stories*. Also "If You Had A Wish" in Association For Childhood Education's *Told Under the Magic Umbrella*.

"The Three Wishes" in Child Study Association's *Castles and Dragons*. All the wishes come true without making a single one. A longer story by Barbara Leonie Picard.

"Wishes" in Babbitt's *The Devil's Storybook*. A search for the perfect wish.

"Did the Tailor Have a Nightmare?" in Blanche Serwer's *Let's Steal the Moon* (Little, 1970). Napoleon grants a poor tailor three wishes.

For Younger Children

Preschoolers enjoy the old favorites such as *The Three Bears, Little Red Riding Hood,* and *The Gingerbread Man.* Extend their horizons by introducing them to other good stories.

"The Cats and the Mouse" in Jacobs's *English Fairy Tales*. A short story with a great deal of action. Use your hands to indicate the movement of the mouse.

"Henny Penny" in Virginia Haviland's *Favorite Fairy Tales* (Little, 1973). A repetitive story.

"The Old Woman and Her Pig" in Jacobs's *English Fairy Tales*. ". . . the piggy wouldn't go over the stile."

"Little Rooster and the Turkish Sultan" in Ross's *The Lost Half Hour*. Originally a story within a story in Kate Seredy's *The Good Master* (Viking, 1935).

The Tale of Peter Rabbit by Beatrix Potter (Warne, 1902). The book is often too small to show to a group, but the story stands by itself.

"Talk" by Harold Courlander and George Herzog in Gruenberg's *Favorite Stories*. An African tale about a yam that talks.

"Cat and the Parrot" by Sara Cone Bryant in Ross's *The Lost Half Hour*. Also in Johnson's *Anthology*. A repetitive story about a cat with a huge appetite. See also Jack Kent's *The Fat Cat* (Parents, 1971), a picture-book version from Denmark.

Bibliography: Illustrated Single Tales

Artists often illustrate traditional and original folktales in single volumes. At first glance these picture books may seem suitable only for preschoolers but this is not always the case. Usually these picture books are excellent for use in telling stories to an older group. In some instances you will want to share the artist's interpretation of the story with the older children just as you do with those who are younger. As a storyteller relying heavily on words, you will occasionally be puzzled by some of the stories that are illustrated. Why illustrate something that is better seen with the mind's eye? There is no ready answer to this question; only the artist's publisher knows.

One way of using these often beautiful books is to display them *after* the story is told. Another way is not to show the pictures during the storyhour at all, but to have the book ready for children to take home and enjoy at their leisure. From time to time you will want to read and show the pictures to a group as you would during the primary book program, and sometimes you will want to use the text of one edition with the pictures of another. A particular story might be told on several occasions, the first time without showing the pictures so that the audience "sees" their own interpretation, the next time showing the artist's work. Whichever way the illustrated books are used, you are in for a treat. All the titles in the bibliography that follows are recommended. Those marked by an asterisk are my particular favorites. Titles preceded by the symbol § are suitable for younger children.

*Aardema, Verna. *Why Mosquitoes Buzz in People's Ears;* il. by Leo and Diane Dillon. Dial, 1975. An accumulative action story with exciting graphics and a surprise ending.

Andersen, Hans Christian. *The Fir Tree;* il. by Nancy Ekholm Burkert. Harper, 1970. Delicate drawings illustrate a small book telling this beautiful Christmas story.

———— *The Nightingale;* tr. by Eva Le Gallienne; il. by Nancy Ekholm Burkert. Harper, 1965. Doublespread paintings could be shown to a group for added interest in this long Andersen classic, well worth learning.

———— *The Swineherd;* tr. and il. by Erik Blegvad. Harcourt, 1958. The detailed drawings are too small to show to a large group, but this edition might be introduced to Andersenphiles.

§ Asbjørnsen, Peter C. and Moe, Jorgen E. *The Three Billy Goats Gruff;* from the translation of G. W. Dasent; il. by Marcia Brown. Harcourt, 1957. Classic Norwegian folktale.

Barth, Edna. *Jack-O-Lantern;* il. by Paul Galdone. Seabury, 1974. The origin of a Halloween custom and the Devil are subjects in this picture book.

Baruch, Dorothy. *Kappa's Tug-of-War with Big Brown Horse;* il. by Sanryo Sakai. Tuttle, 1962. How a farmer outwits a Japanese water imp.

§ Belpré, Pura. *Oté: A Puerto Rican Folktale;* il. by Paul Galdone. Pantheon, 1969. The Devil is outwitted by a Puerto Rican family.

———— *Perez and Martina;* il. by Carlos Sanchez. Warne, 1961. An old Puerto Rican folktale retold by a gifted storyteller.

*Bernstein, Margery, and Kobrin, Janet, retellers. *The First Morning; An African Myth;* il. by Enid Warner Romanek. Scribner, 1976. The animals bring back from above the sky a box that is supposed to contain light. Vivid black-and-white silhouette drawings.

Bianco, Margery. *The Velveteen Rabbit;* il. by William Nicholson. Doran, 1926. A stuffed toy is loved with such intensity it comes to life.

Bierhorst, John, ed. *The Ring in the Prairie: A Shawnee Legend;* il. by Leo and Diane Dillon. Dial, 1970. Waupee and his family are changed into eagles in this dramatically illustrated Native American legend.

Briggs, Raymond. *Jim and the Beanstalk;* il. by author. Coward, 1970. An updated version of a traditional tale.

§ Brooke, L. Leslie. *The Golden Goose Book;* il. by author. Warne, 1906. Preschool favorites such as "The Three Bears" and "The Three Little Pigs." Show the pictures after you tell the stories.

Brown, Marcia. *Once a Mouse;* il. by author. Scribner, 1961. A mouse is given a chance to be a bigger, more powerful animal.

*———— *Stone Soup: An Old Tale;* il. by author. Scribner, 1947. Three soldiers teach the townspeople how to make soup from stones.

Buck, Pearl S. *The Chinese Story Teller;* il. by Regina Shekerjian. John Day, 1971. Why cats and dogs don't get along. A story within a story from China, illustrated with paper cutouts.

Buffet, Guy and Pam. *Pua Pua Lena Lena and the Magic Kiha-Pu;* il. by Guy Buffet. Weatherhill, 1973. Humorous watercolors illustrate this authentic Hawaiian tale.

Byars, Betsy C. *The Dancing Camel;* il. by Harold Berson. Viking, 1965. An original story about a camel named Camilla.

Carlson, Natalie Savage. *Alphonse, That Bearded One;* il. by Nicolas Mordvinoff. Harcourt, 1954. A bear cub is trained to be a soldier in this Canadian folktale.

Ciardi, John. *John J. Plenty and Fiddler Dan;* il. by Madeleine Gekiere. Lippincott, 1963. A familiar fable retold by a poet.

Clarke, Mollie. *Momotaro;* il. by Grace Huxtable. Follett, 1963. Traditional Japanese tale about the adventures of a boy who is found in a peach.

Coalson, Glo. *Three Stone Woman;* il. by author. Atheneum, 1971. An Eskimo story of good and evil illustrated with black-and-white ink drawings.

*Cohen, Barbara. *The Carp in the Bathtub;* il. by Joan Halpern. Lothrop, 1972. A remembrance of a Jewish childhood.

Dayrell, Elphinstone. *Why the Sun and the Moon Live in the Sky;* il. by Blair Lent. Houghton, 1968. Stylized drawings complement the text.

Domjan, Joseph. *see* Hardendorff, Jeanne B.

Elkin, Benjamin. *How the Tsar Drinks Tea;* il. by Anita Lobel. Parents, 1971. This has a folklore feel, but its origin lies in the imagination of the author.

——— *The Wisest Man in the World;* il. by Anita Lobel. Parents, 1968. A story of King Solomon.

Fleischman, Sid. *McBroom Tells a Lie;* il. by Walter Lorraine. Little, 1976. An original tall tale in which a farm is saved by a popcornmobile.

*Gág, Wanda. *Gone Is Gone;* il. by author. Coward, 1935. A man does the housework for a day. A single story for the advanced storyteller.

§*——— *Millions of Cats;* il. by author. Coward, 1928. "Hundreds of cats, thousands of cats, millions and billions and trillions of cats."

Galdone, Paul. *The Gingerbread Boy;* il. by author. Seabury, 1975. The lively pictures in color add to the enjoyment of this classic story.

———*The Monkey and the Crocodile: A Jataka Tale from India;* il. by author. Seabury, 1969. A curious monkey uses his wits to trick a crocodile.

Garrison, Christian. *Little Pieces of the West Wind;* il. by Diane Goode. Bradbury, 1975. The mighty West Wind must find the old man's socks.

Ginsburg, Mirra, reteller. *The Proud Maiden, Tungale, and the Sun: A Russian Eskimo Tale;* il. by Igor Galanin. Macmillan. 1974. A Slavic-Eskimo tale about the origin of the moon.

§ ——— *Two Greedy Bears;* il. by José Aruego and Ariane Dewey. Macmillan, 1976. A Hungarian tale in which a sly fox gets the better of two bear cubs who insist on equal shares of everything.

Grimm Brothers. *King Grisly-Beard;* tr. by Edgar Taylor; il. by Maurice Sendak. Farrar, 1973. Amusing illustrations and "old-world" language make a good storytelling package.

§ ——— *The Shoemaker and the Elves;* tr. by Wayne Andrews; il. by Adrienne Adams. Scribner, 1960. Delicate watercolors illustrate this classic tale. A Christmas favorite.

——— *Snow White;* tr. by Paul Heins; il. by Trina Schart Hyman. Little, 1974. The combination of text and pictures brings this classic tale to life.

——— *Snow-White and the Seven Dwarfs;* tr. by Randall Jarrell; il. by Nancy Ekholm Burkert. Farrar, 1972. Glorious illustrations for group or individual enjoyment.

——— *Tom Thumb;* il. by Felix Hoffmann. Oxford, 1973. Hoffmann's illustrations are good to show after the story is told. For variety, mix and match by using the

Gág or Shub version to tell, followed by the Hoffmann illustrations. Also in picture-book form by Hoffmann: *The Four Clever Brothers* (Harcourt, 1967); *King Thrushbeard* (Harcourt, 1970); *Rapunzel* (Harcourt, 1961); *The Seven Ravens* (Harcourt, 1963); *The Sleeping Beauty* (Harcourt, 1960); and *The Wolf and the Seven Little Kids* (Harcourt, 1959).

——— *The Twelve Dancing Princesses;* tr. by Elizabeth Shub; il. by Uri Shulevitz. Scribner, 1966. Stylistic drawings for this story of a soldier who outwits twelve princesses.

Haley, Gail E. *A Story, A Story: An African Tale;* il. by author. Atheneum, 1970. Explains the origin of the spider tale. A good introduction to African stories.

§ Hardendorff, Jeanne B., reteller. *The Little Cock;* il. by Joseph Domjan. Lippincott, 1969. Colored woodcuts give life to this version of a very popular Hungarian folktale. Tell the story first, then show the pictures.

§*Harper, Wilhelmina. *The Gunniwolf;* il. by William Wiesner. Dutton, 1967. A funny variant of *Little Red Riding Hood.* Tell with or without the pictures.

Hauff, Wilhelm. *Dwarf Long-Nose;* tr. by Doris Orgel; il. by Maurice Sendak. Random, 1960. Jacob is turned into an ugly dwarf for displeasing a witch.

*Hodges, Margaret. *The Fire Bringer: A Paiute Indian Legend;* il. by Peter Parnall. Little, 1972. How the fire came to men. Beautifully illustrated.

——— *The Wave;* il. by Blair Lent. Houghton, 1964. A Japanese tale adapted from Lafcadio Hearn's *Gleanings in Buddha-Fields.*

Hogrogian, Nonny. *The Contest;* il. by author. Greenwillow, 1976. Two men are engaged to the same girl in this Armenian folktale.

Holland, Janice. *see* Huai-nan-tzu.

§ Huai-nan-tzu. *You Never Can Tell;* ad. and il. by Janice Holland from the translation by Arthur W. Hummel. Scribner, 1963. A picture-book version of an easy-to-tell Chinese tale.

Hyndman, Jane A. *Mourka, the Mighty Cat;* by Lee Wyndham (pseud.); il. by Charles Mikolaycak. Parents, 1969. Russian tale.

Jacobs, Joseph. *Master of All Masters;* il. by Marcia Sewall. Little, 1972. This short story from Joseph Jacobs's collection is more effective without pictures, but children might enjoy looking at the book after they've heard the story.

Keats, Ezra Jack. *John Henry: An American Legend;* il. by author. Pantheon, 1965. A simple retelling of the American folk hero's story.

*Kennedy, Richard. *Come Again in the Spring;* il. by Marcia Sewall. Harper, 1976. Old Hark outwits death to feed the birds.

——— *The Parrot and the Thief;* il. by Marcia Sewall. Little, 1974. An intelligent parrot tricks a thief and attains his freedom.

§*Kent, Jack. *The Fat Cat: A Danish Folktale;* il. by author. Parents, 1971. A variant of the gingerbread boy. Use with or without the pictures.

Kimishima, Hisako. *The Princess of the Rice Fields;* il. by Sumiko Mizushi. Weatherhill, 1970. Indonesian folktale illustrated with traditional Indonesian puppets.

Kimmel, Margaret Mary. *Magic in the Mist;* il. by Trina Schart Hyman. Atheneum, 1975. Thomas, studying to be a wizard, meets a small dragon and starts a friendship.

Kipling, Rudyard. *The Elephant's Child;* il. by Ulla Kampmann. Kipling's story with collage illustrations. A long story to learn.

La Fontaine, Jean de. *see* Wildsmith, Brian.

Lang, Andrew. *The Twelve Dancing Princesses;* il. by Adrienne Adams. Holt, 1966. A prince spies on twelve sisters and wins one as his bride.

Leichman, Seymour. *The Boy Who Could Sing Pictures;* il. by author. Doubleday, 1968. Ben teaches a king a lesson in war.

Lexau, Joan M. *It All Began with a Drip, Drip, Drip . . . ;* il. by Joan Sandin. McCall, 1970. A retelling of a funny Indian tale.

Lionni, Leo. *Tico and the Golden Wings;* il. by author. Pantheon, 1964. Kindness rewarded.

Lowe, Patricia Tracey, ret. and tr. *The Tale of Czar Saltan, or the Prince and the Swan Princess;* il. by I. Bilibin. Crowell, 1975. Bilibin's full-color illustrations made for the 1905 edition should be shared to help impart the magic of this ageless fairy tale by Alexander Pushkin of Prince Guidon and his Swan Princess.

McDermott, Beverly Brodsky. *The Golem; A Jewish Legend;* il. by author. Lippincott, 1976. Powerful paintings bring the ancient legend of a man fashioned from clay to all ages.

*McDermott, Gerald. *Anansi the Spider: A Tale from the Ashanti;* adapted and il. by author. Holt, 1972. A picture book based on a film. Stylized illustrations.

——— *Arrow to the Sun;* adapted and il. by author. Viking, 1974. The solar fire as the source of life is presented in a stunning picture book. A film adaptation is also available.

——— *The Magic Tree: A Tale From the Congo;* ad. and il. by author. Holt, 1973. Picture book version based on an animated film to "show and tell."

——— *The Stonecutter: A Japanese Folk Tale;* il. by author. Viking, 1975. Striking illustrations illuminate this story of a lowly worker who wishes for greater power.

McHale, Ethel Kharasch. *Son of Thunder: An Old Lapp Tale Retold;* il. by Ruth Bornstein. Children's Pr., 1974. A troll-like creature tests the adopted son of a childless couple.

Maestro, Giulio. *The Tortoise's Tug of War;* il. by author. Bradbury Pr., 1971. The tortoise challenges the whale and the tapir to a tug of war.

§ Mosel, Arlene. *The Funny Little Woman;* il. by Blair Lent. Dutton, 1972. This Caldecott winner, based on a Japanese tale, is an exciting story to tell.

§ ——— *Tikki Tikki Tembo;* il. by Blair Lent. Holt, 1968. Picture-book version of a popular nonsense story.

Pearce, Anne Phillipa. *Beauty and the Beast;* il. by Alan Barrett. Crowell, 1972. A familiar tale retold with sophistication.

Perrault, Charles. *Cinderella;* il. by Marcia Brown. Scribner, 1954. The crayon drawings add much to this classic fairy tale of magic and romance.

§ ——— *Puss in Boots;* retold and il. by Hans Fischer. Harcourt, 1959. A Swiss artist has added to the charm of this story with his pictures.

§ ——— *Puss in Boots;* retold and il. by Paul Galdone. Seabury, 1976. Jaunty cartoon illustrations give a fresh interpretation to this old tale.

Pollack, Reginald. *The Magician and the Child;* il. by author. Atheneum, 1971. A variety of painting styles gives the reader something to think about. For use with more sophisticated children in small groups.

Pushkin, Alexander. *see* Lowe, Patricia Tracey.

Pyle, Howard. *King Stork;* il. by Trina Schart Hyman. Little, 1973. Fully illustrated version of one of the stories in *The Wonder Clock.*

Ransome, Arthur. *The Fool of the World and the Flying Ship;* il. by Uri Shulevitz. Nelson, 1967. Retold from Ransome's *Old Peter's Russian Tales* (Dover, 1969).

Rees, Ennis. *Brer Rabbit and His Tricks;* il. by Edward Gorey. Young Scott, 1967. Three Brer Rabbit stories retold in picture-book form.

Rockwell, Anne. *The Wonderful Eggs of Furicchia;* il. by author. World, 1969. A retelling of an old Italian tale accompanied by watercolor drawings.

Ryan, Cheli Durán. *Hildilid's Night;* il. by Arnold Lobel. Macmillan, 1971. A delightful story written in folktale style about a woman who hated the night.

§ Sawyer, Ruth. *Journey Cake, Ho!;* il. by Robert McCloskey. Viking, 1953. A variant of *The Pancake* with a mountain feel.

Say, Allen. *Once under the Cherry Blossom Tree: An Old Japanese Tale;* il. by author. Harper, 1974. A wicked landlord swallows a cherry pit and a tree sprouts from his head.

Schiller, Barbara. *Hrafkel's Saga: An Icelandic Story;* il. by Carol Iselin. Seabury, 1972. "But remember that no matter how urgent the need, you must never ride this horse."

Shivkumar, K. *The King's Choice;* il. by Yoko Mitsuhashi. Parents, 1970. An animal tale from India illustrated in the style suggestive of traditional Indian art.

Shulevitz, Uri. *The Magician;* adapted from the Yiddish of I. L. Peretz; il. by author. Macmillan, 1973. A feast is conjured up by Elijah disguised as a magician.

The Squire's Bride; originally collected and told by Peter C. Asbjørnsen; il. by Marcia Sewall. Atheneum, 1975. The bride is a horse in this picture-book version of an old favorite.

Stalder, Valerie. *Even the Devil Is Afraid of a Shrew;* ad. by Ray Broekel; il. by Richard Brown. Addison, 1972. A folktale of Lapland, in which a peasant husband outwits his shrewish wife and the devil, too.

Stamm, Claus. *Three Strong Women: A Tale from Japan;* il. by Kazue Mizumura. Viking, 1962. Three generations of women train a wrestler.

Steel, Flora Annie. *Tattercoats;* il. by Diane Goode. Bradbury, 1976. The Prince insists that Tattercoats dance at a palace ball accompanied by a gooseherd's magic piping.

*Suhl, Yuri. *Simon Boom Gives a Wedding;* il. by Margot Zemach. Four Winds, 1972. Simon Boom wants the best for his daughter. Tell with or without the pictures.

Tarcov, Edith. *Rumpelstiltskin: A Tale Told Long Ago by the Brothers Grimm;* il. by Edward Gorey. Four Winds, 1974. A droll version of the story of a search for a name. For your more sophisticated picture-book audience.

Taylor, Mark. *Jennie Jenkins;* il. by Glen Rounds. Little, 1975. An American folksong is the basis for this story of a spunky gal.

Tom Tit Tot; il. by Evaline Ness. Scribner, 1965. The English version of *Rumpelstiltskin.*

Towle, Faith M. *The Magic Cooking Pot;* il. by author. Houghton, 1975. This folktale from India is illustrated with batik prints that give the book a special traditional quality.

§ Tresselt, Alvin. *The Mitten;* ad. from the version by E. Rachev; il. by Yaroslava. Lothrop, 1964. In this Ukranian tale, animals find shelter in a boy's mitten.

Ungerer, Tomi. *Zeralda's Ogre;* il. by author. Harper, 1967. A little girl tames a hungry ogre with her gourmet cooking.

§ Walker, Barbara K. *How the Hare Told the Truth about His Horse;* il. by Charles Mikolaycak. Parents, 1972. A hare outwits a lion.

§ Walker, Barbara K., and Uysal, A. E. *New Patches for Old;* il. by Harold Berson. Parents, 1974. Hasan alters some trousers, but his wife, daughter, and mother work on the same trousers with hilarious results.

Weiss, Renée Karol. *The Bird from the Sea;* il. by Ed Young. Crowell, 1970. The illustrations add to this story of an unhappy caged bird in India.

Werth, Kurt, and Watts, Mabel. *Molly and the Giant;* il. by Kurt Werth. Parents, 1973. A variant of Molly Whuppie with an Irish background.

§ Wildsmith, Brian. *The Hare and the Tortoise;* based on a fable by La Fontaine; il. by author. Watts, 1966. Vibrant full-color illustrations add to the meaning of this traditional fable. Also illustrated by Wildsmith in single picture-book versions: *The Lion and the Rat* (Watts, 1963), *The North Wind and the Sun* (Watts, 1964), and *The Rich Man and the Shoemaker* (Watts, 1965).

Williams, Margery. *see* Bianco, Margery.

Withers, Carl. *Painting the Moon;* il. by Adrienne Adams. Dutton, 1970. Gouache paintings illustrate an old folktale from Estonia.

Wolkstein, Diane. *8,000 Stones;* il. by Ed. Young. Doubleday, 1972. Picture-book version of a Chinese tale.

Wondriska, William. *The Stop;* il. by author. Holt, 1972. A story is told against the background of Monument Valley in its many moods. Show the paintings.

Wyndham, Lee. *see* Hyndman, Jane A.

Yamaguchi, Tohr. *The Golden Crane;* il. by Marianne Yamaguchi. Holt, 1963. A deaf and dumb child nurses a wounded crane back to health.

Yolen, Jane. *The Bird of Time;* il. by Mercer Mayer. Crowell, 1971. Pieter is given the power to make time go faster or slower.

———— *The Girl Who Loved the Wind;* il. by Ed Young. Crowell, 1972. The art for this book is a mixture of collage and watercolor and gives a Persian air to an original fairy tale.

*Zemach, Harve. *Duffy and the Devil: A Cornish Tale;* il. by Margot Zemach. Farrar, 1973. A hilarious variant of *Rumpelstiltskin.* Use it with or without the wonderful illustrations.

———— *Salt;* from a translation by Benjamin Zemach; il. by Margot Zemach. Follett, 1965. A Russian story amusingly illustrated.

Zimelman, Nathan. *I Will Tell You of Peach Stone;* il. by Haru Wells. Lothrop, 1976. A peach pit takes on the significance of a gift. (Save peach pits to give as favors when you tell this.)

Bibliography: Collections

The collections of good storytelling material could fill an entire library. Editors have gathered together stories with a theme, stories from a particular region or country, and popular or favorite stories. If you are truly interested in the art of storytelling you will want to browse through as many books as you can to find the stories most suited to you and your group. In the following bibliography I have selected a broad range of collections. My particular favorites, those I highly recommend, are preceded by an asterisk. Titles preceded by the symbol § are stories suitable for younger children. Happy browsing.

Aardema, Verna. *Behind the Back of the Mountain: Black Folktales from Southern Africa;* il. by Leo and Diane Dillon. Dial, 1973. Authentic stories from Africa.

———— *Tales for the Third Ear from Equatorial Africa;* il. by Ib Ohlsson. Dutton, 1969.

*Alger, Leclaire G. *Heather and Broom: Tales of the Scottish Highlands,* by Sorche Nic Leodhas (pseud.); il. by Consuelo Joerns. Holt, 1960. If you like these stories, mostly for the intermediate storyteller, try the author's other collections, *Ghosts Go Haunting* (Holt, 1965); and *12 Great Black Cats* (Dutton, 1971).

Andersen, Hans Christian. *The Complete Fairy Tales and Stories;* tr. by Erik Haugaard. Doubleday, 1974. All of Andersen's stories, funny, poignant, satiric, are collected here.

———— *Fairytales;* il. by children from 18 nations. Orion, 1958. The children's drawings might inspire other artists.

*———— *It's Perfectly True;* tr. by Paul Leyssac; il. by Vilhelm Pedersen. Macmillan, 1937. Good translation of these famous stories.

———— *Seven Tales;* tr. by Eva Le Gallienne; il. by Maurice Sendak. Harper, 1959. The most popular of the Andersen stories. Be sure to show the pictures.

The Arabian Nights; ed. by Kate Douglas Wiggin and Nora A. Smith; il. by Maxfield Parrish. Scribner, 1929. The best known tales. Many of these are quite long. Use them for reading aloud if you don't want to learn them.

Arbuthnot, May Hill, comp. *Time for Fairy Tales, Old and New;* il. by John Averill and others. Scott, Foresman, 1961. Also *Time for New Magic* (Scott, Foresman, 1971), and *Time for Old Magic* (Scott, Foresman, 1970). An extensive collection of folk- and fairy tales useful for storytelling and reading aloud.

Arkhurst, Joyce C. *The Adventures of Spider: West African Folktales;* il. by Jerry Pinkney. Little, 1964. Short trickster stories.

*Asbjørnsen, Peter C. and Moe, Jorgen E. *East O' the Sun and West O' the Moon;* tr. by George Webbe Dasent; il. by Erik Werenskiold. Dover, 1970. Fifty-nine Norwegian folk tales. Some of the stories are lengthy, but the mood of oral tradition makes them easy to learn.

———— *East O' the Sun and West O' the Moon;* il. by Kay Nielsen. Doran, 1922. These illustrations are outstanding. Use them with the Dasent text.

———— *East O' the Sun and West O' the Moon;* rev. ed., retold by Gudrun Thorne-Thomsen; il. by Frederick Richardson. Row, 1956. A famous storyteller adapted these famous Norwegian tales for telling.

§ Association for Childhood Education International, Literature Committee. *Told under the Green Umbrella;* il. by Grace Gilkison. Macmillan, 1962. Favorite traditional tales for storytelling. See also *Told under the Magic Umbrella* (Macmillan, 1966); and *Told under the Christmas Tree* (Macmillan, 1962).

Aulaire, Ingri and Edgar d'. *d'Aulaires' Trolls;* il. by authors. Doubleday, 1972. Stories and oversize illustrations of the Scandinavian troll.

——— *Ingri and Edgar Parin d'Aulaire's Book of Greek Myths;* il. by authors. Doubleday, 1962. The myths of Greece, fully illustrated and retold as folktales.

*Babbitt, Natalie. *The Devil's Storybook;* il. by author. Farrar, 1974. Very funny, original stories featuring the Devil. All are easy to learn and gratifying to tell.

Baker, Augusta, comp. *The Golden Lynx and Other Tales;* il. by Johannes Troyer. Lippincott, 1960. Also *The Talking Tree; Fairy Tales from 15 Lands* (Lippincott, 1955). A famous storyteller collected these unusual stories.

Bang, Garrett, comp. *Men from the Village Deep in the Mountains and Other Japanese Folk Tales;* tr. and il. by compiler. Macmillan, 1973. A variety of folk characters are presented in these twelve tales good for storytelling. "The Strange Folding Screen" has an ecological theme.

Bang, Molly, comp. *The Goblins Giggle, and Other Stories;* il. by compiler. Scribner, 1973. Five scary, funny stories from Japan, Ireland, France, Germany, and China.

Bates, Daisy. *see* Wilson, Barbara Ker.

Baumann, Hans. *The Stolen Fire: Legends of Heroes and Rebels from Around the World;* tr. by Stella Humphries; il. by Herbert Holzing. Pantheon, 1974. Little known legends arranged by continent.

Belpré, Pura. *Once In Puerto Rico;* il. by Christine Price. Warne, 1973. A native of Puerto Rico collected these tales, some of which are religious and some historical. Also see *The Tiger and the Rabbit and Other Tales,* Lippincott, 1965.

Belting, Natalia. *Cat Tales;* il. by Leo Summers. Holt, 1959. A collection for cat lovers.

Berends, Polly B. *Jack Kent's Book of Nursery Tales;* il. by Jack Kent. Random, 1970. Seven of the most popular children's tales illustrated with amusing cartoons. Use with a small group; the pictures are small and scattered.

Berger, Terry. *Black Fairy Tales;* il. by David Omar White. Atheneum, 1969. Tales from South Africa.

*Beston, Henry. *Henry Beston's Fairy Tales.* Aladdin, 1958. Use the author's wording when telling these witty, original stories.

*Bianco, Margery Williams. *A Street of Little Shops;* il. by Grace Paull. Doubleday, 1932. American everyday stories of people you might know yourself. These original stories are not difficult to learn or tell.

*Bleecker, Mary Noel, comp. *Big Music, or, Twenty Merry Tales to Tell;* il. by Louis S. Glanzman. Viking, 1946. A basic collection, every story of which is worth learning.

Borski, Lucia Merecka, and Miller, Kate B. *The Jolly Tailor;* il. by Kazimir Klepacki. Longmans, 1957. Stories from Poland.

Botkin, Benjamin A., ed. *A Treasury of American Folklore.* Crown, 1944. The classic collection of stories, legends, tall tales, and folksongs of America.

Bowman, James Cloyd and Bianco, Margery, comps. *Tales from a Finnish Tupa;* from a translation by Aili Kolehmainen; il. by Laura Bannon. Whitman, 1936. Folktales from Finland.

Brand, Christianna. *see* Lewis, Mary Christianna.

*Brenner, Anita. *The Boy Who Could Do Anything and Other Mexican Folk Tales;* il. by Jean Charlot. W. R. Scott, 1942.

These Mexican tales which are mostly humorous are easy to tell.

Brown, Michael, comp. *A Cavalcade of Sea Legends;* il. by Krystyna Turska. Walck, 1972. The sea is represented in fiction, nonfiction, and poetry.

Bryan, Ashley. *The Adventures of Aku;* il. by author. Atheneum, 1976. An African folktale that tells how the cat and dog, once friends, became enemies.

——— *The Ox of the Wonderful Horns and Other African Folktales;* il. by author. Atheneum, 1971. Modern illustrations grace these four animal stories.

Carkin, Helen S. *see* Lerman, Norman.

*Carlson, Natalie Savage. *The Talking Cat and Other Stories of French Canada;* il. by Roger Duvoisin. Harper, 1952. Amusing stories; try telling them with a French accent.

Carpenter, Frances. *Wonder Tales of Dogs and Cats;* il. by Ezra Jack Keats. Doubleday, 1955. *See* also *The Elephant's Bathtub* (Doubleday, 1962). These are but two of this editor's collections for storytellers.

Carrick, Valery. *see* Karrick, Valerian V.

Carter, Dorothy Sharp, comp. *Greedy Mariani;* il. by Trina Schart Hyman. Atheneum, 1974. Folktales from the Antilles.

*Chase, Richard. *Jack Tales;* il. by Berkeley Williams, Jr. Houghton Mifflin, 1943. See also *Grandfather Tales* (Houghton, 1948). Excellent American mountain tales, these are best told in dialect.

*Child Study Association of America. *Castles and Dragons;* il. by William Pène Du Bois. Crowell, 1958. A collection of lesser known fairy tales.

Colum, Padraic. *The Children of Odin: The Book of Northern Myths;* il. by Willy Pogány. Macmillan, 1962. Norse myths.

§ Colwell, Eileen, comp. *The Puffin Storytime Box.* Penguin, 1972. Four books of stories particularly chosen for preschoolers: *Tell Me a Story;* il. by Judith Bledsoe (Penguin, 1962); *Time for a Story;* il. by Charlotte Hough (Penguin, 1967); *Tell Me Another Story;* il. by Gunvor Edwards (Penguin, 1964); and *Bad Boys* (Penguin, 1973).

*——— *A Second Storyteller's Choice;* il. by Prudence Seward. Walck, 1964. All these stories collected from various sources are worth telling. Some are for the advanced storyteller. Hints for storytelling accompany each story.

*——— *A Storyteller's Choice;* il. by Carol Barker. Walck, 1964. Excellent collection especially for storytellers.

*Corrin, Sara and Stephen, eds. *Stories for Eight-Year-Olds and Other Young Readers;* il. by Shirley Hughes. Prentice-Hall, 1971. Includes stories by Walter de la Mare, Hans Christian Andersen, James Thurber, and E. Nesbit. A good, all-around collection for the advanced storyteller.

Courlander, Harold. *The Piece of Fire and Other Haitian Tales;* il. by Beth and Joe Krush. Harcourt, 1964. These tales are spirited and easy to tell.

——— *Terrapin's Pot of Sense;* il. by Elton Fax. Holt, 1957. Traditional tales of American blacks.

——— *A Treasury of African Folklore.* Crown, 1975. Myths, legends, jokes, moral fables, satires arranged by tribal origin and geographical area.

*Courlander, Harold, and Leslau, Wolf. *The Fire on the Mountain and Other Ethiopian Stories;* il. by Robert Kane. Holt, 1950. The wit and wisdom of Ethiopia.

*Courlander, Harold, and Prempeh, Albert Kofe. *The Hat-Shaking Dance and Other Tales from Ghana;* il. by Enrico Arno.

Harcourt, 1957. Anansi, half man, half spider, is a leading character in these stories.

D'Aulaire, Ingri and Edgar. *see* Aulaire, Ingri and Edgar d'.

*Davis, Mary Gould, ed. *A Baker's Dozen;* il. by Emma Brock. Harcourt, 1930. The first storytelling specialist at New York Public Library collected these. Mostly for the advanced storyteller.

De La Mare, Walter. *Animal Stories.* Scribner, 1940. An outstanding children's poet puts some familiar stories into prose. *See also* *Tales Told Again* (Knopf, 1959).

*De Regniers, Beatrice Schenk. *The Giant Book;* il. by William Lahey Cummings. Atheneum, 1966. Giants from myth, legend, and folklore comprise an admirable anthology for giant lovers.

DeRoin, Nancy. *Jataka Tales: Fables from the Buddha;* il. by Ellen Lanyon. Houghton, 1975. Authentic collection of Indian fables.

§*Dobbs, Rose. *More Once-Upon-a-Time Stories;* il. by Flavia Gág. Random, 1961. Short, easy to tell. *See also* *Once-Upon-a-Time Story Book* (Random, 1958).

Dorliae, Peter G. *Animals Mourn for Da Leopard;* il. by S. Irein Wangboje. Bobbs-Merrill, 1970. Linoleum block prints illustrate this collection of West African folktales.

Downing, Charles. *Tales of the Hodja;* il. by William Papas. Walck, 1965. Episodic adventures of the Turkish folk character. Illustrated with bright, gay pictures.

Du Mond, Frank. *Tall Tales of the Catskills;* il. by Peter Parnall. Atheneum, 1968. Stories to learn and stories to read aloud in the oral tradition.

Durham, Mae. *Tit for Tat;* from the translation of Skaidrite Rubene-Koo; il. by Harriet Pincus. Harcourt, 1967. Latvian folktales.

Ellentuck, Shan. *Yankel the Fool;* il. by author. Doubleday, 1972. Funny stories based on the Yiddish oral tradition.

Elliot, Geraldine. *The Long Grass Whispers;* il. by Sheila Hawkins. Schocken, 1968. And *Where the Leopard Passes* (Schocken, 1968). African folktales.

Emrich, Duncan, comp. *The Book of Wishes and Wishmaking;* il. by Hilary Knight. American Heritage, 1971. Wishmaking formulas.

*Evans, Pauline Rush, ed. *Best Book of Read Aloud Stories;* il. by Adolph Le Moult and George Wilde. Doubleday, 1966. From traditional and modern sources.

*Farjeon, Eleanor. *The Little Bookroom;* il. by Edward Ardizzone. Walck, 1956. Farjeon's own favorite stories, all with her special fairytale quality.

Feinstein, Alan S. *Folk Tales from Portugal;* il. by Diana L. Paxson. Barnes, 1972. Eighteen tales by the author of *Folk Tales from Persia* (Barnes, 1971); and *Folk Tales from Siam* (Barnes, 1969).

Felton, Harold W. *Pecos Bill, Texas Cowpuncher;* il. by Aldren Auld Watson. Knopf, 1949. Stories with an American Western mood.

*Fenner, Phyllis, comp. *Fools and Funny Fellows;* il. by Henry C. Pitz. Knopf, 1961. All of Fenner's collections are worthy of a prime spot on the storyteller's shelf. *See* also her *Demons and Dervishes* (Knopf, 1946); *Feasts and Frolics: Special Stories for Special Days* (Knopf, 1949); *Ghosts, Ghosts, Ghosts* (Watts, 1958); *Giants and Witches and a Dragon or Two* (Knopf, 1943); and *Time To Laugh: Funny Tales from Here and There* (Knopf, 1942).

Ficowski, Jerzy. *Sister of the Birds and Other Gypsy Tales;* tr. by Lucia M. Borski; il. by Charles Mikolaycak. Abingdon, 1976. Six stories translated from the Polish. Excellent notes and pronunciation guide.

*Fillmore, Parker. *The Shepherd's Nosegay: Stories from Finland and Czechoslovakia;* ed. by Katherine Love; il. by Enrico Arno. Harcourt, 1958. Wry and romantic folktales.

Finger, Charles J. *Tales from Silver Lands;* il. by Paul Honore. Doubleday, 1924. South American folktales.

Finlay, Winifred, reteller. *Cap O'Rushes and Other Folk Tales;* il. by Victor Ambrus. Hale, 1974. A collection of popular and little known tales told with charm.

Fisher, Anne B. *Stories California Indians Told;* il. by Ruth Robbins. Parnassus, 1957. A good collection of stories of Native Americans.

Gág, Wanda. see Grimm Brothers.

Garner, Alan, ed. *A Cavalcade of Goblins;* il. by Krystyna Turska. Walck, 1969. A fine collection of stories and poems from around the world.

Gilstrap, Robert and Estabrook, Irene. *The Sultan's Fool;* il. by Robert Greco. Holt, 1958. Easy-to-learn folktales.

Ginsburg, Mirra, ed. *How Wilka Went to Sea and Other Tales from West of the Urals;* il. by Charles Mikolaycak. Crown, 1975. The third in a series of collections of non-Russian folktales from Russia. *See also The Kaha Bird: Tales from the Steppes of Central Asia* (Crown, 1971); and *The Master of the Winds and Other Tales from Siberia* (Crown, 1970):

———— *The Lazies: Tales of the Peoples of Russia;* il. by by Marian Parry. Macmillan, 1973. Laziness as represented by Russian folklore. An excellent collection for the industrious storyteller.

The Golden Fleece; Tales from the Caucasus; tr. by Avril Pyman; il. by Juri Krasny. Progress Publishers, 1971. Traditional tales from the USSR. The book may be ordered from Progress Publishers, 21, Zubovsky Boulevard, Moscow, USSR.

The Golden Treasury of Myths and Legends; ed. by Anne Terry White; il. by Alice and Martin Provensen. Golden Pr., 1959. An anthology with dramatic illustrations.

Graves, Robert. *Greek Gods and Heroes;* il. by Dimitri Davis. Doubleday, 1960. The myths of ancient Greece.

§ *Great Children's Stories: The Classic Volland Edition;* il. by Frederick Richardson. Hubbard/Rand, 1972. These nursery tales are lavishly illustrated.

Green, Roger Lancelyn, comp. *A Cavalcade of Magicians;* il. by Victor Ambrus. Walck, 1973. Many sources yield these stories from ancient to modern times.

Greene, Ellin, comp. *Clever Cooks: A Concoction of Stories, Charms, Recipes and Riddles;* il. by Trina Schart Hyman. Lothrop, 1973. Stories about cookery.

Grimm Brothers. *About Wise Men and Simpletons;* tr. by Elizabeth Shub; etchings by Nonny Hogrogian. Macmillan, 1971. Authentic translations of the famous Grimm's tales.

———— *Grimm's Fairy Tales;* il. by Arthur Rackham. Viking, 1973. This edition is best used by showing the illustrations.

———— *Grimm's Fairy Tales;* complete ed.; ed. and tr. by James Stern; intro. by Padraic Colum; commentary by Joseph Campbell; il. by Josef Scharl. Pantheon, 1944. For the professional shelf, a large collection for browsing and telling.

———— *The Juniper Tree and Other Tales from Grimm.* Selected by Lore Segal and Maurice Sendak; tr. by Lore Segal and Randall Jarrell; il. by Maurice Sendak.

Farrar, 1973. Two volumes of the lesser known tales meticulously translated and illustrated.

*——— *Tales from Grimm;* tr. and il. by Wanda Gág. Coward, 1936. Also *More Tales from Grimm;* tr. and il. by Wanda Gág. Coward, 1947. Still the best versions of the Grimm tales for telling.

*Gruenberg, Sidonie M., ed. *Favorite Stories Old and New;* il. by Kurt Wiese. Doubleday, 1942. *See* also *More Favorite Stories Old and New for Boys and Girls* (Doubleday, 1948). Some of these are original modern stories, others traditional favorites.

*Hale, Lucretia. *The Peterkin Papers.* J. R. Osgood, 1880. A ridiculous family always gets into incredible situations.

Hamilton, Virginia. *The Time-Ago Tales of Jahdu;* il. by Nonny Hogrogian. Macmillan, 1969. Mama Luka tells these stories to a little black boy. Also *Time-Ago Lost: More Tales of Jahdu* (Macmillan, 1973).

Hardendorff, Jeanne B., ed. *Tricky Peik and Other Picture Tales;* il. by Tomie de Paola. Lippincott, 1967. Tricksters are the main characters of these stories.

Harman, Humphrey, comp. *Tales Told Near a Crocodile;* il. by George Ford. Viking, 1962. African folktales from Nyanza.

Harris, Christie. *Once upon a Totem;* il. by John Frazer Mills. Atheneum, 1963. Indian tales from the Northwest.

Harris, Joel Chandler. *Brer Rabbit: Stories from Uncle Remus;* adapted by Margaret Wise Brown; il. by A. B. Frost. Harper, 1941. These stories are easier to tell than the original Harris tales.

Harris, Rosemary. *Sea Magic and Other Stories of Enchantment.* Macmillan, 1974. Most of these stories from various regions of the world (China, England, New Zealand) deal with romantic love.

Harrison, David L. *The Book of Giant Stories;* il. by Philippe Fix. American Heritage, 1972. The illustrations in this book rather than the stories are what could be useful in a storyhour. The giant really seems gigantic.

*Hatch, Mary C. *13 Danish Tales;* il. by Edgun. Harcourt, 1947. Amusing tales easy to learn.

§*Haviland, Virginia, comp. *The Fairy Tale Treasury;* il. by Raymond Briggs. Coward, 1972. This selection includes all the familiar favorites, many particularly suited for the preschool storyhour. Profusely illustrated.

*——— *Favorite Fairy Tales Told in India;* il. by Blair Lent. Little, 1973. Haviland's numerous collections are primarily meant for individual reading; however, they can also be used for storytelling. Good source for finding materials from particular countries.

Hodges, Elizabeth Jamison. *Serendipity Tales;* il. by June Atkin Corwin. Atheneum, 1966. Serendipity is the gift of "finding valuable or agreeable things not sought for." Tales from Persia, India, and Ceylon.

Hodges, Margaret, reteller. *The Other Worlds: Myths of the Celts;* il. by Eros Keith. Farrar, 1973. Cuchulain, King Arthur, and Tam Lin are among the legendary heroes of these tales.

——— *Tell It Again: Great Tales from Around the World;* il. by Joan Berg. Dial, 1963. Some new, some old stories, a collection especially for the storyhour.

Hoke, Helen, ed. *Witches, Witches, Witches;* il. by W. R. Lohse. Watts, 1966. Stories, some funny, some scary, are good for Halloween programs. *See* also *Devils, Devils, Devils* (Watts, 1976); and *Dragons, Dragons, Dragons* (Watts, 1972).

Hosford, Dorothy. *Thunder of the Gods;* il. by Claire and George Louden. Holt, 1952. Norse myths.

*Housman, Laurence. *The Rat-Catcher's Daughter: A Collection of Stories;* selected by Ellin Greene; il. by Julia Noonan. Atheneum, 1974. Use the language of the author when telling these special literary folktales.

*Hughes, Richard. *The Spider's Palace and Other Stories;* il. by George Charlton. Looking Glass Library, 1960. Sophisticated original stories.

Hughes, Ted. *How the Whale Became;* il. by George Adamson. Faber & Faber, 1963. A British author's original stories, similar in theme to Kipling's *Just So Stories.*

§ Hutchinson, Veronica. *Chimney Corner Stories;* il. by Lois Lenski. Minton, Balch, 1925. Stories suitable for preschoolers.

Hyndman, Robert. *Tales the People Tell in China,* by Robert Wyndham (pseud.); il. by Jay Yang. Messner, 1971. Myths, legends and sayings of ancient China.

Jablow, Alta, and Withers, Carl, comps. *The Man in the Moon;* il. by Peggy Wilson. Holt, 1969. A collection of stories featuring the moon, stars, and sun.

§*Jacobs, Joseph. *English Fairy Tales;* il. by John D. Batten. Dover, 1967. The classic collection of English tales.

Jagendorf, Moritz A. *Folk Stories of the South;* il. by Michael Parks. Vanguard, 1972. Stories from the eleven states of the old Confederacy.

────── *Tyll Ulenspiegel's Merry Pranks;* il. by Fritz Eichenberg. Vanguard, 1938. A seemingly foolish fellow uses his wit in these lively German stories.

Jagendorf, Moritz, and Tillhagen, C. H. *The Gypsies' Fiddle and Other Gypsy Tales;* il. by Hans Helweg. Vanguard, 1956. Stories about gypsies.

Jewett, Eleanore Myers. *Which Was Witch? Tales of Ghosts and Magic from Korea;* il. by Taro Yashima. Viking, 1953. Notes on source material are helpful. Good for the Halloween storytime.

Jiménez, Juan Ramón. *Platero and I;* tr. by Eloise Roach; il. by Jo Alys Downs. Univ. of Texas Pr., 1957. A quiet portrait of Spanish life as the author talks to his donkey. For a sophisticated group.

§*Johnson, Edna; Sickels, Evelyn R.; and Sayers, Frances Clarke, comps. *Anthology of Children's Literature,* 4th ed.; il. by Fritz Eichenberg and N. C. Wyeth. Houghton, 1970. A large collection of stories for every occasion.

Junne, I. K., comp. *Floating Clouds, Floating Dreams: Favorite Asian Folktales.* Doubleday, 1974. Stories from eleven Asian countries.

Karrick, Valerian V. *Picture Tales from the Russian* by Valery Carrick (pseud.); il. by author. Dover, 1967. Short stories first published in 1926.

Kedabra, Abby, ed. *Nine Witch Tales;* il. by John Fernie. Scholastic, 1970. Collected from various sources, these tales will satisfy the cry for "something scary."

Keely, H. H., and Price, Christine. *The City of the Dagger;* il. by Christine Price. Warne, 1971. A collection of legends. An essay gives some historical background for the stories.

*Kelsey, Alice Geer. *Once the Hodja;* il. by Frank Dobias. Longmans, 1943. Short, funny, easy-to-tell Turkish stories.

────── *Once the Mullah;* il. by Kurt Werth. Longmans, 1954. Short, funny stories from Iran.

Kent, Jack. *see* Berends, Polly B.

*Kipling, Rudyard. *Just So Stories;* il. by author. Doubleday, 1946. These animal stories should be told in the author's own words.

*Lang, Andrew, ed. *The Blue Fairy Book;* il. by Ben Kutcher. Longmans, 1948. The best-known fairy tales. Read and choose tales from the other "color" books in the series—Red, Violet, Yellow, etc.

——— *Fifty Favorite Tales;* il. by Margery Gill. Watts, 1964. Stories chosen from Lang's color series.

Leach, Maria, ed. *How the People Sang the Mountains Up: How and Why Stories;* il. by Glen Rounds. Viking, 1967. Very short stories explaining the ways of nature.

*——— *Noodles, Nitwits, and Numskulls;* il. by Kurt Werth. World, 1961. Funny short stories from many sources. Most are easy to tell.

——— *The Rainbow Book of American Folk Tales and Legends;* il. by Marc Simont. World, 1958. Amusing illustrations are scattered through this anthology of tales from North and South America.

——— *Whistle in the Graveyard: Folktales to Chill Your Bones;* il. by Ken Rinciari. Viking, 1974. Forty short ghost tales that are useful when you need a "quickie but scary."

Lerman, Norman. *Once Upon an Indian Tale;* il. by Helen S. Carkin. Carlton, 1968. Authentic tales from the Pacific Northwest rewritten for today's reader.

Lester, Julius. *The Knee-High Man and Other Tales;* il. by Ralph Pinto. Dial, 1972. Animal tales from American slave lore.

Lewis, Mary Christianna, comp. *Naughty Children,* by Christianna Brand (pseud.); il. by Edward Ardizzone. Dutton, 1963. Most of these selections about children are excerpted from fictional sources.

*Lines, Kathleen, ed. *The Faber Book of Stories;* il. by Alan Howard. Faber, 1961. A large collection of stories from old and new sources.

——— *Nursery Stories;* il. by Harold Jones. Watts, 1960. A familiar choice of fairy tales. The delicate illustrations add to the book's use.

Lundbergh, Holger. *see* Olenius, Elsa.

Maas, Selve. *The Moon Painters and Other Estonian Folk Tales;* il. by Laszlo Gal. Viking, 1971. Short tales that are easy to learn.

McCloskey, Robert. *Homer Price;* il. by author. Viking, 1943. Episode adventures of small town life.

*McCormick, Dell J. *Tall Timber Tales: More Paul Bunyan Stories;* il. by Lorna Lively. Caxton, 1939. Put two or three of these stories together to make a longer story.

Malcolmson, Anne. *Yankee Doodle's Cousins;* il. by Robert McCloskey. Houghton, 1941. Pecos Bill, Paul Bunyan, and Johnny Appleseed are among the American folk heroes featured in this collection.

Manning-Sanders, Ruth. The following collections are excellent sources for storytelling: *A Book of Devils and Demons;* il. by Robin Jacques (Dutton, 1970); *A Book of Ghosts and Goblins;* il. by Robin Jacques (Dutton, 1969); *A Book of Giants;* il. by Robin Jacques (Dutton, 1963); *A Book of Magical Beasts;* il. by Raymond Briggs (T. Nelson, 1970); *A Book of Mermaids;* il. by Robin Jacques (Dutton, 1968); *A Book of Monsters;* il. by Robin Jacques (Dutton, 1976); *A Book of Princes and Princesses;* il. by Robin Jacques (Dutton, 1970); *A Book of Witches,* il. by Robin Jacques (Dutton, 1966); *A Book of Wizards;* il. by Robin Jacques (Dutton, 1967); and *The Red King and the Witch: Gypsy Folk and Fairy Tales;* il. by Victor G. Ambrus (Ray, 1965).

Margolis, Ellen. *Idy, the Fox-chasing Cow and Other Stories;* il. by Kurt Werth.

World, 1962. Easy-to-learn stories collected in the state of Ohio.

Martin, Frances. *Nine Tales of Coyote;* il. by Dorothy McEntee. Harper, 1950. Indian tales featuring the animal god.

Martin, Frances, reteller. *Raven-Who-Sets-Things-Right: Indian Tales of the Northwest Coast;* il. by Dorothy McEntree. Harper, 1975. Ten tales that feature Raven the trickster.

Milne, A. A. *Winnie the Pooh,* il. by Ernest H. Shepard. Dutton, 1926. For storytelling or reading aloud. Pooh, Piglet, Eeyore, and Christopher Robin are the characters in this childhood classic. *See also The House At Pooh Corner* (Dutton, 1928).

Minard, Rosemary, ed. *Womenfolk and Fairy Tales;* il. by Suzanna Klein. Houghton, 1974. Eighteen stories featuring clever women chosen from classic sources.

Nahmad, H. M. *The Peasant and the Donkey: Tales of the Near and Middle East;* il. by William Papas. Walck, 1968. Persian, Armenian, Turkish, and Hebrew tales.

§ Newell, Hope. *The Little Old Woman Who Used Her Head and Other Stories;* il. by Margaret Ruse and Anne Merriman Peck. Nelson, 1973. First published in 1935, this collection contains short stories of silly problems and their improbable solutions.

Nic Leodhas, Sorche. *see* Alger, Leclaire G.

Nye, Robert. *The Mathematical Princess and Other Stories;* il. by Paul Bruner. Hill & Wang, 1971. Original stories by a fine English author.

Olenius, Elsa, comp. *Great Swedish Fairy Tales;* tr. by Holger Lundbergh; il. by John Bauer. Delacorte, 1973. The illustrations in the collection evoke a fairy-tale mood.

Olson, Helen Kronberg. *Stupid Peter and Other Tales;* il. by Jack and Irene Delano. Random, 1970. Humorous original stories.

Opie, Iona and Peter. *The Classic Fairy Tales.* Oxford, 1974. Most interesting for its many illustrations collected from other editions of these popular stories.

Peretz, Isaac L. *The Case against the Wind;* tr. by Esther Hautzig; il. by Leon Shtainmetz. Macmillan, 1975. Ten stories by the nineteenth-century Yiddish author, with useful notes for the storyteller.

Perrault, Charles. *Classic French Fairy Tales;* il. by Janusz Grabianski. Meredith, 1967. Perrault's tales all in one volume.

*———— *Perrault's Fairy Tales;* tr. by Sasha Moorsom; il. by Landa Crommelynck. Doubleday, 1972. Modern line drawings and brilliant colors make the large size illustrations worth sharing.

Picard, Barbara Leonie. *Three Ancient Kings: Gilgamesh, Hrolf Kraki, Conary;* il. by Philip Gough. Warne, 1972. Stories from the epics. Probably better for reading aloud because of their length.

Pilkington, Francis M. *Shamrock and Spear: Tales and Legends from Ireland;* il. by Leo and Diane Dillon. Holt, 1968. Legends and folktales that are purely Irish in origin.

§*Power, Effie L., comp. *Bag O'Tales;* il. by Corydon Bell. Dover, 1969. A reprint of a 1934 selection of stories for storytellers. Includes fables, myths, epics, folktales, and a section for younger children.

Provensen, Alice and Martin, comps. *The Provensen Book of Fairy Tales;* il. by compilers. Random, 1971. Show the illustrations to the group after you've told the stories. Modern original tales. Most appear in other sources.

Pugh, Ellen. *More Tales From the Welsh Hills;* il. by Joan Sandin. Dodd, 1971. Stories from a Welsh country village.

*Pyle, Howard. *The Wonder Clock.* Dover, 1965. Original stories for the advanced storyteller. First published in 1887.

Quinn, Zdenka, and John Paul. *The Water Sprite of the Golden Town: Folk Tales of Bohemia;* il. by Deborah Ray. Macrae Smith, 1971. Many Bohemian folk characters are represented in this collection.

Rackham, Arthur, comp. *Fairy Book;* il. by compiler. Lippincott, 1950. The illustrations make this collection of traditional favorites worthwhile.

*Ransome, Arthur. *Old Peter's Russian Tales;* il. by Dmitri Mitrokhin. Dover, 1969. Longer Russian tales in a classic collection.

Ritchie, Alice. *The Treasure of Li-Po;* il. by T. Ritchie. Harcourt, 1949. Six original tales set in old China.

Rockwell, Thomas. *The Portmanteau Book;* il. by Gail Rockwell. Little, 1974. Includes stories, contests, and cartoons for individual browsing or for storyhour use.

*Ross, Eulalie Steinmetz, ed. *The Blue Rose: A Collection of Stories for Girls;* il. by Enrico Arno. Harcourt, 1966. An excellent collection of romantic tales by Ruth Sawyer, Howard Pyle, Walter de la Mare, Eleanor Farjeon, and other well-known writers.

*———— *The Buried Treasure;* il. by Josef Cellini. Lippincott, 1958. Mostly animal tales.

*———— *The Lost Half Hour;* il. by Enrico Arno. Harcourt, 1963. Excellent collection chosen by a well-known storyteller. Many of the stories are quite long.

Rounds, Glen. *Ol' Paul, the Mighty Logger;* il. by author. Holiday, 1949. An amusing collection of stories about the American tall-tale hero.

Rugoff, Milton. *A Harvest of World Folk Tales;* il. by Joseph Low. Viking, 1949. An excellent collection for the storyteller's shelf.

*Sandburg, Carl. *The Sandburg Treasury;* il. by Paul Bacon. Harcourt, 1970. An anthology which includes *The Rootabaga Stories*—nonsense stories.

*Sawyer, Ruth. *Joy to the World: Christmas Legends;* il. by Trina Schart Hyman. Little, 1966. Also *The Long Christmas* (Viking, 1941); and *The Way of the Storyteller* (Viking, 1962). These stories were collected by a noted storyteller.

§*Sechrist, Elizabeth Hough, and Woolsey, Janette, eds. *It's Time For Story Hour;* il. by Elsie Jane McCorkell. Macrae Smith, 1964. A miscellaneous collection divided into sections for the storyteller.

Seeger, Elizabeth. *The Ramayana;* il. by Gordon Laite. W. R. Scott, 1969. Stories from the great Indian epic.

Sekorová, Dagmar, comp. *European Fairy Tales;* il. by Mirko Hanák. Lothrop, 1971. A selection of tales from eight European countries.

*Serwer, Blanche Luria. *Let's Steal the Moon; Jewish Tales, Ancient and Modern;* il. by Trina Schart Hyman. Little, 1970. Jewish wit and wisdom are featured in this storyteller's collection.

Sheehan, Ethna, comp. *Folk and Fairy Tales from Around the World;* il. by Mircea Vasiliu. Dodd, 1970. Hints for beginning storytellers are included in this collection of tales from 17 countries.

*Sherlock, Philip M. *Anansi, the Spider Man;* il. by Marcia Brown. Crowell, 1954. Anansi in Jamaica. Compare these with the African Anansi stories.

Shub, Elizabeth. *see* Grimm Brothers.

*Simon, Solomon. *More Wise Men of Helm and Their Merry Tales;* il. by Stephen Kraft; ed. by Hannah Goodman. Behrman House, 1965. The silly antics of the mythical Jewish town of Helm.

*Singer, Isaac Bashevis. *When Shlemiel Went to Warsaw and Other Stories;* tr. by author and Elizabeth Shub; il. by Margot Zemach. Farrar, 1969. Eight short stories, some drawn from Jewish folklore, others fantasies of his own imagining.

*——— *Zlateh the Goat;* tr. by author and Elizabeth Shub; il. by Maurice Sendak. Amusing Jewish tales about fools and simpletons.

*Smith, Helen R. *Laughing Matter;* il. by Kurt Wiese. Scribner, 1949. A collection of funny stories.

Spicer, Dorothy. *13 Ghosts;* il. by Sophia. Coward, 1965. Ghosts are a popular subject with storytelling groups.

Stoutenburg, Adrien. *American Tall-Tale Animals;* il. by Glen Rounds. Viking, 1968. Fish, snakes, even insects are featured in this collection of animal stories.

§*Tashjian, Virginia A., comp. *Juba This and Juba That;* il. by Victoria de Larrea. Little, 1969. A collection of rhymes, riddles, and very short stories. Also *With A Deep Sea Smile* (Little, 1974).

Thoby-Marcelin, Philippe, and Marcelin, Pierre. *The Singing Turtle and Other Tales from Haiti;* tr. by Eva Thoby-Marcelin; il. by George Ford. Farrar, 1971. Magic and animals from Haiti.

Thompson, Stith, comp. *One Hundred Favorite Folktales;* il. by Franz Altschuler. Indiana Univ. Pr., 1968. All the world favorites for the professional shelf.

Thompson, Vivian L. *Hawaiian Legends of Tricksters and Riddlers;* il. by Sylvie Selig. Holiday House, 1969. Trickster and riddle stories; good introductions with a pronunciation guide.

Thorne-Thomsen, Gudrun. *see* Asbjørnsen, Peter C., and Moe, Jorgen E.

Titiev, Estelle, and Pargment, Lila, tr. and adapters. *How the Moolah Was Taught a Lesson and Other Tales from Russia;* il. by Ray Cruz. Dial, 1976. Four different peoples of Russia are represented in this collection for the storyteller.

Tolkien, J. R. R. *The Hobbit; or, There and Back Again.* Houghton, 1938. A full-length novel; parts are good for storytelling.

*Uchida, Yoshiko. *The Magic Listening Cap: More Folk Tales from Japan;* il. by author. Harcourt, 1955. Also *The Sea of Gold* (Scribner, 1965). Stories from Japan.

Ungerer, Tomi, ed. *A Story Book;* il. by author. Watts, 1974. Six well-known stories amusingly illustrated. In Ungerer's version Little Red Riding Hood marries the wolf.

Untermeyer, Bryna and Louis, eds. *Unfamiliar Marvels;* il. by Hans Helweg. Golden Pr., 1962. A good mix of folklore and modern tales from many sources.

Untermeyer, Louis. *The World's Greatest Stories: Fifty-five Legends that Live Forever;* il. by Mae Gerhard. Evans, 1964. Stories that have their origins in history.

*Wahl, Jan. *Runaway Jonah and Other Tales;* il. by Uri Shulevitz. Macmillan, 1968. New versions of stories from the Old Testament.

Walker, Barbara. *Watermelons, Walnuts and the Wisdom of Allah, and Other Tales of the Hoca;* il. by Harold Berson. Parents, 1967. Amusing collection of Turkish stories centering around the wise and witty Nasreddin Hoca.

Wheeler, Post. *Russian Wonder Tales;* il. by I. Bilibin. Thomas Yoseloff, 1957. Long stories to tell from old Russia.

White, Anne Terry. *see The Golden Treasury of Myths and Legends.*

Wiggin, Kate Douglas and Smith, Nora Archibald. *see also The Arabian Nights.*

Wiggin, Kate Douglas and Smith, Nora Archibald, comps. *The Fairy Ring;* rev. by Ethna Sheehan; il. by Warren Chappell. Doubleday, 1967. Many different countries are represented in this collection.

*Wilde, Oscar. *The Happy Prince and Other Stories;* il. by Lars Bo. Penguin, 1962. Sensitive stories for the older child and the advanced storyteller. These should be learned word for word in order to profit from the lovely language.

Williams, Margery. *see* Bianco, Margery Williams.

Wilson, Barbara Ker, reteller. *Tales Told to Kabbarli;* aboriginal legends collected by Daisy Bates; il. by Harold Thomas. Crown, 1972. Aboriginal legends of Australia. Difficult vocabulary.

Withers, Carl, comp. *A World of Nonsense: Strange and Humorous Tales from Many Lands;* il. by John E. Johnson. Holt, 1968. The silly and absurd in the world of nonsense.

Wolkstein, Diane. *Lazy Stories;* il. by James Marshall. Seabury, 1976. Easy-to-learn tales from Japan, Mexico, and Laos.

Wyndham, Robert. *see* Hyndman, Robert.

Yolen, Jane. *The Girl Who Cried Flowers and Other Tales;* il. by David Palladini. Crowell, 1974. Original tales in classic fairy tale form. Long to learn, but worthy of the storyhour.

———— *The Moon Ribbon and Other Tales;* il. by David Palladini. Crowell, 1976. Six original fairy tales, each with a special message.

6 / Reading Aloud

It is impossible to memorize all the literature written for children that is worthy of presenting to them. There are stories that are too long or too difficult to learn, but that seem to beg to be heard aloud. You might just as well be honest with yourself too. Hardly anyone will want to devote all their time to learning stories. There are times when an alternate method of presentation needs to be found, and reading aloud is the obvious solution. Families today should find a daily session in which everyone has a chance to read aloud just as enjoyable as did the Victorians. In our household we regularly read to our daughter before bedtime, and often there is time to start a book between breakfast and schooltime.

When I was a child, my best friend's mother had tea at four o'clock every afternoon, complete with a silver tea service and a tray of homebaked yummies for us. For an hour she read to us from the greats of children's literature. We met Walter de la Mare, C. S. Lewis, and Eleanor Farjeon during teatime at Helen's house. Helen now lives in England. She carries on the same tradition of teatime reading even though her children are of high school age. There is no reason why the oral sharing of books needs to stop just because everyone knows how to read to themselves. My former library school dean read aloud to his family after dinner long after his children were adults with children of their own.

If you are a busy classroom teacher a reading aloud session can be a daily occurrence with a formal storyhour taking place as a special treat once a week. But please don't do what Mrs. Morrison did to us in the fourth grade. Halfway through one book she felt the class needed to be punished, so she never finished it. I'm still searching for that story (it's about this elephant . . .) so I can find out what happened.

If you are a public librarian you might find that school vacations are a good time to schedule daily read aloud sessions so that you may offer a chapter or two of a longer book to your patrons.

Choosing Materials to Read Aloud

Choose any materials of high literary quality that appeal to you. These may be short stories, plays, longer folktales, original fairy tales, poetry, picture books, even a longer book to read a chapter at a time. If the selection is too long to learn to tell comfortably, prepare it for reading aloud. If the language of a story or book could be spoiled unless read word for word, consider reading aloud instead of telling the story.

If you are reading this book, then you are probably interested in children and hopefully are already familiar with many children's books. If you read children's books on a regular basis, you are bound to come across titles that you'll want to present. While you are reading, think of some of the elements which make a book a good one to read aloud. Children like action, suspense, and lots of conversation. This doesn't mean that a book which seems slow and contains long descriptive passages doesn't make an excellent read-aloud book. Hearing description gives children time to absorb the images the author presents, imagine the scene, and feel the mood of the book.

Don't choose a book merely because a colleague says it's good. Be sure you have read and familiarized yourself with any recommended book. If you think you will be bored reading aloud a book you've just read to yourself, put it aside for a later reading. When you find a book that you like, you'll be surprised, however, that even the most familiar story will seem different when a new audience is hearing it for the first time, for each group reacts differently to the same book.

You might choose a book the children are unlikely to read on their own. For example, if they are reading Marguerite Henry's horse books, there is little need to introduce them to more of her books. Try *Smoky* by Will James (Scribner, 1926) or John Steinbeck's *The Red Pony* (Viking, 1937), books that are a little more sophisticated and that they might have difficulty reading on their own. This also applies to types of books. If a majority of children in your group are addicted to formula mystery stories, reading aloud might be the perfect opportunity to introduce something entirely different, such as poetry.

Try to vary the mood and type of material each time you read aloud. Don't always read funny books or dog books. Each story should fill a different need for your audience. Fantasy provides a departure from reality and takes the listeners on a voyage to a new and strange world. Humorous books are usually very popular and give your group a chance to share in laughter. On the other hand, sad books often bring an audience closer together. Most adults are reluctant to cry in public, although children are less embarrassed at showing a normal emotion. You might plan in advance for the sad parts of a book. If you are reading aloud *Charlotte's Web* (Harper, 1952), dim the lights so that the audience will have more of a feeling of privacy in their grief. Realistic animal stories will give listeners a chance to broaden their understanding about life in the wild. Books that emphasize human characters are also satisfying to read. These books might stimulate spontaneous discussion questions such as "What would you do in the same situation?" Nonfiction should not be ignored as a source for books to read aloud. A variety of subjects can be introduced in the informal atmosphere of group listening.

If the ages of your group are disparate, and you have time to read only one book, I suggest you choose a book more appropriate for the older children. The younger children will understand enough of what they hear to enjoy the more advanced title. Do not dismiss the picture-book format, however; it is often suitable for an older as well as younger group of children. Picture books are usually short enough so that they can be completed in one session. The fine illustrations should be shared with the children while you're reading, and introducing a worthwhile book in a format often considered "for babies" might overcome some of the prejudices these books face at the checkout desk.

How-To's

If at all possible choose a gentle atmosphere for reading aloud. A warm fire and comfortable seating obviously add to your performance. Even in a drafty classroom or a noisy factory, a little preparation and planning can make reading aloud a more enjoyable experience. An overstuffed chair purchased at a garage sale, a colorful quilt rescued from an attic trunk for your audience to sit on may make the difference between full attention and wandering minds. Make sure that both you and the children are comfortable. Read with expression. There is no point in reading aloud at all if you are going to rush through the reading, mumble, or skip passages. This is true of all reading aloud, including quotes added to a lecture or announcement sent in memo form from the office. Remember, your competition is television. If you don't take your role seriously, your audience might choose mechanical over live entertainment. I still can't imagine a child who would really rather watch television than hear a good story read with feeling and enthusiasm by someone they love.

I could repeat the old adage "Practice makes perfect" on every other page in this book, but the phrase truly does apply to the art of reading aloud. The more you read aloud, the more adept you'll become. When I first became a radio announcer, I panicked every hour just before news time for in the radio world, there was no time to prepare the hourly news bulletin. It was great experience reading cold copy and now I can read almost any news story with a minimum of preparation.

Be sure you have looked up the pronunciation of any unfamiliar words *before* you begin reading. Don't be tempted to change or simplify words because you think your audience will not understand them. Not only is it unfair to an author, but it is unfair to the listeners too. The way we learn new words is to hear them repeated in different contexts. What better way to increase a child's vocabulary than to hear words properly used in an exciting story?

You may be tempted to do less preparation for reading aloud than for a memorized oral presentation. Just keep in mind this picture: a few years ago a student and I were doing a series of story programs at a school arts festival. While we waited for our turn in one classroom we listened to a monitor who was struggling through a reading of Kipling's *The Elephant's Child*. I'm sure she was grateful to be relieved of her task; so were the children. She had obviously never read the story before. And if you meet such Kipling phrases as ". . . the Precession had preceded according to precedent . . ." or ". . . the banks of the great grey-green, greasy Limpopo River, all set about with fever trees . . ." for the first time in front of forty critical children, it has to be a harrowing experience. My companion turned to me and said, "Too bad we can't bring that lady back to class with us, she's the best example of not doing her homework I've ever seen."

High school and college teachers who quote written passages in their lectures often "throw away" these passages by reading too fast, or stumbling through them. The theory must be that because it's someone else's writing it must be boring. Quite the contrary, it is the teachers themselves who, with their unenthusiastic reading, make it boring. Since you choose the book to read, articulate its words with pleasure, and present it with enthusiasm.

Be aware of your phrasing. Do you tend to take a break after exactly the same syllables each time? Does your voice rise or drop at the end of a sentence? Don't bury your head in the print; look up from time to time. Don't always look at the same person; favor different members of the audience each time you glance up. Be careful not to always pick your head up at the same rhythm. It gets monotonous to see a head bobbing up and down after each comma. If you come to an illustration in the text, pause and show it to the group. The pictures are part of the book, after all, and part of the enjoyment of reading. If you are reading to a large group, you might explain at the beginning of the session that the children can come up after the session to examine the pictures. If you come to a spot in the text that contains extensive conversation it might be more effective to leave out the "he said," "she said" since this becomes clear as you read. When you pick up the book again the next evening or day, quickly summarize in a sentence or two the preceding events to refresh your memory and theirs too. At the close of the daily reading, a relaxed discussion of the events may seem in order. I don't think this should be a forced session. It is only worthwhile if questions and comments come out naturally. Some books need a little time to be digested.

If it is at all possible, duplicate copies of the book, and other books by the author or books with a similar theme should be available for take-home reading. As a school librarian I once had a call from a parent whose child wanted to leave the house with a bad case of scarlet fever because she didn't want to miss the daily episode of Esther Hautzig's *The Endless Steppe* (Crowell, 1968). Luckily we had an extra copy to send to her.

A last word: Reading aloud is not to be substituted for traditional storytelling. It's just one other way to present literature orally.

Favorite Books for Reading Aloud

There are no recommended ages on this list because it is almost impossible to pinpoint at what age a child will enjoy which book. Selection of books to read aloud is even more difficult, since a child's ability to understand what he or she hears is usually much higher than his or her reading competence. The members of your group may be disparate in emotional maturity as well. You will probably be familiar with or know about the children in a particular class or group and you will have read the books so you can more easily put the two together. Most of the books have been found useful with children in the fourth through seventh grades, but younger or older boys and girls can enjoy some of the titles too. The books are listed under various broad categories so that you may vary the types of books you read; an animal story followed by a biography, perhaps. As you read new titles each year add to the list a few outstanding titles that might be worthy of reading aloud.

Animals

Adams, Richard G. *Watership Down*. Macmillan, 1972. This is a long book, but each of the chapters (there are fifty) is short enough to read in one sitting. It is an intricate animal fantasy in which wild rabbits search for a better home.

Boston, Lucy. *A Stranger at Green Knowe*; il. by Peter Boston. Harcourt, 1961. Ping, a Chinese orphan, and Hanno, a gorilla, meet at Green Knowe.

Byars, Betsy. *The Midnight Fox*; il. by Ann Grifalconi. Viking, 1968. Tommy reluctantly spends a summer on a farm and learns to respect a fox.

Eckert, Allan. *Incident at Hawk's Hill*; il. by John Schoenherr. Little, 1971. Based on a true frontier incident, this is the story of a boy who lives with a badger.

George, Jean. *Julie of the Wolves*; il. by John Schoenherr. Harper, 1972. A modern Eskimo girl lost on the tundra is befriended by wolves.

Gipson, Frederick B. *Old Yeller*; il. by Carl Burger. Harper, 1956. A boy and his mongrel dog face life in the Texas frontier territory.

James, Will. *Smoky, the Cowhorse*; il. by author. Scribner, 1926. The story of a horse told in cowboy vernacular.

London, Jack. *Call of the Wild*; il. by Robert Todd. Macmillan, 1956. Buck, an Alaskan sled dog, learns the "law of club and fang" during the Gold Rush.

McGowan, Tom. *Odyssey from River Bend*. Little, 1975. In the future other animals will have reached a high degree of civilization and explore the remains of cities built by humans.

Morey, Walter. *Kavik the Wolf Dog*; il. by Peter Parnall. Dutton, 1968. A dog makes his way from Seattle to Alaska to return to the family he loves.

Smith, Ivan. *The Death of a Wombat*; il. by Clifton Pugh. Scribner, 1972. A moving story of the death of a small animal in a brush fire.

Biography

Aldis, Dorothy. *Nothing Is Impossible: The Story of Beatrix Potter*; il. by Richard Cuffari. Atheneum, 1969. The lonely girlhood of the author and illustrator of nursery classics.

Coolidge, Olivia E. *George Bernard Shaw*. Houghton, 1968. An entertaining picture of the unconventional playwright.

Fritz, Jean. *And Then What Happened, Paul Revere?* il. by Margot Tomes. Coward, 1973. A humorous yet historically accurate account of Revere's ride to Lexington.

Hautzig, Esther. *The Endless Steppe: Growing Up in Siberia.* Crowell, 1968. The story of the author's five years in Siberia during World War II.

Klein, Gerda. *All But My Life.* Hill and Wang, 1957. A Jewish girl spends her adolescence in concentration camps.

Singer, Isaac Bashevis. *A Day of Pleasure: Stories of a Boy Growing Up in Warsaw;* photos. by Roman Vishniac. Farrar, 1969. Short incidents from a gifted author's childhood.

Fantasy

Alexander, Lloyd. *The Book of Three.* Holt, 1964. The first in a series based on Welsh mythology which records the clash between good and evil in the mythical land of Prydain. *The Black Cauldron* (Holt, 1965); *The Castle of Llyr* (Holt, 1966); *The High King* (Holt, 1968); and *Taran Wanderer* (Holt, 1967) are subsequent volumes.

Bianco, Margery. *The Velveteen Rabbit;* il. by William Nicholson. Doran, 1926. How toys become real is beautifully explained in a short sentimental fantasy.

Carroll, Lewis. *see* Dodgson, Charles L.

Dodgson, Charles L. *Alice in Wonderland,* by Lewis Carroll (pseud.); il. by Arthur Rackham. Watts, 1966. A grave little girl finds herself in a strange world after falling down a rabbit hole.

Farjeon, Eleanor. *The Little Bookroom;* il. by Edward Ardizzone. Walck, 1956. Short stories by an English author, including "The Seventh Princess."

Hunter, Mollie. *see* McIlwraith, Maureen.

Ireson, Barbara, ed. *Haunting Tales;* il. by Freda Woolf. Dutton, 1974. Supernatural short stories by Ray Bradbury, Sir Arthur Conan Doyle, and H. G. Wells, among others.

Jarrell, Randall. *The Animal Family;* il. by Maurice Sendak. Pantheon, 1965. A hunter collects a strange family that includes a mermaid, a bear, and a baby.

Juster, Norton. *The Phantom Tollbooth;* il. by Jules Feiffer. Random, 1961. Milo journeys into a world of words to rescue the Princesses of Rhyme and Reason. Excellent classroom reading.

Kahn, Joan, comp. *Some Things Strange and Sinister.* Harper, 1973. Fourteen stories of the supernatural.

Kendall, Carol. *The Gammage Cup;* il. by Erik Blegvad. Harcourt, 1959. Some nonconforming Minnipins show the Establishment the need for new ideas.

Leichman, Seymour. *The Boy Who Could Sing Pictures;* il. by author. Doubleday, 1968. The son of a court jester teaches the king a lesson in war. One-session reading.

Macdonald, George. *The Light Princess;* il. by William Pène du Bois. Crowell, 1962. This is short enough for a single "read aloud" session. Another edition is available with illustrations by Maurice Sendak (Farrar, 1969).

McIlwraith, Maureen. *The Kelpie's Pearls,* by Mollie Hunter (pseud.); il. by Josef Cellini. Funk and Wagnalls, 1966. A charming modern fantasy features the Loch Ness monster and a woman who makes friends with a kelpie.

O'Brien, Robert C. *Mrs. Frisby and the Rats of Nimh;* il. by Zena Bernstein. Atheneum, 1971. A group of inventive, literate rats seeks a colony where they can live without fear.

Pearce, Anne Philippa. *The Squirrel Wife;* il. by Derek Collard. Crowell, 1972. Lovely drawings add to this short tale of fairies and evil.

Snyder, Zilpha Keatley. *Below the Root;* il. by Alton Raible. Atheneum, 1975. The Kindar live in the branches of great grundtrees. Raamo explores the forbidden world below. A sequel involving the Erdlings is *And All Between* (Atheneum, 1976).

Tolkien, J. R. R. *The Hobbit; or, There and Back Again.* Houghton, 1938. Bilbo Bag-

gins sets out to recover stolen treasure from Smaug, the dragon.

White, E. B. *Charlotte's Web;* il. by Garth Williams. Harper, 1952. The story of a rare and beautiful friendship between Wilbur the Pig and Charlotte, a spider.

Wilde, Oscar. *The Happy Prince and Other Stories;* il. by Lars Bo. Penguin, 1962. Original philosophical fairytales by an adult author.

Williams, Margery. *see* Bianco, Margery.

Wrightson, Patricia. *The Nargun and the Stars.* Atheneum, 1974. A lonely boy meets beings of another time: The Potkoorok, The Turongs and the Nyob, but he needs Charlie and Edie, an older couple, to help against the Nargun.

Historical Fiction

Chute, Marchette. *The Innocent Wayfaring;* il. by author. Dutton, 1943. A girl's first love in Chaucer's England.

Edmonds, Walter D. *Bert Breen's Barn.* Little, 1975. A boy has a dream of buying and moving a barn to his own land.

Fleischman, Albert Sidney. *Mr. Mysterious and Company;* il. by Eric von Schmidt. Little, 1962. The Hackett family gives magic shows in the early West.

Haugaard, Erik Christian. *Hakon of Rogen's Saga;* il. by Leo and Diane Dillon.

Houghton, 1963. The Viking period is portrayed in this story of Hakon's revenge. *A Slave's Tale* (Houghton, 1965) is a sequel.

O'Dell, Scott. *Sing Down the Moon.* Houghton, 1970. A young Navajo girl is forced to leave her land and her way of life.

Wilder, Laura Ingalls. *Little House in the Big Woods;* il. by Helen Sewell. Harper, 1932. The first in a memorable series of books about pioneering and frontier life based on the author's own childhood.

Folklore

Barth, Edna. *Cupid and Psyche: A Love Story;* il. by Ati Forberg. Seabury, 1976. A retelling of the Greek myth that retains the spirit of this ancient story.

Church, Alfred J. *The Iliad and the Odyssey of Homer, Retold;* il. by Eugene Karlin. Macmillan, 1964. The two stories are linked together in narrative form.

Gates, Doris. *A Fair Wind for Troy;* il. by Charles Mikolaycak. Viking, 1976. This is the sixth of a series of the author's retellings of the Greek myths. See also *The Golden God: Apollo;* il. by Constantine CoConis (Viking, 1973); *Lord of the Sky: Zeus;* il. by Robert Hardville (Viking, 1972); *Mightiest of Mortals: Heracles;* il. by Richard Cuffari (Viking, 1975);

Two Queens of Heaven: Aphrodite and Demeter; il. by Trina Schart Hyman (Viking, 1974); *The Warrior Goddess: Athena;* il. by Don Bolognese (Viking, 1972).

Ish-Kishor, Sulamith. *Master of Miracle;* il. by Arnold Lobel. Harper, 1971. A fantasy based on the Jewish legend of the Golem.

McHargue, Georgess. *The Impossible People;* il. by Frank Bozzo. Holt, 1972. "A History, Natural and Unnatural, of Beings Terrible and Wonderful."

Nye, Robert. *Beowulf: A New Telling;* il. by Alan E. Cober. Hill and Wang, 1968. A beautiful new edition of an old epic.

Robbins, Ruth. *Taliesin and King Arthur;* il. by author. Parnassus, 1970. Taliesin, a poet, entertains King Arthur; from a Welsh legend.

Singer, Isaac Bashevis. *The Fools of Chelm and Their History;* tr. by the author and Elizabeth Shub; il. by Uri Shulevitz. Farrar, 1973. The misadventures of Shmendrick Numbskull, Berel Pinhead, and Shmerel Thickwit.

Humor

Aiken, Joan. *Not What You Expected: A Collection of Short Stories.* Doubleday, 1974. Six-inch humans, ghosts, and dragons all figure in this unusual collection of short stories.

Babbitt, Natalie. *The Search for Delicious;* il. by the author. Farrar, 1969. Gaylen sets out to find a definition for delicious.

Blume, Judy. *Tales of a Fourth Grade Nothing;* il. by Roy Doty. Dutton, 1972. Episodic adventures of a boy and his "impossible" little brother.

Cleary, Beverly. *Ribsy;* il. by Louis Darling. Morrow, 1964. One of the author's many amusing books, this is a series of episodic adventures of a lovable mutt.

Cohen, Barbara. *The Carp in the Bathtub;* il. by Joan Halpern. Lothrop, 1972. Could you eat a friend?

Grahame, Kenneth. *The Wind in the Willows;* il. by Ernest H. Shepard. Scribner,

1953, 1961. The classic animal fantasy starring a water rat, a mole, a toad, and a badger.

Konigsburg, E. L. *About the B'Nai Bagels;* il. by author. Atheneum, 1969. Mark Setzer's Little League team faces a problem in honesty.

Merrill, Jean. *The Toothpaste Millionaire;* il. by Jan Palmer. A twelve-year-old boy and his friends earn a million dollars plus in their hilarious try at big business.

Milne, A. A. *Winnie the Pooh;* il. by Ernest H. Shepard. Dutton, 1926. A cast of toy animals muddles through life in the 100 Acre Wood.

Raskin, Ellen. *The Tattooed Potato and Other Clues.* Dutton, 1975. A tangled and witty web of mystery.

Rodgers, Mary. *A Billion for Boris.* Harper, 1974. A broken TV set turns out to play programs a day before they're broadcast.

Memorable People

Armstrong, William H. *Sounder;* il. by James Barkley. Harper, 1969. A boy takes on family responsibilities when his father is sent to jail.

Burch, Robert. *Queenie Peavy;* il. by Jerry Lazare. Viking, 1966. Queenie is a 13-year-old tomboy growing up in the early 1930s.

Burnett, Frances Hodgson. *The Secret Garden;* il. by Tasha Tudor. Lippincott, 1911. Mystery and enduring characterizations have maintained the popularity of this classic, written in 1903.

Estes, Eleanor. *The Hundred Dresses;* il. by Louis Slobodkin. Harcourt, 1944. Wanda wears the same blue dress every day, but claims she has a hundred dresses all lined up at home, in this short, sensitively told story.

Godden, Rumer. *Mr. McFadden's Hallowe'en.* Viking, 1975. A Scottish accent will come in handy for this charming story about a spunky girl and a cantankerous farmer.

Green, Alexander. *The Scarlet Sails;* tr. from the Russian by Thomas P. Whitney; il. by E. Nesbitt. Scribner, 1967. A romantic story set in a seaport. Highly recommended.

Holm, Anne. *North to Freedom;* tr. by L. W. Kingsland. Harcourt, 1965. David gradually learns to trust people during his flight from a concentration camp.

Holman, Felice. *Slake's Limbo.* Scribner, 1974. A 13-year-old boy hides underground in a New York subway station learning to survive alone.

Neufeld, John. *Edgar Allen.* S. G. Phillips, 1968. A white family adopts a black boy.

Sachs, Marilyn. *The Bears' House;* il. by Louis Glanzman. Doubleday, 1971. Fran Ellen, who sucks her thumb and smells bad, has courage enough to care for a fatherless household.

Southall, Ivan. *Hills End.* St. Martins, 1963. A group of children are separated from all adults in an Australian village and must fend for themselves.

Taylor, Theodore. *The Cay.* Doubleday, 1969. A blind boy and an elderly black man are shipwrecked.

Webster, Jean. *Daddy Long-Legs;* il. by Edward Ardizzone. Hawthorne, 1967. Written in 1912, these letters from a college girl raised in an orphanage still have charm.

Nonfiction

Holling, Holling Clancey. *Tree in the Trail;* il. by the author. Houghton, 1942. The story of a tree.

Lester, Julius, comp. *To Be a Slave;* il. by Tom Feelings. Dial, 1968. Slavery as seen by the slaves of America.

Moore, Janet Gaylord. *The Many Ways of Seeing: An Introduction to the Pleasures of Art;* il. by author. World, 1968. Many illustrations make this a good introduction to art.

Scheffer, Victor B. *The Seeing Eye.* Scribner, 1971. Full-color photographs show form, color, and texture in nature.

Tunis, Edwin. *Chipmunks on the Doorstep;* il. by the author. Crowell, 1971. All about chipmunks.

Van Loon, Hendrik Willem. *The Story of Mankind;* il. by author. Liveright, rev. ed., 1972. A lengthy but relaxed survey of the history of man.

Poetry

Atwood, Ann. *My Own Rhythm: An Approach to Haiku.* Scribner, 1973. Beautiful color photographs enhance the original verse.

Dunning, Stephen; Lueders, Edward G.; and Smith, Hugh L., comps. *Reflections on a Gift of Watermelon Pickle . . . and Other Modern Verse;* il. with photos. Scott, Foresman, 1966. Black-and-white photographs illustrate this excellent collection of poems.

Fraser, Kathleen. *Stilts, Somersaults and Headstands.* Atheneum, 1968. Game poems based on a painting by Peter Breughel.

Hughes, Ted. *Season Songs;* il. by Leonard Baskin. Viking, 1975. Sophisticated poetry and beautiful graphics make this a book to share with older children.

Jones, Hettie, comp. *The Trees Stand Shining: Poetry of the North American Indians;* il. by Robert Andrew Parker. Dial, 1971. Paintings illustrate these short poems.

Jordan, June. *Who Look at Me?;* il. with paintings. Crowell, 1969. "We do not see those we do not know."

O'Neill, Mary. *Hailstones and Halibut Bones;* il. by Leonard Weisgard. Doubleday, 1961. Poems about colors.

Prelutsky, Jack. *Nightmares: Poems to Trouble Your Sleep;* il. by Arnold Lobel. Greenwillow/Morrow, 1976. Well-written poems about ghouls, ogres, vampires, and other creatures.

Silverstein, Shel. *Where the Sidewalk Ends;* il. by author. Harper, 1974. A selection of the poet's funniest poems.

Picture Books for Older Children and Adults

Bradley, Helen. *Miss Carter Came with Us;* il. by author. Little, 1974. Life in Lancashire, England, in 1908 depicted in a short text and detailed drawings.

Grimm Brothers. *Snow White;* tr. by Paul Heins; il. by Trina Schart Hyman. Little, 1974. Full-color acrylic paintings accompany a readable text.

Lawrence, Jacob. *Harriet and the Promised Land;* il. by author. Simon & Schuster, 1968. Stark, almost brutal illustrations tell the story of Harriet Tubman who led her people in an escape for freedom in 1822.

Macaulay, David. *Cathedral: The Story of Its Construction;* il. by author. Houghton, 1973. The author-illustrator shows the step-by-step process of the growth of a Gothic cathedral.

McDermott, Gerald. *Arrow to the Sun;* adapted and il. by author. Viking, 1974. This Caldecott winner recreates an Indian myth celebrating the power of the sun.

Serraillier, Ian. *Suppose You Met a Witch;* il. by Ed Emberley. Little, 1973. A sophisticated poem is illustrated with striking textured drawings.

Viorst, Judith. *Alexander and the Terrible, Horrible, No Good, Very Bad Day;* il. by Ray Cruz. Atheneum, 1972. The day everything went wrong. This can be learned as a story or read aloud, sharing the black-and-white drawings.

PART TWO

Sources for Storytelling

Where will you find material for your own storyhour?
Start at the library. There, collected especially for
you by generations of professional folklorists and
gifted authors, is a wealth of material waiting to be
brought orally to audiences of children, young people,
and adults.

Books are sources of an incredible collection of
folktales from every region in the world. Fables,
myths, and epics will provide you with enough stories
for many years of folklore sessions. And for variety,
the bookshelves offer many short stories by known
authors, written in the time-honored style of the
folktale or in the contemporary language of today.

The poetry shelves in the library will yield an
extraordinary selection of poems, traditional and
modern, for every interest and taste of any audience
you may want to reach.

Don't forget the picture books, once written exclusively for the preschool child; now, however, the
beautifully designed and printed picture story can be
enjoyed and appreciated by all ages.

Authentic folklore that doesn't tell a story can be
stimulating and amusing too when presented as part
of a program. Riddles, jokes, tongue twisters, and
proverbs are all part of non-narrative folklore that is

enjoyed by children and collected by adults for the youngest to the oldest in the program audience.

Do you live in an area without an adequate library facility? Perhaps you can borrow through a county library or other interlibrary loan system some of the books listed in the bibliographies in this section. Owning your own source material might not be a bad idea either. Start small; order one or two books from a local bookstore. Once you are properly addicted to book buying your collection of storytelling books will soon grow (and you'll lose weight because you'll have less money to buy ice cream sundaes or sodas and lollipops).

Don't worry about what you can use for source material. There's a whole world of stories, poems, and riddles, whatever you want, just waiting for you in books.

7 / Narrative Sources

The key to a successful program lies in the story or stories that you use. Planning, production, promotion, and attention to other details are important, but the story remains the single most important element.

Above all, choose a story that you like, one which fits your own individual personality. By finding stories to suit you, I simply mean that if you think of yourself as vivacious and sparkling, you might tend to enjoy telling some of the funny or silly folktales; if you have a quiet, shy personality you might capitalize on it and choose the more romantic or magical tales. You must read a number of stories until you find those which appeal to you.

Although you will begin by using stories familiar to you, you will want to continue your search for new stories. When local collections are exhausted, ask for an interlibrary loan of some of the other collections you've missed. Ask librarians, teachers, and friends who tell stories to name their favorites. When you attend an educational or library conference, ask your colleagues if they tell stories and find out their favorites. On vacations, visit the local library and ask if they keep records of the stories they tell. You might get ideas of already tried and successful stories told. As you read, note selections that seem to you to have possibilities. Some stories might not be appropriate for your present audience, but write down their names for consideration at a later date. Now read some of your selections over again. One may fit into a particular holiday storyhour, a good Christmas story perhaps. It may be from a country that interests you or fits into the school curriculum with which you are associated. The story may be similar to one you liked as a child. The best reason of all is that it seems attractive to you at the time. Some of the literature about storytelling attempts to list the components of a story that make it worthwhile. This may be of use to you; however, when you're just beginning, I suggest that you start with stories that have already been told and loved by hundreds of children through the generations.

A word of caution: Do not feel tempted to make up your own stories. The purpose of storytelling is to interest your listeners in the books the stories are taken from, to stimulate them to read. You want to be able to show the book that the story comes from to your audience. In general, do not try to use periodicals as sources for stories. The best stories to learn are those that have been used with success for generations, so begin with folktales. Folklore in its various forms will be the core of your book program, since storytelling has its basis in folk sources.

And for Your Inspiration

Every serious storyteller in search of program materials should become familiar with the resources that follow. Those marked by asterisks are particularly helpful.

Bettelheim, Bruno. *The Uses of Enchantment: The Meaning and Importance of Fairy Tales.* Knopf, 1976. A scholarly defense of folk literature.

Cather, Laura E.; Haushalter, Marion McC.; Russell, Virginia A. *Stories to Tell to Children: A Selected List.* 8th ed., Univ. of Pittsburgh Press for Carnegie Library of Pittsburgh Children's Services, 1974.

Folklore: An Annotated Bibliography and Index to Single Editions; comp. by Elsie B. Ziegler. Faxon, 1973. Subject, motif, country of origin, type, and illustrator are listed. Companion volume to *Index to Fairy Tales 1949 to 1972.*

Hardendorff, Jeanne B., ed. and rev. *Stories to Tell: A List of Stories with Annotations.* 5th ed. Enoch Pratt Free Library, 1965. Now out of print but it may be on your library's professional shelves.

Iarusso, Marilyn, comp. *Stories: A List of Stories to Tell and to Read Aloud.* 7th ed.

New York Public Library, 1977. Honors the fiftieth anniversary of the New York Public Library's storytelling program.

Index to Fairy Tales 1949 to 1972, Including Folklore, Legends, and Myths in Collections; comp. by Norma Olin Ireland. Faxon, 1973. Analyzes over 400 collections of stories.

*Sawyer, Ruth. *The Way of the Storyteller.* rev. ed. Viking, 1962 (first published in 1942). A classic introduction to storytelling. The eleven stories in the appendix are a bonus for the advanced storyteller.

*Shedlock, Marie L. *The Art of the Storyteller.* Dover, 1951 (first published in 1915). Shedlock is considered responsible for bringing traditional storytelling to American libraries. Good background reading and a collection of stories.

Ziskind, Sylvia. *Telling Stories to Children.* Wilson, 1976. The chapter on mastering technique is particularly useful.

Folktales

Stith Thompson, the recognized authority of the folktale, defines the traditional prose tale as a story "which has been handed down from generation to generation either in writing or by word of mouth." As potential storytellers living in today's world, we usually take our material from printed sources. Few working teachers or librarians will have access to oral story sources. Scholars engaged in the study of folklore might complain that most folktales which have been published no longer belong to the true tradition since they have been frozen in print and therefore can no longer develop and change. For our purposes this may actually be an advantage, for it is not just the plot of the story that we wish to convey but the spirit and style as well. We want to introduce the language of literature.

The audiences that listen to you tell these stories will benefit in a variety of ways too. Some individuals will be influenced by the ethical values inherent in most of the tales; others will be stimulated by the images and situations to create in artistic ways; whereas still others will view the storyhour as pure entertainment, unaware that they are learning about other lands and people. Ultimately you will receive requests for the books in which the stories appear, and this will lead to further reading and study. Familiar stories such as "Goldilocks and the Three Bears," "Little Red Riding Hood," and "Cinderella" are all examples of the folktale. The versions of these stories with which we are most familiar originate in three different countries: "The Three Bears" from England, "Little Red Riding Hood" from Germany, and "Cinderella" from France. All three stories exist in many versions. In fact, more than 400 versions of the Cinderella stories have been recorded around the world. The formula for virtually all folktales is the same: the characters and problem are introduced, an obstacle is set up, and a resolution ends the story. Usually folktales are devoid of long descriptive passages and concentrate almost entirely on plot. Even the characters are not developed to any great extent and tend to be stereotypes of good or evil, cleverness or stupidity. The shorter folktales rely on a single theme: the triumph of good over evil or of a poor man outwitting a rich man. If you wish to pursue a more academic study in this area, you will want to begin with some of the adult studies listed at the end of this chapter. You may also be interested in the notes at the end of the story collections that you read, for some authors and folklorists provide extensive notes regarding the source of the story, the circumstances under which it was collected, what parts were deleted, or what additions were made. Some of the material may be of particular interest to your audience and the background on collecting the story may, in some situations, provide useful introductory material.

Many modern authors have been much influenced by folktales and have attempted to write their own, some quite successfully. These original stories are sometimes referred to as "literary folktales." Some famous storytellers have written both kinds of folktales, those based directly on folklore and literary folktales. Hans Christian Andersen is a good example. His earlier work is based upon folklore, probably the stories he learned as a child. His later work is entirely original and no folk literature has been identified as its source. Usually, the original or literary folktale or fairy tale is more difficult to tell since you will want to retain the beauty of the author's language by virtually memorizing the story word for word. The stories of Hans Christian Andersen, Rudyard Kipling, Eleanor Farjeon, and Laurence Housman all fall into this category.

A newer name among the creators of the literary folktale is Jane Yolen. She is the author of several single illustrated tales and two distinguished original collections. In *The Girl Who Loved the Wind*, Danina, a lonely princess, joins the wind to explore the "ever-changing" world. The pictures in this book by Ed Young remind the reader of Persian miniatures and might be shared with a small group. The stories in *The Girl Who Cried Flowers and Other Tales* and *The Moon Ribbon and Other Tales* not only have the spirit and warmth of some of the older tales but also a special lyrical romantic quality that predict a long shelf life for this contemporary author. Yolen's longer story, *The Transfigured Hart*, is a timeless tale of two children of very different temperament who have an equally strong belief in the existence of the fabled unicorn. This book is probably too long to learn as a story, but should not be overlooked for reading aloud. In her *Writing Books for Children* (Writer, 1973), Jane Yolen states that "The writer lights many candles in a good fantasy novel. The shadows they cast in a child's soul will last for the rest of his life." It is too soon to know if Yolen's stories will become a part of the permanent storytellers' collection, but in the last few years they have made a lasting impression on a new generation of fairy tale readers.

It is useful to be aware of some of the major types of folktales, for it is then possible to identify the particular types that suit your personality for telling. Identification of common themes can help you create thematic programs and broaden your repertoire to include particular types of tales or motifs that appeal to you or your audiences. Following are descriptions of some of the types of stories you will find in your search for program material.

Repetitive and Cumulative Tales

These tales are the easiest to learn since they have a minimum of plot and usually a repetitive rhythm occurs throughout. While some adults may find these stories boring to tell because of the constant repetition, they are particularly popular with young children. After you have actually told one of these tales to a group of preschoolers and have experienced their delighted reaction, you will be more attuned to the attractiveness of this story form.

Typical of the repetitive story is the familiar, foolish Henny-Penny who meets Cocky-Locky, Ducky-Daddles, Goosey-Loosey, Turkey-Lurkey and Foxy-Woxy on the way to tell the king that the sky is falling. In "The Gingerbread Boy" the proud gingerbread hero repeats, "Run! Run! as fast as you can! You can't catch me, I'm the Gingerbread Man!" to a host of would-be captors. A delightful variant to this story is a picture-book adaptation of a Danish tale by Jack Kent of *The Fat Cat* who devours with relish a number of objects, animals, and people until a crafty woodcutter puts an end to the greedy cat. Joseph Jacobs's "The Cat and the Mouse" delights youngsters with its rhythmic refrain:

> Then the baker gave mouse bread, and mouse gave butcher bread, and butcher gave mouse meat, and mouse gave farmer meat, and farmer gave mouse hay, and mouse gave cow hay and cow gave mouse milk, and mouse gave cat milk, and cat gave mouse her own tail again!

A similar story in picture-book form is Nonny Hogrogian's *One Fine Day*, in which a fox loses his tail.

Animal Tales

Many of the folktales deal with talking animals who are often really humans in disguise, exhibiting very recognizable human faults and foibles. The simpler tales such as "The Three Bears," "The Three Pigs," or "The Three Billy Goats Gruff" are easily learned and are appropriate for use with small children. Longer and more sophisticated animal stories often involve animals in relationships with human beings. In the German "The Fisherman and his Wife," a fish can carry on a conversation as well as grant wishes. In the French "Puss in Boots," a cat takes care of his master, while in the Finnish variant, "Mighty Mikko," it is a gentle and clever fox that guides his master into marrying a princess.

Enchanted humans take on animal form in stories collected from around the world. In the well-known German story a prince lives his life as a frog until he is freed by a waspish princess. In the Finnish tale, "The Forest Bride," it is an enchanted mouse that befriends a younger son and then becomes his bride.

How and Why Stories

Sometimes referred to as "pourquoi" stories, these tales explain how and why a physical or cultural phenomenon began. Some of these stories are closely related to myth since a god often intervenes in the climax. The African folktale retold by Elphinstone Dayrell in picture-book form with illus-

trations by Blair Lent explains *Why the Sun and the Moon Live in the Sky.*
A story collected by Pura Belpré (in *Once in Puerto Rico*) from Puerto Rican
folklore explains the origin of the royal palm tree, while Harold Courlander's
story from El Salvador explains the origin of the balsam tree (in *Ride With
the Sun*). A charming Chinese story tells "How the Camel Got his Proud
Look." And a Norwegian story explains *Why the Sea Is Salt.* Maria Leach
has collected a number of how and why stories in *How the People Sang the
Mountain Up.*

You might be able to find Indian "pourquoi" stories that explain why
mountains or rivers in your area exist.

Adventure and Romantic Stories

These two types often join together in one story. A foolish lad, or a clever
prince in search of a wife might be led on fantastic adventures that take him
deep inside a hill or to a glass mountain. The most famous of the romantic
stories is probably "Cinderella." The version we know was collected in France
in the seventeenth century, but there are so many known variants of the
Cinderella story that a storyteller could specialize in telling just this one
story. One of the characteristics of the folktale is the simplicity with which
people, places, and actions are described. Usually the characterizations are
scanty; heroes and heroines are kind and good, while their enemies are often
portrayed as trolls, giants, or witches.

Droll and Humorous Stories

Stories that make your audience laugh are fun to tell. You know through
their laughter if the story has been well received. Drolls are those silly stories
that rely on ridiculous situations or witless characters to create their humor.
In Jewish folklore there is a mythical town called Chelm in which all the
inhabitants are incredibly stupid. The stories of the people of Chelm can be
found in several collections: *Zlateh the Goat* by Isaac Bashevis Singer and
The Wise Men of Helm by Solomon Simon. A typical story of the citizens of
Chelm goes like this:

> Once the people of Chelm thought they could make money by selling
> lumber from the mountain that overlooked their town. For weeks the men
> of Chelm chopped down the largest trees and cut off the branches until
> they had a fine pile of large logs. Then it took a month for the men to carry
> the great tree trunks down the mountain. At last the horrendous job was
> almost done. Two strangers arriving in town on the last day watched in

amusement as the men carried the logs down the mountain. "Why didn't you just roll the logs down the hill instead of carrying them?" suggested one of the strangers. "What a good idea," exclaimed the men of Chelm. "Let's do it." And with that they began the long trek back up the mountain, each man hauling a log so that when they reached the top they could roll them back down again.

Folk Characters

In your reading of folktales you will find many collections that revolve around one folk character, animal or human, who seems to be wise and foolish at the same time. A majority of these folk characters trick their adversaries through their cleverness. Till Eulenspiegel, a German folk character and merry trickster who outwits a variety of established scholars and businessmen with his clever pranks, has had many stories written about him. One of my favorite stories tells of the time that Till tricked the scholars of Bremen into thinking that he had taught a donkey to read. Baron Munchausen, another German tall-tale character, inevitably emerges triumphant from the conflicts in his humorous adventures. The popular Turkish folk character, the "Hodja," is a simple soul who is often taken advantage of and finds his revenge in ingenious trickery. The Haitian "Uncle Bouqui" is often bested by his friend "Ti Malice," just as the American "Br'er Rabbit" takes advantage of his "friends."

Supernatural characters such as the Scandinavian trolls and ogres, the Irish fairies, and the Slavic domovoi are just a few of the unusual inhabitants of the folktale. Some of these creatures are workers of evil; others may be a blessing for those who come in contact with them. If you become interested in one of these folk characters, you can gather a number of stories together to create an entire program.

Regions or Countries

One obvious grouping is to collect stories that are popular in a particular region or country. Well-written collections from every part of the world, ranging from the islands of the Caribbean to the mountains of Russia, are available to the interested storyteller. It is interesting to note that Americans are often more familiar with the folktales of France, Germany, England, and Norway than they are with the native American tales.

France. The first book of "fairy tales" published in France is still read and relished by children in Western Europe and America. The book, *Histoires ou contes du temps passe avec des moralités* (Histories or tales of long ago with morals) and subtitled *Contes de ma mère l'oye (Tales of Mother Goose)* was published in 1697. Charles Perrault (1628–1703), usually credited with their authorship, collected these folktales and rewrote them for the amusement of the adults at the French Court, but the tales became popular with children as well. The eight tales in his collection (whose subtitle, incidentally, seems to be the first mention of the name "Mother Goose") were "The Sleeping Beauty," "Little Red Riding Hood," "Blue Beard," "Puss In Boots," "Diamonds and Toads," "Cinderella," "Riquet with the Tuft," and "Tom Thumb." Perrault added morals to the stories for the amusement of adults, although these are usually omitted for children.

Other French tales, some of which were written in the same period as Perrault's stories, are still enjoyed today. For example, Comtesse D'Aulnoy's "The White Cat" and Madame LePrince de Beaumont's "Beauty and the Beast" both appear in many story collections.

Germany. In Germany, Jacob and Wilhelm Grimm collected folktales as part of their study of philology in order to examine the roots of the German language. Their first volume of Kinder und Hausmarchen (*Children's and Household Tales*) was published in 1812, and subsequent volumes followed in later years. The stories were recorded exactly as the Grimm brothers heard them, usually from country peasants. Although not all the Grimm tales are appropriate for children, many have been consistently popular: "Hansel and Gretel," "Rapunzel," "Rumpelstiltskin," "Snow White and the Seven Dwarfs," and "The Bremen Town Musicians" are just a few of the ever-popular stories they gathered.

The Grimm tales, originally collected in German over a hundred years ago, reach us in many different translations and versions. A large library can easily have a whole shelf of different books all devoted to these tales the Grimms collected. Which version should you use to learn and tell these tales? If you took the time to thoroughly study each version of Grimm, each version of the Arabian Nights, and each version of Perrault you would become an expert folklorist, but you might not ever have time to learn a story. As a beginner in the field you may do well to trust the judgment of experienced storytellers in the matter of choosing a good version for telling. Several libraries have published excellent storytelling bibliographies or you could begin by using the bibliographies at the end of this chapter. There is, of course, no one perfect version. For instance, even though several new translations, beautifully illustrated, have recently been published of the Grimm tales, I still prefer the older retelling by Wanda Gág, who wrote the rhythmic *Millions of Cats.*

As a storyteller you do not need to be convinced that folktales should be introduced to children, but you might be amazed at the amount of violence in some of the tales. It is true that many of the stories are unsuitable for children for various reasons but, as for the concern about violence, the reader will discover, on closer examination, that what is being portrayed is simply symbolic of the struggle between good and evil. The triumph of good often comes out through some sort of sacrifice, but rarely with the graphic presentation of blood and gore so often emphasized in the media of today. For example, "The Seven Ravens" is the story of a sister searching for her seven bewitched brothers. In the course of the story, the girl cuts off her finger to use as a key to open the door of the glass mountain. This act symbolizes a sacrifice in exchange for love and forgiveness. Even so, it is overshadowed by the brothers' return to their human form and their reunion with their sister. If a young child seems to be frightened by a story from Grimm then certainly he or she should not be further exposed to these stories until more mature and able to deal with their frightening aspects.

As a visiting storyteller with the New York Public Library, I was once invited to tell stories to a multiethnic group on the Lower East Side of New York. I told the librarian that I had recently learned Wanda Gág's version of Rapunzel, but that I felt the story was too familiar to tell. She advised me to tell it anyway. The experience really taught me why these stories have remained popular down through the generations, for the children listened with such eagerness and afterwards asked many questions. Did it hurt to have someone climbing up your hair like that? And what happened to the witch? I was too inexperienced to come up with any satisfactory answers but I promised to find out. The next week they were ready for me as I came through the door, but I had done my homework and was prepared to field their questions. I had found two perfect visual answers: Arthur Rackham, the distinguished British artist, had painted a clear illustration of Rapunzel's long tresses wrapped several times around a hook outside her tower window showing that having a prince or a witch climb up your braids might be almost a comfortable experience. As for what happened to the witch, Felix Hoffmann's picture book of *Rapunzel* showed a picture of the witch being carried off by a bird, which satisfied the most curious of the children. It was this experience that made me realize that there is a place for good visual material in a storyhour as well as for exciting words.

England. The name which stands out above all others in the collecting of English tales is that of Joseph Jacobs (1854–1916). His purpose was somewhat different from that of the Grimm brothers; he was deliberately trying to find stories which would be suitable for children. In his versions of the English tales, he left out incidents which he felt would be inappropriate, but each of his omissions is recorded in the notes at the end of his collections. Although he changed the language slightly where the heavy dialects would make reading difficult, the tales still retain their original folk flavor.

The stories which Jacobs collected range from the simple nursery favorites, such as "The Three Little Pigs," "The Three Bears," and "Teeny-Tiny" to the more sophisticated "Cap O'Rushes," a variant of Cinderella. Whereas the German folktales often have a somber mood, many of the English tales contain a measure of gentle humor. Giants and giant killers abound in these tales. One of my favorites features a brave girl, Molly Whuppie, who outwits a giant. Even though Jacobs's tales cannot be considered authentic folklore, since he attempted to give literary character to the stories, his versions have a distinction worth retaining. Think of the bowdlerized versions of "The Three Little Pigs" you've encountered. Now enjoy Jacobs's introduction to the popular story:

> Once upon a time when pigs spoke rhyme
> And monkeys chewed tobacco,
> And hens took snuff to make them tough,
> And ducks went quack, quack, quack, O!

> There was an old sow with three little pigs, and as she had not enough to keep them, she sent them out to seek their fortune.

For years Joseph Jacobs's collections were the only source of English folktales readily available to children. However, well-known folklorist Andrew Lang included English tales with tales from all over the world in his famous "color" fairy books. More recently James Reeves, the English poet, published a collection of English tales, *English Fables and Fairy Stories*.

The popularity of these English stories has inspired some fine picture-book versions. Evaline Ness has illustrated an edition of *Tom Tit Tot* emphasizing the humor of this light-hearted variant of the German Rumpelstiltskin. Marcia Brown used two-color linoleum cuts to illustrate *Dick Whittington and His Cat*. Marcia Sewall's delightful black-and-white sketches adorn a picture-book version of *Master of All Masters*. In my opinion these illustrated versions should be used sparingly in the actual program and reserved, for the most part, for individual reading after the story has been told. An oral presentation of *Master of All Masters* has got to be funnier without pictures, no matter how skillfully they are drawn.

Norway and Sweden. When one thinks of Norwegian folktales, one inevitably comes up with two names. Just as the Grimm brothers collected tales from the German countryside, so two friends, Peter Christian Asbjørnsen (1812–1885) and Jorgen E. Moe (1813–1882), gathered stories they heard from peasant storytellers and published them in a still famous collection, *East O' the Sun and West O' the Moon*. Much of the popularity and success of this collection in English-speaking countries must be attributed to the excellent translation done by the English scholar, George Webbe Dasent (1817–1896). Here, as in the German and English collections, are simple stories for the very youngest like the rhythmic "The Three Billy Goats Gruff" and the short "Why the Bear is Stumpy-tailed." A nonchalant humor prevails in some of the tales, such as "Gudbrand-on-the-Hillside," in which everything that the man does, no matter how foolish, is supported with good humor by his loving wife. A similar story to Wanda Gág's *Gone Is Gone* is "The Husband Who Was to Mind the House," whose housekeeping efforts end in humorous disaster. Trolls and giants appear in the stories with enough frequency for the listeners to call out "Tell another scarey one like the last story."

With the new interest in older drawings you might want to locate Kay Nielsen's strong interpretations of these Norwegian stories to share with your group. Erik Werenskiold and Theodor Kittelsen's black-and-white traditional illustrations for the Asbjørnsen and Moe *Norwegian Folk Tales* are also worthwhile.

Although the Norwegian collection is by far the best known of the Scandinavian collections, a recent English translation of Swedish tales, illustrated by John Bauer in a style reminiscent of Nielsen, makes these Swedish tales come to life. Selected by Elsa Olenius and translated by Holger Lundbergh, *Great Swedish Fairy Tales* is filled with wonderful stories of terrifying trolls usually outwitted by clever simple folk.

The United States. Although it would take several volumes to just introduce the folklore of the world and its storytelling editions, we mustn't forget to mention at least one more folk region.

While many folktales read in the United States are European in origin, distinct American folklore is found in Indian tales, black folktales, folk songs, and tales of American folk heroes. Indian lore, in which animals figure so prominently, seem to hold a never-ending fascination for children. These legends of the origins of our lakes, rivers, and mountains may be difficult to understand, however, without some background explanation. Black folktales have been gathered largely from the South. Many of these stories are written in a dialect which may be difficult for the average reader or storyteller. Folk songs are also a part of American folk tradition. There are collections of the songs, complete with music, and many attractive picture books based on individual songs listed in the bibliography at the end of the music chapter.

Not all of the American tall-tale heroes are authentic derivations from folklore, but the tales of their deeds and their colorful characters have captured the hearts of school-age children who have been introduced to them. Many of these folk stories are based on the adventures of historical personages, such as Davy Crockett, Johnny Appleseed, and John Henry. Others, such as Mike Fink, the river boatman; Pecos Bill, the cowboy; and Paul Bunyan, the mighty logger, are probably not genuine folklore heroes, but stories about them are written in folktale form and are delightful to tell.

Some other American folktales are actually variants of European tales, imported and adapted to the American experience. For example, some of the tales collected by Richard Chase in the southern mountain regions of Appalachia for his *Grandfather Tales* and *The Jack Tales* are European stories transformed by American settings and dialects.

Other countries. France, England, Germany, and the United States have provided familiar folktales for generations of storytellers. For those in search of lesser known folktales for presentation, a wealth of material awaits you. Luckily, talented folklorists have collected authentic tales in book form. Harold Courlander's African collections provide scholarly interpretations suitable for the storyteller. *The Hat Shaking Dance and Other Ashanti Tales from Ghana* and *The Fire on the Mountain and Other Ethiopian Stories* are only two of the books providing material for oral presentation. Yoshiko Uchida's *The Dancing Kettle* and *The Sea of Gold* introduce the English-speaking storyteller to the vigorous Japanese stories. Isaac Bashevis Singer has retold some of the homely stories of the Middle European Jews in *Zlateh the Goat* and *When Shlemiel Went to Warsaw.* Russian, Polish, and South American stories represent just a few of the regions in the story collections waiting for use in your local library or available through your favorite bookstore.

References: Folktales

Asbjørnsen, Peter C. and Moe, Jorgen E. "Gudbrand-on-the-Hillside," "The Husband Who Was to Mind the House," "The Three Billy Goats Gruff," "Why the Bear is Stumpy-tailed," and "Why the Sea is Salt." *East O' the Sun and West O' the Moon;* tr. by George Webbe Dasent; il. by Erik Werenskiold. Dover, 1970.

——— *Norwegian Folk Tales;* tr. by Pat Shaw Iversen and Carl Norman; il. by Erik Werenskiold and Theodor Kittelsen. Viking, 1961.

Belpré, Pura. "The Legend of the Royal Palm." *Once in Puerto Rico;* il. by Christine Price. Warne, 1973.

Brown, Marcia. *Dick Whittington and his Cat;* il. by author. Scribner, 1950.

Chase, Richard. *Grandfather Tales;* il. by Berkeley Williams, Jr. Houghton, 1948.

———— *The Jack Tales;* il. by Berkeley Williams, Jr. Houghton, 1943.

Courlander, Harold. "The Origin of the Balsam Tree." *Ride with the Sun;* il. by Roger Duvoisin. McGraw-Hill, 1955.

Courlander, Harold, and Leslau, Wolf. *The Fire on the Mountain and Other Ethiopian Stories;* il. by Robert Kane. Holt, 1950.

Courlander, Harold, and Prempeh, A. K. *The Hat-Shaking Dance and Other Ashanti Tales from Ghana;* il. by Enrico Arno. Harcourt, 1957.

Dayrell, Elphinstone. *Why the Sun and the Moon Live in the Sky;* il. by Blair Lent. Houghton, 1968.

Gág, Wanda. *Gone Is Gone;* il. by author. Coward, 1935.

Grimm Brothers. *Grimm's Fairy Tales;* il. by Arthur Rackham. Viking, 1973.

———— *Rapunzel;* il. by Felix Hoffmann. Harcourt, 1961.

———— *The Seven Ravens;* il. by Felix Hoffmann. Harcourt, 1963.

———— "Rapunzel." *Tales from Grimm;* tr. and il. by Wanda Gág. Coward, 1936.

Hogrogian, Nonny. *One Fine Day;* il. by author. Macmillan, 1971.

Jacobs, Joseph. "Cap O' Rushes," "The Cat and the Mouse," "Teeny-Tiny," "The Three Bears," "The Three Little Pigs." *English Fairy Tales;* il. by John D. Batten. Dover, 1967.

Kent, Jack. *The Fat Cat: A Danish Folktale;* il. by author. Parents, 1971.

Leach, Maria. *How the People Sang the Mountains Up: How and Why Stories;* il. by Glen Rounds. Viking, 1967.

Master of All Masters; il. by Marcia Sewall. Atlantic-Little, 1972.

Olenius, Elsa. *Great Swedish Fairy Tales;* tr. by Holger Lundbergh; il. by John Bauer. Delacorte, 1973.

Reeves, James. *English Fables and Fairy Stories;* il. by Joan Kiddell-Monroe. Oxford, 1954.

Ross, Eulalie. "How the Camel Got His Proud Look." *The Buried Treasure and Other Picture Tales;* il. by Josef Cellini. Lippincott, 1958.

Simon, Solomon. *The Wise Men of Helm and Their Merry Tales;* tr. by Ben Bengal and David Simon; il. by Lillian Fischel. Behrman House, 1945.

Singer, Isaac Bashevis. *When Shlemiel Went to Warsaw and Other Stories;* tr. by the author and Elizabeth Shub; il. by Margot Zemach. Farrar, 1969.

———— *Zlateh the Goat;* tr. by the author and Elizabeth Shub; il. by Maurice Sendak. Harper, 1966.

Tom Tit Tot; il. by Evaline Ness. Scribner, 1965.

Uchida, Yoshiko. *The Dancing Kettle and Other Japanese Folk Tales;* il. by Richard Jones. Harcourt, 1949.

———— *The Sea of Gold and Other Tales from Japan;* il. by Marianne Yamaguchi. Scribner, 1965.

Yolen, Jane. *The Girl Who Cried Flowers and Other Tales;* il. by David Palladini. Crowell, 1974.

———— *The Girl Who Loved the Wind;* il. by Ed Young. Crowell, 1972.

———— *The Moon Ribbon and Other Tales;* il. by David Palladini. Crowell, 1976.

———— *The Transfigured Hart;* il. by Donna Diamond. Crowell, 1975.

There are, of course, many more folktales for you to choose from in the bibliographies included in chapters 5 and 6. Find some that appeal to you and learn to tell them. Not only will you enjoy telling these stories, your listeners will enjoy them too.

Literary Tales

After you feel comfortable telling the simple and then the more complex folktales, you will want to attempt to learn a literary tale, a short story written with elements reminiscent of folklore. These stories are more appropriate for the advanced storyteller because, to retain the beauty of the language, you will need to almost memorize the entire story, to know it so perfectly that you will be able to concentrate completely on an expressive presentation. Sometimes my graduate students can try a literary tale almost immediately because they have been taking courses for years that have required a good deal of memorization. The more you memorize, the easier the task becomes. It would be impossible to list all those authors who have contributed by writing original fairy tales, but a few should be mentioned. In the course of your storytelling career you may want to examine the work of each of these authors more closely.

Hans Christian Andersen

A favorite interview question is, "If you could meet a famous personage from the past, who would you pick?" My choice would be the Danish author and storyteller Haṇs Christian Andersen who published his first book of fairy tales in 1835. It is my opinion that he was the most talented of all writers, the father of modern storytelling. Although his greatest desire was to be well thought of as a playwright and serious author, his fairy tales were an instant success and are still read with great enjoyment today. Some of his first stories can be traced to folk sources, but his later work is entirely original. Since Andersen wrote in Danish, the work you will be reading will, of course, be a translation. For that reason it is necessary to find an edition which retains the original flavor of Andersen's work. A 1938 translation by Paul Leyssac, *It's Perfectly True,* is the one I still use. Erik Haugaard's *Hans Christian Andersen: The Complete Fairy Tales and Stories,* published in 1974, is also a good edition, with lots of stories but, unfortunately, no pictures.

The fantasy of Andersen's world is suitable for a wide age range. His satirical comments on human nature are universally understood and his stories are enjoyed by children and adults the world over. Although Andersen told his stories while performing intricate paper cuttings, telling an Andersen story usually requires a good bit of concentration. Therefore attempting to emulate his artistry with paper while telling a story may be difficult to do. But if you want an activity after your storyhour, some of the paper-cutting ideas in chapter 19 may be useful and entertaining or maybe you know an amusing and appropriate papercraft trick of your own to demonstrate. Andersen's birthday, April 2, is a good time to plan an Andersen storyhour. This date also happens to commemorate International Children's Book Day, so if you don't want to "tell an Andersen," feature stories from some foreign countries instead.

The Andersen museum in Odense, Denmark, is housed in the cottage where he was born. The collection contains memorabilia as well as Andersen books that have been translated and illustrated around the world. Should you want to send for the museum's catalog of books and souvenirs, the address is: Hans Christian Andersen Museum, Munkemøllestroede, Odense, Denmark. As a gift to yourself or your library, Wedgwood, the English china company, has produced each year since 1971 a children's Christmas plate featuring a scene from an Andersen story.

Ruth Sawyer

Ruth Sawyer, an American storyteller and author of children's books, wrote a classic on traditional storytelling, *The Way of the Storyteller,* which should be required background reading for every serious storyteller. The stories she has collected in the back of her book and those stories she wrote herself are as robust, humorous, and thoughtful as any you will find. "The Flea" in Eulalie Ross's *Buried Treasure* is a tongue-in-cheek romp whose plot hinges on a shepherd boy guessing a cryptic riddle. There are a few Spanish words in the story that add to its enjoyment. "The Princess and the Vagabond" is an Irish version of *The Taming of the Shrew* and is suitable for both young adults and adults. The story I wish I could do justice to is "Wee Meg Barnileg and the Fairies," which appears in the appendix of Sawyer's book on storytelling. The phrases and wording in this story are so perfect that it would be a desecration to change any of it. For some reason I cannot seem to get it right and so have never been able to share it. However, some of my students have managed to tell it with the combination of verve and dreamlike quality it needs. Maybe you can do it justice too. The Sawyer stories are long, so be prepared to take some time to learn them.

Eleanor Farjeon

I first discovered the English Eleanor Farjeon in a full-length novel of hers called *The Glass Slipper,* which is based on the Cinderella story. Naturally I had to read her other full-length novel, *The Silver Curlew,* based on the Tom Tit Tot story. The charm of Farjeon's novels is further enhanced by the Ernest Shepard drawings. Both of these books are good reading-aloud sources, but it is the sensitive charm of her short stories that makes her work a storyteller's dream. In the best fairy-tale tradition her stories transport one to a delicate world of poets and princesses. The theme of personal freedom is beautifully portrayed in "The Seventh Princess," while the quickly learned "The Lady's Room" is reminiscent of "The Fisherman and His Wife." Both stories are from *The Little Bookroom.* My favorite Farjeon, "Elsie Piddock Skips in Her Sleep," from *Martin Pippin in the Daisy-Field,* is perfect for a spring storyhour because the plot revolves around skipping rope. This story takes nearly half an hour to tell, so you can imagine the time and effort it takes to learn. It is worth it, of course, since you don't learn stories for just one performance. Every story you learn can be told over and over again for years of good telling and listening. And with such a long story as this one, you needn't plan to tell another one for that session.

Howard Pyle

Howard Pyle's stories are funny. Many are lengthy, but they should be learned just as Pyle wrote them. *Pepper and Salt,* first published in 1885, and *The Wonder Clock,* published in 1887, provide humorous stories written in a folktale style that are suitable for storytellers and for those who feel Pyle's tales are best read aloud. "How the Good Gifts Were Used by Two" makes an excellent Christmas story. His Cinderella story is entitled "The Apple of Contentment." The beginning of the latter story will give you an idea of Pyle's style: "There was a woman once, and she had three daughters. The first daughter squinted with both eyes, yet the woman loved her as she loved salt, for she herself squinted with both eyes." If you'd like to share pictures with your group, Pyle's own wry illustrations are most appropriate to his stories. For illustrations that are in a more modern style, Trina Schart Hyman has done a broad, colorful interpretation in *King Stork,* a story taken from Pyle's *The Wonder Clock.*

Rudyard Kipling

Rudyard Kipling's longer works are somewhat out of fashion these days, mainly because they seem wordy and decidedly racist to the modern reader. However, two of his works, *The Jungle Book* and the *Just So Stories,* are treasure troves for the storyteller. By learning parts of *The Jungle Book* you can introduce potential readers to this special book and the *Just So Stories* are original pourquoi stories which have great appeal. Kipling imaginatively explains "How the Leopard Got His Spots," "How the Camel Got His Hump," and, in "The Elephant's Child," he tells why elephants all have trunks instead of "a blackish, bulgy nose as big as a boot." The wonderfully imaginative language of these stories is what gives them their authority.

Carl Sandburg

Carl Sandburg is well known for his works for adults, but he wrote successfully for children as well. His *Rootabaga Stories,* which abound in nonsense phrasing and bizarre situations, should be popular with any group. It takes a skilled storyteller, however, to offer these stories with just the right amount of tongue-in-cheek gravity. As with the tales of Andersen, many of Sandburg's *Rootabaga Stories* feature inanimate objects: umbrellas, rag dolls, and even skyscrapers. If you are fascinated by interesting names, Sandburg will supply them in abundance. His "How Bozo the Button Buster Busted All His Buttons When a Mouse Came" is told to three girls named Deep Red Roses, The Beans Are Burning, and Sweeter Than the Bees Humming. Not so elaborate but as jocosely descriptive is Shush Shush, the big buff banty hen who rings the doorbell when she lays an egg, also from the *Rootabaga Stories.* For a potpourri of Sandburg, try *The Sandburg Treasury.* A gay picture-book version of one of his stories, *The Wedding Procession of the Rag Doll and the Broom Handle and Who Was in It,* is illustrated with zany humor by Harriet Pincus.

Laurence Housman

Laurence Housman's stories have a completely different tone than Sandburg's. They grip the reader with a quiet intensity and to capture and transmit to an audience the full flavor of his words a slower, more deliberate telling is most successful. The settings of Housman's stories create vivid pictures in the mind. In "The Rat-Catcher's Daughter," much of the story takes place in the dwelling of a gnome deep underground where a greedy man's daughter must spend three years of her life. In "Rocking-Horse Land" a young prince dreams of his toy rocking horse's success. Although Housman's descriptions tend to be lengthy, they are essential to an understanding of the stories. A new edition of many of Housman's tales has been issued by Atheneum under the title story *The Rat-Catcher's Daughter.* Housman also did an admirable job retelling some of the more familiar stories from the *Arabian Nights*.

John Gardner

One of the happy things about finding a good folk story to learn is that it doesn't become dated or go out of fashion. This does not mean, however, that we should rely solely on the old, the tried and true. We must keep searching for new material. I've already mentioned Jane Yolen as a possible modern source for stories. John Gardner, an author who has written mainly for adults, might be another source of literary fairy tales. In recent years Gardner has written two collections of magical and witty tales for children. His stories are reminiscent of well-known fairy tales, but in a contemporary mood. "The Tailor and the Giant" in *Dragon, Dragon and Other Tales* reminds the reader of the Grimm story, but in the Gardner version the tailor makes signs which say LOVE in big red letters and prepares to demonstrate in front of the king's palace.

The beginning of the title story in *Gudgekin the Thistle Girl and Other Tales* is representative of Gardner's humorous approach:

> In a certain kingdom there lived a poor little thistle girl. What thistle girls did for a living—that is, what people did with thistles—is no longer known, but whatever the reason that people gathered thistles, she was one of those that did it.

Mature audiences familiar with the traditional tales will enjoy Gardner's wry, tongue-in-cheek humor.

References: Literary Tales

Andersen, Hans Christian. *The Complete Fairy Tales and Stories;* tr. by Erik Haugaard. Doubleday, 1974.

———— *It's Perfectly True;* tr. by Paul Leyssac; il. by Vilhelm Pedersen. Macmillan, 1937.

Farjeon, Eleanor. *The Glass Slipper;* il. by Ernest Shepard. Viking, 1956.

———— "The Lady's Room," "The Seventh Princess." *The Little Bookroom;* il. by Edward Ardizzone. Oxford, 1956.

———— "Elsie Piddock Skips in Her Sleep." *Martin Pippin in the Daisy-Field;* il. by Isobel and John Morton-Sale. Stokes, 1938.

———— *The Silver Curlew;* il. by Ernest Shepard. Viking, 1954.

Gardner, John. *Dragon, Dragon and Other Tales;* il. by Charles Shields. Knopf, 1975.

———— *Gudgekin the Thistle Girl and Other Tales;* il. by Michael Sporn. Knopf, 1976.

Housman, Laurence. "The Rat-Catcher's Daughter," "Rocking-Horse Land." *The Rat-Catcher's Daughter;* ed. by Ellin Greene; il. by Julia Noonan. Atheneum, 1974.

Kipling, Rudyard. *The Elephant's Child;* il. by Ulla Kampmann. Follett, 1969.

———— *The Jungle Book;* il. by Fritz Eichenberg. Grosset, 1950.

———— "How the Camel Got His Hump," "How the Leopard Got His Spots." *Just So Stories;* il. by Etienne Delessert. Doubleday, 1972.

———— *Just So Stories;* il. by author. Doubleday, 1946.

Pyle, Howard. *King Stork;* il. by Trina Schart Hyman. Little, 1973.

———— *Pepper and Salt, or Seasoning for Young Folk;* il. by author. Harper, 1885.

———— *The Wonder Clock;* il. by author. Dover, 1965.

Sandburg, Carl. "How Bozo the Button Buster Busted All His Buttons When a Mouse Came." *The Rootabaga Stories;* il. by Maud and Miska Petersham. Harcourt, 1974.

———— *The Sandburg Treasury;* il. by Paul Bacon. Harcourt, 1970.

———— *The Wedding Procession of the Rag Doll and the Broom Handle and Who Was In It;* il. by Harriet Pincus. Harcourt, 1967.

Sawyer, Ruth. "The Flea." *The Buried Treasure;* ed. by Eulalie Steinmetz Ross; il. by Josef Cellini. Lippincott, 1958.

———— "Wee Meg Barnileg and the Fairies," "The Princess and the Vagabond." *The Way of the Storyteller.* Viking, 1962.

Stories from the Arabian Nights; retold by Laurence Housman; il. by Girard Goodenow. Junior Deluxe Editions, 1955.

Fables

Fables are short, didactic tales which attempt to teach a lesson or convey a moral. The main characters are often animals who behave like humans. Some fables are so well known that expressions from them, such as "sour grapes," have become part of our everyday language. Although some of these didactic tales might provoke even young children into thinking about the "message," most will be enjoyed simply for the story. Of course, some fables present philosophical concepts that are too abstract for many children to understand; these are best left for telling to those who are mature enough to comprehend.

However, because so many fables feature animal characters that do appeal to children, there have been many editions of fables published especially for them. In particular, some attractively illustrated picture books by distinguished artists have become very popular. Two adaptations by Doris Dana in picture-book form offer fables in both English and Spanish text by the Chilean poet Lucilla Godoy-Alcayaga, who writes under the pseudonym

Gabriela Mistral. Both books, *Crickets and Frogs* and *The Elephant and His Secret,* are illustrated with colorful woodcuts by Antonio Frasconi.

Tell a fable at the beginning of a storyhour. They are easy to learn and may stimulate some serious thought in young listeners. Only one fable at a time, please; too many at one session tend to be tiresome.

Aesop's Fables

The best-known fables are those in the Greek collection commonly known as *Aesop's Fables*. It is believed that Aesop was a Greek slave who lived about 600 B.C. The earliest known written versions of these stories are the ones recorded in Latin by Phaedrus in the first century A.D. In the third century, Babrius wrote a collection of some 300 of the fables in Greek verse. Subsequent compilations were made by Aviares in the fourth century, and by Romulus in the tenth century. Later, these fables reached Northern Europe, and were among the stories printed by William Caxton. They have survived until the present in various versions. There is no one accepted version, nor is there any classic illustrator of these fables. The Metropolitan Museum of New York exhibited a number of pictures gathered from the last 500 years of illustrated versions of the Aesop fables. *Aesop: Five Centuries of Illustrated Fables* is a book based on this exhibit. It may be an inspiration to any potential illustrators in your folk program.

My favorite modern adaptation of an Aesop's fable is James Daugherty's picture book *Andy and the Lion,* which has the same theme as "Androcles and the Lion" and can also be compared with La Fontaine's "The Lion and the Mouse." For older children there is the picture-book version of Chaucer's "Nun's Priest Tale" (which is adapted from Aesop's "The Cock and the Fox") with scratchboard drawings by Barbara Cooney and titled *Chanticleer and the Fox.* Take your choice of illustrators of the fables of Aesop. For those who enjoy the traditional, there are Arthur Rackham's black-and-white silhouette drawings interspersed with full-color traditional paintings in the V. S. Vernon Jones translation of *Aesop's Fables.* The happy, gay cartoon interpretation of Jack Kent's *Fables of Aesop* gives the old moralistic tales a fresh, new, humorous twist that will make you and your audiences laugh aloud.

Fables of La Fontaine

Jean de La Fontaine used various sources, including Aesop, for his verse fables which first appeared in 1688. French school children know the fables almost as well as American children know their Mother Goose. They hear them when they are young and study them in school, memorizing them for recitation contests. Although La Fontaine suffers somewhat in translation, his poems are still delightful versions of the traditional fables. One of the more exciting ways of presenting these works of La Fontaine to children is by using the single-fable picture books of Brian Wildsmith. Through his use of rich, glowing colors and strong, bold lines, he has added visual excitement to five of the fables.

Fables of Krylov

Just as French children are weaned on La Fontaine, Russian children grow up with Krylov. Ivan Andreevich Krylov worked as a librarian in the St. Petersburg Library. His first collections of fables consisted of translations of La Fontaine's tales; but later he wrote fables which expressed harsh political and social criticism, attacking hypocrisy in particular. The first complete collection of Krylov's fables appeared in 1843. While English editions are not plentiful, the *15 Fables of Krylov*, a fine translation by Guy Daniels, is suitable for older children.

Fables of India

The Pañchatantra which contains the earliest recorded fables of India originated somewhere between 275 B.C. and 275 A.D. In these fables the Vishnu Sarma attempts to teach the three sons of the king some principles of conduct which they are to follow. There are some 200 delightful versions of *The Pañchatantra*, recorded in more than 50 languages. These fables which are much more complex than those of Aesop or La Fontaine have stories within stories. The Arthur W. Ryder translation, *Gold's Gloom; Tales from the Pañchatantra*, tells 34 of the stories separately and in random order, thus making them easier for readers of other cultures to enjoy.

The Hitopadeśa, or *Book of Good Counsels*, is actually a rearrangement of *The Pañchatantra* with a few additional stories that dates from the tenth century. One story from this collection has been made popular in this country, Marcia Brown's excellent picture-book version, *Once a Mouse* which won the Caldecott Medal in 1962 with its bold woodcut illustrations. In this story a hermit befriends a mouse and turns him into various animal forms. When the mouse, now a proud tiger, expresses his ungratefulness to the hermit he is turned once more into a humble little mouse.

The Jatakas are a series of animal stories describing the lessons of life that Gautama Buddha preached in northeast India between 563 B.C. and

483 B.C. The stories, numbering some 500, remained in the oral tradition until several hundred years after Buddha's death, when they were written down in the Pali language. Although they were first translated into English in the nineteenth century, these fables have been told and enjoyed for over two thousand years in various parts of the world.

Two collections by Ellen C. Babbitt that were designed for children have brought these stories to American children. Her version of the fable of "The Turtle Who Couldn't Stop Talking" is my favorite. A turtle meets some geese who are flying back to their home. The turtle would like to join them and the geese suggest that he hold a stick between his teeth while they each take an end and fly into the air. When the village children see the odd sight they jeer and laugh at the turtle. Because he is unable to keep quiet, the foolish turtle lets go of the stick to answer the children and falls to his death. A 1975 book edited by Nancy DeRoin retells thirty of the 500 fables in a more detailed version than Babbitt's.

References: Fables

Brown, Marcia. *Once a Mouse;* il. by author. Scribner, 1961.

Chaucer, Geoffrey. *Chanticleer and the Fox;* adapted and il. by Barbara Cooney. Crowell, 1958.

Daugherty, James. *Andy and the Lion;* il. by author. Viking, 1938.

DeRoin, Nancy. *Jataka Tales; Fables from the Buddha;* il. by Ellen Lanyon. Houghton, 1975.

Godoy-Alcayaga, Lucilla. *Crickets and Frogs,* by Gabriela Mistral (pseud.); adapted and tr. by Doris Dana; il. by Antonio Frasconi. Atheneum, 1972.

————— *The Elephant and His Secret,* by Gabriela Mistral (pseud.); adapted and tr. by Doris Dana; il. by Antonio Frasconi. Atheneum, 1974.

Gold's Gloom: Tales from the Pañchatantra; tr. by Arthur W. Ryder. Univ. of Chicago Pr., 1925.

Jataka Tales; retold by Ellen C. Babbitt; il. by Ellsworth Young. Prentice-Hall, 1912. Also *More Jataka Tales* (Century/Prentice-Hall, 1922).

Jones, V. S. Vernon. *Aesop's Fables;* il. by Arthur Rackham. Watts, 1968.

Kent, Jack. *Jack Kent's Fables of Aesop;* il. by author. Parents, 1972.

Krylov, Ivan A. *15 Fables;* tr. by Guy Daniels; il. by David Pascal. Macmillan, 1965.

McKendry, John J., comp. *Aesop: Five Centuries of Illustrated Fables.* Metropolitan Museum of Art, 1964.

Mistral, Gabriela. *see* Godoy-Alcayaga, Lucilla.

Ryder, Arthur W. See *Gold's Gloom.*

Myths

Traditionally, myths have been regarded as stories which represent the attempts of primitive people to explain the nature of the world around them and human existence. Whether these tales were actually part of the religion of ancient cultures is now in question, but we generally define a myth as having something to do with religion. The Greek, Roman, and Norse cultures have been the major sources of our most familiar myths. These myths, along with stories from the Judaic and Christian religions, are an important part of our literary heritage.

Myths are most suitable for the upper grades of elementary school, junior high, and beyond. Some writers have attempted to adapt them for younger children, but this often necessitates stripping away the beautiful language and more significant philosophical musings, leaving only the bare threads of the plot.

Myths are more difficult to introduce to children than folktales. While a folktale usually can be enjoyed without a knowledge of the culture of its origin, myths usually cannot so easily be removed from their cultural context. The relationships of the gods and the patterns of the culture are expressed in more continuous relationships rather than in individual tales. However, these stories, like most folklore, were originally told orally; and, with some care, they may be read or told aloud. If they seem too long or complicated, some condensation may be desirable; but care must be taken not to shorten or simplify them so drastically that the majesty and power of these ancient tales are lost. Margery Bernstein and Janet Kobrin have successfully retold several myths for younger children. *The First Morning*, a myth told by the Sukuma people of East Africa, charmingly relates how the animals acquire light from the land above the sky. A group of Abo students have collected and illustrated Australian aboriginal myths, such as "How the Kangaroo Got His Tail," in *Djugurba: Tales from the Spirit Time*. And for storytellers, that's pronounced "jook-urr-pa."

It is important to note that the myths we read are not mere translations of the original. The literary styles of writers who do the retellings vary widely. While some versions are well suited for oral storytelling, others can best be enjoyed by individual readers. For instance, Lillian Smith points out in her book on children's literature, *The Unreluctant Years*, that the different literary styles of Charles Kingsley, Nathaniel Hawthorne, and Padraic Colum have produced three vastly different versions of the same Greek myths. Adults who wish to introduce mythology to children should take the time to sample several collections in order to know what styles are available and to become acquainted with them. Don't cross myths off your list of possible storytelling material, however; these are vital, exciting, and meaningful stories to share with an audience.

Greek and Roman Myths

The stories of the gods and heroes of ancient Greece and Rome are among a storyteller's favorite myths. With their fantastic events, abundant action, complex characters, and involved relationships among gods and mortals, these myths comment on human and divine foibles, explain natural phenomena, and describe the beginning of the world. While the capricious cruelty of the gods in those myths often causes painful tragedy for humans, the myths also exude a sunny optimism that celebrates the beauty and excitement in life.

Today, there is a wide choice of retellings, narrative styles, and styles of illustration available. Whichever you or a child chooses, these well-known myths are likely to stimulate the imagination. For a short introduction to Greek mythology, Robert Graves's *Greek Gods and Heroes* offers an entertaining look at the classics. Edith Hamilton's scholarly *Mythology* is a noted classicist's retelling that includes valuable background that can be utilized in your introductions during the folklore program. On the other hand, Ingri and Edgar Parin d'Aulaire's *Book of Greek Myths* has a humorous and earthy folktale quality that is reflected in both the text and illustrations. Charles Kingsley's *The Heroes* relates the classic stories in a simple style that is strong and not condescending. A single tale retold by Margaret Hodges, *Persephone and the Springtime*, explains the seasonal change in climate; with its colorful illustrations by Arvis Stewart this book makes an excellent storytelling tool. Whether you enjoy stark or poetic prose, collections of stories or a single favorite tale, these books offer a rich array of stories to share with your listeners.

Norse Myths

The Norse myths of Iceland are contained in two collections, the *Elder* or *Poetic Edda* and *Younger* or *Prose Edda*. The *Poetic Edda* tells of the creation of the world and the evolution of the gods. It also contains the Norse epic story of Sigurd the Volsung. The *Prose Edda* is a collection of important Norse myths gathered in the thirteenth century. Incidentally, the word "edda" originally meant a great-grandmother, which gives a rather folksy air to these sometimes difficult stories. To some readers the Norse myths may seem considerably more somber and tragic in tone than those of the Greeks and Romans. For instance, unlike the immortal deities of classical Greek and Roman mythology, the Norse gods are mortal and prepare to perish in a tragic battle at the end of the world. If these stories appeal to you, you may choose from several versions. Padraic Colum and Olivia Coolidge relate both the myths and the hero or epic tales in their collections, while Dorothy Hosford devotes her *Sons of the Volsungs* to the Sigurd tales and her *Thunder of the Gods* to the myths about Odin, Thor, Baldur, Loki, and the other gods and goddesses. The d'Aulaires' version, *Norse Gods and Giants,* which is amply illustrated and manages to emphasize points of beauty and humor in these sometimes dark tales of the North, may even appeal to a somewhat younger age group. Margaret Hodges has also rewritten one of the Icelandic myths as a single tale, *Baldur and the Mistletoe,* which relates the story of Baldur's death and why the use of mistletoe stands for hope.

References: Myths

Aulaire, Ingri and Edgar P. d'. *Ingri and Edgar Parin d'Aulaire's Book of Greek Myths;* il. by authors. Doubleday, 1962.

———— *Norse Gods and Giants;* il. by authors. Doubleday, 1967.

Bernstein, Margery, and Kobrin, Janet, re-tellers. *The First Morning: An African Myth;* il. by Enid Warner Romanek. Scribner, 1976.

Colum, Padraic. *The Children's Homer: Adventures of Odysseus and the Tale of Troy;* il. by Willy Pogány. Macmillan, 1962.

Coolidge, Olivia E. *Greek Myths;* il. by Edouard Sandoz. Houghton, 1949.

D'Aulaire, Ingri. *see* Aulaire, Ingri d'.

Djugurba: Tales from the Spirit Time. Univ. of Indiana Pr., 1976.

Graves, Robert. *Greek Gods and Heroes;* il. by Dimitri Davis. Doubleday, 1960.

Hamilton, Edith. *Mythology;* il. by Steele Savage. Little, 1942.

Hodges, Margaret. *Baldur and the Mistletoe;* il. by Gerry Hoover. Little, 1974.

———— *Persephone and the Springtime;* il. by Arvis Stewart. Little, 1973.

Hosford, Dorothy. *Sons of the Volsungs;* il. by Frank Dobias. Holt, 1949.

———— *Thunder of the Gods;* il. by Claire and George Louden. Holt, 1952.

Kingsley, Charles. *The Heroes;* il. by Joan Kiddell-Monroe. Dutton, 1963.

Smith, Lillian. *The Unreluctant Years: A Critical Approach to Children's Literature.* American Library Assn., 1953.

Epics

Whereas the myth focuses on the gods, the epic centers on an earthly hero. Originally the epics were collections of individual songs or poems about a particular hero and his adventures, but modern authors have collected these stories in prose form which makes them particularly useful to the storyteller. Usually the epic hero is one whose character and moral code express not only universal, but national ideals as well, and the tales, therefore, impart a very nationalistic flavor. While one adventure is sometimes extracted from an epic and presented to children as a single tale, the appeal of the epic form lies in following the complete adventures of the hero, often from birth to death. Most adults will recognize some of their old childhood favorites in the epic literature and present-day children continue to enjoy them.

Storytellers might find that an entire series can be built around a popular epic; combining oral storytelling and reading aloud can make such a program series an exciting experience.

English Epics

The exploits of Robin Hood, one of the most popular children's heroes, appear in several forms of literature and film, including prose stories and numerous old English ballads. These stories, abounding with amusing and fascinating characters such as Little John, Will Scarlet, Friar Tuck, and Maid Marian, are filled with wit, courage, and fellowship. Robin Hood is an outlaw, but one who embodies many exemplary traits. His robbing of the rich to give to the poor may be a questionable ethic, but it is heartily approved by his many followers who see it primarily as a brave attempt at justice. Howard Pyle's version, *The Merry Adventures of Robin Hood,* is a superb edition, good for reading aloud or for extracting incidents for a more traditional oral presentation.

King Arthur is the hero of a long series of medieval romances. Arthurian stories in the oral tradition were first written down in French, the language of the English court in Norman times. A progressive elaboration of the material culminated in Sir Thomas Malory's fifteenth-century version, *Le Morte d'Arthur.* Malory's tales of this romantic figure and his chivalrous knights have been the source for later versions, of which Lord Tennyson's *Idylls of the King* is typical. The concept of chivalry exemplified by Arthur and his knights reflects a more sophisticated ethic than that of the Robin Hood epic, but whether or not children understand chivalry as such, they find knights and their ladies particularly fascinating. Howard Pyle, who so aptly portrays Robin Hood, has also written an excellent version of this epic, *The Story of King Arthur and His Knights.* Sidney Lanier's *The Boy's King Arthur* is another continually popular telling which is greatly enhanced by N. C. Wyeth's illustrations.

The oldest epic in English is *Beowulf,* an Anglo-Saxon saga believed to have been written in the eighth century. It celebrates the sheer courage, strength, wit, and cunning by which the hero Beowulf destroys the man-eating monster, Grendel, Grendel's cruel mother, and a fiendish dragon. Robert Nye's *Beowulf: A New Telling* is a strongly dramatic prose version which renders the action with all the gory detail inherent in this tale.

Greek Epics

The Iliad and *The Odyssey* of Homer are the famous Greek epics. *The Iliad,* which relates the events of the Trojan war, is extremely complex and is probably too confusing to be told to very young children. The central figure is Achilles, but many other legendary heroes also take part, among them Agamemnon, Patrocles, Hector, and Priam. *The Odyssey,* which is much easier to understand, relates the strange and wonderful adventures which befall Odysseus on his return voyage to Ithaca after the capture of Troy. Adult versions of these Homeric epics are usually too difficult for children, but there are several adaptations or retellings designed for young readers that give the storyteller some material with which to work. Padraic Colum's *The Children's Homer* emphasizes action, while Barbara Leonie Picard's *The Odyssey of Homer* concentrates on character portrayal. The collaboration of author Jane Werner and illustrators Alice and Martin Provensen has produced yet another exciting version, *The Iliad and The Odyssey.*

Epics of India

The Ramayana, a collection of stories often told through dance, describes the earthly life of the god Vishnu in his human form as Prince Rama. It relates Prince Rama's marriage to Sita and the adventures they share before her death. Two versions particularly suited for children are Joseph Gaer's *The Adventures of Rama* and Elizabeth Seeger's *The Ramayana,* which is much enhanced by Gordon Laite's illustrations.

Other National Epics

Program planners might also enjoy children's versions of the tales of other national heroes. The Irish heroes of Cuchulain and Finn MacCool, the ancient Babylonian hero Gilgamesh, the Cid of Spain, Roland of France, and Siegfried of Germany are examples of other epic heroes. Barbara Leonie Picard retells stories of three hero-kings, "Gilgamesh, King of Erech"; "Hrolf

Kraki, King of Denmark"; and "Conary, High King of Ireland" in *Three Ancient Kings*. These can be adapted for storytelling but would probably be better for reading aloud. An epic poem from the Sudan of West Africa, *Gassire's Lute*, has been translated and adapted by Alta Jablow and is suitable for young adults.

References: Epics

Colum, Padraic. *The Children's Homer: Adventures of Odysseus and the Tale of Troy;* il. by Willy Pogány. Macmillan, 1962.

Gaer, Joseph. *The Adventures of Rama;* il. by Randy Monk. Little, 1954.

Jablow, Alta, tr. *Gassire's Lute;* il. by Leo and Diane Dillon. Dutton, 1971.

Lanier, Sidney, ed. *The Boy's King Arthur;* il. by N. C. Wyeth. Scribner, 1924.

Nye, Robert. *Beowulf: A New Telling;* il. by Alan E. Cober. Hill & Wang, 1968.

Picard, Barbara Leonie. *The Odyssey of Homer;* il. by Joan Kiddell-Monroe. Oxford, 1952.

————— *Three Ancient Kings: Gilgamesh, Hrolf Kraki, Conary;* il. by Philip Gough. Warne, 1972.

Pyle, Howard. *The Merry Adventures of Robin Hood;* il. by author. Scribner, 1946.

————— *The Story of King Arthur and His Knights;* il. by author. Scribner, 1903.

Seeger, Elizabeth. *The Ramayana;* il. by Gordon Laite. W. R. Scott, 1969.

Werner, Jane. *The Iliad and the Odyssey;* il. by Alice and Martin Provensen. Golden Pr., 1964.

Legends

As you read through various studies of folklore you will find many overlappings of types of stories; the words "myth," "legend," "epic" sometimes are used interchangeably, too. A legend, however, usually refers to a story relating to the history of a culture. The story revolves around an incident that is believed to have taken place or a person who may actually have lived, but, in most instances, these tales have been retold so often and embellished to such an extent that it would be all but impossible to discover a factual account. Did Johnny Appleseed and John Henry really live? Was the Swiss William Tell a real personage? Did he actually shoot an apple from his son's head? These, and other legends like them, provide a wealth of material for the storyteller.

Just as you will find similarities in folktales from one country to another, so you will find yourself being led from one book to another when you find an interesting legend. Hans Baumann collected 27 legends from the world of folklore in his book *The Stolen Fire*. In the title story Maui defies the gods to gain for mankind the gift of fire. If this story sparks your interest, you may be led to Westervelt's *Hawaiian Legends of Ghosts and Ghost-Gods,* many of whose stories deal with the same Maui and his exploits. On the other hand, it may be the fire of the story that interests you and you may be led to Margaret Hodges's Indian legend, *The Fire Bringer*, which gives another interpretation of how man acquired fire. Perhaps you are more fascinated by the origin of the legend than by the subject.

Written in a terse style, *The Travels of Atunga* by Theodore Clymer offers us an Eskimo legend of a visit to Moon in a starkly illustrated picture-book format. Louis Untermeyer introduces 55 legends in *The World's Great Stories* by reminding us that while most legends have their origins in history, they survive not because they may be based on facts but because "they touch on fundamental traits of human nature." This collection should give any storyteller a good start with some of the world's great legends.

Myths and epics are usually more difficult to learn and tell than folktales and legends. The language and background is often more sophisticated. They are very much appreciated by older boys and girls, however, and should not be ignored in the storyteller's repertoire.

References: Legends

Baumann, Hans. *The Stolen Fire: Legends of Heroes and Rebels from Around the World;* tr. by Stella Humphries; il. by Herbert Holzing. Pantheon, 1974.

Clymer, Theodore. *The Travels of Atunga;* il. by John Schoenherr. Little, 1973.

Hodges, Margaret. *The Fire Bringer: A Paiute Indian Legend;* il. by Peter Parnall. Little, 1972.

Untermeyer, Louis. *The World's Great Stories: Fifty-five Legends that Live Forever;* il. by Mae Gerhard. Evans, 1964.

Westervelt, W. D., comp. and tr. *Hawaiian Legends of Ghosts and Ghost-Gods.* Tuttle, 1964.

Religious Sources

Oral presentation has traditionally played an important part in the teaching of religion. The teacher or leader stands or sits in front of a group and tells a story based on the religious principles of the order. Today storytelling is still used as a way to teach, as well as a way to entertain.

Many of the stories that have been orally handed down or printed make direct reference to religious incidents or persons. "The Jolly Tailor Who Became King," a Polish folktale, is a humorous nonsense story about an exceptionally thin tailor who sews up a hole in the sky and wins a princess as his wife. In the story the tailor and a friend are entertained by the devil's representatives; the frightened tailor invokes the protection of the Holy Virgin by singing a song in her praise, and the devils disappear. Although this part of the story seems quite incongruous in context, it does illustrate the religious influence on a simple folktale. Oscar Wilde, the talented nineteenth-century playwright, contributed to children's literature by writing a book of original fairy tales. The most impressive of these tells of a selfish giant who lets no one visit his beautiful garden. Because he is so selfish, winter lingers within its walls while it is springtime outside. When the neighborhood children sneak into the garden and the trees burst into blossom, the giant befriends a little boy. Years later the boy, a Christ figure, turns up to accompany the giant to the garden of Paradise. This religious symbolism may not be understood by children, but the story is lovely and beautifully written. It is yet another example of the religious influence on written and oral sources.

For those seeking obviously religious stories, there is a wealth of material. Remember that nearly every story has some sort of worthwhile message to impart. Even a seemingly frivolous nonsense story can be telling us that "happiness is laughter." Just because a story doesn't specifically mention religion, doesn't mean that it might not serve your purpose.

I was once at a religious camp meeting where my friend introduced me as a storyteller. Without warning, the camp PA system announced that a visiting storyteller would now entertain. While my friend cringed, wondering what stories I could use, I simply told two of my favorites. The audience could easily find appropriate morals in them, even though they were not truly religious stories.

Stories involving beliefs of most of the world's great religions can easily be found on library shelves. A brief examination of the availability of books based on Judaic-Christian heritage gives an idea of the variety and types of stories within easy reach for the storyteller. Beginning with the Bible we can choose from many interpretations. *Brian Wildsmith's Illustrated Bible Stories* with text by Philip Turner offers the Old and New Testaments in magnificent combination. The gloriously colored pen-and-ink drawings are matched by a graceful yet scholarly commentary. For those who like a more chatty, informal Bible scattered throughout with British colloquialisms, there is the British Broadcasting Corporation's *Bible Stories*, written originally for television production, which explores the Old Testament. The New Testament as edited by J. L. Klink, *Bible for Children* (volume 2), combines background material, poetry, plays, music, and storytelling material along with the scripture. Of course, the Bible, with its many interpretations, is only one way of presenting religious stories. Meindert DeJong, the Newbery Award winner, has written stories of the people in the Bible: Noah, Abraham, Isaac, Sarah, David, and many others as he remembered them told by his teacher and read to him by his grandfather. Each section of his *The Mighty Ones* begins with a quotation from the Bible and then in strong prose relates an incident from the lives of these Old Testament people. Another modern retelling of the Bible stories is Jan Wahl's *Runaway Jonah and Other Tales* in which five of the more familiar Old Testament stories are given a new and slightly offbeat vitality. Legends based on religion can always be found. Uri Shulevitz, in *The Magician*, writes of Elijah, a favorite figure of Jewish folklore who, on the eve of Passover, conjures up a feast for a needy couple. Another Jewish legend, gloriously illustrated as a picture book but suitable for a large age range, is Beverly Brodsky McDermott's *The Golem* in which a lump of clay fashioned into a man becomes a monster with a power all its own.

Retellings of single Bible stories are popular. The story of Noah and the ark has inspired a number of picture books. *Noah and the Rainbow* as retold by Max Bollinger and illustrated by Helga Aichinger, with stark simplicity, alternating warm with cool colors, is based on that familiar story. Another, *The Endless Party* by Etienne Delessert and Eleonore Schmid, departs from tradition and has Noah inviting all the animals aboard the ark for a party. Isaac Bashevis Singer's picture-book version *Why Noah Chose the Dove*, illustrated by Eric Carle's tissue paper collages, shows the animals arguing about who is the more worthy animal. It is the dove who says, "Each one of us has something the other doesn't have, given us by God who created us all." At that point Noah invites all the animals into the ark. Still another dimension is added to the story of the ark when Noah's grandson is lost before embarkation in Norma Farber's *Where's Gomer?* The illustrator, William Pène du Bois, pictures Noah and his family in trim yachting outfits eating chocolate layer cake and drinking milk. The old folksong *One Wide River to Cross* inspired still another picture-book version of the Noah story by Ed and Barbara Emberley, illustrated in decorative woodblock designs on brightly colored paper. For storytellers who are musically talented, the music is printed in the back of the book. *Will I Go to Heaven?* by Peter Mayle is an informally written picture book that explains various concepts of Heaven and Hell to those who have no direct affiliation with an organized religious group but who wish to impart some moral values to children. The lightly humorous cartoon drawings make it a good book to share with young children. Those interested in using their storytelling skills in their church or synagogue activities can find an endless supply of source materials for visual presentation, storytelling, and reading aloud.

References: Religious Sources

Bleecker, Mary Noel, comp. "The Jolly Tailor Who Became King." *Big Music; or Twenty Merry Tales to Tell;* il. by Louis S. Glanzman. Viking, 1946.

Bolliger, Max. *Noah and the Rainbow;* tr. by Clyde Robert Bulla; il. by Helga Aichinger. Crowell, 1972.

DeJong, Meindert. *The Mighty Ones: Great Men and Women of Early Bible Days;* il. by Harvey Schmidt. Harper, 1959.

Delessert, Etienne, and Schmid, Eleonore. *The Endless Party.* Harlin Quist, 1967.

Farber, Norma. *Where's Gomer?;* il. by William Pène du Bois. Dutton, 1974.

Klink, J. L., and others, eds. *Bible for Children: Vol. 2, New Testament with Songs and Plays;* tr. by Patricia Crampton; il. by Piet Klaassee. Westminster Pr., 1968–69.

Kossoff, David, reteller. *Bible Stories;* il. by Gino D'Achille. Follett, 1969.

McDermott, Beverly Brodsky. *The Golem;* il. by author. Lippincott, 1976.

Mayle, Peter. *Will I Go to Heaven?;* il. by Jem Gray. Corwin, 1976.

One Wide River to Cross; adapted by Barbara Emberley; il. by Ed Emberley. Prentice-Hall, 1966.

Shulevitz, Uri. *The Magician;* an adaptation from the Yiddish of I. L. Peretz; il. by author. Macmillan, 1973.

Singer, Isaac Bashevis. *Why Noah Chose the Dove;* tr. by Elizabeth Shub; il. by Eric Carle. Farrar, 1973.

Turner, Phillip. *Brian Wildsmith's Illustrated Bible Stories;* il. by Brian Wildsmith. Watts, 1969.

Wahl, Jan. *Runaway Jonah and Other Tales;* il. by Uri Shulevitz. Macmillan, 1968.

Wilde, Oscar. "The Selfish Giant." *The Happy Prince and Other Stories;* il. by Lars Bo. Penguin, 1962.

Other Literary Sources

Although traditionally the story program is devoted almost entirely to presenting folklore or original fairy tales, there are other resources in the library or media center for you to draw on. Collections of short stories and chapters from longer works of fiction and nonfiction also can be used in the book program. However, selecting passages and exciting incidents for retelling does take some experience. Obviously it is necessary to be familiar with the work in order to find and identify appropriate program-worthy material.

As you reread your favorite books and come across new ones, make it a habit to take note of those passages which might make a successful presentation, filing them for future reference.

A bookstore owner I know who is also a fine storyteller tells one section from Selma Lagerloff's *The Adventures of Nils* with such gusto that the children argue over who will get to read this lengthy book first. He has also prepared chapters from Lucy Boston's books for storytelling.

Adults will welcome oral renditions of their favorite O. Henry or the more caustic Roald Dahl in their programs. Chapters from Jerome K. Jerome's *Three Men in a Boat* or Ralph Schoenstein's *With T-Shirts and Beer Mugs for All* might precede a travel program. Both authors used the essay approach to write of trips they took. Jerome's summertime trip up the Thames in the late nineteenth century and Schoenstein's family excursion across America in the late 1960s are hilariously funny and are easily adapted for oral presentation. Using selected passages and several different storytellers, the tape-recorded documentary probing into what Americans do for a living and what they think about it from Studs Terkel's *Working* would make an excellent young adult or adult program on careers. The award-winning *A Day of Pleasure*, stories in which Isaac Bashevis Singer recounts his boyhood in Poland, makes for fine nostalgic storytelling. Black history is the basis for Julius Lester's stories in *Long Journey Home*, while Kristin Hunter's short stories in *Guests in the Promised Land* explore with compassion and conviction what it means to be black in a white world.

Science fiction collections of short stories are also excellent sources for oral presentation. Robert Heinlein's early writings and Ray Bradbury's stories are always well received and stimulate library circulation of fantasy as well as science fiction. The popularity of science fiction with young adults has stimulated new authors in the genre. Try one of the nine stories in Jean Karl's *The Turning Place* which she has subtitled "stories of a future past" for some thought-provoking situations with strong female characterizations.

Children's literature will also provide fictional and nonfictional sources for a children's book program. The books and short stories of Joan Aiken make good read-aloud material. Her *Not What You Expected: A Collection of Short Stories* includes stories about tiny people living in a doll house and a three-headed dragon who runs a museum. More realistic are the stories in E. L. Konigsburg's *Altogether, One at a Time* that tell of inviting an unwanted guest to a birthday party and the experiences of a young girl at "Camp Fat." A happier birthday party is described for younger readers in Johanna Hurwitz's *Busybody Nora,* in the chapter, "Daddy's Birthday." Children will appreciate it if you take the time to learn a part of a favorite book and present it as a story. If you are adept at memorizing lists you can contrast parts of two vastly different books; for example, the amusing things that Captain Cook the Penguin stores in the refrigerator in *Mr. Popper's Penguins*, among them ". . . a radish, two pennies, a nickel, and a golf ball . . ." with the wistful collection of Slake in *Slake's Limbo*, which includes "broken or cracked mirrors, aspirin and liquor bottles, several lenses from eyeglasses, colored glass beads from ill-fated necklaces, and a broken drinking glass." Nonfiction can be presented orally too. Try selections from Maxine Kumin's *When Mother Was Young* with recollections of life in America during World War II, or the section on snakes in *Pets*, a handbook on the care, understanding, and appreciation of all kinds of pets.

References: Other Literary Sources

Aiken, Joan. *Not What You Expected; A Collection of Short Stories;* il. by author. Doubleday, 1974.

Atwater, Richard and Florence. *Mr. Popper's Penguins;* il. by Robert Lawson. Little, 1938.

Bradbury, Ray. *Medicine for Melancholy.* Doubleday, 1959.

Chrystie, Frances N. *Pets;* 3d rev. ed.; il. by Gillett Good Griffin. Little, 1974.

Heinlein, Robert. *The Man Who Sold the Moon.* New American Library, 1973 (paper).

Holman, Felice. *Slake's Limbo.* Scribner, 1974.

Hunter, Kristin. *Guests in the Promised Land.* Scribner, 1973.

Hurwitz, Johanna. *Busybody Nora;* il. by Susan Jeschke. Morrow, 1976.

Jerome, Jerome K. *Three Men in a Boat.* Collins, 1957.

Karl, Jean E. *The Turning Place: Stories of a Future Past.* Dutton, 1976.

Konigsburg, E. L. *Altogether, One at a Time;* il. by Gail E. Haley and others. Atheneum, 1971.

Kumin, Maxine. *When Mother Was Young;* il. by Don Almquist. Putnam, 1970.

Lagerloff, Selma O. *The Wonderful Adventures of Nils;* tr. from the Swedish by Velma S. Howard; il. by H. Baumhauer. Pantheon, 1947.

Lester, Julius. *Long Journey Home: Stories from Black History.* Dial, 1972.

McDermott, Gerald. *Arrow to the Sun;* adapted and il. by author. Viking, 1974.

Schoenstein, Ralph. *With T-Shirts and Beer Mugs for All.* Prentice-Hall, 1968.

Singer, Isaac Bashevis. *A Day of Pleasure; Stories of a Boy Growing Up in Warsaw;* photos. by Roman Vishniac. Farrar, 1969.

Terkel, Louis. *Working: People Talk about What They Do All Day and How They Feel about What They Do,* by Studs Terkel (pseud.). Pantheon, 1974.

References: For Adult Study of Folklore

Aarne, Anttia. *The Types of the Folktale.* 2d ed. Helsinki; Suomalainen Tiedeakatemia, 1961.

Briggs, Katherine M., ed. *A Dictionary of British Folktales.* 4 vols. Univ. of Indiana Pr., 1970.

Brunvand, Jan Harold. *The Study of American Folklore; An Introduction.* Norton, 1968.

Dorson, Richard M. *Buying the Wind: Regional Folklore in the United States.* Univ. of Chicago Pr., 1964.

Dundes, Alan. *The Study of Folklore.* Prentice-Hall, 1965.

Grimm Brothers. *Grimm's Fairy Tales.* Pantheon, 1944.

Krappe, Alexander H. *The Science of Folklore.* Norton, 1964.

Lang, Andrew, ed. *The Fairy Books.* 12 vols. Longmans, 1889–1910.

Opie, Iona and Peter. *The Classic Fairy Tales.* Oxford Univ. Pr., 1974.

Reeves, James. *The Idiom of the People; English Traditional Verse.* Norton, 1958.

Rugoff, Milton. *A Harvest of World Folktales.* il. by Joseph Low. Viking, 1968.

Thompson, Stith. *The Folk Tale.* Dryden Press, 1946.

———— *Motif Index of Folk Literature.* 6 vols; Indiana Univ. Pr. 1955–1958.

———— *One Hundred Favorite Folktales.* il. by Fran Altschuler. Indiana Univ. Pr., 1968.

8 / Poetry

Poetry adds an extra touch of magic and sophistication to the storyhour, like having chocolate syrup on your ice cream; while not essential, it certainly adds to the treat. You can have a single poem or a storyhour devoted entirely to poetry, or even a poetry festival in which poetry is featured for a number of storyhours. In any case, consider using at least one poem in each story session. Poems are meant to be read aloud, and your storyhour provides the perfect opportunity.

Choosing a Poem

In addition to traditional favorites, you will find an unending stream of excellent new books of poetry. Almost any good library will have a fine variety of anthologies as well as books by individual poets in its collection. The selected bibliography at the end of this chapter will give you an idea of the variety.

If you are planning a program for younger children, preschool through third grade, you might begin by looking through some of the many editions of Mother Goose. Traditionally, Mother Goose is a child's first experience with formal rhyme. The sounds and rhythms of the language appeal to the ear, and for this reason, adults needn't worry about questions of "relevancy" or about unfamiliar language (such as Miss Muffet's "curds and whey," or Jack's broken "crown"). These verses, along with other childhood rhymes such as jump-rope jingles, are further distinguished by being perhaps the only widespread oral tradition still alive in our society.

Even though you may remember the more familiar Mother Goose rhymes, you will probably want a book not only to refresh your memory but also to show the attractive pictures which accompany the wonderfully rhythmic language. There are many beautiful editions currently in print. Some books contain collections of rhymes (e.g., Raymond Briggs's collection), while in others a single rhyme is profusely illustrated (e.g., Peter Spier's books). There is, in addition, a wide choice in style of illustration, ranging from the traditional (Kate Greenaway) to the ultramodern (Beni Montresor). It is only a matter of exploring to discover which version will please you and your audience.

When a child hears the music of Mother Goose, he or she will want other poetry. Nonsense verse is popular with small children, who love to repeat the sounds. Leslie Brooke's *Johnny Crow's Garden,* written in 1904, is still delighting today's children with its humorous animals and nonsensical verse. In a more recent book, *MA nDA LA,* Arnold Adoff uses nonsense syllables to make music for the child's ear, while at the same time telling a story through pictures. According to the jacket cover, "Ma" is mother, "Da" is father, "La" is singing, "Ha" is laughing, "Ra" is cheering. "Na" is sighing, and "Ah" is feeling good. The child, however, doesn't need this translation in order to joyfully join in the song, "Ma nDa La Ma nDa Ha / Ma nDa LaLaLa Ma nDa HaHaHa / Ma La Da La . . ."

There are also formal poems written expressly for very young children. Usually these poems are about children and their everyday experiences. Two classic poets of early childhood, A. A. Milne and Robert Louis Stevenson, both celebrated the daily events in a child's life. For example, in *A Child's Garden of Verses,* Stevenson wrote of going to bed, the passing of seasons, and the shadow which follows a child on a sunny day. These poets have succeeded in writing of childhood from the point of view of the child. Contemporary children's poets follow this tradition. Marchette Chute's *Rhymes about Us* includes short verses about a younger brother, drawing with crayons, and losing mittens.

Your storyhour can include one of the numerous picture books whose stories are told in rhymed verse. For example, Ludwig Bemelmans's *Madeline* is a rhymed story about twelve little French girls. Robert Charles's humorous verse tale, *A Roundabout Turn*, relates the adventures of a toad who sets off to discover whether the world really is round, but ends up riding round and round on the merry-go-round, 72 times in one day!

It is often said that poetry should be read aloud to be fully enjoyed. Perhaps the younger children, those who do not read yet, are fortunate in that their entire experience with poetry is aural; it is necessary to read aloud to them. Happily, children of today have a rich treasury of books whose poetry is music to the ear, just as the pictures are delights to the eye.

You will also want to search through the poetry collection for poems that appeal to an older group. Obviously, the more familiar you are with poetry the easier it will be to present poems with enthusiasm and to choose subjects or themes that interest a specific audience. Even in the short bibliography at the end of this chapter you will notice the variety of types of poetry. There is lyrical poetry as exemplified by Walter de la Mare, June Jordan's free verse, Ellen Raskin's nonsense verse, Japanese haiku beautifully illustrated by Ann Atwood's photographs and Ezra Jack Keats's color illustrations. A new trend in poetry publishing is the publishing of poems by children or young adults. You might want to further your knowledge about poetry in general by reading one or two adult references about poetry for children, but the best way to begin is to simply start browsing.

If you have had little exposure to the world of poetry you may find that cuddling up with a poetry book for any length of time is confusing and even tedious. But none of us can say that we don't have time to read poetry. We all have odd snatches of time: between making the bed and fixing breakfast, while waiting for a friend to arrive for dinner, or even during television commercials.

You may decide to begin a personal poetry project. Find a number of poems that particularly please you to use with children. Or examine the work of one poet with the view of presenting it to a group of children. Keep a file of poems that you enjoy and, as your file gets larger, divide it by theme (circus poems, dog poems), or type (funny poems, story poems). If you also have a story file, you may want to integrate the two, matching poems with stories. A story about a clever son and a poem about a not-so-clever boy make a good storyhour.

When planning a program I find one type of poetry book especially useful.

This is the poetry book that revolves around a particular theme, for in some instances the subject of the book will inspire an entire storyhour. Richard Shaw has edited several collections, each short volume emphasizing one animal; *The Cat Book*, *The Owl Book*, *The Fox Book*, *The Frog Book*, and most recently *The Bird Book*. Think of the possibilities of planning a storyhour with such a resource available to you. You might tell a fox story such as "Mighty Mikko" from Parker Fillmore's *A Shepherd's Nosegay*, learn a poem or two from *The Fox Book*, and use that same book to show some of the artists' interpretations of foxes.

However, don't feel that the theme of your poems must be related to your stories. A poem might appeal to you simply because it sets a mood or tone, such as one of gaiety or of thoughtfulness. Use it at the appropriate point in your story session—at the beginning, at the end, or in moving from one story to another.

Learning a Poem

Some adults find it difficult to memorize poetry. They may be able to learn a long folktale but freeze at the thought of a poem. This is not unusual. You can take liberties with the text of a folktale, whereas you must memorize a poem word for word. One way to go about it is to copy the poem on a card and carry it with you in your pocket or purse. Take it out several times a day, read it over, put it out of sight, and try to repeat it to yourself line by line. Memorizing the words is only the first step. Once you are comfortable with the words, begin to think of the meaning and you will find that expression will come more easily. After you've learned the first poem, you will, in all likelihood, find that the next one is easier to learn. If you take the project seriously, soon you will have acquired a repertoire of poems.

Experiment to discover which kinds of poetry you can learn most easily. Consider your own personality. You might find that silly rhymes are easier for you to learn than poems that establish moods. Modern poetry which lacks structured rhyme is sometimes easier to memorize since it is more conversational. Also, try Japanese haiku. These short poems may give you confidence for tackling longer, more complicated poetry.

Introducing a Poem

A short introduction to the theme of the poem adds to the enjoyment of it. Usually a simple sentence or question is sufficient: "Have you ever wondered what it feels like to be a turtle?" "Do you ever feel lonely?"

With some groups you may even want to avoid the actual word "poetry." There are those unfortunates who have been introduced to the wonderful world of poetry in a negative way and find it fashionable among their peers to fervently and volubly dislike it. For them, try introducing your poems as "stories" or "thoughts."

The Poetry Program

After you have used an occasional poem in your storyhour successfully, you may want to attempt something more ambitious. Do a session entirely devoted to poetry, perhaps featuring the poems of one writer. Introduce the session with a *short* discussion of the poet's life and a few brief remarks on the major characteristics of his poetry. Give this type of introduction only if you can keep it short, lively, and to the point. By all means, avoid lecturing! Be sure you have books available featuring the poet's poems. Show the children how a poem first published in an individual book of poetry is later used in an anthology. For poets like Edward Lear, exhibit a number of different illustrated versions of the poetry.

Poetry on a single theme makes a lovely program, too. Take any subject (dogs, snow, loneliness, baseball, or the city), and search through your poetry collection for poems worthy of inclusion. Decorate your story room with large cutouts representing the theme. Serve a special treat, such as simple cutout cookies, to emphasize the subject. Create bookmarks listing the authors of the poems you will recite. Now let your audience sit back comfortably, listen, and enjoy.

The Poetry Festival and Children as Poets

A still more ambitious project is a poetry festival to which you invite talented adults or children to perform. This can be a very informal session in which the children perform for each other or it can be a more formal festival, perhaps lasting for several sessions. A poetry festival might feature the works of an individual poet (maybe you can invite the poet as a guest), a particular theme, or just poetry in general.

A festival is a good time for children to present their own creations. If you do have children writing poetry, you may find that the writer does not necessarily want to be the performer. In this situation you might encourage some cooperation between two children with different talents—one who enjoys writing and one who enjoys performing. You might even open the secret doors of the storyhour to interested adults. Let them hear what the talented youngsters have written.

Choral Work

In the "olden days," only a generation or two ago, choral work was extremely popular. The children, arranged by voice pitch, and assigned to parts, practiced poetry just as a choir practices music. As a group exercise and voice training, this kind of performance was probably worthwhile, but it placed a tremendous burden on the leader and the group to work toward perfection, and, as a consequence, risked destroying much of the fun and spontaneity of poetry in general. If you are eager to try choral work, begin with something simple, a short poem that the group can recite in unison or one in which a child recites an entire verse or a single line. I am not, however, particularly enthusiastic about choral work, for, done poorly, it may foster a distaste for poetry. Reading verse seems to me to require more privacy and individual choice, and I prefer encouraging a child to discover his or her own favorite poems.

Recordings and Films

There are many excellent recordings of poems. Some are accompanied by a musical background, while others feature poets reciting their own works. My experience is that recordings are more successfully used with an individual rather than in a group situation, so give the children earphones for listening to poetry records on their own after the program.

Sometimes, a well-done film will increase a child's enjoyment of a poem if the visuals provide an added dimension to the word images expressed by the poet. *Hailstones and Halibut Bones* distributed by Sterling is an excellent example of a film that enhances the original poetry with its abstract visual interpretation.

Illustrations and Poetry

Many children's books of poetry are beautifully and appropriately illustrated. A. A. Milne's *Now We Are Six* and *When We Were Very Young*, for example, would seem empty and incomplete without the charming illustrations by E. H. Shepard. And some stories written in verse, such as Ludwig Bemelmans's *Madeline* or Dr. Seuss's *And to Think That I Saw It on Mulberry Street*, depend upon the illustrations to help tell the story. With other books, you might show the illustrations after you have recited the poetry.

Kathleen Frasers's *Stilts, Somersaults and Headstands* gives you an opportunity to introduce art while enjoying excellent poetry. The poet has written a delightful poem for each game or activity represented in the sixteenth-century painting "Children's Games" by the Flemish artist Peter Brueghel. Ruth Craft also has used a Brueghel painting as inspiration for poems in *Pieter Brueghel's The Fair.*

Often modern books of poetry are beautifully illustrated. Share an appropriate illustration with your group after you have recited or read one or more poems. However, keep in mind that although pictures do add much to the presentation, it is the *sound* of the words you are reciting or reading that makes poetry truly exciting.

Think of the many ways of using poetry while projecting visuals. Try taking 35mm color pictures (to make slides) of children acting out a poem. Or, put acetate (available in your art supply store) in 2x2 slide mounts and draw abstract images on them with permanent color felt pens. Recite poetry as you project the images.

Consider projecting a scratch film of your own making. To do this, ask your photo store for 16mm film leader. With a stylus or any sharp point—a nail or a knife—scrape away the emulsion on the leader to form abstract designs. Play music and recite poems while you project your film. The process is more fully explained in the chapter on film.

Puppets

Have you a favorite hand puppet? It could have a hidden talent. Maybe it can recite poetry better than you can! If you are afraid to recite poetry, lest you forget what comes next, let your puppet do it. After all, if your puppet makes a mistake, you can correct him. Or, you can take a quick peek at the copy, if your puppet appears to need some coaching.

The Poetry Tradition in Your Storyhour

Why not decide that you are always going to begin or end your story sessions with a poem? The children will begin to eagerly expect your poem and this will compel you to build up your poetry repertoire. After you have learned ten poems for ten sessions, you will have an entire poetry program ready for the next poetry festival.

Five Favorite Poems

There are so many, many poems suitable for the storyhour. Following are five of my favorites.

Of the poets who write poems for younger children, A. A. Milne still remains at the top of my list of favorites. The poem that follows captures the imagination of a child and remains in his memory as he grows up. Any adult that you see on a city street walking carefully in the squares and avoiding the lines has probably heard this poem.

LINES AND SQUARES

Whenever I walk in a London street,
I'm ever so careful to watch my feet;
And I keep in the squares,
And the masses of bears,
Who wait at the corners all ready to eat
The sillies who tread on the lines of the street,
Go back to their lairs,
And I say to them, "Bears,
Just look how I'm walking in all of the squares!"
And the little bears growl to each other, "He's mine,
As soon as he's silly and steps on a line."
And some of the bigger bears try to pretend
That they came round the corner to look for a friend;
And they try to pretend that nobody cares
Whether you walk on the lines or squares.
But only the sillies believe their talk;
It's ever so portant how you walk.
And it's ever so jolly to call out, "Bears,
Just watch me walking in all the squares!"

—From *When We Were Very Young* by A. A. Milne, illustrated by Ernest H. Shepard.
Copyright 1926 by E. P. Dutton & Co., renewal 1954 by A. A. Milne.
Reprinted by permission of the publishers, E. P. Dutton & Co., Inc.

I like to use folk rhymes and sometimes the children will contribute rhymes that they have heard out on the playground. The bad grammar in "The Frog" adds to its charm and gives it a colloquial air.

THE FROG

What a wonderful bird the frog are—
When he sit, he stand almost;
When he hop, he fly almost.
He ain't got no sense hardly;
He ain't got no tail hardly either.
When he sit, he sit on what he ain't got—almost.

—Folk rhyme, not attributable

The two voices in the next poem make it almost like a play. The uncertainty of the new boy is a common emotion, but his solution is unique and funny.

RUNNING THE GAUNTLET

Big Neighborhood Boy:
    Want to run the gauntlet?
New Little Boy:
    How do you play?
Big Neighborhood Boy:
    Well, *we* all sit in a row on the grass, across from each other and *you* have to run through our feet from one end of the row to the other.
New Little Boy:
    Through all your knees and all your boots?
Big Neighborhood Boy:
    Yep.
New Little Boy:
    Will you kick and bump? Will you trip me?
Big Neighborhood Boy:
    Well, sort of . . .
New Little Boy:
    Will it hurt?
Big Neighborhood Boy:
    Not if you cross your eyes and wiggle your ears and run as fast as a lizard.
New Little Boy:
    I think I'll just watch for a while.

Children are introduced to a fine poet in the following poem. A school-age child will easily relate to its subject. The conversational style makes it easier to memorize than lyrical poetry.

ARITHMETIC

Arithmetic is where numbers fly like pigeons in and out of your head.
Arithmetic tells you how many you lose or win if you know how many you had before you lost or won.
Arithmetic is seven eleven all good children go to heaven—or five six bundle of sticks.
Arithmetic is numbers you squeeze from your head to your hand to your pencil to your paper till you get the answer.

Arithmetic is where the answer is right and everything is nice and you can look out of the window and see the blue sky—or the answer is wrong and you have to start all over again and try again and see how it comes out this time.

If you take a number and double it and double it again and then double it a few more times, the number gets bigger and bigger and goes higher and higher and only arithmetic can tell you what the number is when you decide to quit doubling.

Arithmetic is where you have to multiply—and you carry the multiplication table in your head and hope you won't lose it.

If you have two animal crackers, one good and one bad, and you eat one and a striped zebra with streaks all over him eats the other, how many animal crackers will you have if somebody offers you five six seven and you say No no no and you say Nay nay nay and you say Nix nix nix?

If you ask your mother for one fried egg for breakfast and she gives you two fried eggs and you eat both of them, who is better in arithmetic, you or your mother?

—From *Complete Poems*, copyright, 1950, by Carl Sandburg.
Reprinted by permission of Harcourt Brace Jovanovich, Inc.

The idea that a list of words can be poetry is intriguing. These are such amusing words that have real meaning.

WORDS

Words to be Said on the Move

Flit	Tiptoe
Fluctuate	Pirouette
Wobble	Twirl
Wiggle	Teeter
Shiver	

Odd Words (to be spoken out loud, for fun)

Hobnob	Oaf
Barley	Egg
Dog-eared	Oboe
Hopscotch	Nutmeg
Windward	Oblong

Light Words (to be said in windy or singing moods)

Ariel	Sibilant
Willow	Petticoat
Spinnaker	Nimble
Whirr	Nib
Lissom	

Heavy Words (to be used in gloom or bad weather)

Duffle	Mugwump
Blunderbuss	Pumpkin
Galoshes	Crumb
Bowl	Blob
Befuddled	

—From *Ounce, Dice, Trice* by Alastair Reid. Little, Brown, 1958.
Copyright © 1958 by Alastair Reid and Ben Shahn. Used by permission.

Bibliography: Poetry to Read or Recite

Choosing poetry to read or recite is an even more personal experience than choosing a story. Certainly no one can really preselect a poem or a poet for you. Simply explore the library's collection until the message, the mood, or the language of a particular poem inspires in you a wish to share it. This bibliography is highly selective. Its purpose is to remind you of some of the delightful books waiting to be enjoyed by you, the children, and the adults you serve. Titles marked with an asterisk have illustrations worth sharing.

Poetry for the Youngest

Anthologies

Agree, Rose H., comp. *How to Eat a Poem and Other Morsels;* il. by Peggy Wilson. Pantheon, 1967. Poems about eating and food.

*Bodecker, N. M. *It's Raining Said John Twaining;* tr. and il. by author. Atheneum, 1973. Danish nursery rhymes amusingly illustrated.

Cole, William, ed. *Oh, What Nonsense!;* il. by Tomi Ungerer. Viking, 1966. Simple humorous poems.

*De Forest, Charlotte B. *The Prancing Pony;* il. by Keiko Hida. Walker/Weatherhill, 1968. Nursery rhymes from Japan.

Frank, Josette, comp. *Poems to Read to the Very Young;* il. by Dagmar Wilson. Random, 1961. Poems about animals, people, seasons, and feelings.

From King Boggen's Hall to Nothing-at-all; il. by Blair Lent. Little, 1967. Rhymes of houses and shelter. A picture book.

*Hyndman, Robert, ed. *Chinese Mother Goose Rhymes;* ed. by Robert Wyndham (pseud.); il. by Ed Young. World, 1968. Nursery rhymes translated from the Chinese.

*Jones, Hettie, comp. *The Trees Stand Shining: Poetry of the North American Indians;* il. by Robert Andrew Parker. Dial, 1971. Beautiful full-color paintings illustrate short Indian verses. Suitable for the youngest, but to be enjoyed by all ages.

Lent, Blair. see *From King Boggen's Hall.*

*Lewis, Richard. *In a Spring Garden;* il. by Ezra Jack Keats. Dial, 1965. Selected Japanese haiku for all ages, beautifully illustrated.

*——— *The Wind and the Rain;* photos by Helen Buttfield. Simon and Schuster, 1968. Poems by New Zealand children.

Livingston, Myra Cohn, comp. *Listen, Children, Listen: An Anthology of Poems for the Very Young;* il. by Trina Schart Hyman. Harcourt, 1972.

Rawlins, Margaret G., comp. *Round About Six;* il. by Denis Wrigley. Warne, 1973. The fourth book in a series for young children. Traditional rhymes, songs, poems by well-known poets, with some by children as well.

Wyndham, Robert. *see* Hyndman, Robert.

Individual Poets

Aldis, Dorothy. *All Together: A Child's Treasury of Verse;* il. by Helen D. Jameson, Marjorie Flack, and Margaret Freeman. Putnam, 1952.

*Bonner, Ann and Roger. *Earlybirds, Earlyworlds.* Scroll, 1973. Brief poems and bright illustrations for the youngest.

*Brown, Margaret Wise. *Nibble Nibble;* il. by Leonard Weisgard. W. R. Scott, 1959. Nature poems for the young, illustrated in green tones.

Caudill, Rebecca. *Come Along;* il. by Ellen Raskin. Holt, 1969. Original haiku poems.

Chute, Marchette. *Rhymes about Us;* il. by author. Dutton, 1974. Kittens, teddy bears, dinnertime, and other pleasures of childhood by the author of *Around and About.*

*Clifton, Lucille. *Some of the Days of Everett Anderson;* il. by Evaline Ness. Holt, 1970. A week in the life of a six-year-old boy. Use this as a picture book.

De Regniers, Beatrice Schenk. *Something Special;* il. by Irene Haas. Harcourt, 1958. The wishes and activities of children.

Fisher, Aileen. *My Cat Has Eyes of Sapphire Blue;* il. by Marie Angel. Crowell, 1973. Short cat verses.

Hoban, Russell. *Egg Thoughts, and Other Frances Songs;* il. by Lillian Hoban. Harper, 1972. Funny poems featuring the thoughts of Frances the badger.

Hopkins, Lee Bennet, ed. *Me! A Book of Poems; il.* by Tālivaldis Atubis. Seabury, 1970. The emotions of early childhood: loneliness, friendship, happiness, hate, and love.

Katz, Bobbi. *Upside Down and Inside Out: Poems for All Your Pockets;* il. by Wendy Watson. Watts, 1973. Short amusing poems that reveal the hidden wishes of childhood.

Kuskin, Karla. *Any Me I Want to Be;* il. by author. Harper, 1972. Each poem is written from the point of view the poem is about. Can you guess who is speaking?

Leichman, Seymour. *Shaggy Dogs and Spotty Dogs and Shaggy and Spotty Dogs;* il. by author. Harcourt, 1973. Poems celebrating dogs.

Livingston, Myra Cohn. *I'm Hiding;* il. by Erik Blegvad. Harcourt, 1961. A child hiding in and around the house.

McGinley, Phyllis. *All around the Town;* il. by Helen Stone. Lippincott, 1948. An adult poet's offering for children.

Merriam, Eve. *It Doesn't Always Have to Rhyme;* il. by Malcolm Spooner. Atheneum, 1974. Lively and spirited poems about poetry.

Milne, A. A. *When We Were Very Young;* and *Now We Are Six;* il. by E. H. Shephard. Dutton, 1924, 1927. Poems of childhood by the author of *Winnie the Pooh.*

*Raskin, Ellen. *Who, Said Sue, Said Whoo?* il. by author. Atheneum, 1973. Nonsense verses that can be read individually or use the whole book as a picture book.

*Riley, James Whitcomb. *The Gobble-uns'll Git You Ef You Don't Watch Out!;* il. by Joel Schick. Lippincott, 1975. Black-and-white drawings enhance this picture-book version of a favorite poem.

*Stevenson, Robert Louis. *A Child's Garden of Verses;* il. by Brian Wildsmith. Watts, 1966. Classic poems of childhood.

Tippett, James S. *Crickety Cricket!;* il. by Mary Chalmers, 1973. Poems concerning childhood activities: wrapping presents, ducks in the rain, and traveling. Easy to learn.

*Tripp, Wallace, comp. *A Great Big Ugly Man Came Up and Tied His Horse to Me;* il. by the compiler. Little, 1973. The funny pictures add to this picture-book collection of nonsense verse. All ages.

*Watson, Clyde. *Father Fox's Pennyrhymes;* il. by Wendy Watson. Crowell, 1971. Original American folk rhymes.

*Whitman, Walt. *I Hear America Singing;* il. by Fernando Krahan. Dial, 1975. A celebration of America.

Single Rhymes and Story Poems

*Adoff, Arnold. *MA nDA LA;* il. by Emily McCully. Harper, 1971. A chant using nonsense words, with pictures which show planting and harvesting of crops.

*Bemelmans, Ludwig. *Madeline;* il. by author. Simon and Schuster, 1939. Rhymed text tells the story of a vivacious little French girl.

*Brooke, Leonard Leslie. *Johnny Crow's Garden;* il. by author. Warne, 1903. All the animals visit Johnny's garden in this nonsense rhyme.

*Charles, Robert H. *A Roundabout Turn;* il. by L. Leslie Brooke. Warne, 1930. A toad sets out to see if the world is round.

*De Regniers, Beatrice Schenk. *May I Bring a Friend?;* il. by Beni Montresor. Atheneum, 1964. A little boy brings a whole zoo full of animals to the king and queen's palace for tea.

*Fisher, Aileen. *Listen, Rabbit;* il. by Symeon Shimin. Crowell, 1964. A child watches a rabbit through the seasons.

*———— *We Went Looking;* il. by Marie Angel. Crowell, 1968. Enchanting pictures, for a small group, contribute to a poetic text. Looking for badgers you meet other animals and birds.

The Fox Went Out on a Chilly Night; il. by Peter Spier. Doubleday, 1961. The old folk song, profusely illustrated.

*Geisel, Theodor Seuss. *And to Think that I Saw It on Mulberry Street;* by Dr. Seuss (pseud.); il. by author. Vanguard, 1937. Marco's imagination turns an ordinary horse and wagon into a mammoth extravaganza.

Graham, Al. *Timothy Turtle;* il. by Tony Palazzo. Robert Welch, 1946. A turtle adventures around Took-a-look Hill and all goes swimmingly.

*Lobel, Arnold. *The Man Who Took the Indoors Out;* il. by author. Harper, 1974. A story told in verse. Bellwood Bocese invites the furniture in his house to come outside and the things run away.

Nash, Ogden. *Custard, the Dragon and the Wicked Knight;* il. by Linell. Little, 1961. A dragon and a little girl strike up a friendship.

*Preston, Edna Mitchell. *Pop Corn and Ma Goodness;* il. by Robert Andrew Parker. Viking, 1969. Watercolor paintings illustrate a nonsense verse of life on a farm.

*Sendak, Maurice. *Nutshell Library;* il. by author. Harper, 1962. Four delightful rhymed books in a slipcase. Pictures need to be enlarged for storytelling.

Seuss, Dr. *see* Geisel, Theodor Seuss.

Spier, Peter. *see The Fox Went Out on a Chilly Night.*

*Walker, Barbara K. *I Packed My Trunk;* il. by Carl Kock. Follett, 1969. Progressive nonsense rhyme.

Selected Mother Goose Books

*Alderson, Brian, comp. *Cakes and Custard;* il. by Helen Oxenbury. Morrow, 1975.

Brian Wildsmith's Mother Goose; il. by Brian Wildsmith. Watts, 1964.

*Brooke, L. Leslie. *Ring O'Roses: A Nursery Rhyme Picture Book;* il. by author. Warner, 1922.

*Caldecott, Randolph. *The Hey Diddle Diddle Picture Book;* il. by author. Warne, 1882.

De Angeli, Marguerite, comp. *Book of Nursery and Mother Goose Rhymes;* il. by compiler. Doubleday, 1954.

*Domanska, Janina. *I Saw a Ship A-sailing;* il. by author. Macmillan, 1972.

*—— *If All the Seas Were One Sea;* il. by author. Macmillan, 1971.

The House That Jack Built; il. by Antonio Frasconi. Harcourt, 1958.

Granfa' Grig Had a Pig and Other Rhymes Without Reason; comp. and il. by Wallace Tripp. Little, 1976.

Lang, Andrew, ed. *The Nursery Rhyme Book;* il. by L. Leslie Brooke. Dover, 1972. Reprinted from a book first published by Warne in 1897.

Lines, Kathleen, comp. *Lavender's Blue;* il. by Harold Jones. Watts, 1954.

London Bridge Is Falling Down!; il. by Peter Spier. Doubleday, 1967.

Mother Goose; il. by Tasha Tudor. Walck, 1944.

Mother Goose; rev. ed.; il. by Frederick Richardson. Rand/Hubbard Pr., 1972.

Mother Goose: The Classic Volland Edition; rearranged and ed. by Eulalie Osgood Grover; il. by Frederick Richardson. Hubbard Pr., 1971.

Mother Goose in French; tr. by Hugh Lathan; il. by Barbara Cooney. Crowell, 1964.

The Mother Goose Treasury; il. by Raymond Briggs. Coward, 1966.

Peppé, Rodney. *Humpty Dumpty;* il. by author. Viking, 1975.

Provensen, Alice and Martin, comps. *The Mother Goose Book;* il. by compilers. Random, 1976.

The Real Mother Goose; il. by Blanche Fisher Wright. Rand, 1916.

The Tall Book of Mother Goose; il. by Feodor Rojankovsky. Harper, 1942.

Poetry for Older Children

Anthologies

There is no such thing as an all-perfect anthology. Browse through these for starters.

Adoff, Arnold, comp. *I Am the Darker Brother: An Anthology of Modern Poems by Negro Americans;* il. by Benny Andrews. Macmillan, 1968.

—— *The Poetry of Black America: An-*thology of the 20th Century. Harper, 1973.

Arbuthnot, Mary, and Root, Shelton L., Jr., comps. *Time for Poetry;* 3d ed. Scott, Foresman, 1968. An extensive collection, useful for the storyteller's shelf.

*Blishen, Edward, ed. *Oxford Book of Poetry for Children;* il. by Brian Wildsmith. Watts, 1964.

Brewton, Sara W. and John E. *Shrieks at Midnight: Macabre Poems, Eerie and Humorous;* il. by Ellen Raskin. Crowell, 1969. "Grave humor."

Brewton, Sara W. and John E.; and Blackburn, G. Meredith, III, comps. *My Tang's Tungled and Other Ridiculous Situations;* il. by Graham Booth. Crowell, 1973. Mostly short and mostly funny for the lighthearted storyhour.

Colum, Padraic, ed. *Roofs of Gold, Poems to Read Aloud.* Macmillan, 1964.

De La Mare, Walter J., comp. *Come Hither, A Collection of Rhymes and Poems for the Young of All Ages;* il. by Warren Chappell. Knopf, 1957.

Dunning, Stephen; Lueders, Edward G.; and Smith, Hugh L., comps. *Reflections on a Gift of Watermelon Pickle . . . and Other Modern Verse;* il. with photographs. Scott, Foresman, 1966. An outstanding collection of modern poetry covering a wide range of subjects of interest to young adults.

———— *Some Haystacks Don't Even Have Any Needle; And Other Complete Modern Poems.* Lothrop, 1969. A somewhat sophisticated collection of modern poetry especially selected for the young adult.

Ferris, Helen J., ed. *Favorite Poems, Old and New, Selected For Boys and Girls;* il. by Leonard Weisgard. Doubleday, 1957.

Grigson, Geoffrey. *The Cherry Tree; A Collection of Poems.* Vanguard, 1959.

McGinley, Phyllis, comp. *Wonders and Surprises: A Collection of Poems.* Lippincott, 1968.

Read, Sir Herbert E., ed. *This Way, Delight; A Book of Poetry for the Young;* il. by Juliet Kepes. Pantheon, 1956. Mostly traditional offerings.

*Summerfield, Geoffrey, comp. *First Voices.* Knopf, 1970. A meaningful selection of poetry accompanied by excellent illustrations from works of art.

Untermeyer, Louis, ed. *The Golden Treasury of Poetry;* il. by Joan Walsh Anglund. Golden Pr., 1959.

Whitlock, Pamela, comp. *All Day Long: An Anthology of Poetry for Children;* il. by Joan Hassall. Oxford, 1954.

Individual Poets

Aiken, Joan. *The Skin Spinners: Poems;* il. by Ken Rinciari. Viking, 1976. Some scarey, some witty, by a noted novelist.

Aldis, Dorothy. *Hello Day;* il. by Susan Elson. Putnam, 1959.

Baylor, Byrd. *Hawk, I'm Your Brother;* il. by Peter Parnall. Scribner, 1976. A boy wishes he could fly in this picture-book poem.

Behn, Harry. *The Wizard in the Well;* il. by author. Harcourt, 1956.

Bodecker, N. M. *Hurry, Hurry, Mary Dear! And Other Nonsense Poems;* il. by the author. Atheneum, 1976. Absurd humor and happy illustrations.

———— *Let's Marry, Said the Cherry, and Other Nonsense Poems;* il. by the author. Atheneum, 1974. Rhythmic nonsense verse.

Ciardi, John. *The Reason for the Pelican;* il. by Madeleine Gekiere. Lippincott, 1959. Nonsense poems.

Coatsworth, Elizabeth. *Poems;* il. by Vee Guthrie. Macmillan, 1957. Poems by a distinguished author of fiction.

*De La Mare, Walter. *Peacock Pie;* il. by Barbara Cooney. Knopf, 1961. Every child should be exposed to this English children's poet. A storyhour is a good time to do it. Enhanced with black-and-white drawings by a Caldecott winner.

Farjeon, Eleanor. *Poems for Children;* il. by Lucinda Wakefield. Lippincott, 1951. Sensitive poems by an English author.

Field, Rachel. *Poems;* il. by author. Macmillan, 1957.

Frost, Robert. *You Come Too;* il. by Thomas W. Nason. Holt, 1959. America's most popular poet gathered these poems for young people.

Giovanni, Nikki. *Ego Tripping and Other Poems for Young Readers;* il. by George Ford. Lawrence Hill, 1974. Memories of a black childhood.

Holman, Felice. *I Hear You Smiling, and Other Poems;* il. by Laszlo Kubinyi. Scribner, 1973. Light and charming poems.

Hughes, Langston. *Don't You Turn Back: Poems;* selected by Lee B. Hopkins; il. by Ann Grifalconi. Knopf, 1969. Selected poems by a black poet.

*Hughes, Ted. *Season Songs;* il. by Leonard Baskin. Viking, 1975.

Lear, Edward. *The Complete Nonsense Book;* il. by author. Dodd, 1958. Famous limericks and other nonsense.

*McCord, David. *Every Time I Climb a Tree;* il. by Marc Simont. Little, 1967. The colorful pictures add to the charm of these rhythmic verses.

Nash, Ogden. *The Old Dog Barks Backwards;* il. by Robert Binks. Little, 1972. Posthumous collection of 77 Nash verses.

Payne, Nina. *All the Day Long;* il. by Laurel Schindelman. Atheneum, 1973. Everyday happenings seen through a poet's eye.

Roethke, Theodore. *I Am! Says the Lamb;* il. by Robert Leydenfrost. Doubleday, 1961.

Sandburg, Carl. *Wind Song;* il. by William A. Smith. Harcourt, 1960.

Silverstein, Shel. *Where the Sidewalk Ends;* il. by author. Harper, 1974. Very funny poems. A good addition to a lighthearted storytime.

Starbird, Kaye. *A Snail's a Failure Socially;* il. by Kit Dalton. Lippincott, 1966. Light comment on animals and people.

Swenson, May. *More Poems to Solve.* Scribner, 1971. Sophisticated thoughts in poetry.

Taylor, Mark. *The Wind's Child;* il. by Erik Blegvad. Atheneum, 1973. A story poem about a black cat who finds a friend, illustrated with black-and-white drawings.

*Thayer, Ernest Lawrence. *Casey at the Bat;* by Paul Frame. Prentice-Hall, 1964. 1964. The classic baseball poem offered as a picture book.

Thurman, Judith. *Flashlight and Other Poems;* il. by Reina Rubel. Atheneum, 1976. Skinned knees, pretending to sleep, and going barefoot are among the subjects of these short, simple poems.

Widerberg, Siv. *I'm Like Me;* tr. from the Swedish by Verne Moberg; il. by Claes Bäckström. Feminist Press, 1973. "Poems for people who want to grow up equal."

Some Poetry Books with Themes

Adams, Adrienne, comp. *Poetry of Earth;* il. by compiler. Scribner, 1972. A collection featuring nature poems.

*Aiken, Conrad. *Cats and Bats and Things with Wings;* il. by Milton Glaser. Atheneum, 1965. Animal poems in a picture-book format.

*Atwood, Ann. *Haiku; The Mood of the Earth;* il. with colored photographs by the author. Scribner, 1971.

*——— *My Own Rhythm: An Approach to Haiku.* Scribner, 1973. Short poems beautifully illustrated with photography by the author.

Babcock, Clarence Merton, comp. *Walk Quietly the Beautiful Trail.* Hallmark, 1973. Lyrics and legends of the American Indian illustrated with authentic American Indian art.

Behn, Harry. *All Kinds of Time;* il. by author. Harcourt, 1950. A sensitive children's poet explores the concept of time.

*Belting, Natalia M., comp. *Whirlwind is a Ghost Dancing;* il. by Leo and Diane Dillon. Dutton, 1974. Indian nature lore related through poetry.

Bierhorst, John, comp. *In the Trail of the Wind: American Indian Poems and Ritual Orations.* Farrar, 1971. A lengthy collection of Indian poems.

Brownjohn, Alan. *Brownjohn's Beasts;* il. by Carol Lawson. Scribner, 1970. Grave humor prevails in a collection of poems about familiar animals.

Cole, William, ed. *I Went to the Animal Fair;* il. by Colette Rosselli. World, 1958.

——— *Poems for Seasons and Celebrations;* il. by Johannes Troyer. World, 1961. Poems for the four seasons and the various holidays we celebrate for those who need a poem for such occasions as Mother's Day, April Fool's Day, or Halloween.

——— *The Sea, Ships, and Sailors: Poems, Songs and Shanties;* il. by Robin Jacques. Viking, 1967.

*Craft, Ruth. *Pieter Brueghel's The Fair;* il. with a repro. of Brueghel's "The Village Fair." Lippincott, 1976. Verses describe the action in a sixteenth-century painting.

*Fraser, Kathleen. *Stilts, Somersaults, and Headstands; Game Poems Based on a Painting by Peter Breughel.* Atheneum, 1968. Poems related to the games shown on a sixteenth-century painting by the famed Flemish painter.

*Hoberman, Mary Ann. *The Raucous Auk: A Menagerie of Poems;* il. by Joseph Low. Viking, 1973. Animal poems each illustrated with a picture.

*Jordan, June. *Who Look at Me?;* il. with paintings. Crowell, 1969. Free verse full of black pride accompanied by 27 paintings of black Americans.

Knudson, Rozanne, and Ebert, P. K. *Sports Poems.* Dell, 1971. A paperback collection of poems about athletes and sports.

Larrick, Nancy, ed. *On City Streets;* il. with photos. by David Sagarin. Evans, 1968. Poetry about people and places.

——— *Room for Me and a Mountain Lion;* il. with photos. Evans, 1974. Poetry of open space.

Livingston, Myra Cohn, ed. *What a Wonderful Bird the Frog Are.* Harcourt, 1973. Humorous verse.

*Mendoza, George. *Poem for Putting to Sea;* il. by Ati Forberg. Hawthorne, 1972. A single poem about the sea.

Moore, Lilian. *See My Lovely Poison Ivy and Other Verses about Witches, Ghosts and Things;* il. by Diane Dawson. Atheneum, 1975. Best ever selection for Halloween.

Morrison, Lillian, comp. *Sprints and Distances;* il. by Clare and John Ross. Crowell, 1965. Sports in poetry, poetry in sports.

O'Neill, Mary. *Hailstones and Halibut Bones;* il. by Leonard Weisgard. Doubleday, 1961. Color poems.

Plotz, Helen, comp. *Imagination's Other Place Poems of Science and Mathematics;* il. by Clare Leighton. Crowell, 1955.

Prelutsky, Jack. *Nightmares: Poems to Trouble Your Sleep;* il. by Arnold Lobel. The ghoul and the bogeyman captured in poetry.

*Rossetti, Christina. *What Is Pink?;* il. by Jose Aruego. Macmillan, 1971. One poem amusingly illustrated.

Sechrist, Elizabeth, comp. *Poems for Red Letter Days;* il. by Guy Fry. Macrae Smith, 1951.

*Shaw, Richard, ed. *The Bird Book.* Warne, 1974. Poems and short stories about birds. Nineteen different artists contributed illustrations. Also see his: *The Cat Book* (Warne, 1973); *The Fox Book* (Warne, 1971); *The Frog Book* (Warne, 1972); *The Mouse Book* (Warne, 1975); and *The Owl Book* (Warne, 1970).

Stewart, Harold. *A Net of Fireflies.* Tuttle, 1960. Haiku.

Weiss, Renée, comp. *A Paper Zoo: A Collection of Animal Poems by Modern American Poets;* il. by Ellen Raskin. Macmillan, 1968.

Poetry in Translation

Behn, Harry, comp. and tr. *Cricket Songs: Japanese Haiku;* with il. selected from Sesshu and other Japanese masters. Harcourt, 1964.

Doob, Leonard, comp. *A Crocodile Has Me by the Leg: African Poems;* il. by S. Irein Wangboje. Walker, 1967.

Gasztold, Carmen Bernos de. *Prayers from the Ark;* tr. by Rumer Godden; il. by Jean Primrose. Viking, 1962. Animal poems from the French.

*Hoffmann-Donner, Heinrich. *Slovenly Peter (Struwwelpeter); or Happy Tales and Funny Pictures;* tr. by Mark Twain; il. by author. Harper, 1935. Children think this funny. Adults may find it violent.

Krylov, Ivan A. *15 Fables;* tr. by Guy Daniels; il. by David Pascal. Macmillan, 1965. Russian fables in verse.

Lewis, Richard, ed. *The Moment of Wonder: A Collection of Chinese and Japanese Poetry;* il. with paintings by Chinese and Japanese masters. Dial, 1964.

Parker, Elinor M., comp. *The Singing and the Gold: Poems Translated from World Literature;* il. by Clare Leighton. Crowell, 1962.

Rasmussen, Knud, comp. and tr. *Beyond the High Hills: A Book of Eskimo Poems;* il. with photos. by Guy Mary-Rousselière. World, 1961.

Some Poets of the Past

Blake, William. *William Blake: An Introduction;* ed. by Anne Malcolmson with il. from Blake's paintings and engravings. Harcourt, 1967.

Chaucer, Geoffrey. *A Taste of Chaucer: Selections from the Canterbury Tales;* ed. by Anne Malcolmson; il. by Enrico Arno. Harcourt, 1964.

Dodgson, Charles L. *The Humorous Verse of Lewis Carroll;* il. by John Tenniel; ed. by J. E. Morpurgo. Grey Walls Pr., 1950.

Rossetti, Christina. *Sing-Song;* il. by Arthur Hughes. University Microfilms (Ann Arbor), 1966.

*Whitman, Walt. *Overhead the Sun;* il. by Antonio Frasconi. Farrar, 1969. Full-color woodcuts enhance these short selections from *Leaves of Grass.*

The Thomas Y. Crowell Series, *The Crowell Poets,* includes volumes of poetry by Robert Browning, Robert Burns, John Keats, Edgar Allan Poe, Shakespeare, and others.

Some Poetry by Children and Young Adults

Adoff, Arnold, comp. *It Is the Poem Singing into Your Eyes.* Harper, 1971.

Allen, Terry, ed. *The Whispering Wind: Poetry by Young American Indians.* Doubleday, 1972. A collection of poetry from the Institute of American Indian Arts.

I Never Saw Another Butterfly; Children's Drawings and Poems from Theresienstadt Concentration Camp, 1942–1944. McGraw-Hill, 1964.

Joseph, Stephen, ed. *The Me Nobody Knows; Children's Voices from the Ghetto.* Avon, 1969.

Larrick, Nancy, comp. *I Heard a Scream in the Street;* il. with photos. by students. Dell, 1970.

Lewis, Richard, comp. *Miracles: Poems by Children of the English-Speaking World.* Simon and Schuster, 1966.

Pellowski, Anne; Sattley, Helen R.; and Arkhurst, Joyce C., comps. *Have You Seen a Comet? Children's Art and Writing from Around the World.* John Day (in cooperation with the U.S. Committee for UNICEF), 1971.

Films

Drummer Hoff, produced by Morton Schindel. Color, 16mm, 5 min. Animated version of the award-winning picture book by Barbara and Ed Emberley. Weston Woods, Weston, CT 06880.

Hailstones and Halibut Bones, produced for NBC-TV by John Wilson. Part I: color, 16mm, 6 min. Part II: color, 16mm, 7 min. Celeste Holm reads selections from Mary O'Neill's book. Animated. Sterling Educational Films, 241 E. 34th St., New York, NY 10016.

In a Spring Garden, Weston Woods, 1967. Color, 16mm, 6 min. Film animation from the book of Japanese haiku of the same name collected by Richard Lewis and illustrated by Ezra Jack Keats (Dial, 1965).

Madeline, produced by Stephen Bosustow for UPA, 1969. Color, 16mm, 7 min. Animated film adapted from Ludwig Bemelmans's book of the same name (Viking, 1939). Learning Corp. of America, 1350 Ave. of the Americas, New York, NY 10036.

Recordings

A *Child's World of Poetry*, 33 rpm. Two 12-inch L.P. records accompany two sets of study prints. Distributed by the Society for Visual Education, 1345 Diversey Pkwy., Chicago, IL 60614.

A *Gathering of Great Poetry for Children*, 4 records, 33 rpm. Produced by Caedmon. Poems by Emily Dickinson, Robert Frost, Langston Hughes, Edna St. Vincent Millay, A. A. Milne, Carl Sandburg, etc., are read by Julie Harris, Cyril Ritchard, David Wayne, and the poets themselves. Richard Lewis selected the poems. D. C. Heath, 2700 N. Richardt Ave., Indianapolis, IN 46219.

Poetry Parade, 2 records, 33 rpm, or 2 cassettes. Produced by Weston Woods. Four poets (David McCord, Harry Behn, Karla Kuskin, and Aileen Fisher) reading their own poetry. Weston Woods, Weston, CT 06880.

Reflections on a Gift of Watermelon Pickle, 33 rpm, price includes a paperback of the book. Produced by Folkways/Scholastic Records. Paul Hecht and Ellen Holly read modern poetry. Folkways, 906 Sylvan Ave., Englewood Cliffs, NJ 07632.

Robert Frost Reading, 33 rpm. Produced by Caedmon. Robert Frost reads some favorites from his own poetry. D. C. Heath, 2700 N. Richardt Ave., Indianapolis, IN 46219.

You Know Who, Fiddler Dan, John J. Plenty and Other Poems, 33 rpm. John Ciardi reads his own poems. Spoken Arts, 310 N. Ave., New Rochelle, NY 10801.

To Read Aloud

De Regniers, Beatrice Schenk. *The Boy, the Rat, and the Butterfly;* il. by Haig and Regina Shekerjian. Atheneum, 1971. Peter the rat recites the poetry of Keats and Shelley.

Adult References

Anderson, Douglas. *My Sister Looks Like a Pear: Awakening the Poetry in Young People*. Hart, 1974. Outspoken ideas from a teacher with the Poets in the Schools project.

Arnstein, Flora J. *Children Write Poetry: A Creative Approach*. 2d ed. Dover, 1967 (paper).

Behn, Harry. *Chrysalis: Concerning Children and Poetry*. Harcourt, 1968.

Brewton, John E. and Sara W., comp. *Index to Children's Poetry*. Wilson, 1942. First supp., 1954; second supp., 1965. Useful for finding sources of poems. Indexed by author, title, subject, and first lines.

Chukovsky, Kornei. *From Two to Five;* tr. and ed. by Miriam Morton. Univ. of California Pr. (Berkeley), 1965. The language and comprehension of the very young child, written by a Russian children's author.

Dunning, Stephen, and Howes, Alan B. *Literature for Adolescents: Teaching Poems, Stories, Novels, and Plays*. Scott, Foresman, 1975.

Haviland, Virginia, and Smith, William Jay, comps. *Children and Poetry: A Selective,*

Annotated Bibliography. U.S. Library of Congress, 1969.

Hopkins, Lee Bennett. *Pass the Poetry, Please!* Citation Pr., 1972. Capsule biographies of children's poets, ideas for presenting poetry, useful bibliographies, and explanations of short verse forms, make up a useful handbook for the program planner in a hurry.

Hughes, Ted. *Poetry Is.* Doubleday, 1970. From a series on the BBC intended for readers and writers of poetry.

Koch, Kenneth. *Wishes, Lies, and Dreams.* Random, 1970. Teaching children to write poetry in a New York City school.

———— *Rose, Where Did You Get that Red?* Vintage, 1974. Teaching great poetry to children.

Larrick, Nancy. see *Somebody Turned on a Tap in These Kids.*

Livingston, Myra Cohn. *When You Are Alone/It Keeps You Capone: An Approach to Creative Writing with Children.* Atheneum, 1973.

Opie, Iona and Peter, comps. *The Oxford Book of Children's Verse.* Clarendon Pr., 1973. Seven centuries of British and American poetry written for children or with children in mind.

Somebody Turned on a Tap in These Kids; ed. by Nancy Larrick. Delacorte, 1971. A collection of articles on the newer trends in appreciation of poetry.

9 / *Non-narrative Sources of Folklore*

Most of the material you will use in your programs has its origins in folk literature, and, if you have been telling stories to a group, its members may already be aware of the various sources—folktales, myths, fables, and the like—from which you have chosen your material. Some of your listeners may even be ready to explore with you the world of folklore in more personal terms. Inasmuch as a folk group is comprised of people who have one thing in common, explain that all of us are members of more than one folk group at any given time. For example, the students in a school belong to a large folk group and within this group there are smaller folk groups—the sophomore class, the track team, the cheerleaders, the science club, among others. Each of these groups may have its own customs and sayings that can be collected. Explain that proverbs, riddle jokes, and tongue twisters are folk sayings and that the games, crafts, food preparation, and graffiti of a group are also considered part of its folklore. Point out too that folklore is transmitted by word of mouth or by means other than books, schools, churches, and other formal institutions.

Apparently the word "folklore" gives some people the impression that to collect "lore" one has to know peasants or old grandmothers. Emphasize that everyone is part of a group. Start collecting for yourself, from your family, your friends. One need not take a trip to some faraway place, for folklore is all around us.

The interest in some forms of folklore has led to collections of riddles, handicrafts, recipes, and the like. Lately there have been books published about such traditional crafts as soapmaking, sheep shearing, and graffiti. Encourage your groups to make collections of their own.

One way to begin a collection of riddles or other folklore of your own is to recite a few folk sayings in a storyhour and hope this will remind your listeners of sayings that they know. To formally collect folklore you should encourage students to write down what they hear exactly as it is related. The person who gives you the material is the "informant" whose name, address, age, background, and education also should be recorded for inclusion in an organized collection. The group might be interested in the notes of origin appearing in some of the books in the library's collection: Richard Chase and Maria Leach, for instance, give notes at the back of their collections. Joseph Jacobs, in his notes, explained how he changed the original stories to make them more appropriate to tell to children.

A haphazard but uninhibited way of collection is to simply put a box in the library or classroom and request jokes and riddles or whatever you are collecting; in some ways, this is the best method of all. You will receive completely authentic, but unsigned responses. I asked several librarian friends to do this recently so that I could get some updated examples for this book. I have included several examples of some of the more popular types of folklore. If some of the examples seem familiar to you, don't be surprised. It always amazes people to see how folklore is transmitted over large geographic areas and over several generations with so few changes. Radio and television communicate their share of folklore too. One children's television show ("Zoom") asks children from all over the country to send in contributions for use on the show. Contributed skits, riddles, and crafts are then performed on the series. Most of the material turns out to be folklore that cannot be traced back to an author.

This non-narrative folklore can be used to create a whole session in your programming; useful in between stories as a change of mood.

Riddles

Riddles have been used as tests in literature and folk stories, but generally they are considered word games to be used just for fun and may be used as such to introduce the reluctant reader to the world of books. It is a pity that today's children often need a manufactured toy to play with, when the realm of words is free, doesn't break, or become outdated. Since riddles are popular you will be able to find a number of collections in your library. You may find, as you search for riddles to use in your storyhour program, that your story-hour group already knows the riddle and shouts out the answer. It's amusing to find a riddle that they cannot guess, but the ones they do know will stimulate the children into contributing riddles of their own. If you become interested in riddles, you might want to identify the country of origin or to mention that a particular riddle was recorded in the Tennessee mountains in 1911, for example.

Ask that each member of your group find a riddle and bring it to the next folk session to present to the group. There may be many duplicates, but you'll also have a lively session. Children participating in extemporaneous story-telling sometimes tend to wander away from the subject, but a riddle gives them a chance to "perform" briefly before a group in a controlled manner.

A *riddle* is a question with an unexpected answer which is supposed to demonstrate the brilliance of the questioner and test the wit and intelligence of the respondent. A *conundrum* is a riddle based on punning or a play on words.

What does a pig use for a sore throat?
Oinkment.

What do you call a general's assistant at the North Pole?
A Kool Aid.

What did the walls say to each other?
Meet you at the corner.

What goes Ho Ho Thump?
Santa Claus laughing his head off.

What did the judge say when the skunk came into the court?
Odor in the court.

What does a tuba call his father?
Um pa pa.

What is black and white and red all over?
    A blushing zebra or a hot fudge sundae with catsup on it.
    (New variations on an oldie.)

What gets wetter and wetter the more it dries?
    A towel.

Why does a school yard get bigger when school starts?
    It has more feet in it. (A nonmetric riddle)

Who is bigger, Mrs. Bigger or Mrs. Bigger's baby?
    The baby is just a little Bigger.

When is a turkey like a ghost?
    When he's goblin.

How do you keep a tiger from charging?
    Take away his credit card. (Modern living.)

Where were the first doughnuts fried?
    In Greece.

What walks on four legs in the morning, two legs in the afternoon, and three
legs at night?
    Man.
    As a baby he crawls on all fours.
    As a young man he walks on two legs.
    As an old man he walks with a cane. (Riddle of the Sphinx)

Why won't you ever see a full moon again?
    Because the astronauts brought back pieces of it. (The Space Age)

What gets bigger the more you take away?
    A hole.

What is the difference between an elephant and peanut butter?
    An elephant doesn't stick to the roof of your mouth. (Elephant joke)

Why do you say "amen" in church instead of a woman?
    Because you sing hymns, not hers. (Women's lib?)

What do you get when you cross a dummy with a flower seed?
    A blooming idiot (with an English accent).

What would you call a country where all the cars were pink?
    A pink carnation.

What's the difference between a donkey and a postage stamp?
    You lick a donkey with a stick and stick a stamp with a lick.

References: More Riddles

Chrystie, Frances. *Riddle Me This;* il. by Elizabeth Ripley. Walck, 1958 (paper). Pocket edition of popular riddles.

Keller, Charles, and Baker, Richard, comps. *The Star-Spangled Banana, and Other Revolutionary Riddles;* il. by Tomie de Paola. Prentice-Hall, 1974. Jokes, puns, riddles featuring the American Revolution.

Leach, Maria. *Riddle Me, Riddle Me, Ree;* il. by William Wiesner. Viking, 1970. Riddles from around the world.

Leeming, Joseph, ed. *Riddles, Riddles, Riddles;* il. by Shane Miller. Watts, 1953.

Lippman, Peter. *The Little Riddle Book;* il. by author. Harper, 1972. Nonsense riddles.

Rees, Ennis. *Riddles, Riddles Everywhere;* il. by Quentin Blake. Abelard-Schuman, 1964. Riddles in rhyme.

Sarnoff, Jane, and Ruffins, Reynold. *The Monster Riddle Book;* il. by Reynold Ruffins. Scribner, 1975. Riddles about vampires, ghouls, and goblins colorfully illustrated.

——— *What? A Riddle Book;* il. by Reynold Ruffins. Scribner, 1974. Five hundred riddles, some in a riddle code.

Tongue Twisters

The tongue twister is a game in which you pronounce a combination of difficult sounds fast and clearly. A few speech teachers use them for the practice of clarity in speech, but usually the tongue twister exists for the simple purpose of playing with words. As with any other folk material, most tongue twisters have been passed orally among children or adults. The most popular have been collected and can be found in books. A tongue twister contest can be great fun. Announce the contest in advance so that the contestants have time to practice. Tongue twisters also make a good ending for a program. The audience leaves the room practicing loudly and reciting as fast as they can such sentences and rhymes as:

Unique New York	Six, slick, slim saplings
Lemon liniment	Sallow Sally
Fruit float, fruit float, fruit float	The sixth sick sheik's sixth sheep's sick.
Double bubble gum gives double bubble trouble	Strange strategic statistics
	Three new blue beans in a new blown bladder

I saw Esau kissing Kate
I saw Esau, he saw me
And she saw I saw Esau

A FLY

A fly and a flea flew up a flue.
Said the flea, "What shall we do?"
Said the fly, "Let us flee!"
Said the flea, "Let us fly!"
So they flew through a flaw in the flue.

A CANNER

A canner, exceedingly canny,
One morning remarked to his granny,
"A canner can can
Anything that he can;
But a canner can't can a can, can he?"

SEASHELLS

She sells seashells by the seashore.
The shells she sells are sure seashells.
So if she sells shells on the seashore
I'm sure she sells seashore shells.

References: More Tongue Twisters

Arnold, Arnold. *The Big Book of Tongue Twisters and Double Talk;* il. by author. Random, 1964. Good source for tongue twisters.

Brown, Marcia. *Peter Piper's Alphabet;* il. by author. Scribner, 1959. An entire tongue twister alphabet, gloriously illustrated.

Emrich, Duncan, comp. *The Nonsense Book;* il. by Ib Ohlsson. Four Winds, 1970. Riddles, tongue twisters, puzzles, and jokes collected from American folklore.

Hayward, Linda. *Letters, Sounds, and Words: A Phonic Dictionary;* il. by Carol Nicklaus. Platt and Munk, 1973. A colorful, amusing dictionary using nonsense sentences as examples.

Schwartz, Alvin, comp. *A Twister of Twists, A Tangler of Tongues;* il. by Glen Rounds. Lippincott, 1972. Good collection arranged by subject.

Jokes

In some instances the stories you will tell are extended jokes; the Turkish Hodja stories are a series of jokes. Children's jokes do differ from adult jokes; the latter tend to be political or ethnic, and of course there is the "dirty" joke, which has a sexual connotation, whereas children's jokes are usually quite simple and often involve a play on words. To adults these jokes often seem silly and inconsequential. Perhaps this is true, but a sophisticated sense of humor is something which must be developed; it doesn't just happen, and nonsense is a good place to begin. Jokes ought to play only a very minor role in the storyhour; they should be used sparingly but are effective to relax a tense group or to set a happier mood after you have told a sad or touching story. Many children's jokes are in the form of riddles, as the following examples indicate.

My sister and I together know everything in the whole world.
> Really? What's the capital of France?
That's one my sister knows.

What is the similarity between a hippopotamus and an elephant?
> Neither one plays golf.

Get up, I heard a mouse squeak.
> What do you want me to do? Oil it?

I can tell the score of this football game before it even begins.
> Nothing to nothing.

Finish your alphabet soup, dear.
> I can't eat another word.

Where was the Declaration of Independence signed?
> At the bottom.

What is a small joke called?
> A mini ha ha.

My cat is lost.
> Why don't you put an ad in the newspaper?
She can't read.

Why did the elephant stand on the marshmallow?
> So he wouldn't fall into the cocoa.

I'm glad that I'm not a bird.
> Why?
I can't fly.

Lady Shopper: I'd like some alligator shoes, please.
> Shoe Salesman: What size is your alligator?

What is history's favorite fruit?
> Dates.

What do elephants have that no other animals have?
> Baby elephants.

Why did the moron throw a watch from the window?
> He wanted to see time fly.

Knock, knock.
>Who's there?

Honeydew and cantaloupe.
>Honeydew and cantaloupe who?

Honeydew you love me? We cantaloupe now.

Knock, knock.
>Who's there?

Boo.
>Boo who (hoo)?

Well, you don't have to cry about it.

You know that you've gained too much weight when you step on a scale and a sign flashes on saying "Only one person at a time please."

They used to call the Middle Ages the Dark Ages because there were so many knights.

A man asked the horse trainer why the racehorse was traveling by train rather than plane. "Oh, he's already seen the movie this week."

A friend was amazed at a dog's obvious attention at a drive-in theater's showing of *The Little Prince*. "I'm amazed too," said the owner. "He didn't enjoy the book at all."

What nut is like a sneeze?
>A cashew (ca-shoo).

What happened when the hippie put dynamite in the refrigerator?
>He blew his cool.

What kind of dog is that?
>A police dog.

He doesn't look like one.
>Of course not. He's in the Secret Service.

References: More Jokes

The Chuckle Book; il. by Mel Crawford. Golden Pr., 1971. Cartoons illustrate a collection of familiar jokes and riddles.

Glovach, Linda, and Keller, Charles. *The Little Witch Presents a Monster Joke Book;* il. by Linda Glovach. Prentice-Hall, 1976. An anthology of witticisms.

Hoke, Helen. *Jokes and Fun;* il. by Tony Parkhouse. Watts, 1972. Many new jokes are included in this collection.

———— *Jokes, Giggles, and Guffaws,* il. by Haro. Watts, 1975. The latest of seven joke books including *Jokes, Jokes, Jokes* (Watts, 1963).

Price, Roger. *Droodles;* il. by author. Price/ Stern/Sloan, 1966. Visual jokes.

Schwartz, Alvin, comp. *Witcracks;* il. by Glen Rounds. Lippincott, 1973. Collected from American folklore.

Seuling, Barbara. *You Can't Eat Peanuts in Church and Other Little-Known Laws;* il. by author. Doubleday, 1975. Very funny yet actual laws in these United States.

Skip Rope Rhymes

School-age children will have no trouble telling you—or showing you—their favorite jump-rope rhymes. If you haven't recently participated in a jump-rope game, you may have forgotten the words of these jingles, but they'll soon come back. You may even be amazed that the rhymes and rhythms you jumped to as a child in Washington, DC, are the same the children are using in a small town in Nebraska today. If your community has super special playground equipment and organized play the children may have forgotten how to jump rope. Re-introduce this traditional spring activity by bringing a length of clothesline rope to school.

Skipping rope and the accompanying jingles are a part of folklore too. To refresh your own memory, a few perennials follow:

House for rent
Inquire within
When I move out, let
Hilary move in.
    (Jumper moves out and next in
    line moves in.)

Sheep in the meadow
Cows in the corn
Tell me the month that you were born.
January, February, March
    (Jump out on the month of your
    birthday.)

Fudge, fudge tell the judge
Mama's going to have a baby.
Wrap it up in tissue paper
Send it on the elevator.
How many floors did it go?
1, 2, 3 (Until the jumper misses.)

Las' night, night before
Twenty-four robbers came to my door.
I got up, let 'em in
Hit 'em on the head with a rollin' pin.
One, two, three, four. . . .

When you fall down
And hurt your knee
Just jump up quick,
And think of me.

HILARY'S CHANT

Miss Mary Mack, Mack, Mack
All dressed in black, black, black
With silver buttons, buttons, buttons
All down her back, back, back
She asked her mother, mother, mother
For fifty cents, cents, cents
To see the elephants, elephants,
   elephants
Jump the fence, fence, fence
They jumped so high, high, high
They reached the sky, sky, sky
And they never came back, back, back
Till the Fourth of July, lie, lie
"It's not good to lie!" (spoken)

SALT, MUSTARD

Salt, mustard, vinegar, pepper,
French almond rock,
Bread and butter for your supper
That's all mother's got.
Fish and chips and coca cola,
Put them in a pan,
Irish stew and ice cream soda,
We'll eat all we can.

Salt, mustard, vinegar, pepper,
French almond rock,
Bread and butter for your supper
That's all mother's got.
Eggs and bacon, salted herring,
Put them in a pot,
Pickled onions, apple pudding,
We will eat the lot.

Salt, mustard, vinegar, pepper,
Pig's head and trout
Bread and butter for your supper
O-U-T spells out.

LITTLE BROTHER

I had a little brother
His name was Tiny Tim
I put him in the bathtub
To teach him how to swim
He drank up all the water
He ate up all the soap
He died last night
With a bubble in his throat
In came the doctor
In came the nurse
In came the lady
With the alligator purse
Dead said the doctor
Dead said the nurse
Dead said the lady
With the alligator purse
Out went the doctor
Out went the nurse
Out went the lady
With the alligator purse

Order in the court
The Judge is eating beans
His wife is in the bathtub
Shooting submarines

As I was in the kitchen
Doing a bit of stitchen
In came a bogey man
And pushed me OUT

Hold 'em up
Stick 'em up
Drop your gun
And pick 'em up
And OUT you go

Fireman! Fireman!
False alarm
There goes Hilary (Jump out)
   in the fireman's arms.

JUMP ROPE RHYME

Orange marginella
Crackers in a pan
I am going to marry
A Minnesota man

He'll be sweet and green-eyed
And just a little stout
Any time we want to
We'll eat our dinner OUT

—Text copyright © 1973 by Nina Payne from *All the Day Long*.
Used by permission of Atheneum Publishers Inc.

References: Skip Rope Rhymes

Butler, Francelia. *The Skip Rope Book;* il. by Gail E. Haley. Dial, 1963. A collection of skip-rope rhymes.

Farjeon, Eleanor. "Elsie Piddock Skips in Her Sleep" in *Eleanor Farjeon's Book;* il. by Edward Ardizzone. Penguin, 1960. Also in her *Martin Pippin in the Daisy-Field;* il. by Isobel and John Morton-Sale. Lippincott, 1963. And in Colwell, Eileen, ed. *A Storyteller's Choice;* il. by Carol Barker. Walck, 1964. Tell this delightful story for the skip-rope season. It is quite long but well worth the trouble to learn.

Skolnik, Peter L. *Jump Rope!;* photos. by Jerry Darvin; il. by Marty Norman. Workman, 1974. Rhymes, tricks, and the physical fitness of jumping rope.

Autograph Rhymes and Mottoes

Autograph books, yearbooks, and autograph dolls appear as summer vacations shine on the horizon. The sayings that are written in memory books are often the same ones your grandmother wrote in her best friend's book way back in the old days. You may find occasion to use these in a storyhour if you are discussing different types of folk sayings.

Yours till banana splits

Yours till dogwood barks

Yours till ice screams

When you're in the kitchen
Learning how to cook
Remember it was Joni
Who wrote this in your book

Happiness is having a friend like you

As you slide down the banister of life
May you always be one of the splinters.

May the bird of paradise never peck a hole in your water-bed

U,R,2 young, and 2 pretty 4 boys

I saw you on the mountain
I saw you in the sea
I saw you in the bathtub
Oops! Pardon me

Roses are red
Violets are blue
The sidewalk is cracked
And so are you

U R 2 good
2 B 4 gotten

We're in a hammock, ready to kiss
In less than a second

We'll look like this.

References: More Autograph Rhymes

Morrison, Lillian, comp. *Remember Me When This You See!;* il. by Marjorie Bauernschmidt. Crowell, 1961. A collection of autograph verses. And also *Yours Till Niagara Falls;* il. by Marjorie Bauernschmidt. Crowell, 1950. And *Best Wishes, Amen: A New Collection of Autograph Verses;* il. by Loretta Lustig. Crowell, 1974. An up-to-date collection that reflects current trends.

Proverbs

　　Proverbs are folk sayings that contain popular advice, state a moral, or confirm a judgment. Different folk groups have their own proverbs, but often they can be recognized as different ways of expressing similar thoughts. You can find proverbs listed in adult folklore collections. Use them in between stories if you wish to begin a discussion. Children might like to remind you of some they are familiar with. Think of the possibilities of these selected proverbs as they relate to today's society:

American Proverbs

Live and let live.

Out of sight, out of mind.

Absence makes the heart grow fonder.

Don't count your chickens before they hatch.

You can't make a silk purse out of a sow's ear.

Don't kill the goose that lays the golden egg.

Penny wise and pound foolish.

A new broom sweeps clean.

A rolling stone gathers no moss.

He couldn't be elected dog catcher in a ward full of cats.

An apple a day keeps the doctor away.

A watched pot never boils.

Two wrongs don't make a right.

The love of money is the root of all evil.

Old soldiers never die; they just fade away.

You can lead a horse to water, but you can't make him drink.

Look before you leap.   Haste makes waste.   No news is good news.

Never criticize a man until you've walked a mile in his moccasins.

All work and no play makes Jack a dull boy.

Lie down with cats, get up with fleas. (My mother, a dog lover, substituted the cat in this familiar saying.)

Jewish Proverbs

The worst informer is the face.

Charge nothing and you'll get a lot of customers.

Do not worry about tomorrow, because you do not even know what may happen to you today.

The sun will set without your assistance.

Your friend has a friend, and your friend's friend has a friend: Be discreet.

The luck of an ignoramus is that he doesn't know that he doesn't know.

An insincere peace is better than a sincere war.

Poverty is no disgrace, but it's no great honor, either.

Everywhere it's good, and at home it's even better.

What is cheap is dear.   At the baths, all are equal.

What three know is no secret.

What good can a lamp and spectacles be when a man just doesn't want to see?

Proverbs from Around the World

You can't make an owl out of a falcon.—Russia.

A hungry cat likes a well-fed mouse best.—Russia.

When the cat's away, the mice do play.—Germany.

An old fox is hard to catch.—Germany.

Even a rooster lays an egg for one who is lucky.—Russia.

Whoever plays with cats must not fear their claws.—Egypt.

He who lives without folly is not so wise as he thinks.—Hungary.

References: More Proverbs

The Bible (Old Testament). *The Proverbs: A Selection,* by Elvajean Hall; il. by Charles Mozley. Watts, 1970.

Kelen, Emery, comp. *Proverbs of Many Nations;* il. by author. Lothrop, 1966.

Mason, Bernard S., and Mitchell, Elmer D. *Party Games for All.* Barnes and Noble, 1946.

Opoku, Kofi Asare, comp. *Speak to the Winds: Proverbs from Africa;* il. by Dindga McCannon. Lothrop, 1975.

Word Games

Words make books, so why not have fun with words? Your group might enjoy playing traditional games that use words as their materials and tools.

I Packed My Trunk (at least two players)

Players sit in a circle. First player says, "I packed my trunk to visit my aunt and in it I put an apple." Then the next player repeats the first player's statement and adds an object beginning with the letter "B." Each player repeats that which went before and adds an object beginning with the next letter in the alphabet. If a player makes a mistake he is out until the next game. If the alphabet is completed, begin again and pack two things beginning with each letter of the alphabet.

Ghost (at least three players)

This spelling game begins when one player calls out a letter. The next one thinks of a word beginning with the letter and calls out a second letter and so one around the group. The object of the game is to keep the word going without saying a letter that will end it. The first time a player loses a round he or she gets a "G," the next time an "H," and so on until he or she is a GHOST. If one player thinks the player before used a letter that cannot be a part of a word, he or she can challenge that player. If the preceding player does have a word in mind, the challenger loses the round and earns a letter; if not, the challenged player loses the round and earns a letter instead.

Hangman (for two players or teams)

This game, a favorite in our family, is similar to Ghost, but in it you "kill" your opponent. First think of a word and draw dashes on paper to indicate the number of letters in the word. The players call out a letter. If it belongs in the word the leader writes it in the appropriate space. If the letter is not in the word draw a part at a time to the hanged man. The player that needs the fewest guesses to guess the word wins. Hints: Start by guessing the vowels. If you're feeling really generous, give your opponent more chances by making the drawing of the hanged man more and more elaborate (add hair, shoes, facial features).

Continuous Story (for two or more players)

The leader begins with the first sentence of a story such as "Once upon a time I went into the woods." Each player in turn, adds another sentence to the story, such as "It was very cold and dark. Suddenly. . . ." The next player might say "I saw a bear" and so on, around the group.

This can also be done as a paper-and-pencil game. Write a sentence of a story on a sheet of paper. Fold the paper over and pass it to the next person all the way around the group, folding each sentence down. Let the last person read the story aloud.

The Newspaper Game (one or more players)

Each player is given a newspaper, scissors, paste, and blank paper. Each player cuts words from a newspaper and pastes them together to make a story. Put a time limit on this game so that no one attempts to write the great American novel.

Telegram (two or more players)

Each player in turn calls out one letter of the alphabet. The other players write down a word beginning with each letter called and then each tries to write a telegram using the words.

Alphabet Salesman (two or more players)

Each player in turn must make up a sentence, the main words of which must begin with the letter of the alphabet in turn; e.g., "My name is Allen and I sell ants in Africa." The next player begins with "B," saying something like "My name is Betty and I sell bananas in Boston," and so on.

Dog to Cat

Change dog to cat in three moves by changing one letter at each move.

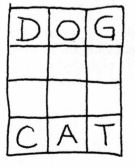 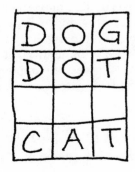 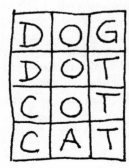

Picto Puzzle

First, select the name of a famous person, perhaps a noted president or a well-known author. Then gather together pictures of objects, the first letter of which, when arranged in the proper order, one below the other, will spell out the name of that person.

L	Lollipop
I	Ice cream
N	Nails
C	Car
O	Octopus
L	Lion
N	Necktie
P	Pie
O	Onion
E	Egg

Homonyms, Homographs, Antonyms

The English language has some weird, yet wonderful, confusions. Some words sound the same, but mean different things; some sound different, but are spelled the same. Instead of sighing at the difficulties these words present, enjoy them. Show your group one of the picture books by Fred Gwynne—*The King Who Rained* (Windmill, 1970) or *A Chocolate Moose for Dinner* (Windmill, 1976). How many others can the children add to the collection? Keep a list of favorites.

Homonyms

Homonyms are words that sound the same but are differently spelled: Hare/hair; flee/flea; bear/bare; flower/flour.

Homographs

Homographs are words that are spelled the same but sound different: tear/tear; dove/dove; wind/wind.

Antonyms

Antonyms are words that are opposite in meaning: hot/cold; high/low; open/closed; hard/soft; rough/smooth.

Word-Game Riddles

What three words contain a silent B?
Doubt, subtle, debt.

What keys are too large to carry in your pocket?
A mon*key*; a tur*key;* a don*key.*

Which word in the English language has the most letters?
Antidisestablishmentarianism (28 letters).

What letters in the alphabet are the opposite of stupid?
Ys (wise).

What two letters are an Indian's house?
TP (teepee).

What two letters in the alphabet spell a word meaning jealousy?
NV (envy)

References: Word Games

Charlip, Remy. *Arm in Arm;* il. by author. Parents, 1969. A few well-chosen endless and circular tables.

Coudrille, Jonathon. *A Beastly Collection;* il. by author. Warne, 1974. An ABC that explores the sound of words.

Gwynne, Fred. *The King Who Rained;* il. by author. Windmill, 1970. From "Daddy says there are forks in the road" to ". . . the Foot Prince in the snow." Also *A Chocolate Moose for Dinner* (Windmill, 1976). Hilarious romps with semantics in picture-book format.

The Hodgepodge Book: An Almanac of American Folklore; collected by Duncan Emrich; il. by Ib Ohlsson. Four Winds, 1972. Rhymes, riddles, jokes, cumulative stories.

Hanlon, Emily. *How a Horse Grew Hoarse on the Site Where He Sighted a Bare Bear; A Tale of Homonyms;* il. by Lorna Tomei. Delacorte, 1976. A clever, funny poem full of homonyms that are listed on the book's last page.

Hanson, Joan. *Homonyms;* il. by author. Lerner, 1972. Also *Homographs* (Lerner, 1972) and *Antonyms* (Lerner, 1972). Cartoon drawings show the differences in these words.

Manchester, Richard B. *The Mammoth Book of Word Games.* Hart, 1976. Five hundred pages of anagrams, crossword puzzles, and other word games.

Schwartz, Alvin. *Tomfoolery: Trickery and Foolery with Words;* il. by Glen Rounds. Lippincott, 1973. Word tricks collected from folklore. Also *Kickle Snifters and Other Fearsome Critters;* il. by Glen Rounds. Lippincott, 1976.

Shipley, Joseph T. *Word Play;* il. by author. Hawthorn, 1972. Excellent collection of word games including puns, cryptograms, palindromes, and more.

Tripp, Wallace, comp. *A Great Big Ugly Man Came up and Tied His Horse to Me;* il. by compiler. Little, 1973. Traditional nonsense verse humorously illustrated.

Wilbur, Richard. *Opposites;* il. by author. Harcourt, 1973. Poems and cartoon drawings celebrate opposites in words.

Sign Language

The idea of communicating nonverbally is not a new one. It has been recently re-explored in a bestselling adult book, *Body Language* by Julius Fast (Evans, 1970). With some of the more familiar hand motions from the

American Indians, or from the sign language of the deaf, see if you can make yourself understood. To begin, try these sentences:

> You (point) come (beckon) with me (point to yourself) to hunt (pull imaginary bow):
>> Deer (fingers at side of head represent antlers)
>> Buffalo (thumbs for ears, index fingers for horns)
>> Bear (hands cupped around ears).
> We all (point to each person and then indicate entire group) dance (move both hands up and down, palms open vertically to group).

References: Sign Language

Amon, Aline. *Talking Hands; Indian Sign Language;* il. by author. Doubleday, 1968.

Charlip, Remy, and Ancona, George and Mary Beth. *Handtalk: An ABC of Finger Spelling and Sign Language;* il. with photos. Parents, 1974. Full-color photographs give a clear introduction to the sign language of the deaf.

Hofsinde, Robert (Gray-Wolf). *Indian Sign Language;* il. by author. Morrow, 1956.

Keller, Charles, comp. *Too Funny for Words: Gesture Jokes for Children;* photos. by Stephen Anderson. Prentice-Hall, 1973. Photographs illustrate jokes that rely on the visual for their effect.

Tomkins, William. *Indian Sign Language;* il. by author. Dover, 1969. Pictures and sample sentences to practice.

Folk Games

Games can be considered folklore too. You may not want to turn your storyhour into a gym period, but games that travel from one generation to the other and from region to region by the private oral route of children can make a fascinating study. Many adults see the passing of street games in favor of Little League and traffic jams as sad. Some of these people have recalled the games of their childhood and compiled books, others have collected the games currently played on the streets and playgrounds of the country. As you browse through these books you will be reminded of games that you played, some quiet, some active.

String Games

You might not have thought of cat's cradle as folklore, but it is a game that is passed on from person to person. If you are familiar with any of the string

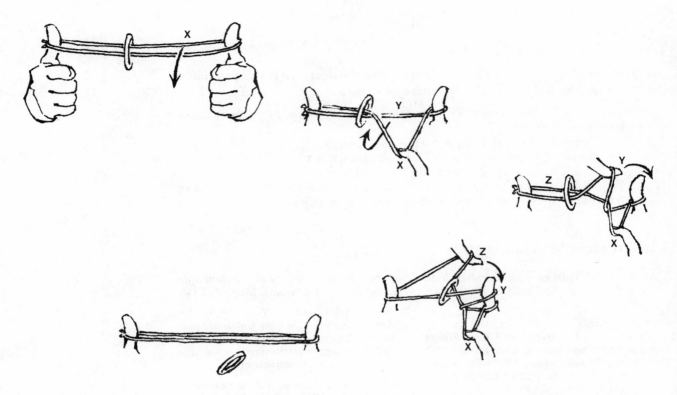

games of your childhood, why not show them to your storyhour group? No doubt they will in turn show you some you don't know.

Ring in the String. To play this game you need a ring, a length of string whose ends are knotted together to form a loop, and a volunteer from the audience.

First draw the string loop through the ring. Then stand facing the volunteer, loop the string around his or her thumbs, and reach across the loop with your right forefinger to catch the far side of the string at X, pulling it downward across the top of the near strand and holding it there. Next, with your left hand reach under the strand you are holding with your right hand and hook the other strand with the left forefinger at Y, pulling it under the strand held by the right hand and *up* over the volunteer's left thumb. Still holding the strand with your right forefinger, reach with left forefinger across the strand, catching it *back* of the volunteer's right thumb at Z, bringing it up and toward you, and looping it over his or her left thumb. Now grasp the ring with the thumb and forefinger of your left hand, at the same time releasing the strand held by the right forefinger. The string will snap free from the ring, leaving the ring free in your hand and the looped string still encircling the volunteer's two thumbs.

References: String Games

Jayne, Caroline Furness. *String Figures and How to Make Them: A Study of Cat's-Cradle in Many Lands.* Dover, 1962. This book gives directions for hundreds of string games, but it takes patience and practice to master many of them.

Haddon, Kathleen. *String Games for Beginners* (2d ed.). W. Heffer (Cambridge, Eng.), 1972. String games collected from many lands with directions for playing them.

Active Games

If you are holding the storyhour outside on a lovely day you might want to play an active "folk" game before settling down to hear a story. Jacks and marble contests can be held indoors for those rainy days.

Kick the Can: a city game. To play Kick the Can as we did when I was growing up in Washington, DC, you will need an empty can, a big paint can or coffee can, and a group of friends.

This is the way you play: The can is placed about 10 feet from "Home Base." One person is "IT." IT faces away from the players, counts to 50 while they run away and hide, and then turns around. The object of the game is to get to Home Base without being tagged. Even though IT has tagged nearly all the players, if anyone succeeds in kicking the can before being tagged, all the players revert to "Free" unless IT retrieves the can and reaches Home Base before the player who has kicked the can.

Pump Pump Pull Away: a country game. This is the way this game was played in Owatonna, Minnesota, by my friend Arvid when he was a boy. You will need lots of room and a group of friends. IT stands in the middle of a playing field. All the players stand on one end of the field. IT yells, "Pump, Pump, Pull Away" and all the players try to run past IT to the other end of the field. Those players that IT manages to tag as they run by then join hands with IT in the center of the field for the next run-through. The winner is the player who has not been tagged after all the remaining players have been tagged and are forming a wall by holding hands.

References: More Folk Games

Arnold, Arnold. *The World Book of Children's Games;* il. by author. World, 1972. A large collection of informal games.

Carlo (pseud.). *The Juggling Book;* il. by author. Vintage, 1974. Directions for juggling, but you still have to practice.

Chase, Richard, comp. *Singing Games and Playparty Games;* il. by Joshua Tolford. Dover, 1967. A compilation by a noted folklorist.

Ferretti, Fred. *The Great American Book of Sidewalk, Stoop, Dirt, Curb, and Alley Games;* photos. by Jerry Darvin. Workman, 1975. A large collection of street games including mumblety peg, Russia, and potsie.

———— *The Great American Marble Book;* photos. by Jay Good. Workman, 1973. More than 50 marble games explained.

Langstaff, John, and Langstaff, Carol. *Shimmy Shimmy Coke-ca-Pop!;* photos. by Don MacSorley. Doubleday, 1973. A collection of city children's street games and rhymes.

Newell, William Wells. *Games and Songs of American Children;* introduction by Carl Withers. First published in 1883. Dover, 1963.

Rockwell, Anne. *Games (And How to Play Them);* il. by author. Crowell, 1973. Big colorful illustrations each show how to play a traditional game, such as sardines, Yankee Doodle cracker, and coffee pot.

Sturner, Fred, and Seltzer, Adolf. *What Did You Do When You Were a Kid?;* il. by Bill Charmatz. St. Martin's Pr., 1973. Cartoon drawings show children how to play stoop ball, territory, and ringolevio.

Vinton, Iris. *The Folkways Omnibus of Children's Games;* il. by Alex D'Amato. Stackpole, 1970. Excellent background material as well as directions for games played around the world.

Wagenvoord, James. *Hangin' Out: City Kids, City Games;* photos. by author; designed by Anita Wagenvoord. Lippincott, 1974.

Weigle, Marta. *Jacks and Jack Games: Follow My Fancy;* ed. by Jessica Hoffman Davis. Dover, 1970 (paper). Directions for all the games of jacks you ever played.

Wood, Clement, and Goddard, Gloria. *The Complete Book of Games;* il. by author. Halcyon House, 1940. Rules for every imaginable game and sport.

Folk Toys

Toys too can be a part of folklore just as jokes, riddles, myths, and folktales are. Folk toys are playthings made by one generation and passed on to the next as a form of entertainment. Collecting some of these old toys, making them yourself or with your group can be part of the story program, especially if you find stories that relate to a particular toy. For instance, displaying or making a hobbyhorse fits in with any horse story. Dress a clothespin doll to portray the main character of a favorite story. Apples, nuts, cornhusks and cobs, twigs, spools, string—all kinds of materials go into the making of folk toys that you and your group can make and enjoy.

Figure 9. Hobbyhorse—
an easy-to-make
folk toy

Hobbyhorse

You need: A large cotton sock
Cotton or polyester batt
Felt scraps
Yarn
3-foot length of ½-inch cotton tubular trim
3-foot length of 1-inch dowel or broomstick

How-to: Make head by stuffing sock with cotton or polyester batt. Make eyes, ears, and nose from felt scraps and sew on or glue to head. Use looped yarn to make mane and forelock. Sew tubular trim to head to make bridle. Attach dowel or broomstick to head with staples or craft glue.

References: More Folk Toys

Comins, Jeremy. *Eskimo Crafts and Their Cultural Background;* photos. and drawings by author. Lothrop, 1975. Instructions and background material for making simple Eskimo toys.

Joseph, Joan, comp. *Folk Toys around the World;* il. by Mel Furukawa; working drawings and instructions by Glenn Wagner. Parents, 1972. Instructions and background material for a toy from each of several selected countries.

Laury, Jean Ray, and Law Ruth, comps. *Handmade Toys and Games: A Guide to Creating Your Own;* photos. by Gayle Smaller and others; drawings by Jean Ray Laury. Doubleday, 1975. Toys, games, puzzles galore, created by various artisans, many of which are easy to reproduce.

Schnacke, Dick. *American Folk Toys and How to Make Them;* il. by author. Putnam, 1973. A practical collection of toy-making crafts.

References: To Find Out More about Folklore

American Folklore Society, Folklore Center, Social Work 306, Univ. of Texas, Austin, TX 78712.

Brunvand, Jan Harold. *The Study of American Folklore: An Introduction.* Norton, 1968. Essays on verbal and nonverbal folklore.

Dorson, Richard M. *American Folklore.* Univ. of Chicago Pr., 1959. Survey of American folklore.

Dundes, Alan. *The Study of Folklore.* Prentice-Hall, 1965. An anthology of 34 essays which "surveys the discipline of folklore."

Epstein, Perle. *Monsters: Their Histories, Homes, and Habits;* il. by author. Doubleday, 1973. Mythical creatures are surveyed for children. Useful for background information.

The Foxfire Book; ed. by Eliot Wigginton. Doubleday, 1972. Articles on folk activities including hunting tales, mountain crafts, and foods. A second volume, *Foxfire 2* (Doubleday/Anchor, 1973), contains ghost stories, spinning, and weaving. A third, *Foxfire 3* (Doubleday, 1975), features animal care, banjos and dulcimers, hide tanning, summer and fall wild plant foods, butter churns, and ginseng.

Frazer, Sir James G. *The New Golden Bough;* ed. by Theodor H. Gaster. Criterion, 1959. An abridged, but still lengthy version, of Frazer's 1890 work. Studies the history of civilization from the point of view of primitive magic, taboos, and superstition.

Funk and Wagnalls Standard Dictionary of Folklore, Mythology and Legend; ed. by Maria Leach and Jerome Fried, 2 vols. Funk, 1949–1950. A reference work that encompasses folklore around the world.

Gladstone, M. J. *A Carrot for a Nose; The Form of Folk Sculpture on America's City Streets and Country Roads.* Scribner, 1974. Illustrated with photographs to use with children.

Krappe, Alexander H. *The Science of Folklore.* Norton, 1964. "A classic introduction to the origins, forms, and characteristics of folklore."

McHargue, Georgess. *The Impossible People;* il. by Frank Bozzo, Holt, 1972. Giants, trolls, witches, pixies, demons, mermaids—a discussion.

Neal, Avon. *Ephemeral Folk Figures;* il. with photos. by Ann Parker. Potter, 1969. Scarecrows, harvest figures and snowmen.

Opie, Ione and Peter. *The Lore and Language of School Children;* il. by authors. Clarendon Pr., 1959.

Panofsky, Dora and Erwin. *Pandora's Box: The Changing Aspects of a Mythical Symbol* (2d ed., rev.). Harper, 1965. A study of the symbol of "Pandora's Box."

Raglan, FitzRoy Richard Somerset, Baron. *The Hero: A Study in Tradition, Myth and Drama.* Vintage, 1956. The myths as fictional narrative.

Thompson, Stith. *The Folktale.* Dryden Pr., 1946. The classic study of the folktale including motif and tale type index.

Periodicals (Available from the library)

Journal of American Folklore (1888– , quarterly). American Folklore Society, Univ. of Texas Pr., Box 7819, Austin, TX 78712.

Southern Folklore Quarterly (1937– , quarterly). Univ. of Florida, c/o Ed. Roger M. Thompson, Anderson Hall, Gainsville, FL 32617.

Western Folklore (1942– , quarterly). California Folklore Society, Univ. of California Pr., Berkeley, CA 94720.

PART THREE

Multimedia Storytelling

You now tell stories in a traditional way using both old and modern sources. Good. You also use a book when telling a story, showing the illustrations while you speak. Fine. Now try something different. Use your storytelling skill, but apply it to the use of media. This type of storytelling includes the use of flip cards; objects; flannel, felt, and magnetic boards; slides, filmstrips, and film. Not every storyteller will be captivated by these techniques, but try a few sessions at least to see whether media are for you. Producing some of these materials may take a considerable amount of time, but they can be used again and again and from year to year. Some of you will be delighted to experiment with making your own materials in the homely tradition of the family craftsman and storyteller. Others may want to rely on professionally produced items. Using media often means making something, or borrowing and learning how to properly use some equipment. If you decide to make your own materials, combine talents with a friend or colleague. One person can cut out felt figures, the other can use them in a presentation. Keep in mind as you are squinting at the 16mm film you are making that anything you create now can go into a permanent storytelling collection to be used again and again.

Many of the ideas in this section use machines to augment the presentation of the story. Machines have long been used to improve methods of instruction and entertainment, but what can they do for storytelling? They can add another dimension. Never to be used to excess, machines, when used creatively, can help improve your book program. However, keep in mind that reliance on any single technique may defeat your purpose. With storytelling, those media techniques which are most successfully used are *multi*media. The combined use of several methods in the same storyhour frequently makes the program more successful than prolonged use of a single technique. Sensitive combinations of traditional and audiovisual techniques can add variety and emphasis to a carefully planned program.

In the following pages you will be exposed to many ideas and mechanical devices. I have not attempted to give you actual technical details; instead my intent is to present enough of an idea of how things work so that you can start experimenting on your own. If you find yourself interested in any one idea or method, I also have provided selected bibliographies that will help you pursue your interest. However, if you want to learn how to do something, the only real way is to DO it.

10 / Pictures and Objects in Storytelling

You've been using a picture book in the intimate storyhour, but it's too small to use with a larger group. A favorite picture book has circulated so much that it is ready to be discarded, but you cannot bear to part with the illustrations. The small, inexpensive paperback editions of picture books cry to be used in a new way. Let us consider different ways in which these pictures and illustrations can be used for storytelling.

Flip Cards

It is possible to reproduce parts of a small book on large cards to use with a large group by enlarging it for presentation or to present a story in a slightly different way for variety. By cards I really mean large sheets of tagboard or heavy paper. "Large" can range from 8 inches by 10 inches to 2 feet by 3 feet. Anything much bigger really becomes physically difficult to handle. Rest the cards on an easel or a table or hold each one up as the story progresses.

Flip cards can be made in a variety of ways. If you enjoy drawing, you may want to illustrate stories yourself. Folktales illustrated by flip cards decorated with your own drawings do at times seem to become more meaningful. Remember that you want to show your story to a group. Keep your pictures simple and uncluttered so that the sense of each will immediately be clear to your audience (*see* fig. 10). Not every scene in the story needs to be illustrated, for you don't want your flip cards to be distracting to the story. Review the story in your mind and pick out the main points for illustration. For example, to tell *Little Red Riding Hood* with flip cards, draw her with her mother as she sets out for Grandma's house; then show the first encounter with the wolf; next illustrate the wolf in bed, pretending to be Grandma; and finally present the scene when the hunter frees Grandma and Little Red Riding Hood. You can also illustrate a chapter from one of your favorite books with flip cards, or even create a picture book of your own for a favorite story that has no suitable illustrations.

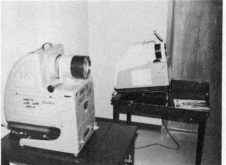

Figure 11. Opaque projectors

Figure 10. Flip card
presentation

Perhaps you have a favorite artist whose books are too small to show a large group. It can easily be argued that the small book should be reserved then for an individual child or the small group. I agree that some books should be cherished in this way, but there is a way for you to "blow up" a picture to use for exhibits or flip cards.

You can become an instant artist by using the opaque projector. This bulky, heavy machine (fig. 11) is used to project books, pictures, or objects on a wall or screen. Many of these machines are gathering dust, unused in schools and libraries, replaced by the overhead projector or other equipment. Resurrect this machine and use it as a copying aid. Insert the book in the machine so that the page you want to reproduce is projected onto a wall. Now attach a posterboard or paper onto the wall with masking tape. Trace around the outlines of the picture with felt pen, crayon, pencil, or whatever you wish. You can fill in the colors later. Remember that excessive reproduction for public use may be violating the author's or illustrator's copyright unless permission is obtained. It is not necessary, in any event, to reproduce the whole work. An outline figure, a portion of a complex figure, or one of several figures is usually enough to convey the sense or flavor of the material. Remember, the ultimate goal in storytelling is to encourage in children an appreciation of books. You will always want to refer a group to the book that inspired you. Have it on hand to show to the children.

Figure 12. Mounted paperback
cut-ups for telling
One Monday Morning

Now that you know how to use the opaque projector to reproduce a picture or draw your own, do something with your pictures that is usually too expensive for a publisher to do with a book. Use fabric, tissue paper, string, and whatever else you can think of to actually dress the characters in the story, thereby creating a three-dimensional effect on your flip cards. The pictures then become tactile, too, so that the children can touch and feel the story after they have seen and heard it.

Many of the picture books in a library or at home eventually meet some kind of disaster in the form of crayons, waterspots, or rips. You may be able to salvage enough of the pictures for use on flip cards. Mount the pages of the book on cardboard. Forget those pictures that are beyond use, but portions of them still may be intact; those you can cut out and mount on cardboard. Now you can tell the story of the book using key pictures, thus saving a book from total discard.

Paperback Cut-ups

Because juvenile paperbacks are relatively inexpensive, sometimes you can afford to buy two, cut them apart and mount the characters or scenes on posterboard. Display them on an easel or stand them up with cardboard stands, use them like stick puppets, or mount them on a roll of paper.

Figure 13. A roll story
drawn on wrapping paper

Books that have repetitive action or sequential characters—perhaps Barbara Emberley's *Drummer Hoff* (Prentice-Hall, 1967) or Uri Shulevitz's *One Monday Morning* (Scribner, 1967)—work well for such use.

Although we are taught never to mutilate a book, some may be put to better use by cutting them up. Take, as an example, the remaindered art books you frequently find on sale at the bookstore. You're tempted to purchase them after which they sit unused on your library shelf or coffee table. Instead, why not put such books to use? Consider cutting up an art book to use for exhibit purposes, bookmarks, posters, or on a magnetic board. Perhaps you own a book whose text is outdated. Why give the book away to an organization that will find the book equally outdated? Perhaps the pictures in it can be used to good advantage in your storytelling programs.

Roll Stories

On a roll of adding machine paper, which is available from your stationer, draw an appropriate story, scene by scene, so that when it is unrolled the scenes and characters of the story will appear in sequence. After the story has been told, the long length of paper can be used on a bulletin board or as a wall decoration. The roll can also be installed in a box cut out to look like a television set. A sturdy shoe box is ideal. Cut a square hole the size of the width of the paper in the bottom of the shoe box. Cut slits above and below the viewing window for the paper to pass through. The paper roll can be pulled through as the story is told or you can use wooden doweling, available at the lumber yard or hardware store, to make a neater roll.

Paper such as newsprint and wrapping paper is also sold in bulk rolls and can be used for this same storytelling technique. The larger the roll, the greater the number of children who will be able to see the story. A handcrafted box can be made to file an oversized roll of paper.

Figure 16. An enormous, handcrafted carrot to use with the last sentence of Ruth Krauss's *The Carrot Seed*

Figure 14. Wearing *Jennie's Hat,* an object story

Figure 15. Model room and objects to tell *Goodnight Moon*

This is a good technique for children to try themselves. After you tell a story, have each child draw a picture. Paste all the pictures onto the roll in a sequence. Now each child will be able to say to himself or herself or more often aloud to the group, "That's my picture." To avoid having too many pictures of the same scene (12 Rapunzels in the tower, for instance, and no witches), you might go over the story, characters, and scenes, reminding the children that other things happen besides the main thing that they remember.

Copying Machine Stories

What can you do with a xerographic copying machine? Reproduce the pictures in a book, color them with felt pens, crayons, or watercolors, and mount them separately on colored posterboard. Use the pictures on a magnetic board or a hook 'n' loop board. Or put them on sticks for use as stick puppets. Remember that books and their pictures are subject to copyright laws. Avoid copying an entire book.

Object Stories

One way of presenting a story is to show objects as you tell the story. For example, if you want to tell Ezra Jack Keats's *Jennie's Hat* (Harper, 1966), you can actually act it out by asking a little girl in the audience to be Jennie. As you tell the story, try on the different objects that Jennie tries on: a TV antenna, a basket, a flowerpot, a saucepan. When the birds bring objects to decorate Jennie's hat, you decorate a hat with the eggs, flowers, and greeting cards, with the fetching results you see in figure 14.

One of my favorite books is Margaret Wise Brown's *Goodnight Moon* (Harper, 1947). The book is probably more appropriately used when children are ready for bed, but as an object story, it becomes a story to use in the storyhour. The book begins:

> In a great green room
> There was a telephone
> A red balloon
> And a picture of the cow
> jumping over the moon.

As each object is named, I place it in the small model room shown in figure 15. I bought dollhouse furniture, but it also would be fun to make furniture yourself. As the narrator says goodnight to each object in the room, I remove that object. It doesn't take long for the children to want to participate by placing and removing the objects as the story is told.

One of my students told *Stone Soup* by Marcia Brown (Scribner, 1947) to a fourth-grade class. Before the story he passed out vegetables: turnips, onions, carrots, beets, and potatoes. As the soldiers in the story asked the town's citizens to contribute to the soup pot the children contributed their vegetables to a large soup pot. That night the storyteller went home and cooked up a big pot of soup to serve at snack time the next day.

Books for Object Story Use

Any ABC book: use objects to represent each letter.

Baylor, Byrd. *Everybody Needs a Rock;* il. by Peter Parnall. Scribner, 1974.

Brown, Marcia. *Stone Soup;* il. by author. Scribner, 1947.

Brown, Margaret Wise. *Goodnight Moon;* il. by Clement Hurd. Harper, 1947.

Hoban, Russell. *A Baby Sister for Frances;* il. by Lillian Hoban, Harper, 1964.

Keats, Ezra Jack. *Jennie's Hat;* il. by author. Harper, 1966.

Kraus, Robert. *The Tail Who Wagged the Dog;* il. by author. Windmill, 1971.

Krauss, Ruth. *The Carrot Seed;* il. by Crockett Johnson. Harper, 1945.

Lionni, Leo. *Tico and the Golden Wings;* il. by author. Pantheon, 1964.

Munari, Bruno. *Jimmy Has Lost His Cap, Where Can It Be?;* il. by author. World, 1959.

Zolotow, Charlotte. *Mr. Rabbit and the Lovely Present;* il. by Maurice Sendak. Harper, 1962.

11 / *Board Stories*

If you have never used props to tell a story and are a bit wary of the whole idea, experimenting with one of the various types of boards is a good way to begin. Using a felt board to tell a story is as much of a tradition in some classrooms and libraries as telling a story without props. Years ago I visited a children's room in a public library in St. Louis. The librarian and I began discussing storytelling and she showed me her felt-board file in which each story was carefully stored in a labeled manila envelope. I was intrigued, yet at the same time alienated, for my first thought was, "But why do you need all that paraphernalia? Why not just tell the story?" Later, returning home to tell stories at the local schools, and thinking of the librarian in St. Louis, I decided to try my own board story. I cut out paper figures and while telling the story, attached the pictures to a window screen using pins. This was, admittedly, a rather crude and unwieldy attempt, yet it was instantly successful. I now had two stories in place of one, for although the children had heard the story many times, they delighted in this new presentation. I now wish I knew the name of that librarian in St. Louis, for I would like to thank her for moving me out of the traditional past into another realm where I can make use of new media and different techniques, all the while retaining the spirit and heritage of the old stories.

With the story board the idea is to tell a story while illustrating it with cutout figures that are placed on the board. As in any storytelling, the most important part is to choose a good story, but you have the added problem of choosing one that is suitable for story board presentation. To do this you want a story that has only a few simple, large characters or objects. You won't want to be putting up a lot of tiny objects that crowd the board. Nor do you want to be constantly changing the pictures. This can be distracting unless you become adept at talking and doing at the same time and can concentrate on telling the story to the audience. Particularly successful is the story which begins with one character and builds up to many. The storyteller simply adds to the cutouts on the board rather than adding and removing. Some stories are just not suitable for board use. I keep wanting to try Polly Goldberg's *Oh Lord, I Wish I Was a Buzzard* (Macmillan, 1968) as a felt-board presentation. I keep thinking what fun it would be to start with a board filled with cotton balls and as I removed them, the animals that the little girl wishes to be could be seen. Yet I know that making a trick out of this particular book would cheapen the message. But there are other books and many stories that are suitable for storyboard use. Try a board story with a group of eager and receptive preschoolers and you'll soon find that you have a drawer full of carefully labeled envelopes containing stories for board use.

Hints for Using Boards

Boards can be used most effectively on an easel, although you may want to sit on the floor and simply lean the board against a wall. You might have your most often used board permanently fastened to the wall. You will also need a table, or a floor area on which to arrange the cutouts that will go on the board. Number these on the back for easy identification. I like to put my pieces behind the board, or in a box or basket so that the audience doesn't see what is coming next.

Care should be observed in using these boards. There is a tendency to talk to the board rather than to the audience. Be sure that you face the audience after you have put the object or picture on the board. If something falls off, simply pick it up and put it back. If you don't, the children will remind you and disrupt the presentation. Try to choose a story in which the placement of the object on the board is not crucial. Otherwise you will take excessive amounts of time carefully arranging your board. The pictures should merely supplement your story. They should not be too detailed. Outline silhouettes may be all you really want because you want to leave room for a child's imagination to work.

Occasionally you may want to use a bird or rabbit from one story in another story. Try to resist the temptation, for you may later find yourself in the middle of a story and discover that you forgot to replace the character. Try to keep all the pictures belonging to one story in a manila envelope that is clearly marked for identification. A copy of the story should also be included in this envelope so that you can easily relearn it for telling without searching for the book. If you do have a copy of the book, it should be shown to the children before or after you tell the story so that they know that the story came from print.

Once you have told the story you might ask for some help in taking down the pictures, for you will discover that the children who handle the figures may be better able to recall the story. You will also find that the children enjoy telling the story to each other and making their own cutouts.

Background music, on a record, tape, or cassette, serves to make your presentation truly professional and is particularly useful during the interlude when you have a lot of pictures to put up or take off a board.

The Chalkboard

Most classrooms, lecture halls, or clubhouses have a chalkboard. Make use of this permanent fixture by illustrating your story as you tell it. Although the same thing may be accomplished with a drawing pad, the chalkboard has the advantage of being reusable and there also is something magical about a story disappearing under an eraser. Choose a story that will require a few simple clues. The audience will become restless if you turn your back and painstakingly complete a master drawing. Although this book emphasizes do-it-yourself projects for people who are not artists, if you are skilled the possibilities of the chalkboard are extensive. Draw your own illustrations while you tell a folktale or relate an author's story. If you don't consider yourself artistic there are some stories and rhymes that require only simple drawings. Among these are the "drawing stories" collected by folklorists which, by their nature, require only minimal drawing ability. Mother Goose rhymes are adaptable to the chalkboard too. Drawing to music is another possibility for using the chalkboard for storytelling. Be sure that you stand to the side as you draw so that everyone can see. Colored chalks may be used to identify or highlight figures. Always practice before presenting a story, so that you feel at ease with the combined drawing/telling activity. The following suggestions should start you on your way to creating with chalk.

Drawing Stories

"T" IS FOR TOMMY

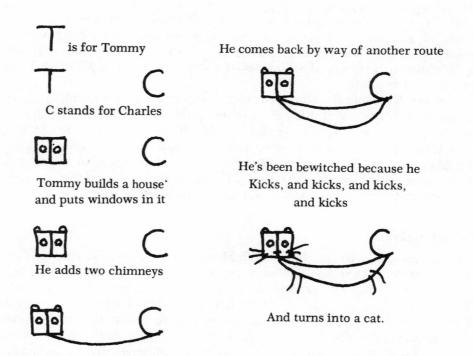

is for Tommy

C stands for Charles

Tommy builds a house' and puts windows in it

He adds two chimneys

Tommy visits Charles' house

He comes back by way of another route

He's been bewitched because he Kicks, and kicks, and kicks, and kicks

And turns into a cat.

Chalkboard Rhymes

April showers
Bring May flowers.

Rain, rain go away
Come again another day.

Jack, be nimble,
Jack be quick,
And, Jack, jump over
The candlestick.

Familiar Folk Songs

(The children sing while leader draws)

Oh where, oh where has my little dog gone?

Oh where, oh where can he be?

With his ears so short

And his tail so long

Oh where, oh where can he be?

Leave the drawing of the dog on the chalkboard, and because it could be a fox as well, direct the children to sing the next song. When they "catch" the fox, draw a box around the animal, erasing it as they sing the last line.

Oh, a-hunting we will go
A-hunting we will go
We'll catch a fox
And put him in a box
And then we'll let him go.

Books for Chalkboard Use

Carle, Eric. *The Mixed-Up Chameleon;* il. by author. Crowell, 1975. A chameleon not only changes colors, but shapes.

Čtvrtek, Václav. *The Little Chalk Man;* tr. from the Czech; il. by Muriel Batherman. Knopf, 1970. Episodic chapters of a magical chalk world.

Dodgson, Charles L. *The Diaries of Lewis Carroll* (pseud.); ed. by Roger Lancelyn Green. Oxford Univ. Pr., 1954, vol. 2, pp. 572–73. "Mr. C and Mr. T," a variant of the black cat drawing story.

Du Bois, William Pène. *Lion;* il. by author. Viking, 1956. Lion is created in heaven after a number of false starts.

Freeman, Don. *The Chalk Box Story.* Lippincott, 1976. Eight pieces of colored chalk change a blank piece of paper into a story.

Langstaff, John. *Oh, A-Hunting We Will Go;* il. by Nancy Winslow Parker. Atheneum, 1974. The familiar folk song with enchanting illustrations.

Leisk, David Johnson. *Harold and the Purple Crayon,* by Crockett Johnson (pseud.); il. by author. Harper, 1958. A little boy draws simple pictures.

Lionni, Leo. *Little Blue and Little Yellow;* il. by author. McDowell, 1959. Use colored chalk in this adventure of two blobs of color which join to create green.

Olsen, Margaret J. *Tell and Draw Stories.* Arts and Crafts, Box 572, Minneapolis, MN 55440, 1963. Gives step-by-step drawings for short original stories.

Silverstein, Shel. *The Missing Piece;* il. by author. Harper, 1976. A circle searches for a missing part, only to discover that life loses its fascination when everything is too perfect. Simple, easy-to-reproduce drawings.

Wilder, Laura Ingalls. *On the Banks of Plum Creek;* il. by Helen Sewell and Mildred Boyle. Harper, 1937. pp. 318–19. A drawing of a duck is the final picture in this drawing story.

Withers, Carl. *The Tale of a Black Cat;* il. by Alan Cober. Holt, 1966. A picture-book version of a well-known drawing tale.

——— *The Wild Ducks and the Goose;* il. by Alan Cober. Holt, 1968. A goose emerges during the telling of this story.

Flannel or Felt Boards

The most popular boards for storytime use are the flannel and felt boards. Their popularity stems from the fact that they are inexpensive to produce and easily stored. Although the felt board is a little more costly to make than the flannel, its versatility more than justifies the extra expense.

A variety of different materials will stick to felt. Felt itself is probably the most popular choice for figure cutouts. It comes in vibrant colors and is readily available, already cut into squares, at craft and fabric shops. Pellon, a material which is used to stiffen fabrics, makes perfect felt board cutouts. It readily adheres to the felt or flannel board and can be colored with paint or crayon. Tagboard or any art paper may also be used. Simply paste sandpaper to the back of the cutout picture and it will stick to the board. Pattern spray, available in fabric stories, sprayed on the back of cutouts will also adhere them to felt. If you use this technique, place paper between the figures when storing them. The felt board is wonderfully useful to tell simple stories and to illustrate riddles and poems, but it may not be the most practical for your particular needs. Larger figures have a tendency to droop or

A red morning sky,
For you, snail;
Are you glad about it?
—Issa

Figure 17. Homemade
felt board

fall off the board, disrupting the story and the viewer's attention. Felt boards may be purchased commercially, but they are also easy to make.

To make a felt board you will need:

An artist's cardboard portfolio. These come in various sizes and can be purchased wherever art supplies are sold. The most versatile for classroom use is 17″ x 22″ folded. A larger size, for stage use in the auditorium, is 34″ x 42″.

Rubber cement

Felt cut to the size of the board. The color of the felt depends on your personal preference. White does show soil more quickly, but a less neutral color has its problems too. My portable felt board is red. I found to my chagrin that one of my favorite stories, Robert Bright's *My Red Umbrella* (Morrow, 1959), didn't work on my board. The leading character, the umbrella, which is red, doesn't show up on a red background and would have to become "My Blue Umbrella" to be seen on my board.

Plastic tape for binding. Simply glue the felt to the portfolio, trim with tape (it covers the edge for neatness), and you have a portable, easily stored felt board.

Figure 18. Magnetic board presentation

Magnetic Boards

A magnetic board utilizes magnets to attach pictures or artifacts to its surface. One of the advantages of the magnetic board is that pictures adhere quickly and securely, almost like magic. Even adults are impressed by the way pictures can be almost thrown onto the surface of the magnetic board, where they really stay put. Those who have had problems with objects falling from felt boards will welcome the use of this more secure method.

The board itself can be any metal surface to which a magnet will cling. For a small board to use with small groups of three or four children, the steel cookie sheet from your kitchen will work. In fact, the kitchen abounds in useful "magnetic boards." The refrigerator is the largest surface, but even your toaster will work. The side of a steel filing cabinet also makes a useful board if it happens to be well placed in your classroom or library. A magnetic board also can be cut to size by your local roofing supplier. Sheet metal shops will sell you sheet metal that can be framed in plywood. Sheet metal comes in different weights. The thinnest is, of course, lighter and more transportable, but it will flex unless mounted on plywood. A metal automobile drip pan, available in auto supply stores, can be used too. Magnetic boards are also available commercially. Look for these in toy departments and stationery stores.

To make the board more useful, buy a can of chalkboard paint which is available in a variety of colors. Paint the surface of the board; you now have a combination chalkboard and magnetic board to use with an easel. If you glue felt on the reverse side of your combination board you will have created a three-in-one board: magnetic, chalk, and felt.

Several types of magnets are now available for use with your magnetic board. The crafts or sewing department of the local variety store or the art department of the stationery store usually sells rubberized strip magnets. These magnetic strips, about ¾-inch wide and 12 inches long, are easily cut to length with scissors. These have an adhesive on one side that readily sticks to fabric, tagboard, or paper. Although the strip magnets might seem expensive, they can be reused again and again; and only a small piece is necessary to hold most cutouts to the board.

The small magnets that are used to stick potholders to a stove are available in the housewares department of your local hardware store, and although these are a little more cumbersome to use since you must affix the glue to them yourself, they are less expensive than the strips. Besides, if you plan to use heavier objects on your board, these small individual magnets are more serviceable since they can hold more weight. If you don't find magnets in your local stationery or department store; order them from a mail order craft and hobby supplier such as Kirchen Bros., Box C1016, Skokie, IL 60076. Write for a catalog. The Highsmith Co., Inc., Fort Atkinson, WI 53538, and Dick Blick, Galesburg, IL 61401, are other sources.

Using Paperbacks with Boards

Many delightful picture books are now in paperback form. You may wish to cut some of these up to use with your felt or magnetic board. Simply cut the figures from the book and mount each on thin cardboard. Glue sandpaper on the backs for use with a felt board or rubberized magnets for a magnetic board. In many instances you will need two copies of the book if you like to use every picture. Telling a favorite story with one of these boards will provide you and your audiences with a new and interesting change of pace.

A Felt or Magnetic Board Story

"The Strange Visitor," which follows, is popular at Halloween because the visitor's head can be represented as a pumpkin or jack-o-lantern. At other times of the year tell it without the aid of the board. The story is from Joseph Jacobs's *English Fairy Tales*, originally published in 1898, and reissued in paperback by two publishers, Schocken and Dover. In some collections the story is titled "Queer Company" and it has a more modern vocabulary. In this version the "reel" has become a spinning wheel, "broad soles" are shoes, and the refrain goes,

> And still she sat
> And still she spun
> And still she waited for someone to come.

I prefer the older version because the strange words add to the feeling of mystery. To heighten the mood this is best told while you are monotonously rocking in a rocking chair, with the felt board within easy reach. During the refrain repeat the same actions each time:

> And still she sat (fold hands)
> And still she reeled (roll hands)
> And still she wished for company (close eyes, rock back and forth)

The stage directions in the story are not mine. They are the collector's hints on how to tell this story effectively.

Cutouts needed for presentation as a felt-board story are the following parts of a man: shoes, legs, waist, shoulders, arms, hands, and a jack-o-lantern head.

> A woman was sitting at her reel one night;
>
> And still she sat, and still she reeled, and still she wished for company.
>
> In came a pair of broad broad soles, and sat down at the fireside;
>
> And still she sat, and still she reeled, and still she wished for company.
>
> In came a pair of small small legs, and sat down on the broad broad soles;
>
> And still she sat, and still she reeled, and still she wished for company.
>
> In came a pair of thick thick knees, and sat down on the small small legs;
>
> And still she sat, and still she reeled, and still she wished for company.
>
> In came a pair of thin thin thighs, and sat down on the thick thick knees;
>
> And still she sat, and still she reeled, and still she wished for company.
>
> In came a pair of huge huge hips, and sat down on the thin thin thighs;
>
> And still she sat, and still she reeled, and still she wished for company.
>
> In came a wee wee waist, and sat down on the huge huge hips;
>
> And still she sat, and still she reeled, and still she wished for company.
>
> In came a pair of broad broad shoulders, and sat down on the wee wee waist;
>
> And still she sat, and still she reeled, and still she wished for company.
>
> In came a pair of small small arms, and sat down on the broad broad shoulders;
>
> And still she sat, and still she reeled, and still she wished for company.
>
> In came a pair of huge huge hands, and sat down on the small small arms;

And still she sat, and still she reeled, and still she wished for company.

In came a small small neck, and sat down on the broad broad shoulders;

And still she sat, and still she reeled, and still she wished for company.

In came a huge huge head, and sat down on the small small neck.

"How did you get such broad broad feet?" quoth the woman.

"Much tramping, much tramping" (*gruffly*).

"How did you get such small small legs?"

"Aih-h-h! . . . late . . . and wee-e-e . . . moul" (*whiningly*).

"How did you get such thick thick knees?"

"Much praying, much praying" (*piously*).

"How did you get such thin thin thighs?"

"Aih-h-h! . . . late . . . and wee-e-e . . . moul" (*whiningly*).

"How did you get such big big hips?"

"Much sitting, much sitting" (*gruffly*).

"How did you get such a wee wee waist?"

"Aih-h-h! . . . late . . . and wee-e-e . . . moul" (*whiningly*).

"How did you get such broad broad shoulders?"

"With carrying broom, with carrying broom" (*gruffly*).

"How did you get such small small arms?"

"Aih-h-h! . . . late . . . and wee-e-e . . . moul" (*whiningly*).

"How did you get such huge huge hands?"

"Threshing with an iron flail, threshing with an iron flail" (*gruffly*).

"How did you get such a small small neck?"

"Aih-h-h! . . . late . . . wee-e-e . . . moul" (*pitifully*).

"How did you get such a huge huge head?"

"Much knowledge, much knowledge" (*keenly*).

"What do you come for?"

"FOR YOU!" (*At the top of the voice, with a wave of the arm and a stamp of the feet.*)

Books for Felt or Magnetic Board Use

Aesop. *The Miller, His Son, and Their Donkey;* il. by Roger Duvoisin. Whittlesey House, 1962. A limited number of figures will work with this fable.

Agostinelli, Maria. *I Know Something You Don't Know;* il. by author. Watts, 1970. An additional element creates a new picture.

Bonne, Rose. *I Know an Old Lady;* music by Alan Mills (pseud.); il. by Abner Graboff. Rand, 1961. Keep adding animals to this folksong.

Bright, Robert. *My Red Umbrella;* il. by author. Morrow, 1959. A small book to enlarge with board cutouts.

Carle, Eric. *The Very Hungry Caterpillar;* il. by author. World, 1970. An engaging story perfect for board telling.

Domanska, Janina. *The Turnip;* il. by author. Macmillan, 1969. Each new figure can be added separately as people and animals try to pull up an enormous turnip.

Elkin, Benjamin. *Six Foolish Fishermen;* il. by Katherine Evans. Children's Pr., 1957. The children will know immediately why one brother seems to be missing.

Geisel, Theodor Seuss. *And to Think that I Saw It on Mulberry Street,* by Dr. Seuss (pseud.); il. by author. Vanguard, 1937. Figures are added until the entire board is a grand parade.

Ginsburg, Mirra. *Which is the Best Place?;* il. by Roger Duvoisin. Macmillan, 1976. Each animal chooses a location to rest that is best suited to it.

Gunthorp, Karen. *Adam and the Wolf;* il. by Attilio Cassinelli. Doubleday, 1968. Adam tells stories to a wolf to keep from being eaten.

Hoberman, Mary Ann. *Bugs;* il. by Victoria Chess. Viking, 1976. Poetry that can be used with storyboards. Find or make your own pictures of insects to illustrate these poems.

Hutchins, Pat. *Good-Night, Owl!;* il. by author. Macmillan, 1972. Keep adding new birds to a tree as you tell the story.

Kahl, Virginia. *The Habits of Rabbits;* il. by author. Scribner, 1957. A lot of rabbit cutouts will be needed to tell this story.

Kunhardt, Dorothy. *Pudding Is Nice;* il. by author. The Bookstore Press (Lenox, Mass.), 1975. Pictures of what the old man is thinking of can be used on the board. Originally published in 1933 (Harcourt) as *Junket Is Nice.*

Lewis, Richard. *In a Spring Garden;* il. by Ezra Jack Keats. Dial, 1965. Japanese haiku to show and recite.

The Little Red Hen/La pequeña gallina roja, by Letty Williams; il. by Herb Williams; tr. by Doris Chávez and Ed Allen. Prentice, 1969. An old favorite retold in Spanish and English.

Morrison, Sean. *Is That a Happy Hippopotamus?;* il. by Aliki (pseud.). Crowell, 1966. Lots of animals and a surprise ending make for happy telling.

Shaw, Charles G. *It Looked Like Spilt Milk;* il. by author. Harper, 1947. A cloud can look like many things.

Slobodkina, Esphyr. *Caps for Sale;* il. by author. W. R. Scott, 1947. Caps and monkeys are the cutouts for this story of imitation.

Teal, Valentine. *The Little Old Woman Wanted Noise;* il. by Robert Lawson. Rand, 1943. The audience makes the animal noises as you tell the story.

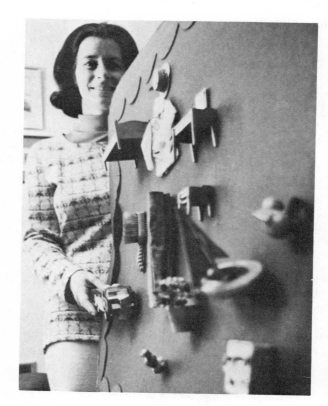

Figure 19. Telling a story
with the hook'n'loop
board

Hook 'n' Loop Board

A man walking in a field was annoyed to find his flannel trousers covered
with burrs afterward. However, his experience inspired him to develop the
two-part nylon fabric closure we all know by the trade name Velcro, which
works on the same principle as the burr: the tiny hooks on the one fabric
catch the tiny loops of the second fabric. If you don't recognize the name,
Velcro is often used as a closure on pockets and jackets in place of zippers
and buttons.

Although Velcro is comparatively expensive, its usefulness far outweighs
its cost, for you can hang almost anything with just a small piece. By anything, I mean anything from a sheet of paper to a heavy book. As you tell a
story, each object that you name can be hung on a board or a strip fastened
to the wall. Commercial boards are available from Charles Mayer, 140 E.
Market St., Akron, OH 44308, or if you want to make your own board, order
the fabric from him by the yard. Another possibility, if you feel that your use
of it would not justify the expense of an entire board, is to buy a strip of
Velcro (available by the yard where sewing notions are sold). Remember, it
comes in two parts and you need both the hook side and the loop side. Small
pieces of the loop side may be fixed to the other side of a felt or magnetic
board, or, if you always tell stories in the same location, you may want to
attach a strip to the wall and use it with stories involving three-dimensional
objects.

Be sure to use strong glue to affix the hook part to the selected object so that it doesn't pull away. It rarely, if ever, will pull away from the loops by itself. Once you have used Velcro you will find many other uses for it, perhaps holding puppet theaters together, and so on. *One caution:* Don't try to use the hooked side of Velcro on a felt board. It does not hold well to the felt. However, the loop side of a Velcro-covered board does function very well as a substitute felt board and sandpaper-backed objects will adhere to it satisfactorily.

Books for Hook 'n' Loop Board Use

ABC and counting books can often be adapted for hook 'n' loop board use. Hang the appropriate objects on the board for each letter and number.

Brandenburg, Aliki. *Keep Your Mouth Closed, Dear;* by Aliki (pseud.); il. by author. Dial, 1966. Hang the objects the crocodile swallows on the board.

Flack, Marjorie. *Ask Mr. Bear;* il. by author. Macmillan, 1958. Use gifts offered the animal as objects for the board.

Reit, Seymour. *The King Who Learned to Smile;* il. by Gordon Laite. Golden Pr., 1960. Dollhouse toys painted gold can represent the king's presents.

Rockwell, Anne and Harlow. *The Toolbox;* il. by authors. Macmillan, 1971. Hang actual tools on the board.

Still wondering what one board will serve all your storytelling purposes? I have no final advice for you. I found I have to have one of each. Keep them under a bed if you are cramped for space.

12 / *Slides and Filmstrips*

A most ingenious invention is the slide projector. It is easy to operate and its flexibility enables you to mix and match slides at your convenience. Since you operate the machine, you also control the speed of the presentation. The slide projector enables a large group of children to see a small book or intricate illustration with great clarity. You can use your own slides: pictures taken to illustrate a poem or folktale, hand-drawn slides to create realistic or abstract pictures, or slides from your own collection to illustrate a book talk. Commercially produced slides are available, too. The possibilities are endless. In fact, once fascinated with slides you might have a problem of overdoing with this medium. I thought that using slides in the classroom was such a wonderful way to teach that the whole quarter was being conducted in the dark and I had to reevaluate the class or be content to never see the faces of my students during that term I was so spellbound.

Equipment and Use

Start with a good piece of equipment. I've found that the carousel type of projector is one of the most versatile. The carousels hold a large number of slides and are easy to load and operate. A good machine enables you to go forward or reverse, to focus, or to voluntarily put a slide out of focus for effect. The machine is also relatively quiet. Some people like to combine their slides with a recorded sound track. I prefer to use slides and narrate them myself. This gives a certain intimacy and sense of sharing that is lost if both the visual and the audio are done mechanically and also lessens the chance of equipment failure since two machines can break down more easily than one. If you do have a projector jam, or any other catastrophe, during a presentation, try to fix it, but if the machine is obviously out of commission move on to another subject that doesn't need slides. Familiarity with the operation of a slide projector will lessen the chances of failure. Be sure that you know, for instance, how to remove a jammed slide. A dime inserted into the center screw of the carousel tray loosens the tray for easy removal. Don't panic—this does not happen often.

The use of a remote control extension cord is essential for an effective presentation. Set the machine in the back of the room and stand in front of the room next to the screen. Don't worry about lighting, the audience will see enough of you from the light spilling over from the screen. Seeing you gives the group a further visual interpretation of the story. They can look at the pictures and at the same time see your face in animated expression. As you tell the story, press the button that automatically advances the slide. It's like turning the page in a picture book. Make sure the image is properly focused before beginning the presentation.

Copying

It is possible to reproduce a book in whole or in part using color slides. Although this generation has been exposed to many machines, there is still something fascinating about turning out the lights and turning on a magic projector. To produce your own slides you will need a 35mm camera, a copy lens, and high speed film. To ensure quality pictures use a tripod or copy stand to make certain the camera does not move during shooting. These copying kits are available commercially—Kodak sells one for the Instamatic camera—or you can convert your own equipment. If you work for a school system, you might have access to a media center which owns copying equipment, or they might have personnel who will take the pictures for you. A photographic workshop may also be available in your community.

This method of presentation may seem expensive. Remember, however, that you are spending your time, effort, and money not for a single presentation, but for many years of stories to be told to many children.

What to Copy

You can copy pictures from books. You can copy art pictures, or pictures drawn by your own students, but whatever you choose, be cautious and avoid violating the author's or artist's copyright.

Handmade Slides

To realize the full potential of the projector, experiment with making your own slides by hand. Cardboard or plastic slide mounts can be purchased for a few pennies each. Three common sizes are: half frame, regular 35mm, and 2x2 super slide size. The larger slide is of course easier to work with, but different sizes add variety. Acetate cut to size can be mounted in the slide holders to produce a drawing surface. The holder is then sealed by using a low heat clothes iron around the edges. Use permanent ink felt pens to draw on your slides and let your imagination and creative instincts run wild.

For a variation on hand-drawn slides, you can draw pictures on a sheet of paper. Use a slide mount as a stencil to show the exact size of the opening. Press the paper with a sheet of transparent film through a thermofax machine that reproduces your pictures as transparencies. Now you can mount the pictures into the slide mounts. One of my students used this method by making tiny drawings to illustrate animal poems. Using the thermofax enables the artist to achieve finer lines and subtleties.

Glass slides, available at your camera store, offer a creative challenge. Between two pieces of thin glass you can mount actual objects: moss, leaves, string, or paper cutouts. You can also make use of the fact that glass slides warm up when projected. This adds a dimension of texture and movement. Use a few drops of cooking oil between the slides, colored with food coloring. The heat of the slide projector will cause the oil to expand and move, giving a colorful, shifting illusion. To prevent the liquid from running into the machine, tape the glass together. Using glass or acetate, experiment with string, sequins, tissue paper, construction paper, gelatins, and any other interesting material you can think of. Remember that if the material is not transparent or translucent, it will appear as a silhouette on the screen. That's all right, of course. I'm just trying to spare you my experience of laboriously pasting string of different colors to 2x2 mounts to give the appearance of a string web growing and contracting in multi-colored shapes. The string appeared solid and all the color turned out to be a black silhouette, but it was an intriguing effect anyway.

Photographic Slides

Take pictures of children acting out a poem or a story. Show them for your next storyhour. Sort through your private collection of slides. Will any of them fit naturally into a story you have already learned, or would like to learn? Could the pictures you took on your trip to Germany introduce a Grimm's tale, or the pictures you took at "Four Corners" make a good finish to an Indian storyhour? Maybe your pictures of New York would set the scene for a program featuring urban stories or books centered in and around New York. Have you been collecting pictures of rain, bridges, sunsets? They might fit into the mood of the stories you are telling at your next session. Always remember, however, that too few are better than too many. If your pictures are of poor quality—out of focus or overexposed—it's better to try again. Show only pictures you can be proud of, and don't tire your audience with too many. Do not subject your audience to the "home movie syndrome."

Screens

Experiment with screens as well as slides. The rear projection screen will give an unusual effect in your presentations and eliminate the beam of light thrown from the back of the room. The screen is translucent; a piece of matte acetate or a white sheet will do. The slide projector is placed behind, instead of in front of, the screen. The storyteller can stand in front of the screen without fear of having the slide project directly on her or him. The rear projection screen is most useful to create unobstructive backgrounds. A single slide can be projected throughout the story of a busy street, a quiet mountain, or a ship at sea to set the scene.

Consider using two projectors and two screens or even three of each. Choose slides that complement each other to show at the same time, or actually plan a three-screen performance. Take a scene in three picture sections, with the idea of multiple projection. You may decide to use two screens simply to give continuity to your program. As one picture fades out, fade the next picture in. You will need an electronic switching device to control both projectors. Ask your local camera store or media department for information.

Another idea for projection is to hang a curved screen around your room—a white sheet hung on a rope will provide a reasonable substitute for a continuous screen. Or simply give a show on a wall, shifting the position of the projector for variety. Try showing your slides, handmade or photographed, on something other than a flat screen. You can experiment with tubes or cylinders made from construction paper taped to the wall. Or use the floor on which you have placed irregular shapes as a screen. You can even use your hands or body. Once you have made the decision to use slides, creative variety in using them may add a new element to the magic of machines.

Filmstrips

Filmstrips are nothing more than a series of slides on a continuous roll of film. They have advantages and disadvantages over slides. A filmstrip projector is so easy to operate that a young child or an uncoordinated Daddy can work it. The danger of misplacing or getting slides out of order is eliminated. On the other hand, because you can't change the order of the slides you can never be creative.

Filmstrips are particularly good for individuals or small groups to use to entertain themselves because the equipment is easy to operate. Consider setting up a storytelling media booth in one area of the library or classroom. If you have a "No Quiet Please" library you won't have to construct a soundproof booth. Simple folding screens will be adequate. Use a dark piece of cloth for the roof to help shield the light. A small screen can be mounted on the wall. Three or four people can then sit on the floor and view a filmstrip.

There are some excellently produced commercial filmstrips of picture books. Threshold Filmstrips/Macmillan, Weston Woods, and Miller-Brody have used the original book illustrations for many of their filmstrips. However, as with the purchase of any book or medium, you must know what you're buying. For some reason, many filmstrips have been the victim of inadequate illustrating; in fact, outrageous imitations of art are often used with flimsy text. A further problem is the practice of adding text to the image enabling the viewer to "read-along" with the pictures. In group viewing this is particularly distracting. Filmstrips are also available with sound. Again, chosen with care, these make for good individual viewing, but some have a "beep" that warns the viewer when the filmstrip is to be advanced—these can make the viewer/operator feel like an automaton.

If you use a sound filmstrip you eliminate the need for a live storyteller, which changes the character of the storyhour. Since the personal interaction of storyteller and audience is lost, sound filmstrips should be used as a supplementary storytelling technique.

I rarely use filmstrips in a group situation. When I first discovered them, there were so few of high quality that it seemed to me the expense of purchasing the filmstrips or the equipment was unwarranted. Since I've discovered that some good ones are being produced I've used them sparingly with classes, mostly because I'm intrigued with "make it yourself" filmstrips and now own a projector.

Making Your Own Filmstrips. Adults may find it fun to draw their own filmstrips, but I've found it a fascinating project for children as well. Illustrating stories or poems with felt tip markers or ballpoint pens can be a creative, fulfilling individual or group project. Some of the films in the kits can be reused, which cuts the cost while experimenting.

Sources for Purchase of Filmstrip Kits

Draw Your Own Filmstrip and Slide Kit, distributed by Scholastic Book Services, 50 W. 44th St., New York, N.Y. 10036, contains materials for making slides and filmstrips.

Multi-Media Learning Materials, produced by Hudson Photographic Industries, Inc., and distributed by Miller-Brody Productions, 342 Madison Ave., New York, NY 10017, contains blank filmstrip or U film, markers, a splicer, and a guide.

U-Film Kit, available from Miller-Brody Productions, 342 Madison Ave., New York, NY 10017, contains blank film, colored markers, storage cans, and a framing guide.

References: Slides and Filmstrips

Cooke, Robert W. *Designing with Light on Paper and Film.* Davis, 1969. Explains how to make pictures without a camera using photographic paper, light, and various objects.

Eastman Kodak. *Classroom Projects Using Photography;* Part I: For the Elementary School Level; Part II: For the Secondary School Level. Eastman Kodak, 1975. Photography ideas in outline form.

Greene, Ellin, and Schoenfeld, Madalynne, comps. *A Multimedia Approach to Children's Literature: A Selective List of Films, Filmstrips, and Recordings Based on Children's Literature.* American Library Assn., 1972. An annotated guide to commercially prepared filmstrips and other media.

Marte, Harold. *Photo Design: Picture Composition for Black and White Photogra-*

phy. Van Nostrand Reinhold, 1971. *Color Design,* Van Nostrand Reinhold, 1972. Outstanding explanations of theories of composition with illustrative pictures.

Scheffer, Victor B. *The Seeing Eye.* Scribner, 1971. An inspiring text complements the color photographs introducing form, texture and color in nature.

Slides with a Purpose: For Business and Education. Kodak, 1972. Pamphlet describes production and presentation of slides. Kodak can answer questions. Write: Eastman Kodak Co., Dept. 412L, Rochester, NY 14650.

Sullivan, George. *Understanding Photography.* Warne, 1972. A basic book primarily for children.

Tiemann, Ernest F. *Production of 2x2 Inch Slides for School Use.* Univ. of Texas, 1970. Simplified directions for copying and processing of slides.

13 / The Overhead Projector

The overhead projector is so versatile that in many instances it is actually replacing that age-old traditional teacher's helper, the chalkboard, probably because the overhead projector, unlike the slide projector, can be used effectively with the lights on. The storyteller may face the audience while writing or drawing on acetate and can also produce transparencies in advance, thereby saving time and allowing preparation of slides of greater clarity. I used the overhead as a teaching device in my children's literature classes for several years before it occurred to me to use it for storytelling; it opened a whole new world of possibilities. Some aspects of using the overhead may not occur to you while you're in the process of telling a story, so consider them in advance. Be sure that your transparencies are in order—they may have become mixed up after your last performance. Make certain that you stand to the side of the projector so that you don't block the screen from the audience. Make sure that the projector lens is in focus. It always amazes me that adults are often so polite that they will let you go through an entire session with your transparencies out of focus or with your arm blocking their view and never say a word. If you are working with children, you needn't worry about these problems. Children will tell you if they can't see properly. Also make sure that you don't leave the overhead on without a transparency, so that all the audience sees as you talk is a distracting, glaring light. The same transparency should not be left on indefinitely. When your audience has

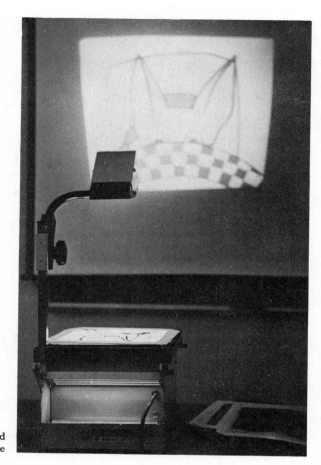

Figure 20. The overhead
projector and storytime

received the information from the transparency, change it or turn off the machine. Most overheads have a fan that automatically turns itself on and off to cool the machine. Remember to speak loudly enough to be heard over the whir of the motor. Practice with your story and the transparencies so that you will give a smooth delivery. If you find yourself without an overhead, but a pile of transparencies, you can hold them up to a window for illumination if the group is small enough. You can also mount them accordion fashion with a light behind them. As you tell your story, move the transparencies past the light.

Experiment with your overhead. The light reflector can be moved in many directions, enabling you to project up, down, and around. You can place acetate on the surface and write or draw on it while you talk. Some machines come equipped with a roll of acetate that rolls out of sight when not in use. You can place an opaque object on the overhead and its shape will project, thereby creating a shadow show. You can even use it to project liquid color, for a light show effect. And, of course, transparencies of all descriptions may be used.

Uses

Light Show Magic

Take a clear glass pie dish and fill it halfway with water. Float a few drops of food coloring and cooking oil on the water. Put the dish and its contents on an overhead and gently turn the dish. Magic shapes will appear on your screen or wall. Tell your story with the moving colors as a background, or simply play music as an accompaniment to the rhythmic designs.

Trace a Transparency

Use either prepared transparencies (these are cut to fit the overhead and mounted with a cardboard frame) or be more economical and buy a roll of acetate and some frames, separately. Materials are available in most art supply shops. You will also need felt pens. Oil-base pens are permanent; water-base pens are for temporary use, made to easily wipe off with a damp cloth. Choose a book that has simple line drawings. Place the acetate over the book and trace some of the pictures. Now you have reproduced pictures to be shown on an overhead projector. Color can be applied to the acetate with felt pens or even paint. The color should be even and translucent so that the light shows through. Make sure that you have a copy of the book available to hold up and show to the group before you show the transparencies and tell the story.

Photocopy Transparency Machines

Many school systems, libraries, or offices have access to machines which can produce transparencies from an original drawing or from photocopied portions of a book. The original sheet, together with a piece of transparency film, is run through the machine producing a black-and-white image which may later be colored with gelatins glued to the surface.

Again, be careful not to violate copyright restrictions when copying.

Overlays

It's possible to create an interesting effect by using one transparency on top of another. Using *Little Red Riding Hood* as an example, you could begin with a transparency of a little girl. The next layer could be her cloak. The next one the basket she carries. Leaving these three slides on the overhead you could add the wolf and so on. Remember too that you can use prepared transparencies and draw on an acetate overlay with a felt pen. You can create movement by having a single character or animal on one transparency and the background on another transparency. By moving one or the other, animation is simulated.

Books for Overhead Projector Use

Burningham, John. *Mr. Gumpy's Outing;* il. by author. Holt, 1970. The addition of animals into a boat suggests the use of overlays.

Burton, Virginia. *The Little House;* il. by author. Houghton, 1942. The progressively growing city around the little house might be effective with overlays.

Flack, Marjorie. *Angus and the Ducks;* il. by author. Doubleday, 1930. Simple illustrations and an easy-to-tell story for young children.

Gág, Wanda. *Millions of Cats;* il. by author. Coward, 1928. This classic picture book readily lends itself to overhead projection at storytime.

Kahl, Virginia. *The Duchess Bakes a Cake;* il. by author. Scribner, 1955. The Duchess bakes a "lovely light luscious delectable cake."

Krauss, Ruth. *Bears;* il. by Phyllis Rowand. Harper, 1948. This can be used with very young children.

Lionni, Leo. *Inch by Inch;* il. by author. I. Obolensky, 1960. Use an inchworm cut-out to move on the drawings.

———— *The Biggest House in the World;* il. by author. Pantheon, 1968. A snail's house grows and grows.

———— *Swimmy;* il. by author. Pantheon, 1963. The underwater scenes in this book suggest overhead possibilities.

14 / *Film*

The film industry has changed in the last generation. There is no longer the mystique of Hollywood and its stars. Yet the film as an art form has flourished, particularly among amateurs or semiprofessionals. Film, of course, is the mainstay of television, but some TV films are hurriedly, if inexpensively, produced. Despite TV, most children still consider a film showing to be a special treat. For this reason you may want to set up a special storytelling film series, or you may want to schedule a film for a particular storyhour.

Commercial Films

There are many good film companies, small and large, producing good and not-so-good films. It takes time and much critical viewing to choose a film for a particular group. Since the objective of a book program is to introduce or enrich a child's experience with books, an obvious choice for your film program is a film based on a children's book or story.

Choosing the Film

Some excellent films based on children's books have been made. Some use animation (*Madeline*); some have actors (*Homer Price*); and some are iconographic (*The Snowy Day*), actually filming the book, but moving the camera in and around the illustrations to give the illusion of movement. The length of a film may be important if you have a scheduling problem such as a school class period. Film lengths range from three and four minutes to two hours. If you decide to use several short picture-book films, you may want to use both iconographic and animated films (real actors are used primarily in longer stories). You may want to keep a particular theme for your film program, perhaps animal stories, fairy tales, adventure stories. If you decide to combine films and storytelling, tell your stories first, then show the film. It may be that the story you tell will be the activity that will remain in the children's memory, but a film, particularly if it is of high quality, is momentarily more exciting. If you are searching for a film based on children's literature, you will want a copy of Ellin Greene and Madelynne Schoenfeld's *A Multimedia Approach to Children's Literature* (American Library Assn., 1972), which lists films and distributors. Other fine children's films with original stories, information, or even abstract themes might be possibilities for your film programs. For recommendations of films (and other nonprint media) see ALA's *The Booklist* which is published twice a month, except in August. The Bowker publication *Previews* now lists and reviews films, and *The Horn Book Magazine* gives reviews of selected films that often are based on children's books. You may buy a film, but depending on your finances, renting films is probably more practical.

Films are not as easy to evaluate as books; you can't usually cuddle up with one on the beach or on a camping trip, but previewing all films before you use them is an absolute necessity. Unhappy surprises can await you if you rely on the brief description in a dealer's catalog. Films with live actors become quickly dated as hair styles and fashions change. No matter how good the story or message, if the people are supposed to be in a present-day setting and look dated and old-fashioned, the children may be distracted from the message. Even a film with an historical fiction setting can become dated. Today's dialogue moves faster, audiences are trained to assume the passage of time, instead of being shown the pages of a calendar flipping.

Films that have a lecturer sitting immobile behind a desk will rarely hold the attention of a group. Even the films you used two years ago should be reviewed again to make sure they are still appropriate. Many books and professionals give a long checklist to be used when previewing a film, and while these may be useful, my personal advice is that if you actually watch a film, you will best know if it fits the group's needs and interests. Do you like it? Show it.

Showing a Film

Films come in a variety of formats: 8mm, Super 8mm, and 16mm. The larger size (16mm) is used by most commercial producers. Each size of film requires its own size projector, so be sure you match the projector to the film and vice versa.

The greatest boon to uncoordinated film threaders is the cassette or film loop which is designed for a child to operate. You just put a box-like affair into a machine, press a button, and view the sequence of pictures. Originally, these loop films were made for instructional purposes, but now many storytelling films are available in this format. In fact you can instruct the film developer to put almost any film into cartridges for easier use. Some of the newer Super-8 projectors can be cartridge loaded if the film is prepared that way. In any event, you must have a competent projectionist to operate the projector. If you are not well versed on the great variety of projectors, either bring one with which you are familiar or make sure that a projectionist is on hand.

Remember that to show a film you will need the film, the proper projector, a screen, and often an extension cord. I usually bring a cord and an adapter (for three prong plugs), even if I've been promised the proper equipment. It's frustrating to arrive at a location and find that the cord doesn't reach to the plug outlet.

Now you are ready to show the film. No one wants to hear a long lecture before a film, but some sort of introduction is in order. You might mention why you chose the film, or explain that it is similar in theme to the rest of the program. Perhaps it has won a prize, or uses an interesting technique. If the book is based on a film, point out that the library has a copy or hopefully several copies of the book to circulate. Other books by the author, or books on the same theme, may also be exhibited.

If there is more than one film on the program, introduce each film just before the showing. Don't try to make announcements or speeches after the program, unless it is to remind the audience of the next program, since people are usually ready to leave after the last film.

Be prepared for the worst. Although films and film projectors seem to be magic, something can go awry. The film can break, the sound can blur. If some disaster of this sort should happen, try to repair the damage, keeping the audience posted of your valiant efforts. People are more patient if they know the cause of the delay. If the damage is irreparable it is better to abandon the film than show one that is impossible to understand. You will now be happy that you are a storyteller, since you can always tell a story in place of the film. However, having the proper equipment and knowing how to run it is still the best insurance against technical problems.

Making Films

With a Camera

You can make your own movies. You may not want to show your first efforts in public, but the making is as much fun as the final effort. Film clubs abound and you can find many kindred souls. Equipment ranges from the very simple to the very professional and may be available on rental basis at your camera store. A simple and inexpensive movie camera can produce surprisingly good shows. The more expensive automatic equipment can give you professional results with a minimum of technical ability. Super-8 cameras are the most popular for the amateur.

Filmmaking can be divided into technical and creative activities. The person who enjoys fiddling with equipment may not be the same person who enjoys the creative aspect of filmmaking. Most of us, however, can't afford to sit in a chair marked "Producer" or "Director" thinking creative thoughts. You'll have to learn a little about both operations in order to begin. This is the important part: if you think you might be interested in filmmaking, begin with an inexpensive or second-hand camera, and, if you enjoy the process and are pleased with the effort, you can take filmmaking more seriously.

Start small. Don't try for too much action at first. If possible, film outdoors in sunlight—it's simply easier than trying to learn about indoor lighting. Hold your camera steady or use a tripod. You must plan what to shoot. Nursery rhymes or simple familiar folktales, such as *The Three Bears,* make good subjects to begin with. Use your own storytelling group as the actors or make your film the culmination of a project in creative dramatics.

Without a Camera

Fiddle-de-dee, a short film put out by the National Film Board of Canada, provided me with my first glimpse into the fascinating world of making films without a camera. The filmmaker, Norman McLaren, pioneered work in animation and drawing directly onto the film to produce fascinating effects. Lines of color drawn directly on the film surface seem to dance to the sound of music. Some adults who are accustomed to a story line have difficulty relating to this abstract art; most children, however, appreciate that not all of life needs to have an understandable theme. They let their imaginations go and simply enjoy what they see on the screen.

I thought it might be fun to try one of these films. As a student with a limited budget, I naturally wanted to experiment as cheaply as possible. I used discarded, overexposed film from the university film department and spliced bits and pieces together. If you do splice, be sure to keep the sprocket holes matched. I tried to time my film to music, laboriously counting the frames per second. My first effort was terribly time-consuming and resulted in only three minutes worth of film, but it was really fun to do, and my students and children I show it to now seem genuinely to like it. There are several techniques that may be used.

Scratch films. If you have access to discarded 16mm film which is underexposed or black, you can try the scratch film technique. A good source of film is a motion picture processing laboratory, so use the yellow pages of your phone book to find the one nearest you. If underexposed 16mm film is not available, the motion picture processing laboratory may sell black leader for sound films (single or double perforation) in rolls of 150 or more feet. The cost for scrap film or black leader should be a few cents per foot.

Take a knife, stylus, or scissors blade and scratch away the exposed emulsion at random. One way to determine the film's emulsion side is to wet your finger and touch it to the film. The surface that sticks to your finger is the emulsion side. Strips, blotches, and spots all create interesting designs that project shapes onto the screen. You may want to experiment a bit attempting to put film to music. Keep in mind that 24 frames (or seven inches of film) equal one second. If you want to set your scratch film to music, theoretically you time sections of the music, then measure off the amount of film, and start scratching, but my own experience is that almost any fast music will seem to fit your handmade film since the abstract blobs and blotches seem to follow any jazzy beat. My advice, therefore, is to experiment with your first film. Find out if you enjoy working with the medium. And, after you have produced a few minutes of film, you can move on to a more sophisticated method.

Hand-drawn films. Now that you have tried the scratch-film technique and found out how much fun it is, you are ready for a more advanced method.

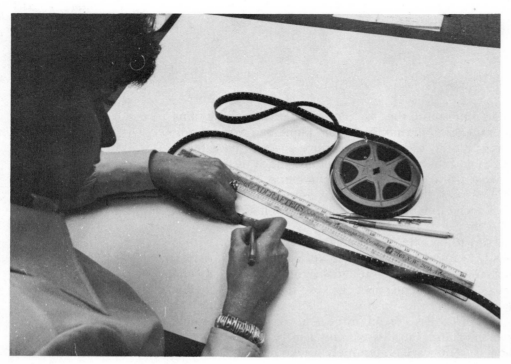

Figure 21. Making a
hand-drawn film

Buy clear 16mm film from the motion picture laboratory or film processor, or, if you have access to discarded film, you can always bleach it yourself. Dip the unrolled film into a strong solution of household bleach. Wait several seconds, then rinse it under water, and hang it up to dry.

Any water-soluble coloring—felt pens, colored inks, watercolors, food coloring—will work on the film. Again, draw on the emulsion side. I prefer working with felt pens, since these dry faster than the other mediums.

Felt pens and film, now what? You can continue with the idea of setting your work to music or try illustrating a story, perhaps Little Red Riding Hood, for example can be represented with a red circle for the heroine, mother can be a somewhat larger blue circle. Don't forget Little Red Riding Hood's basket—a small orange circle. Now you need the forest, represented by green lines and multicolored dots for the flowers. Depict the wolf as a large black circle and grandmother as a purple oblong shape. When the wolf eats the grandmother, put the purple shape inside the black circle. The woodcutter who saves the girl and her grandmother can be a brown circle. A good way to represent the conflict between the wolf and the woodcutter is a series of frames with black fragments flying all about in each.

How to begin. Measure 14 inches of masking tape and affix it to your worktable. This represents two seconds of film time, and enables you to instantly calculate, or guesstimate, film time. The blank film will probably be rolled up on a metal reel. As you work on the film, just let it drop off the edge of your worktable and spill onto the floor. (If you find that this has become a hobby, not just an experiment, you can rent a hand-operated film viewer, which will also have a take-up reel, to examine your work in progress.)

Now time the text of the story. This does not need to be completely accurate but more time allowed rather than less for each scene is advised. To say, "This is Little Red Riding Hood," takes about five seconds, which is approximately 2½ feet of film, or 120 frames. Using your masking tape guide of 14 inches, or 2 seconds, you will have to draw 2½ feet of red circles, one inside each frame.

I strongly advise that if you go beyond the abstract stage and get into a text, that you find a corner where you can set up a permanent worktable. When I'm working on a film, I find an odd 10 minutes here and there, just before dinner, just before going to bed, and so forth. I go into my workshop (the utility room), draw on a foot or so of film, then leave everything as I found it and go on with my life. Eventually the film is finished.

The ultimate in handmade films is the laborious process of actually drawing a story. Each action must be repeated countless times for it to appear as smooth action to the eye. For this kind of film, you will need, besides the proper equipment, infinite patience and a steady hand.

Your children's book group may be inspired to try this noncamera kind of filmmaking, too. You can give each child a length of film to work with or you can let a child work on the film and when he or she finishes, give it to the next child. This eliminates splicing together several short lengths of film. However, if it is more convenient to give each child a separate length of film to work on, the children can learn how to splice the film themselves.

A Final Word

Obviously it would take almost an entire book to explore the intricacies of making a film with camera or without. The basic rule here, as elsewhere, is that you must jump in and try it. Start simply and you may find yourself fascinated and ready to devote some extra time to a new technique.

References: More about Making Films

Andersen, Yvonne. *Make Your Own Animated Movies: Yellow Ball Workshop Film Techniques*. Little, 1970.

Children Are Centers for Understanding Media. Association for Childhood Education International, 1973. Selected articles on the how-tos of filmmaking with children. Animation, flipbooks, and scratch films are discussed.

Colman, Hila. *Making Movies: Student*

Films to Features; il. by George Guzzi. World, 1969. Articulate explanations.

Ferguson, Robert. *How to Make Movies: A Practical Guide to Group Film-Making.* Help for classroom and other filmmakers. Viking, 1969.

Film Library Quarterly. Film Library Information Council, 17 W. 60th St., New York, NY 10023. Reviews of 16mm films and articles on filmmaking.

Helfman, Harry. *Making Your Own Movies.* Morrow, 1970. Preparation, equipment, and actual filming are discussed.

Rynew, Arden. *Filmmaking for Children.* Pflaum/Standard, 1971. Teacher and student handbook.

Weiss, Harvey. *How to Make Your Own Movies.* Young Scott, 1973. For beginners who want to try making films.

References: Films and How to Use Them

Greene, Ellin, and Schoenfeld, Madalynne, comps. *A Multimedia Approach to Children's Literature: A Selective List of Films, Filmstrips, and Recordings Based on Children's Books.* American Library Assn., 1972. A useful tool indeed for the multimedia storyhour program.

Limbacher, James L. *Using Films: A Handbook for the Program Planner.* New York

Educational Film Library Assn., 1967. Film use in libraries, museums, schools, and churches. Lists sources for films.

Rice, Susan, and Ludlum, Barbara, comps. *Films Kids Like, A Catalog of Short Films for Children.* American Library Assn. for Center for Understanding Media, 1973. Annotated list of "child-tested" films.

15 / Television and Radio

Television has become a way of life for many Americans. If you still have the idea that television is a curse, remember that the children you serve take it for granted and enjoy it. Instead of fighting it, use it to your advantage.

There are from time to time really excellent children's specials on commercial television, carefully produced films that are based on children's books. Although television viewing is usually considered a home activity, many schools, libraries and other institutions own television sets. If your library doesn't own a set, you might want to make this a project for your "Friends of the Library" or arrange to have one "donated" by your local TV shop. Keeping informed of good programs can sometimes be a problem if you are not in the habit of reading that section of your newspaper or *TV Guide. Tele-*

vision Highlights, mailed monthly from the Television Information Office (745 Fifth Ave., New York, NY 10019), is an excellent source of information and one which may be put on a bulletin board for parents as well. I wouldn't suggest that a storyhour be held around a TV set, but when there is a worthwhile program, you might plan to turn it on for those children who are in the library at the time.

You should also be aware of offerings on TV if you are working in a school or library. If a television show is based on a children's book you will want to have the book available. The TV series *Lassie* might occasion an exhibit of worthwhile dog books. The cartoon rendition of *Babar* on television should be accompanied by the *Babar* books available and ready to check out.

Occasionally watch some of the more popular programs yourself; then think of books which might have the same appeal or a theme that is similar to a particular series. A family series might suggest the Laura Ingalls Wilder "Little House" books. An adventure series might bring to mind Swift's *Gulliver's Travels*, T. H. White's *Mistress Masham's Repose* (Putnam, 1946), or Mary Norton's *The Borrowers* (Harcourt, 1953). Exhibit such books with a sign that draws a comparison to a favorite TV series. And if Captain Kangaroo or any other program host features a book on the show, why not prominently display a copy of that book, as well as other titles by the same author?

You might remember, too, that if you like or dislike something on television, a letter to the local station and network will be appreciated and noticed. If you'd like to be more actively involved in improving children's programming, write for materials from ACT (Action for Children's Television, 46 Austin St., Newtonville, MA 02160).

Public television was in the past sometimes referred to as "educational television," but that seemed to mean that its programs were not entertaining; now we say "public television" and more viewers tune in as a result. Surprisingly, it was children's television that finally made public television come alive for many people. After years of mediocre children's offerings on commercial TV, the Children's Television Workshop produced *Sesame Street*, a series designed to provide an educational opportunity for culturally deprived preschool children. The program was an instant success, and six months into the first season the Nielsen rating survey indicated that it was watched by over half of America's twelve million three- to five-year-olds. This daily program has inspired similar ones for the primary grades.

Locally produced programs for children are increasing. Storytelling shows take their place in programming. For instance, in Oregon the Oregon Educational Public Broadcasting System offers a series designed for in-school viewing developed as a traditional storytelling program. In its first season the

Oregon Library Association donated funds to help make the series available after school as well. The program, *Caroline's Corner,* is simply conceived. The storyteller tells a traditional folktale in a rather stark setting, relying on the words of the stories and facial expressions to carry the show.

In this age of advanced technology the producer of the show (I'll confess, it's me) was a bit worried that without any films, slides, puppets, or other paraphernalia the show would not be well received. Instead it turned out to be quite a success. There is now a viewer's guide for *Caroline's Corner* that suggests further reading and related individual and group activities for each of the shows.

The public library in Portland (Multnomah County Library), Oregon, successfully produces its own storytelling series for Sunday morning viewing. Using its own children's librarians as talent, the show's format includes reading and showing picture books, riddles, and simple songs. Perhaps your community has interesting storytelling programs too. If not, perhaps you can start one.

Producing a Television Show

Videotape

In today's world, you can make your own television tapes as easily as making an audiotape. The equipment is still prohibitively expensive for most small institutions, but many larger ones already own TV cameras, receivers, and videotape machines.

Videotape is most often used for instructional purposes: for enlarging a small object so that a big group can see it, for taping visiting lecturers, and for teacher and pupil speech practice. Why not use it for storytelling? You could record stories on tape and play them back to individual children or small groups, or you could record the children themselves. Videotape is also one of the most effective means of self-teaching. Your faults become painfully obvious and you can work on correcting them during your next story-hour. Try not to think of videotape exclusively as a performance medium. Think of television as just one more way to tell a story.

Studio Television

If you should have the opportunity to do a single show or a series of shows for an educational or commercial television station, be prepared for a new experience.

The storyteller (or talent) is only one of the many people who make a television program possible. There are camera operators, a floorperson (who gives time cues and directs the performer from camera to camera), audio engineers (who control the sound), switchers (who put the picture on the air), the director (who is responsible for the artistic feel of the show), and the engineer (who ultimately puts the show on tape and into homes). There may be a producer and even an executive producer (the program's idea people).

As the talent you may find the experience frustrating as well as exciting. You will be performing for an unseen audience and will be expected to be your most expressive for a red light on the lens of a television camera. At first I found it difficult to relate to machines. Even the people in the studio seemed mechanical. When I finished a program I'd say to the camera operator, "Did you like that story?" He would apologize and explain that he didn't hear the story, but only saw it. The same was true of the audio engineer. He heard the story, but didn't see it, and anyway he didn't actually listen. Sometimes I would invite a friend to the studio and I'd play to the friend. Afterwards I found they didn't listen either. They were much too interested in the complicated process of filming a show. Now, after several years of television experience, I think I've finally reached the right attitude. The lens of the camera is a "person," the one individual to whom you are talking. The lens may represent hundreds or even thousands of viewers, but you must feel that you are talking to just one person. Look directly into the camera, not at the floorperson or the monitor. If it is your first time on television, you'll probably be better off not having a monitor in view. People get so fascinated seeing themselves on TV that they start watching themselves, instead of performing.

If you appear as a guest on someone's live show, you'll probably be asked to appear a few minutes before the program to meet the host. You may even be asked to rehearse before the show. This gives you a chance to get used to the lights and microphone. If the show is to be taped, there is usually more time allotted so that the show has a better chance of achieving perfection. This will mean a rehearsal, and often many delays while lights are arranged and the sound adjusted. It's possible that you might make a mistake, but there is a chance to re-do your mistake with tape. There may be a make-up man to help you with your make-up. If not, use your street make-up. If you are accustomed to wearing eyeshadow, be sparing. It might make your eyes look cavernous. Larger television stations often have newer sophisticated equipment that can tape almost anything, but the local station may own older cameras so don't wear clothing that is shiny or terribly bright.

If you are thinking of using children on the show, you should be aware that they probably will be awed by the equipment and may not perform as they usually do. Don't try to get too carried away with props and special effects unless you have many people to help you. Because television is a visual medium there is a great temptation for amateurs to over-visualize a show. A single narrator articulately explaining a process or describing an event can be more effective than a poorly filmed or amateurishly drawn picture. Remember the screen on which people will see your show is very small.

Studio television requires an entire production staff to produce the simplest of programs. In my storytelling series I told stories without the aid of props on a simple set, and yet many people were involved in the taping of each program. If you are involved in even the simplest professional production you will need the following personnel:

Executive producer: Responsible for executive decisions that initiate a series or program.

Producer: Responsible for getting together the people, the content, and the props for a series or program.

Director: Coordinates the activities of all the people involved in production. Makes the artistic selection of images and sound for program airing.

Camera operators: Operate the studio cameras on the director's command.

Talent: The person or persons who perform in front of the cameras.

Floorperson: Gives hand signals to the talent that indicate when and in which direction to move or look and how much time remains in the program. The floorperson is the communication link between the director and the talent.

Audio engineer: Responsible for the audio portion of the program. This includes musical backgrounds and sound levels for the talent.

Boom operator: Operates an overhead microphone in the studio.

Video engineer: Responsible for the technical quality of television images.

Lighting technician: Responsible for studio lighting.

Switcher: Switches and mixes images on director's command.

Videotape operator: Operates and maintains videotape machine. Controls the electronic side of editing.

Chain engineer: Responsible for feeding film clips and slides onto videotape.

Graphic designers: Create the visuals, including slide titles.

Set designer: Responsible for designing the studio set.

Don't be awed by this mob of people. They are there to help you put on a fine production. Think of the small family group that used to hear a storyteller's voice. With the aid of television you can tell stories in thousands of homes at once. Keep your part in the performance simple and, above all, have fun.

References: Television

Production

Alkin, Glyn. *TV Sound Operations* (Media Manuals Series). Hastings House, 1975. One of several short, practical handbooks on the media produced by Hastings House, Publishers.

Bermingham, Alan, et al. *The Small TV Studio: Equipment and Facilities* (Media Manuals Series). Hastings House, 1975.

Millerson, Gerald. *The Technique of Television Production* (Library of Communication Techniques Series), 9th ed. rev. Hastings House, 1972. An encyclopedic approach to every aspect of television production, from make-up to pacing and timing.

Sheriffs, Ronald E. *Television Lighting Handbook*. TAB Books, 1977. One of TAB's useful handbooks. This one provides techniques and methods of effective lighting.

Stasheff, Edward, et al. *The Television Program: Its Direction and Production,* 5th ed., paper. Hill and Wang, 1976. Textlike approach for the more advanced student.

The Videotape Book. Bantam Books, 1975. A paperback book that provides the basics of how video works, the equipment needed, and how to operate it.

Zettl, Herbert. *Television Production Handbook,* 3d ed. Wadsworth, 1976. This is the most popular text for beginning students. Best for an overall view of television production.

Criticism and Information

Adler, Richard. *Television as a Cultural Force.* Praeger, 1976. This collection is an outgrowth of the Aspen Institute's program on communications and society. Includes essays by critics, humanists, and scholars. Useful for background reading. A companion volume to Douglass Cater, ed. *Television as a Social Force: New Approaches to T.V. Criticism.* Praeger, 1975.

Bower, Robert T. *Television and the Public.* Holt, 1973. Audience attitudes toward television.

Breslin, Deirdre, and Marino, Eileen. "Television: Its Impact and Influence," in May Hill Arbuthnot and Zena Sutherland, *Children and Books,* 5th ed. Scott, Foresman, 1977. Discusses the stereotypes television presents to children and how these affect youngsters, then suggests ways to teach children to be less passive viewers. Includes an annotated bibliography. pp. 596–602.

Kaye, Evelyn. *The Family Guide to Children's Television;* il. by Edward Frascino. Pantheon, 1974. "What to Watch, What to Miss, What to Change, and How to Do It" written under the guidance of Action for Children's Television.

Lesser, Gerald S. *Children and Television.* Random, 1974. The story of the production of the successful Sesame Street series.

Teachers Guides to Television. 1968- Presently published semiannually. P.O. Box 564, Lenox Hill Sta., New York, NY 10021. Gives pre- and post-viewing activities for selected television specials. Books and films of related interest are listed.

Television Highlights. Television Information Office, 745 Fifth Ave., New York, NY 10022. Quarterly announcements of television programs of special interest. This publication is available in many libraries.

Radio

Radio is no longer the glamor child of the communications industry, but what would we do without it? Storytelling is particularly well suited to this medium. Those of us who grew up in the days of the radio soap operas, *Jack Armstrong,* and *Let's Pretend* know that we didn't need television to stimulate our imaginations. In fact, no television show or film could possibly reproduce the worlds we imagined when listening to a radio story. Storytelling is still a success on radio. Our local radio station carries several storytelling shows, one of which has been on the air for over twenty years. Two broadcasters read daily from two different children's books. There are great advantages for you, the storyteller, on radio. Since there is no viewing audience you can read the story aloud, although I still think there is no substitution for the spontaneity of storytelling without a script. If you are interested in radio work, I think the best way to get started is by visiting the program manager and suggesting that the library would like to have a storytelling show. Keep in mind, of course, that your ideas may receive better reception if you are willing to volunteer your own time and energy.

The Federal Communications Commission (FCC) encourages broadcasters to sponsor local programming, and many stations look for qualified individuals to appear on their stations. My first job on radio was doing a free weekly children's storytelling program. When a vacancy came up for a general announcer, I got that job, and the experience I gained was invaluable training for teaching and later for television work.

One of the more difficult things to learn is the matter of timing. Everything is blocked out into segments and your show has to fit into a prescribed slot. At first you may find it difficult to time yourself exactly. This becomes easy with practice and after a few tries you will find yourself speaking in fifteen-minute intervals, even at parties or on the job.

Almost any of your favorite stories will work on radio. Remember that you can't show illustrations on radio, so choose a story that does not rely on visuals. Be sure you give credit to the authors, publishers, and books that you use.

References: Radio

See also chapter 6, "Reading Aloud," for techniques to use on radio.

Head, Sydney W. *Broadcasting in America: A Survey of Television and Radio,* 2d ed. Houghton, 1972. An excellent introduction to the entire field of broadcasting.

Nisbett, Alec. *The Technique of the Sound Studio* (Library of Communication Techniques Series), 3d ed. rev. Hastings House, 1972. Technical introduction to radio.

16 / Puppetry

To become interested in the art of puppetry all you need to do is watch one child having a conversation with a puppet. Even though the child is well aware that the puppet is not alive, he or she carries on an animated discussion. And, if permitted to put the puppet on his or her own hand, the child instantly switches roles and gives personality to the puppet.

Professional puppeteers and librarians sometimes discourage the budding puppeteer with such caveats as "Puppetry is difficult," or "If you can't do it well, don't do it." Some promising puppeteers may be discouraged, but the warnings are meant well. Any art presented to children must, of course, be of the finest quality. But the beginner must always begin at the beginning.

Indeed, it is imperative to start simply, since putting on a full-scale puppet production is like putting on a play with live performers, except that you must create the performers as well as perform. Puppets, whether used in simple ways by the beginner or more elaborately by the experienced, can make the storytime program a very special event.

The Puppet Tradition

Puppetry has been performed for education and entertainment for thousands of years. It thrived in the society of ancient Egypt and in the religious rituals of Greece and Rome. In all corners of the earth, puppets have survived as a major art form and theatrical institution. In Europe, famous puppet troupes entertain adults as well as children. In Austria's Salzburg, a permanent puppet theater offers entire operas performed by marionettes. The Japanese Bunraku puppets perform serious classical drama, while the Turkish shadow shows feature the comic characters Hachivat and Karaghioz. The Javanese puppets also perform as shadow shows in Java and Bali. The traditional puppets perform in long shows depicting good and evil characters: princes, gods, or kings at war with evil villains, witches, giants, and demons. In Thailand intricately costumed rod puppets perform in temple courtyards. Indian marionettes are manipulated by street performers from Delhi to Calcutta.

The United States has borrowed from other traditions and has, as well, created its own tradition. Early TV favorites included puppets Kukla, Ollie, with live hostess Fran Allison, as created by Burr Tillstrom. Fred Rogers, host of *Mr. Rogers' Neighborhood*, a daily TV show, offers an entire make-believe-land population in the form of hand puppets. And the Muppets of *Sesame Street*'s Jim Henson were an instant success. Many educational films feature puppets in starring roles. Join some of these famous puppeteers and begin your apprenticeship.

Types of Puppets

All puppets take thought, time, and effort to create and use. Although there are many varieties from which to choose, puppets fall basically into two major groups: the hand puppet that fits on the puppeteer's hand, and the marionette which is manipulated by strings.

The puppet aficionados will argue vigorously in favor of one type of puppet over the other. The hand puppet proponents will tell you that because

Figure 22. Some quality
commercially produced puppets

Figure 23. Glove puppets
for *A Handful of Surprises*

Figure 24. Some finger
puppets to use when telling
The Three Billy Goats Gruff

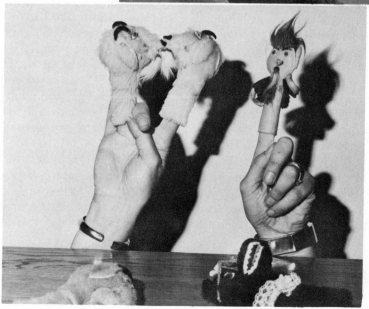

the hand puppet is actually part of the puppeteer, the puppet is more realistic, and the manipulator feels at one with the puppet. Those who favor marionettes say that these puppets, because they are separated from the manipulator, have a life of their own and are therefore better. If this were the time for true confessions, I'd have to tell you that while I argue fairly effectively for the superiority of hand puppets, the real reason I'm a hand puppet person is that marionettes take a lot more skill and patience to manipulate. The differences between the two groups will obviously determine your choice of one over the other. Hand puppets seem most useful in speaking dialogue since the head of the hand puppet is where the audience will be most likely to rivet their attention. The marionettes are better suited to plays with a great deal of physical action. The most sophisticated marionettes have jointed arms, legs, and heads and can dance, pick up objects, and move with ease. They can even fly. If you are a beginning puppeteer there is no need to make a commitment to either major type. Experiment with a variety of puppets until you find the one that gives you the most pleasure and satisfies your needs.

Commercial Hand Puppets

Ordinarily I try to avoid using commercial products other than books in the storyhour. There is enough plastic, mass-produced cuteness on TV, in advertising, and in shops. The traditional and handmade seems to be more suitable. If you feel, however, that you cannot make a good puppet, it is possible to find handmade puppets in shops. Try your senior citizens' shop. They often have knitted or sewn puppets for sale. The renaissance of handicrafts has revived the art of handmade puppets. Your town might have a crafts shop or fair where puppets are sold. If you don't see what you want, special order it from one of these local artisans. They are usually delighted to respond to specific orders. You might even be able to cajole them into donating a puppet: "It's for the library, you know."

If you live in or visit a large city, you might have access to an import store. In the toy department you might find commercially produced puppets that have a handmade look. Spain, Germany, and Poland export quality puppets. And if you visit a resort town, ski or beach, or even a large airport, be sure to wander through the gift shops. Once in a while you'll find exactly what you've been looking for.

Glove Puppets

Most of the puppets that are available commercially or in kits are glove

Figure 26. Little Red Riding Hood and the Wolf stick puppets

Figure 27. Puppets made with tongue depressors or those popsicle sticks you've been saving

Figure 25. Manipulating a marionette

puppets because they are the easiest for beginners to make and manipulate. This puppet, which may be created from a variety of materials, fits onto the hand and is operated either by using the palm and thumb or by putting the index finger into the head, while the thumb operates one hand of the puppet and the remaining fingers operate the other.

It's fun to use an entire glove with each finger representing a different character. Try reproducing the glove puppet story in *A Handful of Surprises* by Anne Heathers and Estéban Francés (Harcourt, 1961). If you can, knit a pair of mittens with three fingers and sew a face in front. Another technique is to use a lunch-size paper bag as a hand puppet. Or take an odd sock, attach three buttons (two eyes and a mouth) with safety pins or needle and thread. Another idea is to split the back of a stuffed animal. Remove the stuffing and you have a hand puppet. Can you sew a tiny bit? Sew together two pieces of muslin or cotton. Turn it inside out and paint a character on it. This can be a hand puppet; if you don't paint anything on it, open it at the top and you have a costume for a hand puppet with a styrofoam ball as a head.

Finger Puppets

Little puppets that fit onto one or more fingers have the advantage of being extremely portable. The fit into a pocket or purse for those odd times when you might find yourself with a group of children. If I meet a child on the bus, or at a friend's house, I take out the finger puppet and shyness on both sides disappears.

Experiment with anything that fits over your finger: a cut-off glove makes a good beginning. Since finger puppets cannot be seen from far away, they should be reserved for storytelling with a small group. You will probably want to let them do the talking while you act as narrator simply introducing the characters as they appear.

Use your hand as a puppet. Washable felt tip pens are available if you choose to draw right on your fingers. Or use rubber cement to glue construction paper or felt to the hand to make faces and costumes.

Marionettes or String Puppets

There are puppeteers who feel that only the marionette can effectively create the illusion of life and an experienced marionetteer is a special treat to see. Marionettes vary in complexity, but since their strings tend to tangle easily they are probably not the best starting point for the beginning puppeteer.

The simplest marionette of all is a handkerchief tied onto a string. Make the handkerchief twist, dance, and go to sleep. Tie two inanimate objects on strings: for example, a comb and brush. Have them talk about their owner. Attach two strings to anything pliable: a chain, a bead necklace. Make your abstract puppet dance to music. Can you give it, him, or her a personality? Is she shy? tired? happy? Move your puppet to show the emotions and personality of your marionette.

Stick Puppets

A stick puppet is made by attaching a solid rod or stick to the back of the puppet, and is held by the performer. It is one of the simplest of all for beginners to use. Puppet characters can be cut from cardboard or plywood. Sticks are then attached and you have a puppet which is quick and easy to use. A more sophisticated rod puppet uses several long rods to manipulate the arms, legs, or head of a jointed puppet.

Puppets can be made with popsicle sticks or with tongue depressors which may be purchased at a drugstore. Seat the children around big tables. In the center put cloth scraps, yarn, sequins, other findings, scissors, and glue for them to share. Then, just let them create. I've done this with many adult groups as well, letting them make up skits after the puppets are completed. Use the Improvisational Skit idea that appears later in this chapter.

Use a wooden spoon. Paint or paste a face on it. You have a simple rod puppet. Cut out figurines of plywood or posterboard. Tape, staple, or glue the cutout characters and scenery to ¼-inch doweling, available at the hardware store or lumber yard. These will work as shadow-show characters as well as on-stage puppets.

Masks and Body Puppets

Most of the puppet types already mentioned are manipulated with your hands. There are puppets that can be operated with other parts of the body. Masks carved from wood and fitting over the head were used by many American tribes in the performance of stories and plays. The whole body is used in the body puppet in which the performer sticks his head and hands through openings in an immobile costume. Draw a figure without a face or arms on a large 2 ft. x 3 ft. posterboard. Cut a hole for the face and arm holes. Preschoolers can wear these costumes to act out a play.

Use a large paper bag to make masks for your group, or, better yet, let them create their own. Plan a show based on Maurice Sendak's *Where the*

Wild Things Are (Harper, 1963), Pat Hutchin's *Good Night, Owl* (Macmillan, 1972), or Grimm's *Snow White and the Seven Dwarfs* (Farrar, 1972).

Shadow Puppets

When you watch a shadow show, you see only the silhouette or shadow of the puppet rather than the puppet itself. Shadow shows usually are performed behind a screen, with the light source coming from behind the puppet and with the performer below the level of the screen. You can use hand puppets or cutouts or even human beings to create shadow shows. Any translucent material, such as thin paper or a sheet, will serve as a screen, and small spot reflector lights may be purchased at the supermarket. The art of shadowgraphy is an ancient one. Most children have used their hands to create figures on the wall; as a storyteller you can manipulate your hands to tell an entire story. Some books that can help you with the basic hand movements are available.

Magnetic Puppets

Magnetized rubber strips can be fastened on the backs of small dolls or posterboard cutouts. Make a screen from posterboard on a cardboard box and use a piece of iron or steel to manipulate the puppets from behind the screen.

Stages

Stage construction ranges from a curtain hung over a door to complex permanent theatres. Start simply. Remember, you'll want to store and maybe transport your stage. Any number of items will serve as a stage for your performance.

You can use an empty refrigerator box as a stage, but since it is bulky to store, plan to use it also as a playstore or individual reading corner. Curtains over a doorway or strung on a rope across a corner make an instant stage. If you can't find a willing volunteer to construct a three-part screen puppet theater for you, a beautifully constructed plywood puppet theater is available from Creative Playthings, Princeton, NJ 08540. Tables will serve as an instant puppet stage too; kneel behind one that has been tipped on its side. An empty picture frame also can serve as a quick substitute for a more complicated stage. If you have nothing else suitable around, cover your head with

Figure 28. Body puppets

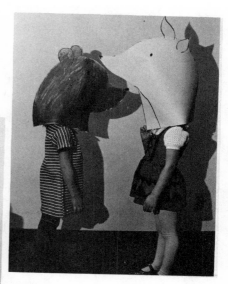

Figure 29. Winnie the Pooh
and Piglet paper masks

Figure 30. Easy-to-make
paper-bag masks

Figure 31. Illustration of
shadow puppetry from
a bygone era

black cloth and cut two openings for your eyes and one for your mouth and simply stand or sit behind your puppets. Actually, it often adds to the puppet performance for the puppeteer to be entirely visible. Just hold the puppet up and start talking. The audience will immediately transfer your voice to the puppet.

Make sure that there is adequate light on your puppets. You may need to use auxiliary lighting since your puppets will usually be small and may be hidden by side curtains.

Following are directions for making a simple theater for hand puppets.

Portable Doorway Puppet Theater

This puppet theater can be easily stored. It works in most doorways, is portable, and, best of all, it can be raised or lowered depending on the height of the puppeteer, child or adult.

You will need:

A spring curtain rod 2½ feet long

A half-inch wood dowel 2½ feet long

3½ yds. heavyweight fabric, such as denim or duck, cut and hemmed to make a screen approximately 26" x 54" (*see* fig. 32).

How to: Sew a two-inch open hem across one width of the fabric for inserting the spring rod. This is the top of the screen. Then cut a 12" x 17" opening a foot (12") from the top and hem around it to give it body. Sew a one-inch open hem across the other (bottom) width of the fabric for the half-inch wood dowel you will insert to give weight to the screen and keep it hanging evenly.

Figure 32. Doorway puppet stage

Figure 33. Self-contained
and ambulatory, the Chinese
hat theater

Chinese Hat Puppet Theater

Totally contained, one-person puppet theaters have been used for centuries in China. One idea for making your own requires the adaptation of a
Chinese coolie hat, or even a Mexican sombrero, either of which may be
bought at import or gift shops. Attach to the hat's brim solid-color fabric that
is long enough to reach to the floor and wide enough to encircle you and the
hat. Sew a zipper in the front, leaving a two-foot opening for the puppets to
perform (*see* fig. 33). You, the puppeteer, wear the puppet theater on your
head. At the end of the story and performance, the entire production—puppets, puppeteer, and stage—walks off.

Uses for Puppets

Puppets may be used as incidental visitors to the book program or as the
basis for an entire story session as performers in a puppet show. Begin simply. Exaggerate your puppet's actions, but don't feel compelled to have your
puppet moving continuously without a purpose. Haphazard movements dis-
tract from a finished looking show. Rather, plan each action so that it is
meaningful. Be sure to speak up and out because the stage will muffle your
voice. You might experiment with using a taped soundtrack so that the puppeteers can concentrate on moving the puppets. Don't try to use elaborate
scenery or involve yourself in complicated scene changes. Music between
acts or scenes helps the continuity of your performance. Lighting need not
be complex, but it must be sufficient to light the action. Try using clip-on
spot lights for flat bright lighting. Don't try to do everything yourself. Enlist
the aid of friends, colleagues, and children. If you decide to perform for an
invited audience, which after all is the point of puppetry, be sure you have
rehearsed your show. If you think you would be proud to have your mother-
in-law see your puppet show, then you are ready for an audience.

The Puppet as Host

You may wish to plan your preschool storyhour around a theme. If this
is not feasible you might want to use a puppet to greet the children and introduce each story. If you have just one puppet (named Arnold, perhaps, by the
children?) that you reserve for use for the preschool storyhour, you will find
the children asking for "Arnold the Elephant" and they will come to associate Arnold with books, poems, and stories.

If you have a puppet—a dog, for example—that you feel comfortable with, take a few minutes to think about your dog's personality. Is it a girl or a boy? Shy, aggressive, knowledgeable, or naive? Introduce the puppet to your group as soon as they are settled. A simple "Boys and girls, this is my friend Arnold" will do. "Hello everybody," says your puppet. "What is your name?" "Would you like to pat me?" Surprisingly, you needn't change your voice when the puppet is speaking. In fact, I caution against a voice change unless you feel fairly confident that you can remember to use it consistently when the puppet is speaking. It can be embarrassing if you start speaking in a high puppet voice, and later your puppet's voice changes tone because you forgot. Children will respond to your puppet just as they will talk to a pet or stuffed animal. Most children understand make-believe much better than most adults. You can have a dialogue with your puppet introducing the stories:

You: "This morning we are going to read a story all about a boy's very first experience in the snow."

Puppet: "Oh good. What's it called?"

You: "*The Snowy Day* by Ezra Jack Keats."

Puppet: "Hurry and read it."

Now just put your puppet down and read the story. At the end of the storyhour you might use the puppet again to say goodbye, and remind the children of the date of the next storyhour. If you use your puppet enough you will begin to think that it is alive, so don't lose it. You'll worry that it may have run into foul play!

Practice with Your Puppet

Here is a list of common emotions to practice with your puppet:

Happiness	Fright	Sleepiness	Curiosity
Loneliness	Sadness	Excitement	Thankfulness
Bravery	Anger	Repentance	Thoughtfulness.

First practice with your puppet using actions alone to express emotions, then act out these feelings using simple phrases or sentences. Add to this list other feelings that might characterize your puppet. Each movement should be planned and fulfill a purpose, but they usually need to be exaggerated to be interpreted by an audience. Simplify all movements. Puppets are too small for subtleties and yet they can be as graceful as dancers. Puppets should per-

Figure 34. The story
*An Anteater Named
Arthur* performed as
a puppet show

form to each other, but as producer you should be aware of the audience as well. The puppets should not be facing the puppeteer or constantly be seen in side view.

Plays

One way to begin your work with puppetry is to find a story or play that appeals to you and then make the puppets to suit the play. If you are working alone, you will want to find a story with only two characters, three at the most. Only two puppets can be on the stage at once, but a third character can appear when one of the main characters is offstage. Remember that you will have to remove one puppet and exchange it for another. This may take time and fumbling while the audience waits.

You may want to have one of your puppets tell the story, or you, as narrator, can give the descriptive passages while the conversational parts are acted by the puppets. Another way to use a puppet is simply to hold each character up while you, the narrator, tell the story. In this way the puppet acts as a three-dimensional illustration of the story.

Some puppeteers script their plays. Each character has a set speech to deliver at a particular time. This has advantages and disadvantages. For one thing, if you're planning on using a published script your search may be a long and hard one, for many of them tend to be overly simplistic. A script also means that parts must be memorized, and if one person forgets his lines, there is liable to be an upset in the entire operation. If adults are presenting a skit or play to children, I think folklore sources are the best. Since there are many variables to putting on a play, it is sometimes worthwhile to use something that your audience and cast are already familiar with. Start with "The Three Bears" or another of the nursery fairy tales. As you become more proficient, you can graduate to a more intricately plotted story. If students are presenting your play, let them write their own script. After you have decided on a story, cast the characters and improvise the story without the puppets. Tape the action or write it down. Now read it over and edit your script. This may be easier to memorize than a script from a book.

Scripting a play seems to make your project more formal and static. Improvising dialogue sometimes works better. Decide on the story you are going to present. Read it aloud. Discuss with your group the different characters and their personalities. Outline the plot so that everyone is sure what happens when. Decide who will take which parts. Try rehearsing your show, criticizing the dialogue and puppets' movements as you go. When the play is refined enough for presentation you will find that some of the speeches have become set while others vary. This often gives more spontaneity to a show. Of course, you must do what works best for you.

An Instant Play to Perform

"*Finding a Friend.*" If you are shuddering at the thought of making puppets and costuming them, constructing a stage, writing a script, and rehearsing a show, perform this simple playlet. It needs only two props: the hands.

Bend down behind a table, counter or lectern. Talk loudly, the table will muffle your voice.

There was once a hand. (Show your hand to the audience.) He was very proud because he could do so many things. He could point (point); he could count one, two, three, four, five (show each finger); he could say "stop" (hold up hand palm outward); he could scratch himself (little finger scratches next finger); he could say "come here" (beckon); he could wave goodbye (wave); he could shake himself (shake your hand, fingers relaxed); he could chastise (shake a finger); he could be tough (make a fist); but he was very sad (fold fingers down in a droop) because he couldn't make any noise. Then the ring finger told the thumb about a noise the first three fingers could make. The hand tried it (snap your fingers); but the hand was dissatisfied. Then one day the hand met another hand (bring other hand up to audience). They discovered that they could make a noise together (clap hands). The moral of this story is (stand up and look at audience), it takes two hands to clap.

Exercise in Performance

If your students have made puppets and you are searching for a play to produce, divide them into groups of five. Let each group pick three pieces of paper from a hat: one indicating a character, one a setting, and one an object. The group must decide on a skit involving the character, setting, and object that they picked. Suggest a time limit for the preparation and performance. Caution them to speak up and out, so that they can be heard as they perform. The greatest failing for amateur puppeteers is their inaudibility.

Here are some ideas for the big three:

Characters	Setting	Object
Teacher	Jungle	Diamond bracelet
Musician	New York City	Book
Explorer	Desert island	Treasure chest
Witch	Sailing ship	Telephone
Librarian	Haunted house	Magic wand
Monster	Department store	Roast turkey
Storekeeper	Cave	Baby elephant
Indian	Art museum	Flashlight
Pirate	Theater	Uncle Jonathon's will
King	Mars	Secret message
Ghost	Hotel	New shoes

Bibliography: Puppetry

This is a selected listing to inspire amateur puppeteers and guide them through their first steps in making puppets and deciding on which stories to produce. If you become particularly interested in puppetry I suggest that you join one of the puppetry organizations where you will find kindred souls willing to share their knowledge and talents with you. Titles marked by an asterisk are particularly recommended.

Background and History

*Baird, Bill. *The Art of the Puppet;* il. by author. Macmillan, 1965. A lavishly illustrated survey by an accomplished puppeteer.

Boehn, Max von. *Dolls and Puppets;* tr. by Josephine Nicoll; with a note on puppets by George Bernard Shaw. Cooper Sq., 1966. Over 500 illustrations make this history a fascinating account.

*Scott-Kemball, Jeune. *Javanese Shadow Puppets.* Trustees of the British Museum, 1970. A history and discussion of the puppets of Java. Illustrated with photographs from the British Museum's Raffles collection.

Simmen, René. *The World of Puppets;* photos. by Leonardo Bezzola. Crowell, 1975. A history of puppets with excellent photographs in color.

Speaight, George. *Punch and Judy; A History.* Plays, 1970. Old illustrations give authenticity to this fine history of these popular folk characters.

Designing and Making Puppets

The first rule in making puppets is: *Never* throw anything away. Save buttons, beads, odd earrings, scraps of material, and anything else that may seem remotely useful. These books will help you begin, but use your own imagination.

Binyon, Helen. *Puppetry Today;* il. by author. Watson-Guptill, 1966. Designing and making marionettes, hand puppets, rod and shadow puppets.

Boylan, Eleanor. *How to Be a Puppeteer;* il. by Tomie de Paola. McCall, 1970. Directions for making puppets and stages.

*Bursill, Henry. *Hand Shadows to Be Thrown upon the Wall.* Dover, 1967. A reprint of a book first published in 1859.

*Chernoff, Goldie Taub. *Puppet Party;* il. by Margaret Hartelius. Walker, 1971. Colorful drawings give directions for simple puppets children can make.

Cochrane, Louise. *Shadow Puppets in Color;* il. by Kate Simunek. Plays, 1972. Patterns for puppets and theaters. Short scripts included.

*Currell, David. *The Complete Book of Puppetry.* Plays, 1975. Clear directions for making hand puppets, marionettes, finger puppets. Includes hints for production and a short chapter on the history of puppetry. Excellent source.

Dolls and Toy Animals; by Vibeke Lind and Lis Albrectsen; tr. from the Danish by Christine Hauch. Van Nostrand, 1973. Directions for sewing dolls and some puppets.

Fling, Helen. *Marionettes: How to Make and Work Them;* il. by Charles Forbell. Dover, 1973.

French, Susan. *Presenting Marionettes.* Van Nostrand, 1968. How to make and manipulate marionettes for the more advanced puppeteer.

*Hopper, Grizella H. *Puppet Making Through the Grades;* ed. by John Lidstone; il. by Sarita R. Rainey. Davis, 1966. Clear photographs give many ideas for simply produced puppets.

Jackson, Sheila. *Simple Puppetry.* Watson-Guptill, 1969. Clear directions for making hand puppets and marionettes, but not really "simple" at all.

*Kampmann, Lothar. *Creating with Puppets.* Van Nostrand, 1972. Excellent ideas for simple puppetry with photographs.

Mulholland, John. *Practical Puppetry;* il. by Jack Parker. London, H. Jenkins, 1961. Design and construction of four main puppet types for the more advanced puppeteer.

Philpott, A. R. *Let's Make Puppets.* Van Nostrand, 1972. Simple puppets to make in a pamphlet form.

Richter, Dorothy. *Fell's Guide to Hand Puppets; How to Make and Use Them.* Frederick Fell, 1970. A guide to making hand puppets. Directions for lighting, stage making, playscripts.

Ross, Laura. *Finger Puppets;* il. by Laura and Frank Ross, Jr. Lothrop, 1971. Simple ideas for finger puppets.

———— *Hand Puppets: How to Make and Use Them;* il. by author. Lothrop, 1969. Includes easy to follow directions for paper bag, rod, and papier-mâché puppets.

Scott, Louise Binder, May, Marion E., and Shaw, Mildred S. *Puppets for All Grades.* F. A. Owen (Dansville, NY 14437), 1970. This short pamphlet has clear photographs illustrating easy ideas.

Organizations

It will make you feel like a real expert if you join a puppetry club.

The American Center of UNIMA
(Union Internationale de la Marionette)
  Mollie Falkenstein
  General Secretary
  132 Chiquita St.
  Laguna Beach, CA 92651

Ontario Puppetry Association
  D. Jeff Essery
  President

  2681 Younge St.
  Toronto 310, Ontario, Canada

Puppeteers of America
  Olga Stevens
  Executive Secretary
  Box 1061
  Ojai, CA 93023
  (Publishes *The Puppetry Journal* six
    times a year.)

Supplies

Pollock's Toy Theaters
  Box 1184-P
  Santa Monica, CA 90406
  (Cardboard theater and puppets—
    replicas)

Thomas Valentine, Inc.
  150 W. 46th St.
  New York, NY 10036

The Puppetry Store
  3500 Tyler N.E.
  Minneapolis, MN 55418

Any variety store for glitter, spangles, felt, feathers.

Materials Adaptable for Puppetry

The following titles are especially adaptable for puppet shows. Types of puppets are suggested too. Keep in mind that puppets also can tell jokes and riddles (*see* "Non-narrative Sources," chapter 9), as well as dance and sing to recorded music.

Bishop, Claire H., and Wiese, Kurt. *The Five Chinese Brothers;* il. by Kurt Wiese. Coward, 1938. (Body puppets)

Brown, Marcia. *Once a Mouse;* il. by author. Scribner, 1961. (Shadow puppets and a narrator)

Emberley, Barbara. *Drummer Hoff;* il. by Ed Emberley. Prentice-Hall, 1967. (Stick puppets)

Flack, Marjorie. *Angus and the Ducks;* il. by author. Doubleday, 1930. (Shadow show)

Harper, Wilhelmina. *The Gunniwolf;* il. by William Wiesner. Dutton, 1967. (Paper-bag masks)

Heathers, Anne, and Francés. Esteban. *A Handful of Surprises;* il. by Esteban Francés. Harcourt, 1961. (Finger puppets)

Joslin, Sesyle. *What Do You Say, Dear?;* il. by Maurice Sendak. Young Scott, 1958. (Shadow show)

Kent, Jack. *The Fat Cat: A Danish Folktale;* il. by author. Parents, 1971. (Stick puppets)

Leach, Maria. *Noodles, Nitwits, and Numskulls;* il. by Kurt Werth. World, 1961. Short, silly riddles, stories, jokes adaptable to your favorite type of puppet.

Lionni, Leo. *Frederick;* il. by author. Pantheon, 1967. (Paper-bag puppets)

Mahy, Margaret. *A Lion in the Meadow;* il. by Jenny Williams. Watts, 1969. (Paper-bag puppets)

Sawyer, Ruth. *Journey Cake, Ho!;* il. by Robert McCloskey. Viking, 1953. (Stick puppets)

Sendak, Maurice. *Pierre,* in *Nutshell Library;* il. by author. Harper, 1962. (Hand puppets)

———— *Where the Wild Things Are;* il. by author. Harper, 1963. (Paper-bag masks)

Sharmat, Marjorie. *Gladys Told Me to Meet Her Here;* il. by Edward Frascino. Harper, 1970. (Hand puppets)

Waber, Bernard. *An Anteater Named Arthur;* il. by author. Houghton, 1967. (Hand puppets)

Wildsmith, Brian. *The Hare and Tortoise,* based on a fable by La Fontaine; il. by author. Watts, 1966. Also *The North Wind and the Sun* (Watts, 1964); *The Rich Man and the Shoemaker* (Watts, 1965). (Hand puppets) And *The Lion and the Rat* (Watts, 1963). (Hand puppets and paper-bag puppets)

Fiction about Puppetry for Storytellers

Read these longer titles aloud.

Lorenzini, Carlo. *The Adventures of Pinocchio;* by Carlo Collodi (pseud.); tr. by Carol Della Chiesa; il. by Attilio Mussino. Macmillan, 1969. The classic Italian story of a carved wooden puppet, written in 1880.

Paperny, Myra. *The Wooden People;* il. by Ken Stampnick. Little, 1976. A moving, family story involving the making and performance of puppets.

Peterson, Katherine. *The Master Puppeteer;* il. by Haru Wells. Crowell, 1975. Jiro is an apprentice puppeteer in a traditional Japanese theater.

Figure 35. Paper-bag hand puppets that children can make

Familiar Folktales for Puppet Improvisations

"Cinderella" (*Cinderella;* retold by C. S. Evans; il. by Arthur Rackham. Viking, 1972. Rackham's silhouettes make a good shadow show.)

"Little Red Riding Hood"

"Noah's Ark"

"Sleeping Beauty" (*Sleeping Beauty;* retold by C. S. Evans; il. by Arthur Rackham.

Viking, 1972. More of Rackham's silhouettes.)

"The Three Bears"

"The Three Billy Goats Gruff"

"The Traveling Musicians"

Plays

Adair, Margaret Weeks, and Patapoff, Elizabeth. *Folk Puppet Plays for the Social Studies.* John Day, 1972. Scripts based on folk sources.

Alexander, Sue. *Small Plays for You and a Friend;* il. by Olivia H. Cole. Seabury, 1974. Very short scripted skits for two performers.

Baumann, Hans. *Caspar and His Friends: A Collection of Puppet Plays;* tr. by Joyce Emerson; il. by Richard Lebenson. Walck, 1968. Short scripts for Caspar, the German Punch.

Carlson, Bernice Wells. *Funny-Bone Dramatics;* il. by Charles Cox. Abingdon, 1974. Riddles, jokes, skits appropriate for puppet presentation.

John, Diana. *St. George and the Dragon* and *Punch and Judy.* Penguin, 1966. Script and directions for making papier-mâché and sock puppets.

Punch and Judy: A Play for Puppets; il. by Ed Emberley. Little, 1965. Short skits for Punch and Judy shows with colorful action illustrations.

Skelton, Red. *Gertrude and Heathcliffe;* il. by the author. Scribner, 1974. Short two-voice jokes suitable for puppets or live performers.

Thane, Adele. *Plays from Famous Stories and Fairy Tales.* Plays, 1967. Twenty-eight brief royalty-free plays.

17 / Magic

The birthday party I remember most clearly was one for which my parents had a magician come and perform. He really did make a live rabbit appear out of a hat. I was fascinated, but until a few years ago it never occurred to me that I too could be a magician. I was helping a friend move when I noticed an entire shelf of very odd looking things. "That's my magic," he said. We stopped packing and he gave me a short performance. I now belong to the Society of American Magicians and the International Brotherhood of Magicians and although I must confess that I'm no expert I, too, have a whole shelf filled with magic tricks. Like any other endeavor you undertake, to be good, you have to take time to learn and practice.

The performing of magic tricks is a natural addition to the storyhour. Many traditional folktales deal with magic or magicians, and the art of conjuring is as old as the tales themselves.

You can use conjuring, or the performing of magic tricks, to introduce a story you have learned. Many of the simple magic tricks that you will begin with are as traditional as the stories you will tell. From a simple trick you will advance to an entire "routine," and once you have performed these for a group of children and have seen their excited reaction you will become hopelessly addicted to the world of magic.

To give you an idea of how you can use magic in the storyhour this is the routine I use after I've told Parker Fillmore's story, "Mighty Mikko," whose hero is a fox.

I tell the audience that I have a fox I'd like them all to meet, and that we must prepare for his arrival. First he needs a soft bed to lie on. I make three small silk handkerchiefs turn into a giant colored silk banner. Next I explain that in order to hold the fox once he arrives you have to be a skilled knot tier. I tie two silks together and examine the first large silk; then I suggest that maybe it has to be even softer and magically my two silks become three. Of course the fox would enjoy something good to drink. My teakettle then pours four different colored glasses of liquid that the audience can sample. When it seems to be empty, I open the teakettle and out springs a bouquet of flowers to make the fox feel at home. To further tempt the fox, I show an empty can that then magically becomes full of cereal. Mixing the cereal with shredded paper in a pan, I light the mixture and it bursts into multicolored flame. To extinguish the fire I put the lid on the pan. When I remove the lid, the fire and cereal have disappeared and a fox puppet appears, and this I manipulate as though it were alive. At the end of the program I make the fox disappear. The tricks used in this routine can be purchased in almost any shop that sells novelties or magic supplies. Naturally as a good magician I won't reveal how the tricks are performed, but I will tell you which tricks to ask for. These may, of course, be used in other ways to introduce other stories:

The blendo	A change bottle
20th-century silks	A dove pan
Teakettle with loading compartment	A puppet
Spring flowers	A change box.

Conjuring—magic for entertainment—may have originated in Greece. In the second century a Greek author, Alciphron, described a still-popular sleight-of-hand trick known as the "cups and balls." Conjuring as performed by a conjurer or magician—but not to be confused with witches, sorcerers, or demons—was a major form of entertainment in many different parts of the world. Today, even with the magic of television, space travel, and other marvels, a good magician, or conjurer, can entertain and delight an audience with some of the tricks that were invented centuries ago. The video engineer where I taped a TV series entertains his coworkers with magic tricks on a weekly basis. Adults watch and are fascinated as he produces an elephant from a matchbox and other tricks.

Children are particularly fascinated with magic tricks. Just like their parents, they want to figure out how the trick was done. Interestingly enough, very young children do not make good audiences for conjurers. Perhaps they take miraculous events for granted, or it may be that they do not have the same reactions as older children or adults. Some magical tricks depend on *misdirection*. For example, the conjurer hides a ball in one hand while the other hand is moving in an eye-catching manner. The adult eye usually follows the larger action automatically and misses the smaller, more important action. Young children, however, are more likely to follow the smaller action, frustrating the magician. Children in the middle and upper grades, however, react in the same way as most adults and are excited by the simplest of tricks.

Magic shows are really suitable for all ages. A recent Broadway show, *The Magic Show*, featuring a magician, attracted adult and child audiences. The adult audience at a Las Vegas extravaganza, in this age of space magic, was astounded and delighted when a magician made a live tiger appear and disappear, and many came back just to see this one act performed. "Quick on the Draw," the Tampa, Florida, TV show features magic for in-school viewing.

The mixture of awe and scepticism which accompanies the performance of magic at a storyhour will make the effort to learn the tricks worthwhile.

Types of Conjuring

There are several ways we can distinguish magic tricks. There are mechanical tricks, sleight-of-hand, table magic, and platform and stage magic. There are also different classes of effects. Although not really necessary for a beginning interest in performing, the history of magic makes a fascinating subject for study.

Magic effects usually come under one of seven categories. The more successful magic tricks include two or more of the following effects:

A *production or creation*. The magician produces something out of nothing, such as a rabbit from a seemingly empty hat.

A *disappearance*. The opposite of production, the rabbit will vanish.

A *transformation*. An object changes from one thing into another. For instance, a rabbit might seem to change into a duck.

A *transposition*. Two objects exchange places with each other. A red handkerchief seems to change places with a blue handkerchief in another location.

Defiance of natural laws. Tricks that seem physically impossible, such as cutting off someone's head or climbing an unsupported rope.

Secret motive power. Tricks in which inanimate objects appear to move under their own power, such as a gyrating walking stick.

Mental tricks. The performer apparently reads the thoughts of those in his audience.

Table and Stage Magic

Some magicians like to specialize in one form of magic. For instance, you might get interested in doing table or closeup magic. These would include card or coin tricks or some of the many tricks to be performed with silk handkerchiefs. These tricks are most appropriate for small audiences at a storyhour in a library or home. Those magicians that get interested in stage magic are usually professional entertainers who will perform before larger audiences. The magic effects will need to be seen from greater distances and are therefore larger. Most amateurs don't have the space to store or transport a box big enough to make a large animal disappear. And, they may not want to care for a tiger to use at an occasional magic show.

Mechanical Magic and Sleight-of-Hand

If you are more than just casually interested in the art of conjuring, you will probably want to get involved with some sleight-of-hand. These are magical effects that rely mainly on manual dexterity. A typical sleight-of-hand maneuver is to show a single ball to an audience and with a series of hand movements seemingly make the one ball disappear or multiply. Undoubtedly because I've not taken the time to perfect any sleight-of-hand movements, I am entirely in awe of this type of magic. There are books to teach you the basics of sleight-of-hand. Another way of learning the fundamentals is to find a magician willing to demonstrate. This really isn't as difficult as it appears. It's true that magicians don't like to give away secrets, but giving magic lessons is different. Those merchants in the business of selling tricks or books on magic will be happy to demonstrate techniques after a purchase. But, as with many ideas and techniques in this book, practice makes perfect.

We've finally arrived at my kind of magic, a trick whose secret you can buy. There are many magic suppliers in the country today. You can buy a trick through the mail from a catalog (instructions included) or you can shop in a retail store that sells novelties and magic. In most cases, the store clerks are magicians themselves. They will demonstrate its secret. What sort of things can you buy? A cane that appears from thin air, a teapot that pours a variety of colored liquids, a milk pitcher that never empties, or a pan that produces endless silk scarves or even a rabbit. Try not to buy on impulse; rather, plan how you can use an item in your programs.

Books About Magic

There are many, many books that give clear directions on magic tricks. In fact, you can buy an entire at-home course (*Tarbell Course in Magic*, published by Louis Tannen) and once you have seen a trick or two performed, you will find it much easier to understand written directions. It's rather like reading a cookbook. You may wonder that the secrets of the magicians are so freely revealed. A famous magician once said that to publish a secret was the best way to keep it, meaning that no one will bother to learn it. This really isn't true, as attested by the number of magicians who write and collect books, but there are few hidden secrets.

Organizations of Magicians

There are two nationally active magicians' organizations, the Society of American Magicians and the International Brotherhood of Magicians. They publish magazines complete with ideas for magic tricks and presentations, book reviews, and news of local groups. They hold conventions featuring magic shows and have local clubs. To join either group you must be sponsored (almost like a fraternal organization). Most local affiliates require an initiation magic performance by you. Don't panic, it's fun. The older magicians are delighted at whatever you do and will be kind and helpful.

Using Magic

Magic ties in well with storytelling. I tell the Japanese story *The Magic Teakettle* and then show my magic teakettle. In fact, first I produce a copy of the book from a flaming pan.

If you feel you are proficient enough to do a whole storyhour featuring magic, wonderful. It will be a real treat. Most amateurs, however, have too small a repertoire to sustain more than a few minutes of magic. There are many stories that have magical elements in them. In fact, all stories create a magical mood. Use a trick or two at the end of the storyhour and inspire others. I suggest only that you do perform your magic after any traditional storytelling, since it's very hard to maintain a mental image of magical events after you have seen miracles performed under your very eyes.

Learn a trick thoroughly before performing. Don't repeat a trick in the same show and don't tell the secret of the trick. It spoils the entertainment value. To misdirect the audience, remember that an audience looks where you look, will look at anything that moves, and will look where you point. They will also look at a light, toward noise, or in the direction of a sudden movement. Practice. Become adept. Then perform.

Patter and Presentation

One of the fascinating aspects of magic is the psychology of entertaining which is employed. The examples of misdirection mentioned above suggest some insights into the performer-audience-action relationship. This type of showmanship can be useful to the storyteller even when he or she is not using magic. As you study and practice in this area, be aware of the performing techniques involved and how they might be applied to other aspects of the storyhour.

Magic Tricks

These tricks don't need any equipment, but require some advance preparation. They are standard tricks which have been adapted to fit into a book oriented program.

Book Telepathy

Use three books you've planned to use in the storyhour. You will need three books (or their covers) and a library card.

Suppose the books are *English Fairy Tales, Oh, What Nonsense!*, and *Big Music.*

Before the trick prepare the following:

On a piece of paper write "You will choose *English Fairy Tales.*" Put the paper into an envelope.

On the underside of the library card print "You will choose *Oh, What Nonsense!*"

On the underside of *Big Music* attach a sign that says "You will choose *Big Music.*"

Line up the three books in a row. Ask a child from the group to think of one of the three books. Now ask him to place the library card on his choice of one of the three books.

If *English Fairy Tales* is chosen, have him look inside the envelope.

If *Oh, What Nonsense!* is chosen, have him turn over the library card.

If *Big Music* is chosen, turn the book over and let him read what is written there.

Now you read or tell a story from the book the spectator selected, but don't repeat this trick with the same group.

Riddle Trick

Use this at the end of a storyhour featuring stories about riddles:

Tell the group you are about to show them something that *you* have never seen before, and that *they* have never seen before. After they see it no living person will ever see it again. Then, take out a walnut. Crack it open and eat the nut inside.

Prediction Pencil

In this trick a rising pencil can answer yes and no questions such as "Did Harve Zemach write *Duffy and the Devil?*" or "Was Hans Christian Andersen a Dane?"

> *Preparation:* Take a pencil and cut a slit in the eraser. Fasten a piece of dark thread to a button on your jacket or shirt about eight inches long. Slip the other end into the slit on the eraser. Drop the pencil eraser side down into an empty soda bottle. As you slowly draw the bottle away from you the pencil will rise in the glass. (The thread can be fastened with beeswax, sometimes called magician's wax, available from magic supply stores.)

If you make the pencil rise, the answer to a question to the magician is "yes"; if you let it drop back into the bottle the answer is "no."

A Word from Smokey the Bear

This trick can be used after telling stories with forest settings. Tell the group that they must be careful to always put out fires and be careful of matches. Remind them that matches should be broken in two to make sure that they are out. Show the group a wooden match which you then place under a scarf. Ask a child to break the match with the scarf still wrapped around it in two. When you take hold of the scarf, the match drops out unharmed. "You can never be too careful," you exclaim.

> *Preparation:* Sew a match inside the hem of a scarf. When the child breaks the match he is really breaking the one sewn into the scarf. Meanwhile you take the match that you displayed into your hand. When you open the scarf, let the match in your hand fall out.

A Proverb Trick

Tell the La Fontaine fable about the milkmaid who, coming home from work with a jug of milk on her head, thinks about all the things she will buy when she sells the milk. "With the money I'll buy some chickens. The chickens will lay eggs. Chicks will hatch from the eggs; I'll sell them, then I'll buy a new dress and go to a dance. I'll dance with all the young men."

As the milkmaid danced in anticipation, the jug fell off her head and broke. There went milk, money, chickens, chicks, and party dress. *Moral:* Don't count your chickens before they hatch.

One version of this story appears in picture-book form in Ingri and Edgar Parin d'Aulaire's *Don't Count Your Chicks* (Doubleday, 1973); yet another version is Hans Christian Andersen's *The Woman with the Eggs* (Crown, 1974).

> *Preparation:* Blow out an egg by putting a pinhole in both ends of an egg and literally blowing the egg out. (Scrambled eggs for breakfast!) Let the eggshell dry for a few days or dry it out in a warm oven. Fill the egg with confetti through one of the holes. Seal the egg with tape or beeswax. After you've told the story crack the egg and let the confetti scatter. Make sure you have a broom and dustpan handy. This is a spectacular trick, but very messy.

The Four Thieves

Do this trick after you've told the Grimm's tale *The Bremen Town Musicians* (McGraw-Hill, 1968). To do so you will need a pack of playing cards. Hold up the four Jacks which, you tell your audience, represent the four robbers. Remind the audience that to spend the night the robbers each went into the house, which is represented by the rest of the deck of cards. Tell them you are going to put the robbers into different rooms in the house but they will all end up at the door ready to run away.

> *Preparation:* Place any three cards behind the Jacks before you fan them out to show them. Show only the Jacks and keep the three extra cards behind the last Jack. Then explain:
> "Here are the four robbers ready to enter the house. The deck of cards can represent the house." (Show the Jacks, then place them face downward on top of the deck. The three extra cards are now on the top of the deck.)
> "The first robber went in and made himself comfortable in the basement." (Place one of the extra cards on the bottom of the deck.)
> "The second robber went into the house and sat in the kitchen." (Place the second card anywhere in the deck.)
> "The third robber went into the bedroom and lay down." (Place the third extra card anywhere in the deck.)
> "The fourth robber stood guard at the door." (You can show this last card, the first Jack on the top of the pile.)
> "The cock, the cat, the dog and the donkey began their concert. The robbers all ran out the door" (show each Jack—one, two, three, four, that seem to have risen to the surface) "and were never seen again."

Television versus Books

Tell your audience that books are better than television. Every time you sit down to look at television you get poor reception. (Show a posterboard with a screen drawn on it. There are wavy lines on the screen.) So you usually switch to another channel. (Place the card inside an envelope. Turn the envelope around and pull out the card. The other side has a screen painted with stars and stripes.) The reception is just as bad on that side. (The audience knows that you are just showing the other side of the card.) So I switch to another channel. (You put the card inside the envelope again and take out the card with the wavy lines on it. The audience expects to see stars and stripes on the other side, but instead when you turn the card around a notice is printed on the other side that says, "Next time read a book.") Now open the manila envelope, tearing it in pieces so that the audience knows there is nothing inside.

Preparation: You need a manila envelope just large enough to hold and easily permit removal of an 8"x10" card. Draw differing TV call letters on each side so that the audience can tell when you have turned the envelope over.

Then you need an 8"x10" card with a screen and wavy lines drawn on one side and a screen with stars and stripes drawn on the other. Carefully trim about ⅛" from each side of this card. The reason for this soon will become clear.

You also need to make a "sheath" card. To do this, tape two 8"x10" cards together, on the inside. On one side of the sheath card, draw the screen with the wavy lines again; on the other side, draw the screen with the words: NEXT TIME READ A BOOK.

The trick is that the second time you place the card inside the envelope you insert the first card in the "sheath" card and hold it up. The audience will never notice that it is slightly larger.

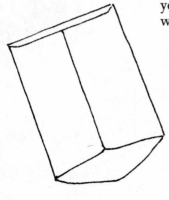

Manila envelope

Back of smaller card

Front of sheath card

Front of smaller card

Next time Read a Book

Back of sheath card

The Dove Pan

My favorite magic trick to buy for the storyhour is the Dove or Chick Pan. Show an empty pan to your audience. Fill it with "what makes a book"; cut up words and pictures. Light a match and it flames up instantly into a blaze which you cover with a pan top. When you remove the top the fire has been replaced with "spring" flowers, streamers, and a book or books which you proceed to read. A spectacular trick which you can use over again.

Almost any magic supplier will demonstrate the Dove Pan for you. The cost is approximately $10 to $14. Flash paper that burns so spectacularly, leaving no ash, and tissue paper flowers that spring to life are also readily available.

References: Magic

The following bibliography includes references, references to organizations of magicians, places to visit, and some suggestions for obtaining supplies. Those marked with an asterisk are particularly recommended.

Background and History

Charney, David H. *Magic; The Great Illusions Revealed and Explained.* Quadrangle/New York Times, 1975. Based on a 1897 publication, this book explains famous tricks with old drawings.

Christopher, Milbourne. *The Illustrated History of Magic;* il. by author. Crowell, 1973. Great conjurers and great tricks in a large book, profusely illustrated. A wealth of background information.

———— *Panorama of Magic.* Dover, 1962. Mostly pictures of magic memorabilia; photographs, lithographs, woodcuts, engravings, posters—all relating to the history of magic.

Cyclopedia of Magic; ed. by Henry Hay (pseud. of June Barrows Mussey); il. with photos. by Audrey Alley. McKay, 1949. Alphabetically arranged; tricks, magicians.

Dexter, Will. *see* Pritchard, William.

Evans, Henry Ridgely. *History of Conjuring and Magic.* Kenton, Ohio, International Brotherhood of Magicians, 1928.

Hay, Henry. *see Cyclopedia of Magic* by June Barrows Mussey.

*Hopkins, Albert A., comp. *Magic: Stage Illusions and Scientific Diversions.* Benjamin Blom, 1967. This is a reprint of an 1897 book and contains over 400 photographs.

*Hunt, Douglas and Kari. *The Art of Magic;* il. by author. Atheneum, 1967. An excellent introduction to the subject of magic. Includes step-by-step photographs of several traditional magic tricks.

Pritchard, William T. *This Is Magic; Secrets of the Conjurer's Craft,* by Will Dexter (pseud.). Citadel Pr., 1958. An informal history of magic.

Salverte, Eusèbe. *The Philosophy of Magic,* vols. 1 and 2. Harper, 1855.

Severn, William. *Magic and Magicians;* il. by Yukio Tashiro. McKay, 1958.

Biographies

Burlingame, Hardin J. *Herrmann the Great.* Laird and Lee, 1897.

Gresham, William Lindsay. *Houdini, The Man Who Walked through Walls.* Holt, 1959.

Scarne, John. *The Odds against Me.* Simon and Schuster, 1966.

Thurston, Howard. *My Life of Magic.* Dorrance, 1929.

Magic Tricks

Amateurs and professional magicians have authored a number of how-to-do-it magic books. Privately printed books and pamphlets abound. This is a selected list to start you on your magic hobby. Asterisked titles are especially recommended.

Adair, Ian. *Magic, Step-By-Step.* Arco, 1970. Photographs give easy-to-follow directions in this paperback.

Bedford, Charles M. *101 Magic Tricks.* S. S. Adams Co., Neptune, NJ. Easy-to-do magic and word tricks.

*Elliott, Bruce. *Magic as a Hobby;* il. by L. Vosburgh Lyons. Harper, 1948. Also, *Professional Magic Made Easy;* il. by Arthur Seymour. Harper, 1959. And *Classic Secrets of Magic;* il. by Stanley Jaks. Harper, 1953. For beginners, easy-to-follow directions for simple magic.

Fleischman, Albert Sidney. *Mr. Mysterious's Secrets of Magic;* il. by Eric von Schmidt. Little, 1975. Tricks for beginners.

Frederick, Guy. *101 Best Magic Tricks;* il. by Doug Anderson. Sterling, 1956. Tricks for beginners to intermediates.

*Gibson, Walter B. *Magic with Science;* il. by Ric Estrada. Grosset, 1973. Magic tricks based on scientific principles. Beginner to intermediate.

*_____ *Secrets of Magic.* Grosset, 1973 (paper). Well-known magic tricks from Egypt, the Middle Ages, and the Orient are revealed. Intermediates. Mostly for relaxing reading.

Hunter, Norman. *The Puffin Book of Magic;* il. by Jill McDonald. Penguin, 1968 (paper). Divided into sections, this original paperback reveals secrets of magic tricks to do with ordinary things, special things, and for small children and groups.

Jonson, Wilfrid. *Magic Tricks and Card Tricks;* ed. by Chesley V. Barnes; il. by author. Dover, 1952. Intermediate.

*Kaye, Marvin. *The Stein and Day Handbook of Magic;* il. by Al Kilgore. Stein and Day, 1973. Chapters on magic for children, showmanship, and how to develop it make this a "bible" of magical style.

Kettelkamp, Larry. *Spooky Magic;* il. by author. Morrow, 1955. For children to read and follow.

Lopshire, Robert. *It's Magic;* il. by author. Macmillan, 1969. Simple magic for beginning readers.

Merlini the Great. *see* Rawson, Clayton.

Mulholland, John. *Book of Magic;* il. by author. Scribner, 1963. For older children. Well-written explanations of magic (older tricks) by a famous magician.

*Nelms, Henning. *Magic and Showmanship: A Handbook for Conjurers;* il. by author. Dover, 1969. This has good ideas for patter and presentation of tricks.

Page, Patrick. *Bell's Magic Book;* il. by Dennis Patten. Bell, a div. of Crown Pub., 1973. Clear instructions and patter for some "oldie but goody" tricks. For the beginner.

*Rawson, Clayton. *How to Entertain Children with Magic You Can Do,* by Merlini the Great (pseud.); il. by author. Simon and Schuster, 1962. Inexpensive magic for adults to perform with children.

*Rice, Harold R. *Encyclopedia of Silk Magic,* vols. 1–3; il. by Francis B. Martineau. Wynnewood, Pa., Silk King Studios, 1948–1962. Everything there is to know about working with silks. This is for adults, intermediate to advanced, and involves the purchase of silks and equipment.

Ripley, Sherman. *141 Magic Tricks;* il. by author. Sentinel, 1973. Directions for simple magic.

*Severn, William. *Bill Severn's Magic Trunk;* il. by author. McKay, 1973. Four paperback volumes in a slipcase: *Magic Comedy, Magic in Your Pockets, Magic Shows You Can Give, Magic with Paper.* Tricks to be performed with materials and objects found in the home. Good for children and beginners.

———— *Magic across the Table;* il. by Katharine Wood. McKay, 1972. Easily prepared tricks for the beginner.

Stoddard, Edward. *The First Book of Magic;* il. by Robin King. Watts, 1953. Easy magic for young children to learn and perform.

*Tarbell, Harlan E. *Tarbell Course in Magic;* il. by author. vols. 1–7; Louis Tannen, Inc., 1941–1954. For the serious student, a *complete* course in magic for beginner to expert. Adults.

*Tarr, Bill. *Now You See It, Now You Don't! Lessons in Sleight of Hand;* il. by Barry Ross. Vintage/Random, 1976. Excellent step-by-step drawings help the beginner to become an expert in sleight-of-hand techniques.

*Wyler, Rose, and Ames, Gerald. *Funny Magic: Easy Tricks For Young Magicians;* il. by Tālivaldis Stubis. Parents, 1972. Directions for simple magic.

Catalogs

Abbot's Magic Co.
  Colon, MI 49040
  ($2 charge for catalog)

Emporium of Magic
  17220 W. 8 Mile Rd.
  Southfield, MI 48075

Bob Little
  27 Bright Rd.
  Hatboro, PA 19040

Louis Tannen, Inc.
  1540 Broadway
  New York, NY 10036
  ($3.50 charge for catalog)

Organizations

International Brotherhood of Magicians
  114 N. Detroit St.
  Kenton, OH 43326
  (Membership includes subscription to
    monthly magazine, *Linking Ring*)

The Society of American Magicians
  66 Marked Tree Rd.
  Needham, MA 02192
  (Membership includes subscription to
    monthly magazine, *MUM*)

Periodicals

Abracadabra (1946– , weekly)
Goodliffe, Arden Forest Industrial Estate
Alcester, Warwickshire, England

Genii—The Conjurors' Magazine (1936– ,
monthly)
c/o Box 36068
Los Angeles, CA 90036

Linking Ring (1923– , monthly, only available to members of the International Brotherhood of Magicians)
International Brotherhood of Magicians
114 N. Detroit St.
Kenton, OH 43326

The Magic Magazine
20 E. 46th St.
New York, NY 10017

MUM, Magic Unity Might (1911– , monthly, only available to members of the Society of American Magicians)
Society of American Magicians
c/o 66 Marked Tree Rd.
Needham, MA 02192

Tops
Magazine of Magic
Abbott's
Colon, MI 49040

Fiction about Magic for Storytellers

Some of the titles that follow are suitable for storytelling; others for reading aloud.

Dickinson, Peter. *Chance, Luck and Destiny.* Little, 1976. Perfect browsing for the storyteller in search of background material.

Emberley, Ed. *Wizard of Op;* il. by author. Little, 1975. An extraordinary exercise using optical art.

Fleischman, Albert Sidney. *Mr. Mysterious and Company;* il. by Eric von Schmidt. Little, 1962. A conjurer and his family travel the old West in a covered wagon. Full-length book.

Green, Roger Lancelyn, comp. *A Cavalcade of Magicians;* il. by Victor Ambrus. Walck, 1973. A complete collection of stories from history and folklore.

Kastner, Erich. *The Little Man;* tr. from the original German by James Kirkup; il. by Rick Schreiter. Knopf, 1966. The hero, only two inches high, is involved with a kidnapper and a magician. Full-length book.

Langstaff, John. *The Two Magicians;* il. by Fritz Eichenberg. Atheneum, 1973. Two magicians try to outdo each other. Picture book.

Manning-Sanders, Ruth. *A Book of Wizards;* il. by Robin Jacques. Dutton, 1967. A collection of stories from Hungary, Wales, Italy, and Russia, all involving wizards and their magic.

Mayer, Mercer. *A Special Trick;* il. by author. Dial, 1970. An amusing picture-book variant of "The Sorcerer's Apprentice."

Newman, Robert. *Merlin's Mistake;* il. by Richard Lebenson. Atheneum, 1970. The old magician gives a boy knowledge of the future instead of the past with amusing results. Full-length book.

Pollack, Reginald. *The Magician and the Child;* il. by author. Atheneum, 1971. "Paintings are the look of feelings. Music is the sound. Dance is the movement.

Stories are the history." "Then what is magic?" the child asked. "All of these put together." A picture book for those willing to understand.

Selden, George. *see* Thompson, George Selden.

Snyder, Zilpha Keatley. *Black and Blue Magic;* il. by Gene Holtan. Atheneum, 1966. "He could fly! He, Harry Houdini Marco, could fly like a bird!" in this story of a magician's son. Full-length book.

Steig, William. *Sylvester and the Magic Pebble;* il. by author. Windmill, 1969. A donkey is turned into a rock in this award-winning picture book.

Thompson, George Selden. *The Genie of Sutton Place,* by George Selden (pseud.). Farrar, 1973. A boy and his dog adventure in New York's Greenwich Village with a genie who can do magical feats. Full-length book.

Wiesner, William. *Magic Tales and Magic Tricks.* Scribner, 1974. Easy tricks accompany short folktales.

18 / Music

When you decide that your storyhour is to be a cultural experience, you may want to include some music. If you can accurately carry a tune, or play a musical instrument, you probably are already aware of most of the ideas to be presented in this chapter. Remember, however, that the storyhour is primarily a time for stories. It should not be turned into a music period, but music can provide your sessions with background, group participation, and an opportunity for presenting talented visitors.

Some storytellers would like to use incidental music in the storyhour, but the idea of locating a record player and toting it about seems like a lot of trouble. Today there are new machines that make recorded music much easier to use. The reel-to-reel tape enables the storyteller to record from many sources: live performances, radio, or recordings to be used in any order and at any time. The cassette recorder is as small as some books; the cassette that it uses is smaller than most paperbacks. The cassette is most useful for background music, but the fidelity may not be satisfactory for larger group listening.

Music in Multimedia Presentations

There may be times during the presentation of a multimedia story when nothing is actually happening, perhaps a scene change in a puppet show or while changing transparencies on an overhead projector. Then it is a good idea to plan for a musical interlude. Use a record, tape recorder, or cassette tape player; if you have a pianist, all the better. Background music can be useful. One time when music is almost a must is when you are showing a book without words on film slides or transparencies. When an individual is looking at such a book, his own thoughts make words or music, but in a group situation this is not so. Choose your music carefully to suit the mood of your story. Ask a friend or the local music store for suggestions if you are unfamiliar with the world of recorded music. Many libraries have extensive collections of records and the librarian is often well versed in what is contained in the collection. A local radio station may have a disc jockey delighted to share his knowledge of music and help you. Sometimes you may even prefer to tape your own background music and sound effects. This is worth experimenting with, but it may be more difficult than it appears. Extraneous noises (the dog barking, the baby crying) may make your tapes less than perfect.

A Storyhour Theme

Just as some disc jockeys have a musical theme to announce their program segments, you may want to choose a theme for the storyhour. Choose a recorded piece of music that suits you and play it throughout the library for a few minutes before the storytime is scheduled to begin.

Settling Down Music

If you are knowledgeable about music, or have a friend or colleague who is, you can choose a different piece of music for every story session. This works well even if you have a theme for your storyhour. For example, you can use circus music for a circus program, quiet music for thoughtful books, folk songs or dances originating from the source country of the stories. Play the music as the children enter the room, find their seats, remove their coats, and place their toys or books on the floor. You might even leave the music on softly as you introduce the stories. When you open the first book, or light your wishing candle, turn the music down. You can turn it up again at the end of the storyhour when the children are leaving. This works rather like the overture of a musical comedy that is played as the audience enters and leaves the theater. If you or a friend can play a musical instrument with proficiency, you can accomplish the same purpose with "live" music.

Singing

Lucky you if you are blessed with a good singing voice. You can find folk songs to fit the stories you tell and incorporate the singing of songs in your storytime. Open the session with a song. Use music as a change of pace between stories and as an ending to your program.

Some storytellers greet the children with the same greeting song at each session and the children sing along. Depending on the sophistication of the song, the idea may not be suitable for all ages. If the storyhours tend to attract a majority of new children each time, singing a group song will be impractical since it will take too much time to learn it each session.

There are times when you may want to make singing the focal point of your storyhour. Celebrate the Christmas season with group singing. Most children know the words of a variety of Christmas carols. In fact, they'll remind you of the words and contribute an idea for a song or two. Last Christmas I was with a group of adults who attempted to sing Christmas carols. We couldn't seem to get past *Jingle Bells* until the ten-year-old daughter of the hostess wandered in. She knew many songs, and we remembered them after she started to sing.

Making up Songs

Encourage the children to make up songs about their daily life. They may sing off key, but it's a delight to hear a preschooler singing happily about getting up or going to bed.

To the Nonmusical

Some stories from folklore contain a song to sing. If the character singing is meant to have a sweet, lilting young voice and you croak like a frog, you might consider another story. However, many songs may be treated like poetry if the audience is first told that the character sang the song.

Do you have a friend who plays an instrument? Invite him or her to perform as a guest at your storyhour. After the performance, he or she may enjoy showing the instrument to the children and explaining a little about it. Books about music and instruments also can be exhibited.

Dance

Again, you don't want to turn your storyhour into a dance class, but you might want your audience to respond to a story rhythmically. Let the children tap out the rhythm of a tongue twister, or the repeated rhyme in a story. Encourage them to respond with dance movements to the mood of a story or record.

If there is a ballet or modern dance studio in your community, invite their special students to your storyhour. Make absolutely certain that you provide a workable phonograph, or tape machine or whatever they need. A good dance program may be hopelessly marred by a faulty musical background. Also don't forget that they will need enough floor space on which to perform.

Field Trips

Some adults have never attended an opera, ballet, or concert. You can insure that this doesn't happen to any of the future adults who come in contact with you in the storyhour. Plan a field trip to a dance festival or musical event in your town. If the nearest such event is some miles away, enlist the aid of parents or local businessmen to provide funds to rent a bus and purchase tickets. Let those families that can afford to help with the costs pay their way. Those children who cannot afford such a trip can be subsidized with donations or put the field trip idea into your next budget. It is an item that voters might just understand and accept. Of course, to transport a group of any size you will need the help of your mothers, but the event, including the getting there and the sack lunches in the park, will be long remembered by the children. At the next session, appropriate stories and books can be presented and discussed.

Homemade Rhythm Instruments

Fill cottage cheese containers, jewelry boxes, hosiery "eggs," film cans, match boxes with buttons, rice, macaroni, marbles, pebbles, or anything else that will rattle.

Use a large nail to thump a rhythm on a cake rack, pot top, tin can.

Put rubber bands across an open box, sugar scoop, or plastic cup to make a homemade stringed instrument you or a child can strum.

Use two of a kind to bump together: a variety of sizes of large bolts, jar lids, pot tops, tin cans. Drill a hole in the center of the tin can or lid so you can tie a string on the instrument which then can hang around your neck, leaving your hands free to tap, pound, or strum.

Make a glass piano by filling several water glasses to different levels, tune them, then tap them with a spoon to produce a melody.

Make a comb kazoo by wrapping tissue paper around a comb. Hum a tune through the paper.

Figure 36. Homemade rhythm instruments

Use these instruments for children to participate in your storyhour. They can tap out a rhythm while singing. After you've told a suitable story let the audience chant a nonsense sentence and "play" the instruments in time to the chant.

Songs with familiar choruses make good material for rhythm instruments. Good and familiar folksongs appear in *The Fireside Book of Folk Songs* (Simon and Schuster, 1947). Try "Clementine," "Sweet Betsy From Pike," "Funiculi, Funicula," "The Bluetail Fly," "Turkey in the Straw," "Oh Susanna," "The Erie Canal."

Following are some stories and poems to use as rhythm activities.

References: Stories with Rhythmic Phrases

Adoff, Arnold. *MA nDA LA;* il. by Emily McCully. Harper, 1971. This is a chant using nonsense sounds. It will take a bit of practice to make it flow easily.

Brown, Jeanette Perkins. "Ticki, Ticki Tembo" in *The Storyteller in Religious Education.* Pilgrim Pr., 1951. A spare telling of a popular nonsense story.

Chase, Richard. "Soap, Soap, Soap!" in *Grandfather Tales;* il. by Berkeley Williams, Jr. Houghton, 1948. "So he headed for the store, arunnin' along and sayin,' 'Soap! Soap! Soap!—so he wouldn't forget."

Hughes, Richard. "The China Spaniel" in *The Spider's Palace and Other Stories;* il. by George Charlton. Looking Glass Library, 1960. A nonsense phrase is quickly learned by the audience.

Milligan, Spike. "On the Ning Nang Nong" in Cole, William, ed. *Oh, What Nonsense!;* il. by Tomi Ungerer. Viking, 1966. A nonsense poem with good rhythm. Each instrument can have a solo in this one.

Songs to Use with Rhythm Instruments

IF YOU'RE HAPPY

Sing this as a group or divide your group so that some are singing and some are playing their instruments. Many verses can be sung by adding actions such as: stamp your feet, turn around, touch the ground, raise your hands, or whatever you can think up.

If you're happy and you know it, clap your hands;

If you're happy and you know it, clap your hands;

If you're happy and you know it, then the whole world will know it;

If you're happy and you know it, clap your hands.

TIN FORD

Sing the chorus of this jingle three times in a row, using actions for each word. Sing the chorus faster each time.

Collected by Robert Rubenstein

I've got a little pile of tin.
Nobody knows what shape it's in.
It's got four wheels and a running board.
It's a Ford. Oh! It's a Ford.

Chorus:

Honk, Honk
Rattle, Rattle
CRASH
Screech, Screech
Beep, Beep.

Using Picture-Book Versions of Songs

Even if you can neither sing nor play a musical instrument, you can introduce children to music through picture books. There are many fine books that use as their subject a folksong or opera. Use these books with or without the music. The book can be read aloud like poetry, showing the pictures, before, during, or after the music is heard. If the music is unavailable don't attempt to sing the song if you are really unmusical—just chant or read the words as you would any picture book. Simply tell the children the story is really a song. My own daughter objects to me singing a picture book. At first I was a bit hurt because I thought she was commenting on my tuneless croak. Now I understand; she feels books are to be read but music is to be played on the piano. With a storyhour group I am not so cowed and plunge into my singing if the children know the song and I think they will join me.

Songs to Sing

If you can sing and/or play, no doubt you have your own favorites to perform. Following is a short selection of folksongs to introduce to your groups. Three of these selections ("Large Boots," "Old Joe Finley," and "Dunderbeck's Machine") are funny songs. You'll notice, however, that each of them has an element of violence or sadness. The children seem to accept this part as inevitable and ask for the songs, again and again.

"The Little Birds' Ball" and "Hush Little Children" are quieter songs for a change of pace. "Rocking Horse" is a short song to sing with very young children. Appropriate hand motions can be used with the participation song "Cows and Horses Walk on Four Feet."

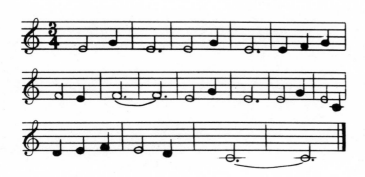

ROCKING HORSE

Collected by Norma Borba

Rocking horse, rocking horse
Give me a ride to Spain.
Rocking horse, rocking horse,
Bring me back home again.

OLD JOE FINLY

From Mrs. E. F. Gaines, Pullman, Wash., 1963
Collected by Edmund F. Soule

Old Joe Finly had a pig . . . Unh-huh!
Old Joe Finly had a pig,
It was so little it never got big . . . Unh-huh!

He went and put it in a sty . . . Unh-huh!
He went and put it in a sty,
And fed it on a sheaf of rye . . . Unh-huh!

The old woman went out to feed the pig . . . Unh-huh!
The old woman went out to feed the pig,
But when she got there the piggy was dead . . . Unh-huh!

The old woman she nearly grieved to death . . . Unh-huh!
The old woman she nearly grieved to death,
To think the piggy had lost its breath . . . Unh-huh!

The old woman she died soon after . . . Unh-huh!
The old woman she died soon after,
The old man he hung himself from a rafter . . . Unh-huh!

And that was the end of one, two, three . . . Unh-huh!
And that was the end of one, two, three,
The old man, the old woman, the little pig-ee . . . Unh-huh!

The lamp and book lie on the shelf . . . Unh-huh!
The lamp and book lie on the shelf,
If you want any more you can sing it yourself . . . Unh-huh!

LARGE BOOTS

Australian marching song
Collected by Edmund F. Soule

Now there was a man named Anthony Dare,
And he was famous everywhere,
As a conjurer and a man of repute,
Because he could play with his boots!

Chorus:

For they were LARGE BOOTS, LARGE BOOTS,
Boots as heavy as lead,
With a circular twist of his muscular wrist
He could swing 'em right over his head!
Dee-dle-dee Um pum pum,
Dee-dle-dee Um pum pum!

As he was walking down the street,
He met a young lady so charming and sweet,
Who thought it would be such a wonderful treat
To see the man play with his boots . . .

As he was swinging them round and round,
One came down with a deuce of a bound
On the hairy head of her faithful hound
Who was watching him play with his boots.

She saw two policemen passing by
And loudly cried "Hi-Hi, Hi-Hi,
My faithful dog has been hit in the eye
By a man who has played with his boots!"

They took him to a magistrate
And lodged him in a cell of state
And there he had time to cogitate
And play with his wonderful boots.

Now the trial was held for straight away,
In fact it was held the very next day,
And the magistrate was heard to say:
"Why shouldn't he play with his boots?"

Now Anthony Dare has gone to his rest;
As a swinger of boots he was the best;
He swung with a zoom and he swung with a zest,
That wonderful pair of boots!

THE LITTLE BIRDS' BALL

Anglo-American folk song as heard in Lewistown, Montana
Collected by Beverly Soule

Said the springbird to the nightingale
I mean to give the birds a ball;
Birdies great and birdies small
All will fly to the little birds' ball.

Chorus:

Tra-la-la-la-la, Tra-la-la-la-la
*Tra-la-la-la-la-*la . . . (Repeat)

O the woodpecker flew from his hole in the tree
And brought his bill to the companee;
Berries ripe and berries red,
A very large bill the little birds said.

O the awkward owl and the bashful jay
Bade each other a very good day;
The lark and the linnet danced for life
And the blackbird danced with the yellowhammer's wife.

They danced and sang till the sun was low
And the mother birds prepared to go;
Birdies great and birdies small
All flew home from the little birds' ball!

HUSH, LITTLE CHILDREN

Traditional Southern lullaby
Collected by Edmund F. Soule

Hush, little children, don't say a word;
I'll give you a mockingbird.

If that mockingbird don't sing;
I'll give you a golden ring.

If that ring should turn to brass;
I'll give you a looking glass.

If that looking glass gets broke;
I'll give you a billy-goat.

If that billy-goat won't pull,
I'll give you a cart and bull.

If that cart and bull fall over,
I'll give you a dog named Rover.

If that dog named Rover won't bark,
I'll give you a horse and cart.

If that horse and cart fall down,
You're still the prettiest little children in town.

DUNDERBECK'S MACHINE

Traditional text. Tune: A Rambling Wreck from Georgia Tech.
Collected by Edmund F. Soule

There was a little Dutchy, and his name was Dunderbeck;
He kept cold meat and sauerkraut and sausage by the peck.
He had a little butcher shop, the finest ever seen
And one day he invented a sausage-meat machine.

Chorus:

O Dunderbeck, O Dunderbeck, how could you be so mean;
I'm sorry you invented that terrible* old machine;
The longtailed cats and billy-go-ats# will never more be seen,
For they'll all be ground to sausage-meat in Dunderbeck's machine!

One day a very little boy came walking into the store;
He wanted to buy a sausage that was lying on the floor.
While he waited for it, it whistled a merry tune
And all the sausages got up and danced around the room.

Now something was the matter, the machine it would not go,
And Dunderbeck he crawled inside the trouble for to know.
His wife was having nightmares and walking in her sleep;
She gave the crank a terrible yank and Dunderbeck was meat!

*horrible
#Variants can be invented: The short-haired cats and pussy-rats, etc.

THANKSGIVING SONG

This song will get your group in the mood for a celebration. Sing it to the tune of Brother John.

Tune: Brother John (Frère Jacque)
Collected by Nell Givler

Turkey dinner, turkey dinner
Gather round, gather round
Who will get the drumstick?
Yummy, yummy drumstick
All sit down, all sit down.

Cornbread muffins, chestnut stuffing
Puddin' pie, one foot high
All of us were thinner,
Until we came to dinner
Me-o-my, me-o-my.

COWS AND HORSES WALK ON FOUR FEET

Collected by Alfred Bates

Cows and horses walk on four feet
Little children walk on two feet
Birdies fly high in the air
Fishes swim in water clear
One, two, three, four, five
Catching fishes all alive
Heads and shoulders, knees and toes
Knees and toes, knees and toes
Heads and shoulders, knees and toes
We'll all clap hands together.

Bibliography of Music in the Storyhour

Entries marked with asterisks represent books that are especially recommended.

General Collections

*Boni, Margaret, ed. *Fireside Book of Folk Songs;* arr. for piano by Norman Lloyd; il. by Alice and Martin Provensen. Simon and Schuster, 1947. A favorite collection of traditional American and foreign folksongs.

Chase, Richard, comp. *Hullabaloo, and Other Singing Folk Games;* six piano settings by Hilton Rufty; il. by Joshua Tolford. Houghton, 1949. A folklorist's collection for older children.

Engvick, William, ed. *Lullabies and Night Songs;* music by Alex Wilder; piano arr. by Seymour Barab; guitar chords by Happy Traum; il. by Maurice Sendak. Harper, 1965. A Caldecott winner has illustrated this book for use at home.

Langstaff, Nancy, and John M., comps. *Jim Along, Josie;* il. by Jan Pienkowski. Harcourt, 1970. Silhouettes illustrate this ALA Notable Children's Book. Includes directions for singing games.

Lloyd, Norman, ed. *The New Golden Song Book;* il. by Mary Blair. Simon and Schuster, 1955. Typical Golden Book format includes games and nursery songs.

Song Collections for Children

Bley, Edgar S., comp. *The Best Singing Games, for Children of All Ages;* piano arr. by Margaret Chase; il. by Patt Willen. Sterling, 1957. Easy-to-follow directions for familiar singing games.

Blyton, Carey. *Bananas in Pyjamas.* Transatlantic, 1973. Musical nonsense.

*Langstaff, John, comp. *Hi! Ho! The Rattlin' Bog, and Other Folk Songs for Group Singing;* piano settings by John Edmunds and others; guitar chords by Happy Traum; il. by Robin Jacques. Harcourt, 1969. Less familiar folk songs for children.

Mitchell, Donald, comp. *Every Child's Book of Nursery Songs;* arr. by Carey Blyton; il. by Alan Howard. Crown, 1968. Music for old favorites such as "Bobby Shafto," "The Muffin Man," "Little Jack Horner," and "Jack and Jill," with drawings in both color and black and white.

Ohanian, Phyllis Brown, comp. *Favorite Nursery Songs;* il. by Marjorie Torrey. Random, 1956. Familiar play and nursery songs.

Poston, Elizabeth, comp. *The Baby's Song Book;* il. by William Stobbs. Crowell, 1972. Songs from America, England, France, Italy, and Spain for young children to enjoy.

Seeger, Ruth. *American Folk Songs for Children; in Home, School and Nursery School;* il. by Barbara Cooney. Doubleday, 1948. Complete directions and music for singing games are included.

Titra, Stephen. *Be Nice to Spiders, Be Kind to Snakes, and 26 Other Songs.* Hubbard, 1973. Nonsense rhymes with musical accompaniment.

Winn, Marie, ed. *The Fireside Book of Children's Songs;* arr. by Allan Miller; il. by John Alcorn. Simon and Schuster, 1966. Singing games, nonsense and nursery songs with simple piano and guitar chord notations.

Collections with a Theme

Boy Scout Songbook. Boy Scouts of America, 1974. Particularly useful for camps and children's groups.

Bryan, Ashley, comp. and il. *Walk Together Children: Black American Spirituals.* Atheneum, 1974. Two dozen spirituals illustrated with stark woodcuts.

Chase, Richard. *Singing Games and Play-party Games;* six piano settings by Hilton Rufty; il. by Joshua Tolford; Dover, 1967. A collection of traditional English and American folk games and dances with music and directions.

Free to Be . . . You and Me; conceived by Marlo Thomas; developed and edited by Carole Hart and others; ed. by Francine Klagsbrun. McGraw-Hill, 1974. Songs, poems, and stories to free children from sexism.

Keller, Charles, comp. *Glory, Glory, How Peculiar;* il. by Lady McGrady. Prentice-Hall, 1976. Song parodies that might inspire a group to collect their own.

*Langstaff, John. *Sweetly Sings the Donkey: Animal Rounds for Children to Sing or Play on Recorders;* il. by Nancy Winslow Parker. Atheneum, 1976. Rounds for two, three, or four parts to sing or play.

*Langstaff, John and Carol. *Shimmy Shimmy Coke-Ca-Pop! A Collection of City Children's Street Games and Rhymes with Piano Arrangements;* photos. by Don MacSorley. Doubleday, 1973. Directions and black-and-white photos explain how to play these games.

Ritchie, Jean. *The Swapping Song Book;* piano arr. by A. K. Fossner and Edward Tripp; photos. by George Pickow. Oxford, 1952. Appalachian folk songs by a distinguished folk singer.

Robinson, Adjai. *Singing Tales of Africa;* il. by Christine Price. Scribner, 1974. Stories that revolve around singing retold from African sources.

Simon, Henry William, ed. *A Treasury of Christmas Songs and Carols;* new piano arr. by Henry William Simon and Rudolph Fellner; il. by Rafaello Busoni. Houghton, 1955. A good basic collection.

Stoutenburg, Adrien. *The Crocodile's Mouth; Folk-song Stories;* il. by Glen Rounds. Viking, 1966. No music, but the words for 14 story songs; e.g., "Sweet Betsy from Pike," "The Sow Got the Measles," and others.

*Winn, Marie, ed. *The Fireside Book of Fun and Game Songs;* musical arr. by Allan Miller; il. by Whitney Darrow, Jr. Simon and Schuster, 1974. A large collection of action, question and answer, and cumulative songs.

——— *What Shall We Do and Allee Galloo!;* musical arr. by Allan Miller; il. by Karla Kuskin. Harper, 1970. Familiar activity and game songs for young children.

Yolen, Jane H., comp. *The Fireside Song Book of Birds and Beasts;* arr. by Barbara Green; il. by Peter Parnall. Simon and Schuster, 1972. Music for animal enthusiasts.

Foreign Language Songbooks

Grüger, Heribert and Johannes. *Images qui chatent: initiation au chant et à la musique.* Fleurus, 1970. Translated from the German into French by Geneviève Ploquin. The notes of each tune are presented pictorially.

Rockwell, Anne, comp. *Savez-vous Planter les Choux? and Other French Songs.*

World, 1960. French songs translated and illustrated.

Yurchenco, Henrietta, comp. *A Fiesta of Folk Songs from Spain and Latin America;* il. by Jules Maidoff. Putnam, 1967. Spanish favorites in two languages.

Songs from Films and Television

Raposo, Joseph and Moss, Jeffrey. *Sesame Street Songbook;* arr. by Sy Oliver; il. by Loretta Trezzo. Simon and Schuster, 1971. Words and music for the familiar songs written for, and presented on, the successful television series.

*Rogers, Fred. *Mister Rogers' Songbook;* il. by Steven Kellogg; piano arrangements by John Costa. Random, 1970. The charming patter songs from *Mister Rogers' Neighborhood* appear in this book. Colorfully illustrated.

The Walt Disney Song Book. Golden Pr., 1971. Disney drawings decorate this collection of songs from his films which include "Zip-a-Dee Doo Dah" and "Who's Afraid of the Big Bad Wolf?"

Children's Books Set to Music

*Fraser-Simson, Harold. *The Pooh Song Book;* words by A. A. Milne; il. by E. H. Shepard. Dutton, 1961. Containing the "Hums of Pooh," "The King's Breakfast" and 14 songs from *When We Were Very Young.* Difficult but beautiful musical arrangements from the Winnie the Pooh stories.

Garson, Eugenia, comp. *The Laura Ingalls Wilder Songbook;* arr. for piano and guitar by Herbert Haufrecht; il. by Garth Williams. Harper, 1968. Music from the *Little House* books for piano or guitar.

Glass, Dudley. *The Songs of Peter Rabbit.* Warne, 1951. Words and music based on Beatrix Potter's *The Tale of Peter Rabbit.*

*Sendak, Maurice. *Maurice Sendak's Really Rosie;* music by Carole King; design by Jane Byers Bierhorst. Harper, 1975.

Picture-Book Versions of Single Songs

Show the book before, during, or after singing or reciting the song.

Abisch, Roz, and Kaplan, Boche. *Sweet Betsy from Pike;* il. by authors. McCall, 1970. Illustrated with collage.

Bangs, Edward. *Steven Kellogg's Yankee Doodle;* il. by Steven Kellogg. Parents, 1976. Colorful, detailed drawings illustrate this song of the American Revolution.

Bonne, Rose. *I Know an Old Lady;* music by Alan Mills (pseud.); il. by Abner Graboff. Rand, 1961. Modern illustrations for a funny song.

Child, Lydia Maria. *Over the River and Through the Wood;* il. by Brinton Turkle. Coward, 1974. The classic Thanksgiving poem illustrated with scenes from the 19th century. Score for piano and guitar included.

Conover, Chris. *Six Little Ducks;* il. by author. Crowell, 1976. Music is included for this rhythmic folk song. Color and black-and-white drawings.

The Fox Went Out on a Chilly Night; il. by Peter Spier. Doubleday, 1961. Detailed drawings illuminate this folksong. Available on film (16mm, color, 7:50 min.) and filmstrip (41 fr., color, 7:32 min.) from Weston Woods.

Frog Went A-Courtin'; retold by John Langstaff; il. by Feodor Rojankovsky. Harcourt, 1955. Gaily illustrated picture-book version of an old song.

Grimm Brothers. *The Story of Hansel and Gretel: A Story of the Forests;* music by Engelbert Humperdink; il. by Warren Chappell. Knopf, 1944. The famous opera brought to life in picture-book form.

Hush Little Baby; il. by Aliki Brandenburg. Prentice-Hall, 1968. A colonial setting for this lullaby.

Hush, Little Baby; adapted and il. by Margot Zemach. Dutton, 1976. A Victorian setting to compare with that of Aliki Brandenburg's. Music included.

Keats, Ezra Jack. *Over in the Meadow;* text based on the original version by Olive A. Wadsworth; il. by author. Four Winds, 1972. The art rather overpowers the simple counting rhyme, but choose for yourself. This version has no music.

Langstaff, John. *Oh, A-Hunting We Will Go;* il. by Nancy Winslow Parker. Atheneum, 1974. Music is included in this retelling of a traditional nursery song. Children will enjoy acting out this story-song.

———— *Over in the Meadow;* il. by Feodor Rojankovsky. Harcourt, 1957. The children enjoy counting the animals in this picture-book version of an old song.

London Bridge is Falling Down!; il. by Peter Spier. Doubleday, 1967. The panoramic drawings show the history of the building of London Bridge.

Mendoza, George. *A Wart Snake in a Fig Tree;* il. by Etienne Delessert. Dial, 1968. A sophisticated parody of "The Twelve Days of Christmas."

Mother Goose. *Hurrah, We're Outward Bound!;* il. by Peter Spier. Doubleday, 1968. Young sea admirers will love this picture-book version of an old sea song.

Old MacDonald Had a Farm; il. by Robert Quackenbush. Lippincott, 1972. Colorful illustrations accompany the familiar song.

*Paterson, Andrew B. *Waltzing Matilda;* il. by Desmond Digby. Collins, 1970. Winner of the Australian award for children's illustrated books, this is a lovely version of the song, but with no music.

Prokofieff, Serge. *Peter and the Wolf;* foreword by Serge Koussevitzky; il. by Warren Chappell. Knopf, 1940. Music and pictures for the famous children's orchestral narrative.

Quackenbush, Robert. *Go Tell Aunt Rhody;* il. by author. Lippincott, 1973. Bright illustrations with hidden objects complement the verses of this familiar folksong.

*Spier, Peter. *The Erie Canal;* il. by author. Doubleday, 1970. Pictures from the American past.

*Zemach, Harve. *Mommy, Buy Me a China Doll;* adapted from an Ozark children's song; il. by Margot Zemach. Follett, 1966. Eliza Lou wants to "trade our daddy's feather bed" for a china doll.

Ballads

The Derby Ram; il. by Rick Schreiter. Doubleday, 1970. Picture-book version of a nursery ballad.

Ferris, Helen, comp. *Love's Enchantment;* il. by Vera Bock. Doubleday, 1944. Romantic ballads.

Manning-Sanders, Ruth, comp. *A Bundle of Ballads;* il. by William Stobbs. Lippincott, 1961. More than 60 traditional ballads in this collection.

*Plotz, Helen. *As I Walked Out One Evening: A Book of Ballads.* Greenwillow/ Morrow, 1976. Divided into six categories with a useful introduction.

Serraillier, Ian. *Robin and His Merry Men; Ballads of Robin Hood;* il. by Victor G. Ambrus. Walck, 1970. Robin Hood in ballad form.

Stories about Music and Dance for Younger Children

*Baylor, Byrd. *Sometimes I Dance Mountains;* photos. by Bill Sears; il. by Ken Longtemps. Scribner, 1973. A young girl tells how she feels while dancing. Picture-book format.

Belpré, Pura. *Dance of the Animals: A Puerto Rican Folktale;* il. by Paul Galdone. Warne, 1972. Señor and Señora Lion give a party.

*Carr, Rachel. *Be a Frog, a Bird, or a Tree: Creative Yoga Exercises for Children;* photos. by Edward Kimball, Jr.; il. by Don Hedin. Doubleday, 1973. Illustrations and poems demonstrate simple yoga positions in a creative way.

*Goffstein, M. B. *A Little Schubert;* il. by author; record by Peter Schaaf. Harper, 1972. A record played by Peter Schaaf of five Schubert waltzes is part of this multimedia book. A delightful introductory biography.

Grimm Brothers. *The Twelve Dancing Princesses;* tr. by Elizabeth Shub; il. by Uri Shulevitz. Scribner, 1966. Stylistic drawings for this traditional tale.

Isadora, Rachel. *Max;* il. by author. Macmillan, 1976. A young baseball player discovers the delights of ballet. A picture book.

Johnson, D. William. *The Willow Flute: A North Country Tale;* il. by author. Little, 1975. A magic flute brings spring to deep snow country.

Lang, Andrew. *The Twelve Dancing Princesses;* il. by Adrienne Adams. Holt, 1966. Rich, warm illustrations for the story of a cowherd who wants to marry a princess.

Levoy, Myron. *Penny Tunes and Princesses;* il. by Ezra Jack Keats. Harper, 1972. When Janos Ady plays his violin, it laughs, cries, and leaps like an acrobat.

*McCloskey, Robert. *Lentil;* il. by author. Viking, 1940. A boy who can't carry a tune saves the day with his harmonica.

*Partch, Virgil Franklin. *Ludwig, The Dog Who Snored Symphonies,* by VIP (pseud.); story by Robert Kraus. Windmill, 1971. A very funny story about a dog whose snores became famous.

Perrault, Charles. *Cinderella;* il. by Marcia Brown. Scribner, 1954. Crayon drawings by a Caldecott winner.

———— *Cinderella;* il. by Beni Montresor. Knopf, 1965. Modern illustrations for this old tale, also from a Caldecott winner.

Quin-Harkin, Janet. *Peter Penny's Dance;* il. by Anita Lobel. Dial, 1976. Peter dances around the world accompanied by gaily colored drawings. The story is based on an English ballad.

Stories about Music and Dance for Older Children

*Andersen, Hans Christian. "The Nightingale," in *It's Perfectly True;* tr. by Paul Leyssac; il. by Richard Bennett. Harcourt, 1938. Andersen's classic is for the advanced storyteller, but well worth learning.

Bang, Molly, comp. "The Old Man's Wen," in *The Goblins Giggle and Other Stories;* il. by compiler. Scribner, 1973. An old man dances with the goblins and is rewarded in a strange way.

Byars, Betsy C. *The Dancing Camel;* il. by Harold Berson. Viking, 1965. A whimsical story about a talented camel for telling or reading aloud.

*Ewing, Juliana H. "Murdoch's Rath," in Sechrist, Elizabeth Hough, and Woolsey, Janette, eds., *It's Time for Storyhour;* il. by Elsie Jane McCorkell. Macrae Smith, 1964. A long delightful Irish story, in which Pat dances with the fairymen.

Farjeon, Eleanor. *The Glass Slipper;* il. by Ernest Shepard. Viking, 1956. A full-length novel based on Cinderella, and excellent for reading aloud.

*Leichman, Seymour, *The Boy Who Could Sing Pictures;* il. by author. Doubleday, 1968. The son of a jester teaches the king a lesson.

"The Rose and the Violinist" in Ficowski, Jerzy. *Sister of the Birds and Other Gypsy Tales;* tr. by Lucia M. Borski; il. by Charles Mikolaycak. Abingdon, 1976. An enchanted rose is freed by music.

Recordings

There is a wealth of recorded music and musical stories available to those who wish to use them. I've explained that I personally have found that group listening to a record is unsatisfactory, and for this reason I've included only a small selection in this bibliography. For at-home listening ask your librarian or record dealer for suggestions.

Amahl and the Night Visitors, RCA Victor, 33⅓ rpm. Gian-Carlo Menotti's Christmas opera with the original cast of the 1963 NBC-TV production. RCA Educational Sales, 1133 Ave. of the Americas, New York, NY 10036.

Folk Songs for Young Folk—Animals, v. 1. Folkways/Scholastic Records, 33⅓ rpm. Alan Mills sings "A Frog He Would A-Wooing Go," and "Who Killed Cock Robin?," among other favorites. Folkways, 906 Sylvan Ave., Englewood Cliffs, NJ 07632.

Free to Be . . . You and Me, Bell Records, 33⅓ rpm. Marlo Thomas and friends sing stories and songs. Columbia Pictures Industries, Inc., 1776 Broadway, New York, NY 10019.

The Little Prince, ABC Records, 33⅓ rpm. Original soundtrack from the Paramount film based on Antoine de Saint-Exupery's book. ABC Records, Inc., Los Angeles, CA 90048.

Mister Rogers: A Place of Our Own, Small World Enterprises, 33⅓ rpm. Songs sung by Fred Rogers from the television show, "Mr. Rogers' Neighborhood." Small World Enterprises, Inc., 4716 Ellsworth Ave., Pittsburgh, PA 15213.

Really Rosie, Ode Records, 33⅓ rpm. Carole King and Maurice Sendak teamed to create this original soundtrack from the television production. A & M Records, Inc., P.O. Box 782, Beverly Hills, CA 90213.

Winnie the Pooh and Christopher Robin,

Decca Records, 33⅓ rpm. Frank Luther sings stories and songs from the books by A. A. Milne. Decca Records, Div. of MCA, Inc., 445 Park Ave., New York, NY 10022.

Films

The Sorcerer's Apprentice. 16mm, color, 14 min. Weston Woods, 1963. A talented artist (Lisl Weil) gracefully draws the story while Paul Dukas's symphony is played. Some adults find this film dated because of the artist's dress, but children seem to be intrigued by it.

Picture Books to Set to Music

The enjoyment of these books might be enhanced by playing music while you show the book. Those preceded by an asterisk have few, if any, words but really do seem to beg for musical background.

*Carle, Eric. *I See a Song;* il. by author. Crowell, 1973. A burst of color and no words represent an artist's interpretation of the sounds of music.

Hazen, Barbara. *The Sorcerer's Apprentice;* il. by Tomi Ungerer. Lancelot Pr., 1969. A humorous retelling. Use Columbia's recording of Dukas's music as performed by the New York Philharmonic (33 rpm, 1969).

*Keats, Ezra Jack. *Psst! Doggie—;* il. by author. Watts, 1973. A cat and a dog wordlessly dance to music of foreign lands.

Paterson, Andrew B. *Waltzing Matilda;* il. by Desmond Digby. Collins, 1970. Sing this Australian song while showing the book.

*Wildsmith, Brian. *Brian Wildsmith's Circus;* il. by author. Watts, 1970. Glorious pictures of the circus. Use circus music.

PART FOUR

Now is the time to put it all together. You have learned and told a few stories, recited some poems, performed a magic trick or two, and even given a puppet show. In this section the first four chapters examine different audiences and their particular characteristics, providing, in addition, examples of specific books and activities suited to them.

Extending the actual telling of stories to include the audience in an expanded program might be your next goal. The last three chapters show through examples how to involve your listeners and turn them into active participants with book parties, activity programs, and creative dramatics.

19 / Preschool and Primary Programs

The Preschool Storytime is for children aged three to five who will enjoy simple stories, songs, and books. My experience suggests that you be cautious about accepting children under three, even if the parent insists that the child listens to stories at home with rapt attention. A new group situation is an entirely different experience and the child will not react the same as in his own home. This doesn't mean that children under three should be neglected. You might plan to work with the parents and guide them in storytelling at home. An occasional special storyhour for the very young might be planned. Keep the session short and the group small—no more than four or five children. Obviously if you work in an infant-toddler day-care center you will want to plan and provide book experiences for the children.

The Primary Storyhour is for the five- to seven-year-old group. In a public library situation you may not have enough staff or energy to separate preschool and primary age groups, but ideally they should be. This age group will be interested in the longer picture books. The old favorites, such as *Cinderella,* that the children already know in picture-book form will be good stories for you to learn and tell in the traditional manner. By separating the younger children from the primary children you will be able to wean the children away from a reliance on pictures, puppets, and board stories. They need to learn to listen as well as to see. By telling rather than showing some of the stories, the children will begin to develop their powers of concentration and become aware of the subtle nuances of the story, the characterizations, the words themselves.

Planning and Production

You may want to hold your preschool or primary book programs in a location where the parents can watch. The major problem with this kind of an arrangement is the way a child acts in the presence of her or his parents, and for this reason I prefer having all my programs without mothers and fathers. A colleague of mine was giving a lecture-demonstration of book programs for the young child. She had invited a local nursery school to come and hear a story while the adult group observed. The children were accompanied by their teacher and one mother. The mother was carrying a baby and her three-year-old son was a member of the class. He was utterly impossible. He stood while his peers sat, ran around and through the children, and screamed as loud as he could. When the baby the mother was carrying began to cry, she left the room. Her little "Dennis the Menace" completely changed almost instantly. He stopped running, quietly walked over to the group, sat down and became the most attentive of listeners. I am sure that no one in that workshop audience will ever allow a mother into a storyhour in their library. However, one librarian I know encourages parents to attend with their preschoolers, her reason being that it helps to give those adults the guidance which they also need.

An assistant is very useful with the preschool storytime. Sometimes a child "forgets" to visit the restroom and needs help. Often a young child really objects to being separated from his mother or father, and an assistant can reunite the child with a parent without disrupting the other children. If you are short of staff and need help, one of the mothers can act as a substitute helper. If possible, recruit a volunteer who is not the parent of a group member.

Some storytellers like the children to be seated on the floor, often on cushions. The storyteller then sits on a chair in front of them. I prefer to have both children and storytellers on chairs. Even though children seem to be more comfortable on the floor than adults, I still think it is unpleasant for any length of time. Seating both the leader and the audience in the same way increases the informality of the session too, a desirable mood for this age group.

Introducing the Program and Follow-up Activities

Opening the storyhour is dealt with at length in another section of this book. This is only to remind you that you should specifically plan what you are going to do to begin the storytime. The settling down period is a time to get acquainted with the audience. I often use a puppet or an interesting artifact to introduce myself and the stories I am going to tell. I may encourage the children to talk to the puppet or comment on the artifact before the stories actually begin. This get-acquainted period should be kept brief, or the children might begin to chatter, becoming more interested in themselves than in the stories. During the actual telling of stories or books I usually ignore comments or questions until the presentation is finished. Between stories the children are encouraged to relax and rearrange themselves for the next book. Often this is accomplished through the participation in a group action such as a finger play or song. At the close of the session there should be enough time allowed for the children to look at the books, touch the display if there is one, and articulate any thoughts they might have about the story they just heard, or one presented on another day.

Program Content

The majority of time spent in the preschool and primary sessions will be devoted to the reading and showing of picture books. Folktales with simple plots and repetitive action will be well received. Rhymes, short poems, and finger plays may be introduced, and singing and games may be used as a secondary activity.

Picture Books

Since books are to be the focal point of your entire program, you will naturally want to choose books of the highest literary and artistic quality. There are many lists to help you decide which books to read. The American Library Association's Children's Services Division (50 E. Huron St., Chicago, IL 60611) puts out annual lists (*Caldecott Medal Books*, *Newbery Medal Books*, and *Notable Children's Books*) as do organizations like the Association for Childhood Education International (3615 Wisconsin Ave. NW, Washington, DC 20016). Reviews of books in professional journals, and the annual lists can keep you up to date and aware of the latest books. Nothing, however, can take the place of your own reading to determine which books will best suit your interests and the needs and interests of your particular group. Many good editions of children's paperbacks have recently been published. Although paperbacks are useful, I highly recommend the use of hardcover editions, whenever possible, in storytelling situations. It is not only the story and beauty of the pictures you want to communicate, but the very essence of the book itself: fine paper, binding, and design. Beware of using the very small sized picture books for a large group; these are better reserved for taking home or for "individual reading."

Always give the title and name the author of the book. Books are by people and there is no reason why children can't learn to associate names with books. And, if you like, you can give a one-sentence introduction to the book so the children know what to expect. "This is the story of a badger that didn't like to go to bed" (*Bedtime for Frances*) or "In this book an old lady receives a boa constrictor as a pet" (*Crictor*).

Despite the fact that you will be holding the book as you tell the story, you should be familiar enough with the text that you need only to glance at it now and then. It's even better if you've actually memorized the text or know it so thoroughly that you can use the book only as a display for the group's benefit. Hold the book in any way that seems comfortable for you and still enables the audience to see the pictures. Move the book slowly around the semicircle so that each child gets a chance to clearly see each and every picture. You might want to point out details in the pictures, "Does everyone see the mouse?", but keep interjections of this kind to a minimum. Children often see more detail than adults anyway. My own child had to show me the mouse on every page in Margaret Wise Brown's *Goodnight Moon* (Harper, 1947); I'd never noticed it before. Give the children time to discover that the pictures tell the story as well as the words.

For a new group unfamiliar with picture books, you will want to begin with shorter, simpler books. After the children have attended several sessions, they will be ready for longer, more complicated stories. It is not necessary to have the two or three books you use in each storyhour relate to each other. However, books that complement each other do make a more cohesive session.

Naturally, you will want to present the new and unusual, but don't feel that you have to present something different at each session. Remember that to the children all the books are new, even those published when Mommy was a little girl. Moreover, it doesn't bore a child to hear a story again and again. Each telling is slightly different, and they will learn something new. At the end of the story session encourage the children to look at books on their own.

Bibliography of Picture Books for Preschool and Primary Children, Arranged by Theme and Subject

The following bibliography lists only a few of the hundreds of books that can be successfully used in the preschool and primary storyhours. They are grouped by subject and/or theme to suggest possible "go together" books, but books listed under a heading are not necessarily to be used at the same time. More than one book about death, for instance, at one sitting would probably be too much. The same is true of birthday books, and yet if you are a classroom teacher, you probably would like a collection of books to read on this special day for the children. The books that are too small to be seen by a group larger than four should be taken home and enjoyed or lovingly looked at before and after the program on an individual basis. Books that are completely unrelated by a theme are fine too. Choose books you personally enjoy and would like to use with children. Try to keep current through reviews and lists of new books published, but at the same time, don't forget all those books that you and others have enjoyed and loved through the years.

ABCs and Counting

Anno, Mitsumasa. *Anno's Alphabet;* il. by author. Crowell, 1975.

Brown, Marc. *One Two Three: An Animal Counting Book;* il. by author. Atlantic/ Little, 1976.

Carle, Eric. *1, 2, 3 to the Zoo;* il. by author. World, 1968.

Feelings, Muriel. *Moja Means One; Swahili Counting Book;* il. by Tom Feelings. Dial, 1971.

Gág, Wanda. *The ABC Bunny;* il. by author and Howard Gág. Coward, 1933.

Miles, Miska. *Apricot ABC;* il. by Peter Parnall. Little, 1969.

Oxenbury, Helen. *Numbers of Things;* il. by author. Watts, 1968.

Ants

Brenner, Barbara. *If You Were an Ant;* il. by Fred Brenner. Harper, 1973.

Freschet, Berniece. *The Ants Go Marching;* il. by Stefan Martin. Scribner, 1973.

Portal, Colette. *The Life of a Queen;* tr. by Marci Nardi; il. by author. Braziller, 1964.

Apples

Hogrogian, Nonny. *Apples;* il. by author. Macmillan, 1972.

Rothman, Joel. *A Moment in Time;* il. by Don Leake. Scroll, 1973.

Scheer, Julian. *Rain Makes Applesauce;* il. by Marvin Bileck. Holiday, 1964.

Bears

Craft, Ruth. *The Winter Bear;* il. by Erik Blegvad. Atheneum, 1975.

Du Bois, William Péne. *Bear Party;* il. by author. Viking, 1963.

Freeman, Don. *Beady Bear;* il. by author. Viking, 1954.

Galdone, Paul. *The Three Bears;* il. by author. Seabury, 1972.

Ginsburg, Mirra. *Two Greedy Bears,* il. by José Aruego and Ariane Dewey. Macmillan, 1976.

Krauss, Ruth. *Bears;* il. by Phyllis Rowand. Harper, 1948.

Kuratomi, Chizuko. *Mr. Bear Goes to Sea;* il. by Kozo Kakimoto. Judson Pr., 1970.

Birthdays

Barrett, Judith. *Benjamin's 365 Birthdays;* il. by Ron Barrett. Atheneum, 1974.

Bornstein, Ruth. *Little Gorilla;* il. by author. Seabury, 1976.

Carle, Eric. *The Secret Birthday Message;* il. by author. Crowell, 1972.

Hutchins, Pat. *The Surprise Party;* il. by author. Macmillan, 1969.

Kellogg, Steven. *Won't Somebody Play With Me?;* il. by author. Dial, 1972.

Munari, Bruno. *The Birthday Present;* il. by author. World, 1959.

Zolotow, Charlotte. *Mr. Rabbit and the Lovely Present;* il. by Maurice Sendak. Harper, 1962.

Cats

Birnbaum, A. *Green Eyes;* il. by author. Golden Pr., 1973.

Brown, Marcia. *Felice;* il. by author. Scribner, 1958.

Carle, Eric. *Have You Seen My Cat?;* il. by author. Watts, 1973.

Clymer, Eleanor. *Horatio's Birthday;* il. by Robert Quackenbush. Atheneum, 1976.

Gág, Wanda. *Millions of Cats;* il. by author. Coward, 1928.

Gantos, Jack. *Rotten Ralph;* il. by Nicole Rubel. Houghton, 1976.

Keats, Ezra Jack. *Hi, Cat;* il. by author. Macmillan, 1970.

Kent, Jack. *The Fat Cat: A Danish Folktale;* il. by author. Scholastic, 1972 (paper).

Newberry, Clare Turlay. *Percy, Polly, and Pete;* il. by author. Harper, 1952.

Seignobosc, Françoise. *Minou,* by Françoise (pseud.); il. by author. Scribner, 1962.

Zimelman, Nathan. *The Lives of My Cat Alfred;* il. by Evaline Ness. Dutton, 1976.

Circus

Allen, Jeffrey. *Bonzini! The Tattooed Man;* il. by James Marshall. Little, 1976.

De Regniers, Beatrice Schenk. *Circus;* il. with photos by Al Giese. Viking, 1966.

Goodall, John S. *The Adventures of Paddy Pork;* il. by author. Harcourt, 1968 (small size).

Munari, Bruno. *The Circus in the Mist;* il. by author. World, 1969.

Peppé, Rodney. *Circus Numbers: A Counting Book;* il. by author. Delacorte, 1969.

Piatti, Celestino, and Huber, Ursula. *The Nock Family Circus;* tr. from the German by Barbara Kowal Gollub; il. by authors. Atheneum, 1968.

Prelutsky, Jack. *Circus;* il. by Arnold Lobel. Macmillan, 1974.

Wildsmith, Brian. *Brian Wildsmith's Circus;* il. by author. Watts, 1970.

Colors

Asch, Frank. *Yellow, Yellow;* il. by Mark Alan Stamaty. McGraw-Hill, 1971.

Carle, Eric. *The Mixed-Up Chameleon;* il. by author. Crowell, 1975.

Haskins, Ilma. *Color Seems;* il. by author. Vanguard, 1973.

Lionni, Leo. *Little Blue and Little Yellow;* il. by author. McDowell, 1959.

Reiss, John. *Colors;* il. by author. Bradbury, 1969.

Rossetti, Christina. *What Is Pink?;* il. by Jose Aruego. Macmillan, 1971.

Tison, Annette, and Taylor, Talus. *The Adventures of the Three Colors;* il. by authors. World, 1971.

Death

De Brunhoff, Jean. *The Story of Babar;* tr. from the French by Merle Haas; il. by author. Random, 1937.

De Paola, Tomie. *Nana Upstairs and Nana Downstairs;* il. by author. Putnam, 1973.

Dobrin, Arnold. *Scat!;* il. by author. Four Winds, 1971.

Kantrowitz, Mildred. *When Violet Died;* il. by Emily McCully. Parents, 1973.

Miles, Miska. *Annie and the Old One;* il. by Peter Parnall. Little, 1971.

Ross, G. Max. *When Lucy Went Away;* il. by Ingrid Fetz. Dutton, 1976.

Viorst, Judith. *The Tenth Good Thing about Barney;* il. by Erik Blegvad. Atheneum, 1975.

Zolotow, Charlotte. *My Grandson Lew;* il. by William Pène Du Bois. Harper, 1974.

The Desert

Baylor, Byrd. *The Desert Is Theirs;* il. by Peter Parnall. Scribner, 1975.

Caudill, Rebecca. *Wind, Sand, and Sky;* il. by Donald Carrick. Dutton, 1976.

Ducks

Conover, Chris. *Six Little Ducks;* il. by author. Crowell, 1976.

Flack, Marjorie. *Angus and the Ducks;* il. by author. Doubleday, 1930.

——— *The Story about Ping;* il. by Kurt Wiese. Viking, 1933.

McCloskey, Robert. *Make Way for Ducklings;* il. by author. Viking, 1941.

Ecology

Chen, Tony. *Run, Zebra, Run;* il. by author. Lothrop, 1972.

Cheney, Richard E. *Really Eager and the Glorious Watermelon Contest;* il. by Ib Ohlsson. Dutton, 1970.

Mizumura, Kezue. *If I Built a Village;* il. by author. Crowell, 1971.

Olsen, Ib Spang. *Smoke;* tr. by Virginia Allen Jensen; il. by author. Coward, 1972.

Peet, William B. *The Wump World;* il. by author. Houghton, 1970.

Folk and Fairy Tales

(*See also* the single tale bibliography in chapter 5)

Berends, Polly B. *Jack Kent's Book of Nursery Tales;* il. by Jack Kent. Random, 1970.

Brooke, Leonard Leslie. *The Golden Goose Book;* il. by author. Warne, 1906.

Brown, Marcia. *Stone Soup;* il. by author. Scribner, 1947.

Galdone, Paul. *Three Billy Goats Gruff;* il. by author. Seabury, 1973.

Garrison, Christian. *Little Pieces of the West Wind;* il. by Diane Goode. Bradbury, 1975.

Suhl, Yuri. *Simon Boom Gives a Wedding;* il. by Margot Zemach. Four Winds, 1972.

Food

Carle, Eric. *The Very Hungry Caterpillar;* il. by author. World, 1970.

Gaeddert, Lou Ann. *Gustav the Gourmet Giant;* il. by Steven Kellogg. Dial, 1976.

Kahl, Virginia. *The Duchess Bakes a Cake;* il. by author. Scribner, 1955.

Lord, John Vernon. *The Giant Jam Sandwich;* story and pictures by John Vernon Lord; verses by Janet Burroway. Houghton, 1973.

Mosel, Arlene. *The Funny Little Woman;* il. by Blair Lent. Dutton, 1972.

Paterson, Diane. *Eat!;* il. by author. Dial, 1975.

Stamaty, Mark Alan. *Who Needs Donuts?* Dial, 1973.

Friends

Carle, Eric. *Do You Want to Be My Friend?;* il. by author. Crowell, 1971.

De Regniers, Beatrice Schenk. *May I Bring a Friend?;* il. by Beni Montresor. Atheneum, 1964.

Ets, Marie Hall. *Gilberto and the Wind;* il. by author. Viking, 1963.

Rabinowitz, Sandy. *The Red Horse and the Blue Bird;* il. by author. Harper, 1975.

Schweitzer, Byrd Baylor. *Amigo;* il. by Garth Williams. Macmillan, 1963.

Sharmat, Marjorie. *I'm Not Oscar's Friend Anymore;* il. by Tony De Luna. Dutton, 1975.

Steig, William. *Amos and Boris;* il. by author. Farrar, 1971.

Udry, Janice. *Let's Be Enemies;* il. by Maurice Sendak. Harper, 1961.

Funny Animals (or Are They Children?)

Brandenburg, Aliki. *Keep Your Mouth Closed, Dear,* by Aliki (pseud.); il. by author. Dial, 1966.

Leaf, Munro. *The Story of Ferdinand;* il. by Robert Lawson. Scholastic, 1961.

Rey, Hans A. *Curious George;* il. by author. Houghton, 1941.

Zion, Gene. *Harry, the Dirty Dog;* il. by Margaret Bloy Graham. Harper, 1956.

Good Night Books

Children are invited to a storyhour in their pajamas.

Brown, Margaret Wise. *Goodnight Moon;* il. by Clement Hurd. Harper, 1947.

Hoban, Russell. *Bedtime For Frances;* il. by Garth Williams. Harper, 1960.

Horwitz, Elinor Lander. *When the Sky Is Like Lace;* il. by Barbara Cooney. Lippincott, 1975.

Hush Little Baby; il. by Aliki Brandenburg. Prentice-Hall, 1968.

Hutchins, Pat. *Good-Night, Owl!;* il. by author. Macmillan, 1972.

Krauss, Ruth. *The Bundle Book;* il. by Helen Stone. Harper, 1951.

Levine, Joan Goldman. *A Bedtime Story;* il. by Gail Owens. Dutton, 1975.

Mayer, Mercer. *There's a Nightmare in my Closet;* il. by author. Dial, 1968.

Plath, Sylvia. *The Bed Book;* il. by Emily Arnold McCully. Harper, 1976.

Ryan, Cheli Durán. *Hildilid's Night;* il. by Arnold Lobel. Macmillan, 1971.

Sugita, Yutaka. *Good Night 1, 2, 3;* il. by author. Scroll Pr., 1971.

Zolotow, Charlotte. *Sleepy Book;* il. by Vladimir Bobri. Lothrop, 1958.

Hats

Geisel, Theodor Seuss. *The 500 Hats of Bartholomew Cubbins,* by Dr. Seuss (pseud.); il. by author. Vanguard, 1938.

Keats, Ezra Jack. *Jennie's Hat;* il. by author. Harper, 1966.

Lexau, Joan M. *Who Took the Farmer's Hat?,* by Joan L. Nodset (pseud.); il. by Fritz Siebel. Harper, 1963.

Slobodkina, Esphyr. *Caps For Sale;* il. by author. W. R. Scott, 1947.

Ungerer, Tomi. *The Hat;* il. by author. Parents, 1970.

Wiseman, Bernard. *The Hat that Grew;* il. by author. Hale, 1967.

Hippos

Brown, Marcia. *How, Hippo!;* il. by author. Scribner, 1972.

Duvoisin, Roger. *Veronica;* il. by author. Knopf, 1961.

Marshall, James. *George and Martha;* il. by author. Houghton, 1972.

———— *George and Martha Rise and Shine;* il. by author. Houghton, 1976.

Holidays

Adams, Adrienne. *A Woggle of Witches;* il. by author. Scribner, 1971. (Halloween)

Bolognese, Don. *A New Day;* il. by author. Delacorte, 1970. (Christmas)

Briggs, Raymond. *Father Christmas;* il. by author. Hamilton, 1973. (At-home use)

Dalgliesh, Alice. *The Thanksgiving Story;* il. by Helen Sewell. Scribner, 1954.

Serrailler, Ian. *Suppose You Met a Witch;* il. by Ed Emberley. Little, 1973. (Halloween)

Viorst, Judith. *My Mama Says There Aren't Any Zombies, Ghosts, Vampires, Creatures, Demons, Monsters, Fiends, Goblins, or Things;* il. by Kay Chorao. Atheneum, 1973. (Halloween)

Watson, Clyde. *Father Fox's Pennyrhymes;* il. by Wendy Watson. Crowell, 1971. (Thanksgiving)

Homes

Burton, Virginia Lee. *The Little House;* il. by author. Houghton, 1942.

Hogrogian, Nonny. *Handmade Secret Hiding Places;* il. by author. Overlook Pr., 1975.

Krauss, Ruth. *A Very Special House;* il. by Maurice Sendak. Harper, 1953.

Lionni, Leo. *The Biggest House in the World;* il. by author. Pantheon, 1968.

Horses

Anderson, Clarence W. *Billy and Blaze;* il. by author. Macmillan, 1962.

Dennis, Wesley. *Flip;* il. by author. Viking, 1941.

Jeffers, Susan. *All the Pretty Horses;* il. by author. Macmillan, 1974.

Rabinowitz, Sandy. *The Red Horse and the Blue Bird;* il. by author. Harper, 1975.

The Squire's Bride; originally collected and told by Peter C. Asbjørnsen; il. by Marcia Sewall. Atheneum, 1975.

Hunting

Burch, Robert. *The Hunting Trip;* il. by Susanne Suba. Scribner, 1971.

Jeffers, Susan. *Three Jovial Huntsmen;* ed. and il. by author. Bradbury, 1973.

Langstaff, John. *Oh, A-Hunting We Will Go;* il. by Nancy Winslow Parker. Atheneum, 1974.

Imagination

Geisel, Theodor Seuss. *And to Think that I Saw It on Mulberry Street,* by Dr. Seuss (pseud.); il. by author. Vanguard, 1937.

Hazen, Barbara Shook. *The Gorilla Did It;* il. by Ray Cruz. Atheneum, 1974.

Himler, Ronald. *The Girl on the Yellow Giraffe;* il. by author. Harper, 1976.

Kent, Jack. *There's No Such Thing as a Dragon;* il. by author. Golden Pr., 1975.

Leisk, David Johnson. *Harold and the Purple Crayon;* by Crockett Johnson (pseud.); il. by author. Harper, 1958.

Lightfoot, Gordon. *The Pony Man;* lyrics by G. Lightfoot; il. by Etienne Delessert. Harper's Magazine Pr., 1972.

McPhail, David. *The Bear's Toothache;* il. by author. Little, 1972.

Mahy, Margaret. *The Boy Who Was Followed Home;* il. by Steven Kellogg. Watts, 1975.

Rees, Ennis. *Potato Talk;* il. by Stanley Mack. Pantheon, 1969.

Riley, James Whitcomb. *The Gobble-uns'll Git You Ef You Don't Watch Out!* il. by Joel Schick. Lippincott, 1975.

Russ, Lavina. *Alec's Sand Castle;* il. by James Stevenson. Harper, 1972.

Sendak, Maurice. *Where the Wild Things Are;* il. by author. Harper, 1963.

Wahl, Jan. *Grandmother Told Me;* il. by Mercer Mayer. Little, 1972.

Zemach, Harve. *The Judge; An Untrue Tale;* il. by Margot Zemach. Farrar, 1969.

Imitation

Aruego, José. *Look What I Can Do;* il. by author. Scribner, 1971.

Suba, Susanne. *The Monkeys and the Pedlar;* il. by author. Viking, 1970.

Indoor Gardening

Barrett, Judith. *Old MacDonald Had an Apartment House;* il. by Ron Barrett. Atheneum, 1969.

Graham, Margaret B. *Plant Sitter;* il. by Gene Zion. Harper, 1969.

Maestro, Giulio. *The Remarkable Plant in Apartment 4;* il. by author. Bradbury, 1973.

Language

Gross, Ruth Belov. *What Is That Alligator Saying?;* il. by John Hawkinson. Hastings, 1972.

Rand, Ann. *Sparkle and Spin: A Book about Words;* il. by Paul Rand. Harcourt, 1957.

Steptoe, John. *My Special Best Words;* il. by author. Viking, 1974. Make sure to review this before you use it.

Williams, Barbara. *Albert's Toothache;* il. by Kay Chorao. Dutton, 1974.

Wilson, Gahan. *The Bang Bang Family;* il. by author. Scribner, 1974.

Lions

Daugherty, James H. *Andy and the Lion;* il. by author. Viking, 1938.

Du Bois, William Pène. *Lion;* il. by author. Viking, 1956.

Fatio, Louise. *The Happy Lion;* il. by Roger Duvoisin. Whittlesey House, 1954.

Mahy, Margaret. *A Lion in the Meadow;* il. by Jenny Williams. Watts, 1969.

Me

Adoff, Arnold. *Big Sister Tells Me that I'm Black;* il. by Lorenzo Lynch. Holt, 1976.

———— *Black Is Brown Is Tan;* il. by Emily McCully. Harper, 1973.

Charlip, Remy, and Moore, Lillian. *Hooray for Me!* il. by Vera B. Williams. Parents, 1975.

Hoban, Tana. *Where Is It?* il. by author. Macmillan, 1974.

Kellogg, Steven. *Much Bigger than Martin;* il. by author. Dial, 1976.

Mice

Freeman, Don. *Norman the Doorman;* il. by author. Viking, 1959.

Holl, Adelaide. *Moon Mouse;* il. by Cyndy Szekeres. Random, 1969.

Monsters

Crowe, Robert L. *Clyde Monster;* il. by Kay Chorao. Dutton, 1976.

Flora, James. *The Great Green Turkey Creek Monster;* il. by author. Atheneum, 1976.

Mosel, Arlene. *The Funny Little Woman;* il. by Blair Lent. Dutton, 1972.

Sendak, Maurice. *Where the Wild Things Are;* il. by author. Harper, 1963.

Native Americans

Bierhorst, John. *The Ring in the Prairie: A Shawnee Legend;* il. by Leo and Diane Dillon. Dial, 1970.

Clark, Ann Nolan. *In My Mother's House;* il. by Velino Herrara. Viking, 1941.

Clymer, Theodore. *Four Corners of the Sky:*

The New Sibling

Alexander, Martha, *Nobody Asked Me if I Wanted a Baby Sister;* il. by author. Dial, 1971.

Burningham, John. *The Baby.* Crowell, 1975.

Greenfield, Eloise. *She Came Bringing Me That Little Baby Girl;* il. by John Steptoe. Lippincott, 1974.

Viorst, Judith. *Alexander and the Terrible, Horrible, No Good, Very Bad Day;* il. by Ray Cruz. Atheneum, 1972.

Kraus, Robert. *Whose Mouse Are You?;* il. by José Aruego. Macmillan, 1970.

Lionni, Leo. *Frederick;* il. by author. Pantheon, 1967.

Ungerer, Tomi. *The Beast of Monsieur Racine;* il. by author. Farrar, 1971.

Viorst, Judith. *My Mama Says, There Aren't Any Zombies, Ghosts, Vampires, Creatures, Demons, Monsters, Fiends, Goblins, or Things;* il. by Kay Chorao. Atheneum, 1973.

Zemach, Harve. *The Judge;* il. by Margot Zemach. Farrar, 1969.

Poems, Chants, and Oratory; il. by Marc Brown. Little, 1975.

McDermott, Gerald. *Arrow to the Sun;* adapted and il. by author. Viking, 1974.

Perrine, Mary. *Salt Boy;* il. by Leonard Weisgard. Houghton, 1968.

Holland, Viki. *We Are Having a Baby;* photos. by author. Scribner, 1972.

Keats, Ezra Jack. *Peter's Chair;* il. by author. Harper, 1967.

Manushkin, Fran. *Baby;* il. by Ronald Himler. Harper, 1972.

Ness, Evaline. *Yeck Eck;* il. by author. Dutton, 1974.

Scott, Ann Herbert. *On Mother's Lap;* il. by Glo Coalson. McGraw-Hill, 1972.

Steptoe, John. *Stevie;* il. by author. Harper, 1969.

On My Own

Freeman, Don. *Beady Bear;* il. by author. Viking, 1954.

Iwasaki, Chihiro. *Staying Home Alone on a Rainy Day;* il. by author. McGraw, 1969.

Lexau, Joan. *Benjie on His Own;* il. by Don Bolognese. Dial, 1970.

Pigs

Brooke, Leonard Leslie. *The Three Little Pigs;* il. by author. Warne, 1905.

Jewell, Nancy. *Cheer Up, Pig!;* il. by Ben Shecter. Harper, 1975.

Oxenbury, Helen. *Pig Tale;* il. by author. Morrow, 1973.

Peet, William B. *Chester the Worldly Pig;* il. by author. Houghton, 1965.

Rayner, Mary. *Mr. and Mrs. Pig's Evening Out;* il. by author. Atheneum, 1976.

Ungerer, Tomi. *The Mellops Go Flying;* il. by author. Atheneum, 1957.

Princes and Princesses

Lobel, Arnold. *Prince Bertram the Bad;* il. by author. Harper, 1963.

Thurber, James. *Many Moons;* il. by Louis Slobodkin. Harcourt, 1943.

Rain

Foster, Joanna. *Pete's Puddle;* il. by Beatrice Darwin. Harcourt, 1969.

Garelick, May. *Where Does the Butterfly Go When It Rains;* il. by Leonard Weisgard. W. R. Scott, 1961.

Howell, Ruth. *Splash and Flow.* Atheneum, 1973.

Shulevitz, Uri. *Rain Rain Rivers;* il. by author. Farrar, 1969.

Yashima, Taro (pseud.). *Umbrella;* il. by author. Viking, 1958.

The Sea

Ardizzone, Edward. *Little Tim and the Brave Sea Captain;* il. by author. Walck, 1955.

Goudey, Alice E. *Houses from the Sea;* il. by Adrienne Adams. Scribner, 1959.

Lionni, Leo. *Swimmy;* il. by author. Pantheon, 1963.

Mendoza, George. *The Alphabet Boat: A Seagoing Alphabet Book;* il. by Lawrence Di Fiori. American Heritage, 1972.

Snow

Keats, Ezra Jack. *The Snowy Day;* il. by author. Viking, 1962.

Knotts, Howard. *The Winter Cat;* il. by author. Harper, 1972.

Welber, Robert. *The Winter Picnic;* il. by Deborah Ray. Pantheon, 1970.

Zolotow, Charlotte. *Hold My Hand;* il. by Thomas di Grazia. Harper, 1972.

Spanish and English

Clifton, Lucille. *The Boy Who Didn't Believe in Spring;* il. by Brinton Turkle. Dutton, 1973. *El niño que no creía en la primavera;* tr. by Alma Flor Ada. Dutton, 1976.

Du Bois, William Pène, and Po, Lee. *The Hare and the Tortoise and the Tortoise and the Hare (La liebre y la tortuga y la tortuga y la liebre);* il. by William Pène Du Bois. Doubleday, 1972.

Kouzel, Daisy. *The Cuckoo's Reward;* il. by Earl Thollander. *El premio del cuco;* tr. by Daisy Kouzel. Doubleday, 1977.

Ness, Evaline. *Do You Have the Time, Lydia?;* il. by author. Dutton, 1971. *¿Tienes tiempo, Lidia?;* tr. by Alma Flor Ada. Dutton, 1976.

Frasconi, Antonio. *The Snow and the Sun (La nieve y el sol);* il. by author. Harcourt, 1961.

Godoy-Alcayaga, Lucilla. *The Elephant and His Secret,* by Gabriela Mistral (pseud.); tr. by Doris Dana; il. by Antonio Frasconi. Atheneum, 1974.

Strange Animals

Barrett, Judith. *Animals Should Definitely Not Wear Clothing;* il. by Ron Barrett. Atheneum, 1970.

Gág, Wanda. *The Funny Thing;* il. by author. Coward, 1929.

Lear, Edward. *The Scroobious Pip;* completed by Ogden Nash; il. by Nancy Ekholm Burkert. Harper, 1968.

Lionni, Leo. *Inch by Inch;* il. by author. I. Obolensky, 1960.

Ungerer, Tomi. *The Beast of Monsieur Racine;* il. by author. Farrar, 1971.

Visual Games

Agostinelli, Maria. *I Know Something You Don't Know;* il. by author. Watts, 1970.

Emberley, Ed. *The Wizard of Op;* il. by author. Little, 1975. Optical illusions.

Hirsh, Marilyn. *Where Is Yonkela?;* il. by author. Crown, 1969.

Hoban, Tana. *Look Again!;* il. with photos. by author. Macmillan, 1971.

Hutchins, Pat. *Changes, Changes;* il. by author. Macmillan, 1970.

Livermore, Elaine. *Find the Cat;* il. by author. Houghton, 1973.

Shaw, Charles G. *It Looked Like Spilt Milk;* il. by author. Harper, 1947.

Ungerer, Tomi. *Snail, Where Are You?;* il. by author. Harper, 1962.

War

Cowley, Joy. *The Duck in the Gun;* il. by Edward Sorel. Doubleday, 1969.

Emberley, Barbara. *Drummer Hoff;* il. by Ed Emberley. Prentice-Hall, 1967.

Friesel, Uwe. *Tim, the Peacemaker;* il. by Jozef Wilkon. Scroll Pr., 1971.

Fitzhugh, Louise, and Scoppettone, Sandra. *Bang, Bang, You're Dead;* il. by Louise Fitzhugh. Harper, 1969. Make sure you review this before you use it.

Wiesner, William. *Tops;* il. by author. Viking, 1969.

Women

Brown, Margaret Wise. *The Steamroller: A Fantasy;* il. by Evaline Ness. Walker, 1974.

Lawrence, Jacob. *Harriet and the Promised Land;* il. by author. Windmill, 1968.

Parrish, Peggy. *Granny and the Desperadoes;* il. by Steven Kellogg. Macmillan, 1970.

Stamm, Claus. *Three Strong Women: A Tale from Japan;* il. by Kazue Mizumura. Viking, 1962.

Zemach, Harve. *Duffy and the Devil: A Cornish Tale;* il. by Margot Zemach. Farrar, 1973.

The Youngest in the Family

Arkin, Alan. *Tony's Hard Work Day;* il. by James Stevenson. Harper, 1972.

Byars, Betsy. *Go and Hush the Baby;* il. by Emily McCully. Viking, 1971.

Kellogg, Steven. *Much Bigger than Martin;* il. by author. Dial, 1976.

Scott, Ann Herbert. *Sam;* il. by Symeon Shimin. McGraw-Hill, 1967.

Zolotow, Charlotte. *Do You Know What I'll Do?;* il. by Garth Williams. Harper, 1958.

Books to Bring Home

Goffstein, M. B. *A Little Schubert;* il. by author; record by Peter Schaaf. Harper, 1972. (Includes a recording)

Goodall, John S. *Jacko;* il. by author. Macmillan (London), 1971.

Potter, Beatrix. *The Tale of Peter Rabbit;* il. by author. Warne, 1903.

Sendak, Maurice. *Nutshell Library;* il. by author. Harper, 1962.

Zacharias, Thomas. *But Where Is the Green Parrot?;* il. by author and Wanda Zacharias. Delacorte, 1968.

Books for Children One to Three

Brooks, Leonard Leslie. *Johnny Crow's Garden;* il. by author. Warne, 1903.

Brown, Margaret Wise. *Goodnight Moon;* il. by Clement Hurd. Harper, 1947.

———— *The Runaway Bunny;* il. by Clement Hurd. Harper, 1942.

Hutchins, Pat. *Rosie's Walk;* il. by author. Macmillan, 1968.

Kunhardt, Dorothy. *Pat the Bunny;* il. by author. Simon and Schuster, 1940.

Memling, Carl. *Hi, All You Rabbits;* il. by Myra McGee. Parents, 1970.

Petersham, Maud and Miska. *The Box with Red Wheels;* il. by authors. Macmillan, 1949.

Provenson, Alice and Martin. *Our Animal Friends at Maple Hill Farm;* il. by the authors. Random, 1974.

Seignobosc, Françoise. *Jeanne-Marie Counts Her Sheep,* by Françoise (pseud.); il. by author. Scribner, 1951.

Spier, Peter. *Gobble, Growl, Grunt;* il. by author. Doubleday, 1971.

Thomson, Ross. *A Noisy Book,* by Ross (pseud.); il. by author. Scroll Pr., 1972.

Stories

Along with picture books you will enjoy presenting simple stories without books. Freed from using the actual book, you can concentrate on telling the story with expression and will be able to occasionally use your hands and even your body to help convey the message.

Start with the old familiar tales such as "The Old Woman and Her Pig" or "The Three Wishes." As the children learn to listen you can attempt slightly longer and less well-known stories such as *Oté* (Pantheon, 1969), a Puerto Rican folktale retold by Pura Belpré in which a devil is outwitted by a family shouting "Tam ni pu—tam ni be."

Authored stories such as the short and amusing "Cheese, Peas and Chocolate Pudding" in *It's Time for Storyhour,* edited by E. H. Sechrist and Janette Woolsey (Macrae Smith, 1964) will be understood by the younger children. It can also be exciting to tell rather than show a picture book. Try Wanda Gág's *Millions of Cats* (Coward, 1928) as a picture book one time, but as a story the next time.

The following is a story that my Grandpa used to tell when I was a child. I've found variants in several collections, but of course I like the way my Grandpa told it best. Make sure that you imitate the sounds made by all the animals. Add as many animals to the house as you wish for as long as you have the children's attention. This is an old Yiddish story, so don't have a pig move into the house. That wouldn't be authentic.

HOW TO MAKE A SMALL HOUSE INTO A LARGE ONE

There was once a man and a woman who lived in a small one-room cottage. It was very tiny. A table, some chairs, a bed, and a stove were the only furniture. It was really crowded, even for the old couple. One day the man received a letter from his daughter. She and her husband and their baby wished to come and live with their parents. The man was outraged. How could two more people and a baby possibly fit into their small house? The old woman suggested that her husband visit the Rabbi, the wisest man in town, and ask his advice.

The man explained his problem to the Rabbi. "Of course you must write immediately and tell your daughter's family to come. Your house may not be as small as you think." In no time at all the daughter, her husband and the baby arrived. Now the house was very crowded. The baby woke up every morning at six o'clock and cried,

"Wah, wah, wah."

The man returned to the Rabbi and asked his help.

"Ah, ha. I see you do have a problem. Indeed, I'm sure that I can help. Do you own a cow?"

Yes, of course, the man owned a cow. Her name was Yasha.

"Go home. Bring Yasha the cow into the house to live with you."

The man was astonished, but no one argued wih the Rabbi. He went home and put Yasha the cow into the house. The baby cried "Wah wah," the cow mooed "Moo, moo," and indeed it was very cramped in the house. Yasha kept swishing her tail back and forth into the man's face. The baby crawled between the cow's legs.

The man returned once more to the Rabbi and pleaded for his help. This time the Rabbi ordered the man to let his rooster, the five hens and the twelve baby chicks live in the house with the man and his family. What a ruckus this caused.

The baby cried "Wah, wah, wah."

The cow mooed, "Moo, moo, moo."

The rooster woke up at 4 every morning: "Cock-a-doodle-doo."

"Cluck, cluck," screamed the hens.

"Wah, wah, wah," cried the baby.

"Moo, moo, moo," lowed the cow.

The hens had no place to lay their eggs. One lay an egg right on top of the man's head. The chicks darted in and out of the woman's path. "Here, chick, chick, chick" called the woman.

The man, in desperation, called on the Rabbi again. The Rabbi stroked his long white beard and suggested that still more animals be brought to live in the house.

Now the house was cramped and noisy.

Wah, wah, wah.

Moo, moo, moo.

Cock-a-doodle-doo.

Cluck, cluck.

Here chick, chick.

And now the sheep baaed "Baa, baa."

The ducks quacked "Quack, quack."

The geese honked "Honk, honk."

The horse neighed "Neigh, neigh."

There was no place for anyone to sleep, work, play or eat.

The man trudged back to the Rabbi's house haggard with lack of sleep. All the animals he owned were now living in the house with him and his wife, their daughter, her husband and their baby.

"Help us, Rabbi. Our house is bursting and the noise is unbearable."

Moo, moo.

Quack, quack.

Cock-a-doodle-doo.

Baa, baa.

Neigh, neigh.

Honk, honk.

Cluck, cluck.

Here chick, chick, chick.

Wah, wah, wah.

"Go home," said the Rabbi, "and take the animals out of the house. Take the cow, the sheep, the ducks, the horse, the geese, the rooster, the hens and chicks all out of the house." The man was relieved. He went home and took all the animals out of the house. It seemed so large without the animals. With only four people and one small baby, the house felt empty. The only noise was the baby making a satisfying crying sound.

So, if you want to make a small house into a big house, just buy a few animals.

Multimedia Storytelling

It is well known that small children have a short attention span. This doesn't mean that they can't sit and listen to stories for 20 minutes to a half hour. It means that the book activities during that time should be varied. Try letting the children participate in the storytelling between the more formal presentations of stories and poetry. If you are interested in trying any of the multimedia ideas suggested in other parts of this book you will find a most receptive audience in preschool and primary children. They will be delighted with the use of boards: felt, magnetic, or hook 'n' loop. Attaching and removing the objects will create a new center of attention, and they may even want to help you. The overhead projector and the slide projector will be particularly useful if you'd like to show and tell stories to larger groups. And don't forget puppetry with its many possibilities.

Finger Plays and Action Rhymes

Finger plays should be repeated several times so that the children can copy your actions. There is no need to stop and explain each action. Those children who couldn't follow you the first or second time will catch on at a later recitation. Although these rhymes do help with reading readiness through finger coordination, they also give the children a chance to stretch a bit between stories. Primarily, they are meant to be fun. This short collection of finger plays and action rhymes are all traditional rhymes. You may know them, but not remember them. In any case, it will take only a minute or so for you to learn or relearn one or two for your preschool and primary story sessions.

THE ANT HILL

Here's the ant hill, with no ants about; (Make a fist)
And I say, "Little ants, won't you please come out?" (Look at fist)
Out they come trooping in answer to my call, (Lift each finger from fist
One, two, three, four, five and that's all.   and have the ants crawl
    about)

THE FROGS

Five little froggies sitting on a well (Cup hands)
One peeped in and down he fell (Raise one finger)
Froggies jumped high (Raise hands and wave
Froggies jumped low   above head)
Froggies jumped everywhere to and fro. (Lower hands to the floor)
   Continue rhyme: Four little froggies, etc. (Wave arms in all
    directions)

TOUCH YOUR NOSE

(suit action to words)

Touch your nose
Touch your chin
That's the way this game begins.
Touch your eyes
Touch your knees
Now pretend you're going to sneeze.
Touch your hair,
Touch one ear,
Touch your two red lips right here.
Touch your elbows
Where they bend.
That's the way this touch game ends.

FINGER PLAY

(suit action to words)

Draw a *little* circle in the air, in the air,
Draw a little circle in the air.
Draw with all your might
Keep it up all night.
Draw a little circle in the air.

Draw a *bigger* circle in the air, in the air,
Draw a bigger circle in the air.
Going 'round in the breeze,
Keep it going, if you please!
Draw a bigger circle in the air.

Draw a *great* big circle in the air, in the air,
Draw a great big circle in the air.
Draw it higher, draw it lower,
Draw it slower, slower, slower . . . .
And now there's no more circle in the air!

THE TURTLE

Vachel Lindsay

There once was a turtle   (Make a fist and open it
He lived in a box   to allow the turtle to
He swam in a puddle   climb out)
He climbed on the rocks.

He snapped at a mosquito,
He snapped at a flea,
He snapped at a minnow,
He snapped at me.

He caught the mosquito   (Snap your fingers)
He caught the flea
He caught the minnow
But he didn't catch me.

—Reprinted with permission of Macmillan Publishing Co., Inc.
from *Collected Poems* of Vachel Lindsay. Copyright 1920 by Macmillan
Publishing Co., Inc., renewed 1948 by Elizabeth C. Lindsay.

Figure 37. Performing "A Bunny" finger play

A BUNNY

I'm a little bunny	(Make a first)
With nose so funny.	(Wiggle thumb)
This is my home in the ground.	(Opposite hand on hip)
When a noise I hear	(Put two fingers of fist up)
I perk up my ears	(Put fist into "hole" of
And jump into the ground.	arm)

THE DUCKS

Five little ducks went out to play	(Ducks are fingers of right
Over the hills and far away	hand. The head is the
Mother duck said "Quack, quack, quack"	hill they go over; the left
But only four little ducks came back.	hand makes the mother
	duck's bill.)

Repeat rhyme with four little ducks until the mother duck is all alone. She quacks loudly and all five ducks come back.

THE LADY

Here are lady's knives and forks	(Intertwine your fingers, palms up)
Here is lady's table	(Turn hands over to make table)
Here is lady's looking glass	(Make a triangle)
Here is baby's cradle	(Clasp hands and rock)

JAPANESE RHYME

Hana, hana, hana, kuchi	(Nose, nose, nose, mouth)
Kuchi, Kuchi, Kuchi, Mimi	(Mouth, mouth, mouth, ear)
Mimi, mimi, mimi, me	(Ear, ear, ear, eye)

THE ELEPHANT

An elephant goes like this and that.	(Stamp feet)
He's terrible big,	(Raise arms)
And he's terrible fat.	(Spread arms)
He has no fingers,	(Wiggle fingers)
He has no toes,	(Touch toes)
But goodness, gracious, what a nose!	(Draw hands out indi-
	cating long curly trunk)

THE MOUSE

There is such a little tiny mouse   (Show how small he is with
Living safely in my house   thumb and forefinger
Out at night he'll quietly creep   —walk fingers across table)
When everyone is fast asleep   (Fold hands next to head)
But always by the light of day   (Open arms wide to show sun)
He'll quietly, quietly creep away.   (Walk fingers across table)

GRANDMA AND GRANDPA

(suit actions to words)

Here are Grandma's glasses   Here are Grandpa's glasses
Here is Grandma's hat   Here is Grandpa's hat
Grandma claps her hands like this   This is the way he folds his arms
And folds them in her lap.   And takes a little nap.

TEN LITTLE GYPSIES

(your fingers are the gypsies)

Ten little gypsies stand up straight   (Raise both hands, fingers rigid)
Ten little gypsies make a gate   (Fingers of both hands interlaced)
Ten little gypsies make a ring   (Make a circle with thumbs and forefingers)
Ten little gypsies bow to the queen   (Fold fingers of both hands forward)
Ten little gypsies dance all day   (Bend wrists, wiggle fingers downward)
Ten little gypsies run away   (Both hands behind back)

LION HUNT

(Storyteller stands in front; children follow with voice and actions)

Everyone get ready
We're going on a lion hunt
Ready?
Ready!
Get set, go

I see
I see
I see a road
Let's walk down the road   (Tap hands on thighs)
Tramp, tramp, tramp

I see
I see
I see a field
Let's walk through the field   (Make wide swinging
Swish, swish, swish   motions with arms)

I see
I see
I see a swamp
Let's walk through the muck   (Lift legs up high)
Squish, squish, squish

I see
I see
I see a tree
Let's climb up it   (Climbing hand over
Climb, climb, climb   hand)

I see
I see
I see a bridge   (Running motion)
Let's run over the bridge   (Click tongue to roof of
Tap, tap, tap   mouth)

I see
I see
I see a cave
Let's go into the cave   (Drag feet slowly)
Slowly, slowly, slowly

I see
I see
I see . . . . . a lion   (Make running motions
                      in place)

(Repeat all actions in reverse quickly, then say, "WOW, WE MADE IT!")

Bibliography: More Finger Plays

Carlson, Bernice Wells. *Listen! and Help Tell the Story;* il. by Burmah Burris. Abingdon, 1965. Action stories and rhymes for the youngest.

Croft, Doreen J. and Hess, Robert D. *An Activities Handbook for Teachers of Young Children.* Houghton, 1972. Ideas for art, music, cooking, and language art activities.

Glazer, Tom. *Eye Winker, Tom Tinker, Chin Chopper;* il. by Ron Himler. Doubleday, 1973. Fifty musical finger plays.

Leighton, Audrey Olson. *Grandma Moon's Fingerplays;* il. by author. Audrey O. Leighton, 911 Tenth St. S.W., Lake Oswego, OR 97034. An excellent collection, some traditional, some more recent.

Matterson, Elizabeth. *Games for the Very Young: A Treasury of Nursery Songs and Finger Plays;* il. by author. McGraw-Hill, 1969.

Montgomerie, Norah, comp. *This Little Pig Went to Market;* il. by Margery Gill.

Watts, 1966. 150 rhymes arranged by category, from hand clapping to tickling.

Poulsson, Emilie. *Finger Plays for Nursery and Kindergarten;* music by Cornelia C. Roeske; il. by L. J. Bridgman. Dover, 1971 (paper). First published in 1893 by Lothrop.

Scott, Louise Binder and Thompson, J. J. *Rhymes for Fingers and Flannelboards;* il. by Jean Flowers. Webster, 1960.

Yamaguchi, Marianne. *Finger Plays;* il. by author. Holt, 1970.

Fold-and-Cut Stories

Paper and scissors will provide the tools for still another way of presenting stories or reciting nursery rhymes. This is the paper-cutting idea that Hans Christian Andersen used somewhat more ambitiously while he told stories. Try colored origami paper which is thin and easy to cut; as you become more adept, construction paper can be used. The rhymes are very short and should be repeated several times, the children joining the leader. During the second and third recitation fold and cut the shape. Until you have done this several times, prefold the paper and draw the appropriate outline on the fold so that you need not think, only cut, while you are reciting. The grand finale is when you open up your cutout to reveal a shape or object relevant to the rhyme. All the children will want to have a shape, so choose the lucky one carefully each time.

Rain on the green grass
And on the tree.
Rain on the house-top
But not on me.
 Why not?
Because I have an umbrella.

Mary, Mary, quite contrary,
How does your garden grow?
With silver bells and cockle shells
And pretty maids all in a row.

Make accordion folds in wide sheet of paper

Peter, Peter pumpkin eater,
Had a wife and couldn't keep her.
He put her in a pumpkin shell
And there he kept her very well.

HENRY AND MARY

Henry was a worthy king,
Mary was his queen.

He gave to her a lily
Upon a stalk of green.

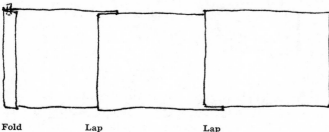    

Fold   **Lap**   **Lap**   **Roll**   **Cut**   **Pull up center**

Make a roll of paper (painted green beforehand, if you like). A rubber band around the middle will keep it rolled. If you don't want to invest in wrapping or shelf paper, use three double-spread sheets of newspaper. To facilitate the rolling, fold down a few inches along the outer edge of the first sheet (a bit of masking tape at the top of the fold will be of help later) and start rolling. Lap each succeeding sheet several inches as you proceed. Hold the roll together with a rubber band and use a heavy-duty shears, sharp knife, or single-edged razor blade to make three or four vertical cuts into the roll. Fold back the "leaves" and pull upward gently at the center of the roll to form the lily stalk. If you used a piece of tape at the top of the fold when you started, the center will be very easy to find. Of course, the more paper you use, the leafier the talk.

Hickety, pickety, my black hen,
She lays eggs for gentlemen.
Sometimes nine and sometimes ten,
Hickety, pickety, my black hen.

Fold five sheets of thin paper in fourths lengthwise and you will have ten eggs to give away.

Little Miss Muffet
Sat on a tuffet
Eating her curds and whey.
Along came a spider
And sat down beside her
And frightened Miss Muffet away.

Wee Willie Winkie runs
through the town,
Upstairs and downstairs
in his nightgown
Rapping at the windows,
crying through the lock,
"Are the children in their
beds, for now it's
eight o'clock?"

Fold and cut to make the figure "8."

Old Betty Blue
Lost a holiday shoe
What can old Betty do?
Give her another
To match the other,
And then she may swagger
in two.

Fold lengthwise.

Show single shoe then open to show the pair of shoes.

See-saw sacradown
Which is the way to
London town?
One foot up and the other down,
And that is the way to
London town.

Little Bo-Peep has lost
her sheep
And can't tell where
to find them;
Leave them alone, and
they'll come home,
And bring their tails
behind them.

Fold lengthwise.

Use triple thickness to make three sheep that will stand up.

Roses are red
Violets are blue
Sugar is sweet
And so are you

And here's a heart for you.

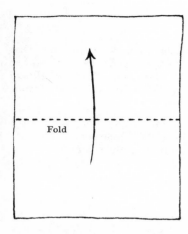

Ring around the rosie
Pocket full of posies
Ashes, ashes
We all fall down.

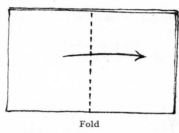

Fold

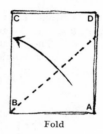

Fold

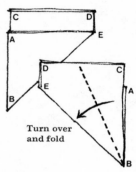

Turn over
and fold

Ring around the Rosie:

1. Fold a large sheet of paper, such as a newspaper double-spread, in half.
2. Fold in half again.
3. Fold corner A diagonally to bring folded edges AB and BC together.
4. Turn over and fold diagonally in half again, bringing edges BE and BAC together.
5. Draw figure on surface AFB and cut to make ring.
6. To make strip of dolls, recut as shown below.

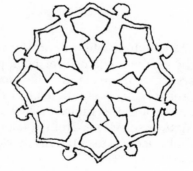

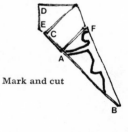

Mark and cut

Like finger plays, fold-and-cut stories and rhymes are fun for listener and leader alike and are good between tales or as a grand finale.

References: More Papercraft Ideas

Johnson, Pauline. *Creating with Paper.* Univ. of Washington Press, 1966. Clear instructions and photographs for the simple to the complex in paper constructions.

Miyawaki, Tatsuo. *Happy Origami: Whale Book;* il. by author. Japan Publications, n.d. The Japanese art of paperfolding to make a whale, a penguin, a frog and several other animals and objects. One of a series. *See also* by the same author *Happy Origami: Butterfly Book, Happy Origami: Swallow Book, Happy Origami: Tortoise Book.*

Yadama, Sadami. *Paper Playtime.* Japan Publications, 1966. Instructions for making zoo animals with paper.

20 / Programs for the Intermediate Grades

The children who attend the third through sixth grades are my choice for the perfect audience for book programs. They are the most receptive listeners, their interests are the most varied, their curiosity boundless. There is probably not a single idea in this book that would not be appreciated by a group of these children. They are ready not only to listen to longer and more mature selections from folklore and literature, but they are fascinated by multimedia presentations as well.

Storytelling for the Middle Graders

In your traditional storyhours when you will be telling stories without the help of film or other media, the selection of what to tell becomes even more important. The children are now ready for longer, more sophisticated stories and will particularly appreciate the folktales of Hans Christian Andersen, Eleanor Farjeon, and Oscar Wilde. Some of the short stories by present-day writers also might be enjoyed. Try those by Joan Aiken and Kristin Hunter for a start.

Poetry should be more frequently used in the sessions. Story poems are particularly popular as is the nonsense poetry of Shel Silverstein and the humorous collections of William Cole. If you are meeting on a regular basis with the same children, you might try using a series of myths from the folk history of a particular country. This would eliminate the necessity of over-long introductions to provide the necessary background material before each story. This age group listens with great enjoyment for a longer period of time than do preschoolers and you can schedule these pure storyhours for about 40 minutes.

In presenting a preschool story session many storytellers prefer to remain seated. In the storyhour for older boys and girls I suggest that you consider standing. It can be argued that the story program is meant to create the close family gathering feeling reminiscent of sitting around a campfire, in a log cabin, or in an Irish stone cottage. I agree that this is also a good mood to capture. It's just that I prefer to appeal to the instinctive sense of the dramatic inherent in the middle years and feel that it can be better ex-pressed by standing. Moreover, with television the resident storyteller in the majority of homes, it is preferable to be presented with "live" theater when attending a program in person. In this type of book program, when you will not be encouraging actual participation, it seems to me that by creating a theatrical atmosphere with the storyteller separated from the audience and with the lights lowered, the listener will be encouraged to "see" the scene as the storyteller narrates.

Program your session in any way that is comfortable for you. A theme is not necessary, although I find that it helps to pull a program together. The longest story should be presented first while the audience is still fresh. A transitional poem might bridge the gap to a second long story. Save the short nonsense story for the end. Some of the favorite stories in your preschool repertoire might even be used in this period of "tell one more story please." The bibliography in chapter 5 lists short, short stories suitable for ending the storyhour.

Here is one of those short stories that I collected when I was living in Europe at the time of the construction of the Berlin Wall, although it takes place just after World War II.

THE SMUGGLER

After the Second World War Berlin was divided into sectors. To pass from Western Berlin to Eastern Berlin one had to go through control gates. Guards at the gates inspected identity cards and packages to guard against smuggling goods from one area to the other.

Each day Peter arrived at "Checkpoint Charlie" riding his bicycle on the way to work. Resting on the handlebars each morning was a large muslin bag filled with sand. Every morning Eric, the American guard, stopped Peter.

"May I see your identity card, please?" he would ask. "Have you anything to declare?"

Peter always answered no, but still Eric was suspicious. Every morning he would eye the large bag of sand. And nearly every morning, but not every morning, he would dump the sand out onto a piece of burlap and run it through his fingers looking for something illegal. Eric was certain Peter was a smuggler, but he never found anything in the bag of sand no matter how carefully he searched.

For three months, five days a week, Peter crossed through "Checkpoint Charlie" on his bicycle carrying a muslin bag of sand on the handlebars.

The search became a morning ritual.

"Guten Tag, Herr Peter."

"Grüss Gott, Herr Eric."

"May I see your identity card, please."

"Certainly."

"Anything to declare?"

"No, sir."

"What's in the bag?"

"Nothing, sir, only sand."

"Sand? Empty it here and I will see for myself. Everything seems in order. You may pass. Have a good day."

"Thank you. Auf wiedersehen."

The months passed. One day Peter arrived on his bicycle carrying a large muslin bag on the handlebar. This time Eric talked to him in a low whisper. Eric was to leave that day to return to his home in the United States. He was to return to civilian life.

"Please," begged Eric, "Before I leave tell me what you have been smuggling all these months. I promise to tell no one."

"Certainly," answered Peter. "BICYCLES!"

Participation Programs

A participation program can be anything from group singing to the more complicated activity programs suggested at the end of this book. I have separated the pure storytelling program from the participation program because I think there is a danger in too much participation. It is primarily the book, the story, the word which we are trying to promote. I totally enjoy and encourage activities and crafts in conjunction with book programs. However, it is essential that they do not overwhelm the story. By differentiating between a pure storytelling session and combination storytelling and activity session you will be more fully aware of the possible domination of one over the other.

Begin your participation programs in a small way. After you have presented a story or two, explain how folklore is passed from one person to another. You might say that riddles and tongue twisters are a part of folklore. Recite a few yourself and then encourage the children to offer riddles or tongue twisters they have heard. A later session might involve a tongue twister contest. A guitar and a folksinger might be another simple participation program encouraging a sing-along atmosphere. Simple dramatizations of a folktale might constitute another story session.

The following play is adapted from a West African folktale, and is most effective when simply performed. The characters may sit on the floor or on the edge of a desk while the narrator stands. As each character speaks he should perform the same mechanical action that his character dictates.

DOWN WITH PRESIDENT STOMACH

THE CAST of ten and the exaggerated actions they perform:

Narrator: Stands and narrates action

Feet: Lifts feet up and down

Hands: Moves hands up and down and sideways mechanically

Nose: Wrinkles nose

Teeth: Opens and closes mouth, clicking teeth

Eyes: Circles eyes with hands and opens wide

Stomach: Sits up straight and pats stomach with both hands

Throat: Strokes throat

God: Speaks without moving; arms folded in front of chest

Mouth: Circles hands around mouth

Narrator: God created man with feet, hands, eyes, nose, teeth, throat, and a stomach. God made the heart the Secretary and the stomach the President. Each part of the body had a particular job to perform.

Eyes: We see.

Nose: We smell.

Teeth: We chew.

Hands: We hold, cut, and grab.

Stomach: I keep all the things that come into the body.

Narrator: Once the parts of the body began to feel jealous. They seemed to be working for Stomach and getting nothing in return.

Throat: Listen, all the food that goes through me is gone in a minute. I think Stomach ties a rope around it and pulls it down for himself. Let's elect a new president and do away with Stomach.

Teeth: You're right. We chew the food, but Stomach is the one who takes it in and enjoys it by himself. You better vote against this president or I will leave and go to live in a foreign country.

Eyes: You're in a better situation than we are. After all, at least friend Throat, the food does pass through you; all we do is get to look.

Narrator: Now Feet wished to be heard.

Feet: We are also unhappy. We only walk to the food, but never get anything to eat.

Hands: Let's go and talk to God. We will tell him that Stomach is greedy and makes a poor president.

All: Yes! Yes! Let's go.

Narrator: The body parts all agreed. A delegation was sent to God.

All (Except Stomach): We are against President Stomach.

Narrator: God asked them if they knew what they were talking about.

God: Do you know what you are talking about?

Nose: You made us. Yes, we know what we are talking about. We do not want Stomach for President. Look, he even looks like an overstuffed lady's handbag.

God: Say nothing that you will be sorry for in the future.

Narrator: God suggested that they return to their home to decide who they wanted for President. He cautioned them not to eat anything lest President Stomach keep using their work. They were happy.

Mouth: Stomach thinks he is the only one created by God. We'll show him we don't need him.

Throat: I'm glad God said we shouldn't feed him.

Narrator: God had promised to meet them in two days' time.

All (except Stomach), chanting: No! No! Down with President Stomach!

Narrator: On the morning of the third day the opposition had not eaten for two long days. Each part of the body was mighty hungry. They asked Left Eye to be President, but Left Eye said:

Eye: I cannot see very well today, I cannot be President.

Narrator: Then they asked Left Foot.

Foot: Sorry, I cannot be President. I can hardly stand up today.

Teeth: I couldn't chew anything even if there was somehing to chew. I cannot be President.

Nose: I haven't smelled anything for at least a day. I cannot be President.

Hands: It is hard for me to hold, cut, or grab. I must decline any suggestion that I be President.

Narrator: They returned to God and explained that they had reconsidered. They wanted Stomach to be their leader since he could hold so much. Now they could see that Stomach had been fair dividing the food equally among them.

Hands: Lord, we want Stomach to be our leader.

Teeth: Yes, we would like him for our king.

God: Hands, cook dinner and feed it to the Stomach. He shall be your king.

Narrator: Hands made supper and the body ate it. A short time later everyone was feeling better.

Eyes: I can see again.

Feet: I can walk again.

Throat: I feel better.

Teeth: I feel better.

Nose: I can smell again.

Mouth: Let us sing to our new leader.

All (except Stomach): Long Live King Stomach! Long Live King Stomach!

Stomach: (Stomach smiles and pats his stomach).

CURTAIN

Media and the Intermediate Grades

If you have any interest at all in any of the multimedia techniques, you will find yourself anxious to present them to this responsive age group. Devote entire programs to multimedia or use sparingly in the storyhour or folklore program. Film programs, puppet shows, overhead light shows will all appeal to these children. Most board stories, with the exception of poetry presentations, are less satisfactory. Talks about magic accompanied by demonstrations, music, and dance programs will all be popular. The interest in these programs can lead to more advanced participation with the youngsters. You can devote entire series to working with slides, producing a hand-drawn or moving picture film, making and performing with puppets, learning Indian sign language or dance steps. You will be limited only by time and your own resources, not by the enthusiasm of your listeners.

Again, since there is the danger of placing the story itself in the background, you may want to separate the media from the pure storytelling programs. After you have gained experience, however, the two will fuse and you will arrive at a successful combination of media and traditional storytelling which will delight the audience and support the story.

21 / The Young Adult Program

The idea of scheduling a series of "storyhours" for the young adult may at first seem ludicrous, especially if you have been brainwashed into thinking that stories are only for little children. Do not be deterred though, for the experience might turn out to be one of your most rewarding. Before embarking on such a series, however, I suggest that you call it something else: "Folklore," "Book Program," "Library Club," or some other title. In every category of folklore and literature there is material available that will be worthwhile to present to the young adults in your school, church, or library. It is my experience that a good story, well told, should interest any age group in the same way that a good television or theater performance does.

Besides offering pure storytelling on a regular basis in the three high school libraries where I've worked, I have also offered young adult programming in a public library on a volunteer basis. As a radio announcer, one of the shows I did was a weekly storytelling series. After preparing the stories for the radio it seemed a waste to present them only once, so I offered my services to the library and told the same stories to an interested young adult group.

It will be natural for you to extend your storytelling sessions, or rather your "Studies of Folklore," to an enthusiastic introduction of other literature that might also interest your audience. A combination of storytelling and book reviewing evolves to the "Book Talk Program" where you can use your skill as a storyteller, your knowledge of books, and your enthusiasm. The "Book Talk" becomes, then, the storyhour for young adults.

Book Talk Programs

A book talk is just what the words say: a talk about books. It's really another way of giving a book report, or a book review. A book "report" may sound too much like a school assignment while a book "review" has an air of formality. There are a variety of techniques and methods you can use to structure a book talk.

Teaser

I've searched for a more academic term for what is really a short oral introduction to one book. But, although it may not sound sophisticated, a teaser is just what it is. It is an informed, brief summary of a book, a technique of storytelling. Suppose you are standing in front of the shelves in a bookstore or library and you take a book off the shelf and quickly introduce it. What you are really doing is giving an oral annotation. Later, you might want to incorporate one or several of these oral annotations into a more formal book talk. Try to get into the habit of mentally composing a teaser after you've read a new book. This way you minimize use of such uninformative comments such as "This is a wonderful book," "a darling book," or "a cute book." Since I'm addicted to buying books I take constant mental inventory at the paperback racks in airline terminals, drug stores, and bookstores, and I can't resist giving a book teaser when someone picks out a book I know. No doubt some of the people I talk to think I'm a raving maniac, and I'll admit I do oversell occasionally. One Christmas a few years ago I recommended so many books to people standing around in an Aspen bookshop that the owner offered me a job selling. Here are a few sample teasers:

"Harriet spies on her friends and neighbors and writes everything she sees in a notebook. One day the notebook is discovered." (*Harriet, the Spy* by Louise Fitzhugh, Harper, 1964.) The diary entries in *Harriet, the Spy* are printed in bold type so it's easy to randomly open the book and read one or two short sentences from the diary. Wouldn't you be a little tempted to read a book that preaches: "Ole Golly is right. Sometimes you have to lie."?

"A mouse is born to human parents." (*Stuart Little* by E. B. White, Harper, 1945.)

"Mary Poppins appears to be quite proper and therefore unapproachable, but she can walk through pictures and float in the air." (*Mary Poppins* by P. L. Travers, Reynal & Hitchcock, 1934.)

"The true story of the survivors of a plane crash in the Andes. Rather than starve to death they ate the bodies of their dead companions." (*Alive* by Piers Paul Read, Lippincott, 1974.) This book has photographs of the crash site and the survivors. In addition to the curt, to-the-point sentences you could take the time to flip open the book and have the prospective reader take a look.

These short introductions can ignore particular titles, but concentrate on the author. A few sentences about Dick Francis's credentials for writing mystery stories ought to spark an interest:

"Dick Francis is a former jockey, sport columnist, and airline pilot. The settings of his mysteries include movie sets and horse-racing tracks. But mostly his books are about people you'd like to meet yourself."

Don't be disappointed if the reader doesn't take your suggestion immediately. Perhaps the next time they're looking for a book to read they will select the title you suggested.

Introducing One Book

Teasers are short, informal book introductions. In a more formal setting such as a classroom or a meeting of your young adult group, given a block of time, and some young adults, you can plan something more structured.

The longer you talk about a particular book, the more the audience will be interested in reading it. Naturally you will want to talk in an organized and enthusiastic fashion. Don't concentrate on the plot of a book; that can usually be summed up quickly. It is far more effective to take one incident, expand on it either by telling it as a story or by reading it aloud. You may learn the section to tell just as you would any literary tale. Be sure to prepare the passage to read aloud. Do not read a lengthy passage; a sampling will do. Try expounding on a character in the book, not necessarily a major character; sometimes a minor character will be just as intriguing.

If the book is nonfiction you may want to demonstrate something you've learned to make. For example, are you talking about a cook book? Pass out some caramels made from a recipe in the book. Describe briefly a few of the facts that can be learned from reading the book.

Introducing Several Books

Perhaps you want to introduce several books connected by a common theme at one time. You can talk about one or two books at length and then give teasers for three or four more. It becomes confusing to talk about too many books at one time. As a college teacher I am often guilty of crowding too much material into a single class session in order to cover a subject. I find, however, that the books I've discussed in depth are the ones the students remember. Be sure to clearly state the author and title of each book, or better yet, distribute a list, including short annotations, of the books you discuss. Hints on the preparation and delivery of Young Adult Programs:

Keep the program brief, 15–20 minutes.

Keep a detailed record of what you presented to whom; this is how you build a repertoire for future use.

Have copies of the books you mention available for circulation or examination.

Prepare the program well in advance.

Reread books listed in your files; they may have lost their appeal.

Putting a Book Talk Program Together

This is how I prepared and presented a book talk that I've used successfully a number of times. It may or may not work for you, but it gives you some indication of the process. I arrive at a subject in various ways. Sometimes an idea pops into my head while I'm waiting at a stoplight; sometimes I agonize for days before a subject that pleases me comes to mind. The theme not only has to appeal to me, but it has to be suitable to the group as well. Start with your audience. Who are they? What are their interests?

In this example I was asked to talk to a membership meeting of the "Friends of the Library." The purpose of the program was to create a feeling or mood about the subject and to spark a little interest in books, not necessarily in the books I was going to talk about, but just books in general. My move from a dry climate to a wet one gave me the idea of using rain as a program subject.

After I have an idea I go to the library to see if someone has published a bibliography on the subject. In addition I wander about looking at the titles on the shelves, hoping a title will remind me of a useful book or article. I ask everyone I meet questions like "Read any good rain books lately?" or more specifically, "Can you think of any books that have incidents that take place in the rain?" Once you have a few titles you'll find that more will occur to you. What is most important is that you do not limit yourself; think in terms of poetry, nonfiction, realistic fiction, fantasy, and folklore.

Now is the time to start reading. Reject any passages which you think are of inferior quality or don't fit into the broad concept of your program. List those that have possibilities. It's a good idea to get into the habit of recording bibliographic data on cards for future use. I say it's a good idea, but I personally have never managed to do it consistently.

For the rain program, I had planned originally to use slides or transparencies, so I began collecting illustrated books. The program I was planning was for young adults or adults, but most of the pictures I found were from preschool picture books, and so I decided to confine the program to printed matter.

After I had gathered a significant amount of material I found that I had several references relating to drought or waiting for rain. One was a passage from Pearl Buck's *The Good Earth*. Another was from a nonfiction book, Chester Wilmot's *The Struggle for Europe* (Greenwood, 1975), in which General Eisenhower is faced with a decision to hold up the D-Day invasion because of stormy weather. Another nonfiction quote seemed to be a possibility for an opening. It came from Archie Binns's *The Sea in the Forest* (Doubleday, 1953): "Visitors who have experienced the wet season at its wettest have given the Puget Sound region the reputation of being one of the rainiest places in the civilized world." In the end I rejected these passages as interesting but unnecessary.

I read several folktales that I thought would be appropriate. One was a Chinese story that begins, "It rains and rains in Kiang Sing, and then it rains some more." Another was the Polish story, "The Jolly Tailor Who Became King," in which a hole in the sky causes constant rainfall over one town.

The story I finally chose for inclusion in the program was one that related better to the Northwest—a Paul Bunyan story that takes place in Oregon. My final program was something like the following:

RAIN

Introduction: Lights turned off and a tape of a train traveling through a rain storm, borrowed from a local radio station. The lights go on, the tape is turned off.

In a deep "radio" voice: "This is the latest official weather forecast for the KUGN country. Partly cloudy with showers or thunderstorms today and tonight. Increasing shower activity on Saturday. Chance of rain 80 percent today and

70 percent on Saturday, 80 percent chance on Sunday. The five-day forecast calls for rainfall to average more than normal through next Wednesday."

In a conversational manner: "When I first came to the Northwest I was a little depressed by the rain until I read Ray Bradbury's 'All Summer in a Day.' Apparently it rains even more on Venus."

Read: "All Summer in a Day" from *Medicine for Melancholy* by Ray Bradbury Doubleday, 1959). This story takes nearly 20 minutes to read aloud in its entirety. It concerns a group of children on Venus who have never seen the sun. At last, after seven years the sun is scheduled to appear for a few hours. The children tease one little girl who has boasted of having seen the sun when she lived on earth. The children lock her in a closet, but forget about her until after it has begun to rain again. The story is thought-provoking and exciting, but it leaves the reader and listeners with a churning sensation in the stomach. It would seem as though a bit of fun is called for, but too abrupt a change is unfair to the material. An appropriate poem makes a good transition, but a long pause is essential between story and poem.

"Even here on earth rain is sometimes bothersome to children."

Recite: Then I recited a short poem written by a 10-year-old boy from Richard Lewis's *The Wind and the Rain* (Simon and Schuster, 1968), which begins
"What a terrible day.
Too wet to play,
Bored stiff,
Nothing to do. . . ."

Listen to or tell: Now the audience is ready for something funny. To provide it, I took the cut "Noah and the Ark" from a Bill Cosby album, *Bill Cosby Is Very Funny, Right?* (Music Corporation of America). Since I'm not very fond of group listening to a record I chose to try to capture the spirit of the record myself. Of course, no one can really equal Bill Cosby's performance. This part of the record only takes a few minutes to hear. Cosby imagines what Noah must have been going through, with jeering neighbors and actually collecting all the animals and fitting them into a home-built ark. Noah complains to the Lord about all the work: "You let me go out and bring in a pregnant elephant, no manual for delivery or nothing, never told me the thing was pregnant. There's old Noah waiting under the thing." When it begins to rain, Noah abruptly stops complaining and the segment ends, "O.K. It's me and you, Lord, right?"

Tell a story: The last segment of the program was a story. This is easy to learn and shouldn't be read, but told:

"When the Rain Came Up from China" from *Tall Timber Tales* by Dell J. McCormick (Caxton, 1939). In this story Paul Bunyan tries to prepare for the Northwest rains in a logging camp in Oregon, but is astonished to discover that the rain comes not from the sky, but from the ground up.

The program took about half an hour. The Bradbury story is much longer than most read-aloud passages should be, but it's such a good story it should hold the interest of any young adult or adult group. I also planned some extras:

Exhibit: An open umbrella with the books listed on the bibliography arranged underneath it.

Favors: Chinese paper umbrellas available at import shops. A favor of course is optional, but it added just the right touch to this program.

Bibliography: The bibliography was intended to simply remind the audience that there are books available in the library. It is an advertisement rather than a reading list. It therefore deliberately had no bibliographic information on it at all. The bibliography for my rain program was mimeographed on sheets of different colored paper. It was a 3"x3" booklet. The cover was a cartoon of Snoopy "borrowed" from a French edition of Charles Schulz's comic strip. Snoopy is standing in the rain hoping to be adopted by a rich lady. I reprinted the text in French so that the audience would be forced to really study the booklet. (Bibliographic information was added for your convenience in this instance, however.)

PAGE 1: Cover with cartoon

PAGE 2: The tried and true childhood rhyme:
  Rain, rain go away,
  Come again another day,
  Little Johnny wants to play.

PAGE 3: POEMS FOR CHILDREN
  "Waiting at the Window," A. A. Milne
  "Spring Rain," Marchette Chute
  "Rain Sizes," John Ciardi
  "Rain in Summer," Henry Wadsworth Longfellow
  "Autumn Rain," Eleanor Farjeon
  "Winter Rain," Christina Rossetti

PAGE 4: POEMS FOR ADULTS
  "April Rain Song," Langston Hughes
  "Conversation With Rain," L. D. Gunn
  "Summer Rain," Sir Herbert Read
  "Spring and All," William Carlos Williams
  "Oregon Winter," Jeanne McGabey

PAGE 5: BOOKS FOR CHILDREN
Staying Home Alone on a Rainy Day, Chihiro Iwasaki (McGraw-Hill, 1969)
And It Rained, Ellen Raskin (Atheneum, 1969)
Rain Makes Applesauce, Julian Scheer (Holiday, 1964)
Rain Rain Rivers, Uri Shulevitz (Farrar, 1969)

PAGE 6: BOOKS FOR ADULTS
Sometimes a Great Notion, Ken Kesey (Bantam, 1971), paper
Henderson the Rain King, Saul Bellow (Viking, 1965), paper
Return of the Native, Thomas Hardy (Norton, 1969), paper
The Cay, Theodore Taylor (Doubleday, 1969)

PAGE 7: STORIES
"The Herd Boy and the Weaving Maiden" in *The Chinese Fairy Book,* Richard Wilhelm; tr. by Frederick Martens (Frederick Stokes, 1921).
"All Summer in a Day," Ray Bradbury
"When the Rain Came up from China," Dell McCormick
"Rain," Somerset Maugham
"Noah's Ark," Genesis

PAGE 8: SONGS
"Rain in Spain"
"April Showers"
"Singin' in the Rain"

FILMS
Rainshower, Churchill Films
The Umbrellas of Cherbourg (Parc-Madeleine Films) Macmillan Films

RECORD ALBUM
"Bill Cosby Is Very Funny, Right?," MCA

PAGE 9: *Library imprint*

Activity (optional):

Rain Walk: I did not include this in the original program. Such an activity does not always fit in, it may not be practical at the time, but it just might work someday, especially if I continue to live in the Northwest.

Bundle up warmly with boots, slickers, and hats. Take a walk. As you walk, take a look around you. What has been blown down from the trees or swept down in a puddle of water? Take a plastic bag with you to collect plants, leaves, or whatever you find. When you get home, dry out your finds and use them to make a collage.

P.S. This program is more meaningful on a rainy day. Schedule it and pray for rain.

22 / *Programs for Parents and Other Adults*

Adults can appreciate storytelling just as much as children. After all, the art of storytelling was originally confined to adult listeners. I've been asked to tell stories to women's clubs, at faculty meetings, senior citizen homes, and even the local bar association. One college professor asked me to tell stories to her remedial English class. "Wear that leather miniskirt," she instructed. So, wearing my miniskirt and boots I proceeded to present stories to a class full of burly athletes. It turned out later that my appearance was an exercise in composition. The professor had announced that a librarian was going to visit the class. After my performance the class was asked to write about what sort of person they imagined was coming and the actuality. Of course, this was all a long time ago, when miniskirts (and my being able to wear one) were current and the old stereotype of the fuddy-duddy librarian was still a generally held notion. You might not always be invited for the right reasons, but I repeat, adults do enjoy a good story.

Planning Programs for Parents

Parents are a special group of adults. You can plan special programs for them, including telling stories and reading aloud. Let's think about what might be accomplished with a particular group of parents: the preschool parent. Preschool children are almost always brought to the library by an adult. This means that you may have nearly as many adults in the library as children. The time period during which you have the children is usually too short for the adults to leave the library. What will they do? Hopefully, they will be looking for books for themselves and their families. Most often, however, they sit together exchanging small talk or glancing at a magazine. Why not plan an activity for this captive audience? This may take extra staff, but not necessarily. It certainly will take extra planning, but it is well worth it. Consider making an exhibit of books for children or adults, and placing it on a small table. If you point out that these books have been particularly chosen for them, the adults will be more apt to browse through them, perhaps even take home one or two.

Now suppose that you would like to get a bit more ambitious. Maybe you will want to have a special program for adults at the same time that the storyhour for their children is being held. The story series for children may have been planned for six or eight weeks. You might want to schedule an adult program three or four times during the series. If your story programs are held in a school, you might interest the teachers or the parents' association in an adult program. Utilize the talents and interests of other library staff to give a half hour to the library. If you have a visitor, plan to accompany his or her talk with a small exhibit of related books for the parents to take out. You want to keep the programs informal, providing an opportunity for the exchange of ideas rather than a lecture. Use your imagination for program ideas. Poll the parents and find out what their concerns and interests are. Suggestions for combined use of program topic, exhibit, and bulletin board follow.

Programs for Parents and Other Adults—A Few Ideas

Simple picture-taking pointers for amateur photographers by a photographer. Ask a parent who is knowledgeable and experienced or a professional, perhaps a teacher of photography. A good follow-up at a later date would be a session on simple darkroom techniques.

EXHIBIT: Photography books, books illustrated with photographs (travel or animal books), biographies of famous photographers, photography equipment.

BULLETIN BOARD: Snapshots taken by library staff, by children, or pictures of parents when they were children.

Reading readiness activities discussed by a teacher or librarian.

EXHIBIT: Books on the teaching of reading, books by bibliophiles, ABC books and picture books with simple, easy-to-read vocabularies.

BULLETIN BOARD: Reading readiness games, such as lotto, or the alphabet spelled out in block letters.

Flower arranging by a local florist or a member of the garden club.

EXHIBIT: Flower identification books, gardening books, novels like *The*

Good Earth, Episode of Sparrows; for children, *The Plant Sitter, Rain Makes Applesauce.*

BULLETIN BOARD: Tissue-paper flowers, perhaps photographs of floral arrangements. Of course, you will want an arrangement of fresh cut flowers too.

How to choose a nursery school by a representative from Association for Childhood Education International or a professional with the early childhood training program at the university. A teacher from the local Head Start program and a teacher from a private nursery school to briefly describe the programs in their respective institutions could be an alternative or a follow-up program.

EXHIBIT: Books on Montessori, English, and American early education.

BULLETIN BOARD: Pamphlets and a listing of nursery schools in the area.

Tools and simple repairs demonstrated by a local carpenter or the high school's woodworking shop teacher to show parents the names and uses of tools in his tool box (the children might enjoy this program, too) and demonstrate proper way to use such tools as a hammer, plane, and saw.

EXHIBIT: "How to" woodworking books, popular craft manuals. For children, *The Toolbox* by Anne and Harlow Rockwell.

BULLETIN BOARD: Pictures of objects made by children or adults in the community.

Paperback exchange. Don't necessarily get carried away and plan a big sale. Each person could bring a paperback they enjoyed to exchange for another. Have a few extras on hand for those who forget.

EXHIBIT: Quality and "slick" paperbacks.

BULLETIN BOARD: List of current bestselling paperbacks. Addresses of local bookstores that sell paperback books.

Reviews of movies by local newspaper reviewer or someone on the staff who's seen everything.

EXHIBIT: Books from which movies have been made.

BULLETIN BOARD: Movie reviews from magazines and newspapers; listing of local offerings.

Toys exhibited by a local toy shop owner or manufacturer's representative to show some of the new toys on the market and especially the games that are always sealed in the shop. Particularly useful around Christmastime.

EXHIBIT: Books about antique toys, how to make toys, and a few of the toys and games to be mentioned.

BULLETIN BOARD: A list of the ten most popular toys for particular age groups and their prices.

Communicable childhood diseases and preventive medicine discussed by a pediatrician or public health officer.

EXHIBIT: Books about health, novels about doctors.

BULLETIN BOARD: Directions to nearest hospital, first aid hints.

How to plant a tree, described by a forestry expert or nurseryman. These experts can suggest when and where to plant a tree for each of the children in a family.

EXHIBIT: Books identifying trees, novels about the lumber industry.

BULLETIN BOARD: A tree with each leaf bearing the name of a child in your regular preschool storyhour.

Making ice cream by someone on the staff. Demonstrate the way to make ice cream with an electric or hand-cranked ice cream maker. Serve the ice cream to the children after the storyhour.

EXHIBIT: Dessert and ice cream cookbooks.

BULLETIN BOARD: Ice cream recipes. Pictures of ice cream desserts.

HANDOUT: Recipes for ice cream.

Creative dance demonstrated by local dance teacher or students to show parents basic movements to dance with their children.

EXHIBIT: Novels about dancers and dancing as well as books illustrating technique.

BULLETIN BOARD: List local dance schools in the area.

Music discussed and performed by a local musician or piano teacher and/or a few students. When to begin music lessons, which instrument to begin with, what records or music experiences a child should have.

EXHIBIT: Music books, musical instruments, novels about music and musicians.

BULLETIN BOARD: List music groups and teachers in the area.

Still More Ideas

Meal planning guidance by the dietician from a local institution or a home economist. Hints on nutrition, special diets, the school lunch are possible topics.

Art activities presented by a local artist or art teacher. Simple ideas for developing a child's artistic talents could be featured.

Book talks given by a librarian on the staff. Just a quick rundown on current best sellers or any book or books that might appeal to the group.

Pets by a pet shop owner or dog breeder. Hints for selecting, training, and caring for a pet.

Hair styling for children demonstrated by a local beautician. Use a model from the children's group.

Parks and recreation activities described by a representative from the parks and recreation department to tell about community offerings.

TV reviews made by one of the parents asked to critique the TV shows aired for children. Open the discussion to everyone.

Magazine evaluations prepared by the serials librarian could give a quick indication of titles available.

Books for gift giving, teasers prepared by a librarian to help parents and others select books for every member of the family. Prepare a mimeographed list to hand out.

Holiday decorations. Ask the parents of each child in the group to bring in an idea for decorating the house at Christmas or another holiday.

Birthday party ideas. Ask parents to describe decorations, refreshments, games they play at birthday parties.

Reference books for the home library. Arrange for the reference librarian to show some of the kinds of books essential in a home library.

Volunteer activities. Invite a representative from the volunteer bureau to discuss volunteer needs in the community.

Adult Storytelling

You may meet with adult groups for different reasons. Some may be interested in storytelling because they would like to learn the skill themselves. In such instances, demonstrate the art by actually telling stories with or without media. Don't concentrate too much on philosophy or background. An adult audience wants to see what storytelling is all about.

When you are asked to tell stories to a group of adults who just want to hear a good story, choose stories whose subjects will be of interest to them. For example, stories involving marriage might be appealing. Quite often a story that you originally learned for presentation to children or young adults will appeal to an adult group as well. Know your intended audience and plan your program accordingly.

Be aware that adults react much differently than children. They are so anxious to be polite and prove their attentiveness that they often seem not to react at all. Sometimes they will laugh, but rarely will they show awe, fright, or sorrow overtly. Do not be alarmed at this seeming lack of enthusiasm. Your adult listeners will remember your stories with pleasure, just as a six-year-old will; they've just learned to keep their feelings to themselves.

At the university where I teach we have held adult storytelling festivals for several years. They are always well attended by people who are interested in oral presentations. Schedule one of these at your library or school. Invite your favorite storytellers to come and perform. Just don't forget those adults who still retain the awe and wonder and contented feeling from a story well told.

23 / *Activity Programs*

Ordinarily, we think of the storytelling program as primarily a performer activity in which the audience participates only by listening. If you're considering a change in this leader-listener relationship, the activity or participation program is an alternative to the traditional storyhour. It should be used as an extension of rather than a replacement for the regularly scheduled storyhour. Book clubs, summer reading activities, and organized group meetings such as the Camp Fire Girls, or camp meetings lend themselves to these participation programs.

In this type of session the leader presents a conventional storyhour which is followed by a period during which the group responds to the stories by drawing a picture, discussing the stories, or making something related to the stories. The idea is to carry the book program beyond the stories. Each of the activities include books to exhibit and to take home and read after the program.

However, before embarking upon such a program there are many things that must be considered. Is the group small enough for all to participate? If you are planning to learn a folk dance more people can be accommodated than if you will be using special equipment such as a stove. Do you have enough scissors or paper and working space to make Japanese lanterns? Before you begin, think about the interests of the group, the facilities available, and the cost of any ambitious projects. Begin with a theme and develop the program from there. The projects which follow have all been successful in a group situation. Your own imagination together with some searching, reading, and experimenting will result in equally successful programs.

Sample Programs

BATHS

For children 8–12 yrs.

Tell as a story or read aloud from one of the following:

"The Bath" in *Mouse Tales* by Arnold Lobel and illustrated by the author (Harper, 1972). For beginning readers, this is a funny episode about a mouse who enjoys bathing.

"A Bear in Hot Water" from *A Bear Called Paddington* by Michael Bond and illustrated by Peggy Fortnum (Houghton, 1960). In this chapter Paddington puts too much water in the bathtub and has to be rescued by his human friends. "But why on earth didn't you pull the plug out?" they ask. "Oh! I never thought of that."

"The Cleanest Dog in the USA" from *Ribsy* by Beverly Cleary and illustrated by Louis Darling (Morrow, 1964). Ribsy, Henry Huggins's dog, gets a bubble bath from the five Dingley children.

"The Elephant's Bathtub" in *The Elephant's Bathtub*, edited by Frances Carpenter and illustrated by Hans Guggenheim (Doubleday, 1972). The king of Thailand wants to bathe his favorite elephant.

Harry, the Dirty Dog by Gene Zion and illustrated by Margaret Bloy Graham (Harper, 1956). Harry hides the scrub brush to avoid taking a bath in this delightful picture book.

Books to Exhibit

Put any books not used in the actual program on exhibit. Baths or bathtubs are mentioned secondarily in the following books:

De Brunhoff, Jean. *The Story of Babar;* tr. from the French by Merle Haas; il. by author. Random, 1937.

Cohen, Barbara. *The Carp in the Bathtub;* il. by Joan Halpern. Lothrop, 1972.

Duvoisin, Roger. *Veronica;* il. by author. Knopf, 1961.

Kraus, Robert. *The Tail that Wagged the Dog;* il. by author. Windmill, 1971.

McCloskey, Robert. *Lentil;* il. by author. Viking, 1940.

Viorst, Judith. *Alexander and the Terrible, Horrible, No Good, Very Bad Day;* il. by Ray Cruz. Atheneum, 1972.

Activity

Decorate soap. This activity MUST have adult supervision; hot wax can be dangerous.

Figure 38. Decorated soap

Materials needed:

Plain white soap (such as Ivory)
Glue
Paraffin
Tongs
Double boiler
Electric hot plate
Knife
Pictures

How to: Scrape the imprint off the soap with a knife. Glue an original picture —or a picture cut from a book or card—onto the soap. Melt paraffin (available in grocery store canning section or hobby shop) in a double boiler. Hold soap with tongs and dip picture side of soap into hot paraffin and remove immediately. If wax has dripped down the side of the bar, it can be neatened by scraping with a knife.

The picture on the soap will last as long as the soap is used; that is, if you can bear to use it. This activity doesn't take a lot of time after the pictures are chosen and glued on the soap. An adult MUST tend the wax pot and assist the children with the dipping.

BEADS

All ages

This program features the showing and reading of just one book. An exhibit of books featuring American Indians and crafts can be used to encourage leisure reading.

Read aloud and show the pictures in Byrd Baylor Schweitzer's *One Small Blue Bead,* illustrated by Symeon Shimin (Macmillan, 1965). Both the language and art of this book are worthwhile and absorbing. Prehistoric cave dwellers wonder if there are other people like themselves in the world beyond. After many months of exploration an old man returns with a strange boy. One small blue bead is given to the boy as a symbol of friendship. There will be many things to discuss after reading the story: curiosity, prehistory, friendship, artifacts, responsibility.

Activities

Make your own beads. Two alternative methods for making beads follow.

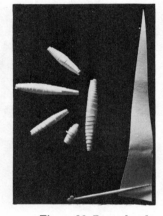

Figure 39. Paper beads

Paper beads

> Materials needed: Paper; newspaper, magazines, wrapping paper
> Liquid starch or paste
> Toothpicks
> Needle and thread
> Paint and shellac optional

> How to: Cut out triangles 6″ high with 1″ bases. The triangle can be varied to make smaller or larger, fatter or thinner beads. Spread paste on back of triangle or dip entire triangle into liquid starch, passing through the fingers to remove excess moisture. Roll triangle around toothpick starting at wide end. Let beads dry. If you are in a hurry beads can be dried in a slow (250°) oven. Remove toothpick when beads are dry and paint and/or shellac. Beads can be strung on coarse thread.

"Clay" Beads

> Materials needed: 1 cup cornstarch
> 2 cups baking soda
> 1¼ cups cold water

> How to: Heat together stirring constantly until mixture looks like moist mashed potatoes. Turn out onto a plate and cover with a damp cloth until cool enough to handle. The doughy material which results can be shaped like clay. Store in an airtight container. This recipe will make at least 100 beads. Use a toothpick to poke a hole in each bead to permit stringing. Poster paints can be used to decorate the beads after they harden. Shellac or polyurethane clear varnish should be applied to keep the beads from disintegrating.

For those who don't feel like making their own clay, an easy commercial product to work with is *Sculpty,* available at your craft supply store. It stays soft until baked.

MANY MOONS

Tell

Tell *Many Moons* by James Thurber and illustrated by Louis Slobodkin (Harcourt, 1943). In this story Princess Lenore wants the moon. The Lord High Chamberlain, the Royal Mathematician, the Royal Wizard find the task impossible. The Court Jester finally gets the moon.

Then tell "How the Hare Became" in *How the Whale Became* by Ted Hughes and illustrated by George Adamson (Faber, 1963). This short story tells why the hare can leap, run, and has long ears.

Books to Exhibit

These books may be exhibited to encourage leisure reading or you may find among them a story that is better suited to your style of telling than the two mentioned above. The list includes mostly folktales and fiction, but now that man has actually set foot on the moon, you might want to find an account of modern space travel. New developments in this area happen so fast it is difficult to recommend any one book on the subject. Use your library to help you find out about journeys to the moon since 1969. The list that follows also will give you an idea of the number of worthwhile books you can find featuring a particular theme or subject.

Brown, Margaret Wise. *Wait Till the Moon Is Full;* il. by Garth Williams. Harper, 1948. When the moon is just right a baby raccoon and his mother can enjoy the night.

Colum, Padraic, ed. "Hina, the Woman in the Moon," in *Legends of Hawaii;* il. by Don Forrer. Yale Univ. Pr., 1937. "I am going to the Moon, to a place I can rest myself."

Dayrell, Elphinstone. *Why the Sun and the Moon Live in the Sky;* il. by Blair Lent. Houghton, 1968. Adapted from an African folktale, this story explains why the sun, moon, and water came to be where they are.

Fuchs, Erich. *Journey to the Moon;* il. by author. Delacorte, 1969. Modernistic pic-tures represent Apollo 11's eight-day journey to the moon.

Gallob, Edward. *City Rocks, City Blocks and the Moon;* photos. by author. Scribner, 1973. Simple geology with photographs.

Garrison, Christian. *Flim and Flam & the Big Cheese;* il. by Diane Goode. Bradbury, 1976. Flim tricks Flam into thinking he can eat the moon, the big cheese.

Ginsburg, Mirra, reteller. *The Proud Maiden, Tungale, and the Sun: A Russian Eskimo Tale;* il. by Igor Galanin. Macmillan, 1974. The origins of the moon are told in this Slavic-Eskimo tale in which a young girl resides in the sky as the moon after marrying the sun.

Holl, Adelaide. *Moon Mouse;* il. by Cyndy

Szekeres. Random, 1969. A curious mouse sets off to see the moon and finds it, he thinks.

Jablow, Alta, and Withers, Carl. *The Man in the Moon;* il. by Peggy Wilson. Holt, 1969. Folktales about the moon.

Kondo, Herbert. *The Moon;* rev. ed.; il. with photos. Watts, 1971. A nonfiction exploration of the moon.

Levitin, Sonia. *Who Owns the Moon?;* il. by John Larrecq. Parnassus, 1973. A nonsense tale with illustrations for showing while telling.

Lewis, Claudia. *When I Go to the Moon;* il. by Leonard Weisgard. Macmillan, 1961. Rhythmic verse describes the marvels of the earth and moon.

Oakley, Graham. *The Church Mice and the Moon;* il. by author. Macmillan, 1974. The mice are captured and trained to be astronauts in a rocket project.

Preston, Edna Mitchell. *Squawk to the Moon, Little Goose;* il. by Barbara Cooney. Viking, 1974. A goose outwits a fox in a variant of "The Boy Who Cried Wolf."

Reeves, James. *How the Moon Began: A Folktale from Grimm;* il. by Edward Ar-dizzone. Abelard-Schuman, 1972. The mayor bought a moon for two pounds ten and hung it in an oak tree.

Serwer, Blanche Luria. *Let's Steal the Moon: Jewish Tales, Ancient and Modern;* il. by Trina Schart Hyman. Little, 1970. The title story concerns the efforts of the people of Chelem to capture the moon.

Sleator, William. *The Angry Moon;* il. by Blair Lent. Little, 1970. The retelling of a Tlingit legend from Alaska. Distinguished illustrations.

Turska, Krystyna. *The Magician of Cracow;* il. by author. Morrow, 1975. Spectacular pictures illustrate the story of a man who longs to visit the moon.

Udry, Janice May. *The Moon Jumpers;* il. by Maurice Sendak. Harper, 1959. Children play outside enjoying the mystery of nighttime.

Ungerer, Tomi. *Moon Man;* il. by author. Harper, 1967. The Moon Man is curious about earth and comes for a visit.

Withers, Carl. *Painting the Moon;* il. by Adrienne Adams. Dutton, 1970. The devil tries to paint the moon so that it will be dark enough to do a bit of evil.

Activity

People used to say the moon was made of green cheese. Princess Lenore's gold moon would be very expensive to make. Instead, what would the moon be like if it was made of peanut butter and honey? Yummy. This recipe for Moon Cookies requires no stove and no cooking.

Ingredients: ½ cup wheat germ   3 cups dried milk
1½ cups peanut butter   ¾ cup graham cracker crumbs
1½ cups honey   Powdered sugar

How to: Mix thoroughly. Form into balls. Roll in sugar. Makes about five dozen moons.

WITCHES

Children 7–12 years old

Tell

"Rapunzel" from *Tales from Grimm* translated and illustrated by Wanda Gág (Coward, 1936). This story has been popular for generations of children. It may be familiar to you, but is always worth repeating.

Then tell "Baba Yaga and the Little Girl With the Kind Heart" from *The Lost Half Hour*, edited by Eulalie Steinmetz Ross and illustrated by Enrico Arno (Harcourt, 1963). This story also appears in *Witches, Witches, Witches*, edited by Helen L. Hoke and illustrated by W. R. Lohse (Watts, 1966), and is the classic Russian witch story.

Books to Exhibit

These books to encourage leisure reading feature real and imaginary witches:

Carleton, Barbee Oliver. *The Witches' Bridge;* il. by author. Holt, 1967. New England witchcraft and a large black dog are involved in this mystery when a young boy sets out to put an end to a family curse.

Gregor, Arthur S. *Witchcraft and Magic: The Supernatural World of Primitive Man;* il. by Laszlo Kubinyi. Scribner, 1972. Beliefs about witchcraft and magic from Africa to Siberia are explained and justified.

Glovach, Linda. *The Little Witch's Black Magic Cookbook;* il. by author. Prentice-Hall, 1972. Bewitching recipes charmingly illustrated for young witches.

Hildick, Edmund W. *The Active-Enzyme Lemon-Freshened Junior High School Witch;* il. by Iris Schweitzer. Dell, 1974. An incorrigible 12-year-old sorceress conjures up the weird, the hilarious, and the impossible.

Hoke, Helen, ed. *Witches, Witches, Witches;* il. by W. R. Lohse. Watts, 1966. Modern and traditional stories abound in this collection of sometimes terrifying, sometimes amusing witches.

Jones, Diana Wynne. *Witch's Business.* Dutton, 1973. A group of children find themselves in competition with a real witch.

Konigsburg, E. L. *Jennifer, Hecate, Macbeth, William McKinley, and Me, Elizabeth;* il. by author. Atheneum, 1967. Jennifer, a self-confessed witch, allows Elizabeth to become her apprentice.

Lively, Penelope. *The Whispering Knights;* il. by Gareth Floyd. Dutton, 1976. Three contemporary children make a witch's brew and conjure up Morgan le Fay, the legendary sister of King Arthur.

Manning-Sanders, Ruth. *A Book of Witches;* il. by Robin Jacques. Dutton, 1966. Short traditional stories of witches, mostly evil.

Norton, Alice Mary. *Lavender-Green Magic,* by André Norton (pseud.); il. by Judith Gwyn Brown. Crowell, 1974. "A world of witches, rare herbs, and a curse."

Petry, Ann. *Tituba of Salem Village;* il. by

author. Crowell, 1964. A slave from Barbados is accused of witchcraft while serving the family of the Rev. Samuel Parris in Salem.

The Puffin Book of Magic Verse; selected by Charles Causley; il. by Barbara Swiderska. Penguin, 1974. Incantations, curses, elves, changelings, wizards, and ghosts in verse.

Serraillier, Ian. *Suppose You Met a Witch;* il. by Ed Emberley. Little, 1973. Ed Emberley gloriously illustrates a poem about what it would be like to be under a witch's spell.

Snyder, Zilpha Keatley. *The Witches of Worm;* il. by Alton Raible. Atheneum, 1976. Was Worm a witch's cat?

Speare, Elizabeth George. *The Witch of Blackbird Pond.* Houghton, 1958. Kit outrages her Puritan relatives by making friends with a suspected witch.

Starkey, Marion. *The Visionary Girls;* il. by author. Little, 1973. The nightmare of the 1692 Salem witch trials is explored in depth in a fascinating account.

Witch, Witch!; Stories and Poems of Sorcery, Spells and Hocus-Pocus; ed. by Richard Shaw; il. by Clinton Arrowood. Warne, 1975. Twenty-five stories about witches from folklore and original sources. Find a Halloween or campfire story here.

A record to listen to: Vincent Price tells *A Coven of Witch's Tales.* Caedmon T.C. 1338.

Activities

Grow your own witch's crystal garden.

Materials needed:

Porous bricks or charcoal briquettes	¼ cup salt
Food coloring	¼ cup laundry bluing
1 tablespoon of ammonia	¼ cup water

How to: Put two drops of food coloring on the brick or charcoal. Mix together remaining ingredients and slowly pour onto brick. Enough for 4–6 bricks. The garden will begin to grow into weird and wonderful shapes in a few **hours.**

Mix up a "Witch's Brew" with which to concoct a delicious potion to give to a friend or to brew for your group to sip while you tell them a story about witches.

Ingredients:

⅔ cup instant tea	2 cups sugar
14 ounces Tang (orange flavor)	2 teaspoons cinnamon
2 packages dry lemonade mix	2 teaspoons powdered cloves

Mix together and store in jars.

To brew: Add 1½ to 2 teaspoons mix to 1 cup boiling water. Be sure to give directions for brewing on the jar's label if you give some as a gift.

Figure 40. Witch's crystal garden,
step by step

FASHION

Young adults

Tell

"The Emperor's New Clothes" from *It's Perfectly True* by Hans Christian Andersen, translated by Paul Leyssac; illustrated by Vilhelm Pedersen (Macmillan, 1937). The Emperor is so vain he'll believe anything. This classic story can be found in most Andersen collections. Then go on to tell "Dinner with Halil" in *Once the Hodja* by Alice Geer Kelsey and illustrated by Frank Dobias (Longmans, 1943). The Hodja thinks that a dinner invitation was issued to his clothes rather than to him.

Introduction

Have you ever wondered why we wear clothes? An obvious reason is for insulation against rain, wind, and cold. Protection against animals, insects, brambles, and plants might be another reason. Add to these the need for modesty, and we have many of the reasons for being dressed. Clothing also serves to show others a certain social position. In order to be different, ladies and gentlemen of money and position adopt new clothing ideas. If enough people copy the new style, a fashion trend is born. Before 1900 only royalty could afford to play the game of fashion, but after the first World War, magazines, films, and "ready-to-wear" clothing brought the changes in fashion to millions of people. Today, paid designers invent new fashions for clothing manufacturers who, in cooperation with fashion magazines and textile manufacturers, promote new styles which influence current ideas about clothes.

Where do clothing designers get their ideas? The most talented use their own imaginations. The less experienced and less ingenious copy ideas from many different sources, including their competitors. Just standing on the street corner in what is considered the "fashionable part" of a large city might produce a few ideas. What are the trend setters wearing?

Costume design in film and theater can constitute a source of ideas. Current fashion magazines which concentrate on "high fashion," or the most extreme fashions can yield ideas for the trend-conscious. A look into the past will often yield ideas—what is "in" today may have been the height of fashion hundreds of years ago.

Can books be the source of fashion ideas? People wear clothes in books. Do picture-book artists for young children have active imaginations where clothing is concerned, or are they less imaginative than trained fashion experts?

Let's look at some of the children's books for possible ideas.

Activities

Fashions in children's books. Choose books from your library's collection which show contemporary clothing as well as "fairy tale" or imaginative clothing. Let the group browse through the books. If possible, the audience should be seated around tables so that they can better share the books. They may come to the conclusion that artists aren't very imaginative when it comes to clothing, or they might find that fairy-tale people seem to be more creatively dressed than characters in contemporary stories. This is one way of getting young adults to take a close look at some of our better picture books, too.

Here are three brief fashion analyses:

De Brunhoff, Jean. *The Story of Babar;* tr. from the French by Merle Haas; il. by author. Random, 1937. This book was first published in France in 1933, but it is still enjoyed today by adults as well as children. Like many children's stories, this book is about an animal, in this instance an elephant, that dresses like a person.

In the forest where he is born Babar wears no clothes but when he arrives in the city he buys "a shirt with a collar and tie, a suit of a becoming shade of green, then a handsome derby hat, and also shoes with spats"; then he has his picture taken. Although this book was written so long ago, and maybe men (or elephants) no longer wear hats, the artist gives the feel of Babar as a well-dressed gentleman. The old lady, his friend, wears a black fur-trimmed suit or long black dress throughout the book, and the reader feels she is properly attired for the gentle friend that she is. When Babar's cousins Arthur and Celeste arrive from the forest, they also arrive with no clothes and Babar buys them "some fine clothes"—for Arthur a red and white sailor suit and for Celeste a polka dot dress. The clothes seem to be ageless and clearly tell the story.

Buck, Pearl S. *The Chinese Story Teller;* il. by Regina Shekerjian. John Day, 1971. The children are wearing colorful, sim-ple summer clothes and the grandmother a classic long-sleeved dress of simple cut.

The story then shifts to a scene in pre-World War China. The crowd is wearing traditional Chinese peasant costumes: cotton coats with frog closings and pants. Cloth slippers cover their feet.

The next part of the book is a retelling of an old Chinese folktale. The people are wearing more formal classic Chinese dress. The artist has used a folk art of China: paper cutouts to dress his characters. The story ends with a return to the modern scene, but this time Grandma is drawn only in outline and her dress could almost be an old Chinese gown.

Zemach, Harve. *Duffy and the Devil: A Cornish Tale;* il. by Margot Zemach. Farrar, 1973. Margot Zemach won a Caldecott award for the illustrations in this book, mostly of people.

At the beginning of the story Duffy is described as a "lazy bufflehead" who "gallivants with the boys all day long and never stops at home to boil the porridge, nor knit the stockings, nor spin the yarn!" The artist shows this "gashly" girl with untidy braids, overweight, her stockings falling down and her weskit unbuttoned.

When the girl marries and becomes Lady Duffy Lovel of Trove, she wears "satin gowns and the best of silks and laces and red-heeled shoes from France."

Despite her new riches, Duffy is still the same girl and the artist shows her overdressed and hair still straggling from under her bonnet.

As for the artist's interpretation of Squire Lovel's clothes, well, what could be funnier than the climax of the story when the Squire's "stockings dropped from his legs and the homespun from his back. He had to come home with nothing on but his hat and his shoes."

References to Exhibit

Bocker, François. *10,000 Years of Fashion.* Abrams, 1966.

Harris, Christie, and Johnston, Moira. *Figleafing through History: The Dynamics of Dress;* il. by Moira Johnston. Atheneum, 1971.

Squire, Geoffrey. *Dress and Society: 1560–1970.* Viking, 1974.

Women's Wear Daily. (1910– , daily). The fashion industry's daily newspaper. Fairchild Publications, 7 E. 12th St., New York, NY 10003.

Up for discussion. Voice your opinions about body coverings:

a. Do you wear what you feel comfortable in or what your friends are wearing, or what your parents choose for you?

b. Who are the "trend setters" in your class? What gives them this distinction?

c. Do clothes seem to be more comfortable today than 100 years ago? What does this show about changing life styles?

d. Do clothes give a person status? Can you tell by what a person is wearing which his or her profession is?

e. Does your school have a dress code? Do you think this should be enforced? Is it useful or necessary?

f. What does the expression "white collar" or "blue collar" mean? Does the blue-collar worker have less status than a white-collar worker?

g. Do you think it is improper to wear a bikini to church on a hot day? Why or why not?

h. What is the purpose of wearing a uniform?

i. Which would you rather have: one costly pair of pants or several less expensive ones? Why?

j. Which would you rather have if you were a skier: good equipment or fashionable clothes? Why?

k. Is being one of the "Ten Best Dressed People in America" an enviable position?

l. Do hair styles, shoe styles, and skirt lengths reflect something about our society?

Fashion observation. Stand in a busy intersection or the high school campus. Take notes on what most people seem to be wearing. Summarize the fashion of that particular group. The same thing can be done with those in a room. Include hair styles in your observations. Provide each observer with his or her own fashion notebook (see Favor).

Fashion design. Provide paper and felt tip pens, crayons, charcoal, pencils, scraps of fabric, a collection of buttons, beads, trim, and glue. Individually, or as a group, solve one of the following fashion problems by drawing or making a collage:

> Design shoes for the year 2000
> Design a hat to wear to a coronation
> Design a child's outfit for Christmas morning
> Design a ballgown for Cinderella
> Design an ornament for a man or woman
> Design a fabric for a dress or tie
> Design an outfit for your first trip to Venus.

If your group has designed individually, let them give a fashion show by describing the fabric, style, price, and function of the clothes they have designed.

Newspaper Fashion Show.

Provide: A stack of newspapers
Several pairs of scissors
A roll of masking tape.

How to: Divide the larger group into groups of five. Have each group design and make some sort of body covering in 15 minutes to model before the class. Each small group should choose a fashion commentator to describe each model's costume.

Favor

Fashion notebook. Use the pages of a mail-order catalog or fashion magazine as the covers for a notebook. Staple sheets of blank paper to the cover for the fashion observers to use in taking notes on current fashions.

Note: This program should include both sexes. Some of us tend to believe that only girls are interested in clothes, yet the multibillion dollar fashion industry is dominated by men.

24 / Book Parties

If you agree that enjoying books and stories is as important as eating, you will probably understand that storytelling should not be confined to a particular time and place: between math and science, or between dinner and bed. For instance, combine your interest in books with your enjoyment of food. At the next organized party you give, you can feature books and serve book-related food. Snacktime can also be book- and food-oriented. When you plan a special storyhour or book program serve a treat appropriate to the occasion. Parents might be called upon to volunteer their time and talents for this project. My friend Johanna, a school librarian, almost always serves a book treat along with stories. Wouldn't you like to go to her school?

Placecards and Placemats

In the more formal party situation, you can begin by setting the table with a book theme. Choose a book or subject to feature. Tell a story. When the story is finished, provide the guests with paper and crayons to design their own placecards and placemats. Suggest that they illustrate the story they just heard. Less creative, but still decorative, is to make outline drawings of the book and allow the children to color them. For a more permanent book placemat, use posterboard and cover the drawing with clear contact paper or plastic. Felt cutouts can also be used to decorate colored posterboard and covered with acetate. A commercial company (Mat Maker, Roselle, NJ 07203) makes plastic placemats that actually are empty envelopes that will accommodate original art work.

Book Decorations to Look at or Eat

Make book-shaped ornaments to decorate a home, library, classroom, Christmas tree, or for that special party.

Baker's Clay Decorations

This dough is inedible, to be used for decorative purposes only. Although these "cookies" are not meant for eating, they are certainly not poisonous. My dog ate an ornament in the shape of a "Wild Thing" with great relish and was still full of energy to beg for more.

> Materials needed: 4 cups unsifted all purpose flour
> 1 cup salt
> 1½ cups water

> How to: Combine ingredients and mix thoroughly with hands. More water can be added, a little at a time, if dough is too stiff. When dough is thoroughly mixed, remove it from the bowl and knead from four to six minutes. Shape as desired. Bake on a cookie sheet in preheated 350° oven for an hour or more, depending on the size of the "cookies." Some larger pieces will take two hours, perhaps longer. Test with a toothpick for doneness. Use a spatula to remove forms to cake rack to cool.

Figure 41. Baker's clay decorations

When completely cooled, decorate with paint. Spray finished pieces with clear fixative to keep dough from breaking or softening. The cookies are attractive without paint too, but do cover them with fixative, shellac, or varnish to make them last. Decorations can be hung by piercing the dough shapes before baking.

Ethel's Book Cookies

These are edible ornaments to make in the shape of book characters.

Ingredients:
¾ cup shortening (part butter or margarine)   2½ cups flour
1 cup sugar   1 teaspoon salt
2 eggs   1 teaspoon baking powder
½ teaspoon lemon or vanilla flavoring

How to: Mix shortening, sugar, eggs, and flavoring thoroughly. Measure flour. Stir flour, baking powder, and salt together; blend in egg mixture. Chill at least one hour.

Heat oven to 400°. Roll dough ⅛" thick on lightly floured board. Cut with cookie cutters or use cardboard patterns. Place on ungreased baking sheets. Bake six to eight minutes, or until cookies are a delicate golden color. Decorate with egg yolk paint or icing. Yields about 4 dozen cookies.

Egg Yolk Paint: Blend well one egg yolk and ¼ teaspoon water. Divide mixture into cups. Add different food colorings. Paint on the cookies.

Icing: 1 cup sifted confectioners sugar
        ¼ teaspoon salt
        ½ teaspoon vanilla or other flavoring
        1½ tablespoons cream or 1 tablespoon water

How to: Blend sugar, salt, and flavoring. Add cream to make it easy to spread. If desired, tint with food coloring. Spread on cookies with spatula. This makes enough icing for 3 to 5 dozen cookies.

Commercial cookie cutters in the shape of animals or other objects appropriate to a story or book often can be found at the hardware store or housewares section of department stores. You can also make your own special cookie patterns.

How to: Draw a shape or trace an illustration, transfer it to stiff cardboard, then cut it out. Place the cardboard pattern on the cookie dough and cut around it with a sharp paring knife.

Book and Food Tie-In

Following are a few of the treats, snacks, main, and side dishes which are suggested by books. Perhaps we have a cooking-oriented campus, but we always turn our university programs into a party by preparing a little something reminiscent of the stories that are told. If this is not always a possibility for you, don't forget your own family. Serve a story-oriented treat for them.

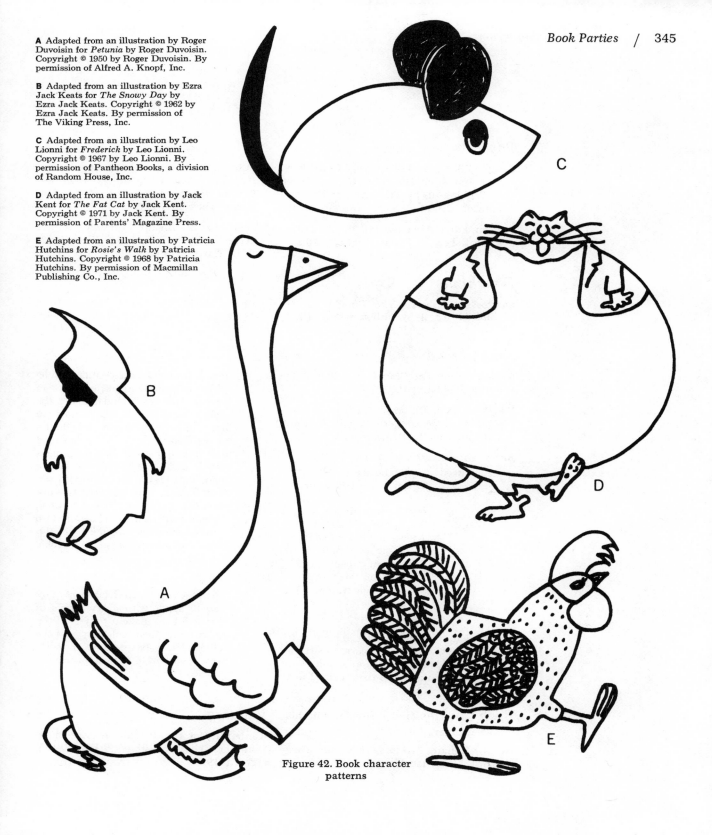

A Adapted from an illustration by Roger Duvoisin for *Petunia* by Roger Duvoisin. Copyright © 1950 by Roger Duvoisin. By permission of Alfred A. Knopf, Inc.

B Adapted from an illustration by Ezra Jack Keats for *The Snowy Day* by Ezra Jack Keats. Copyright © 1962 by Ezra Jack Keats. By permission of The Viking Press, Inc.

C Adapted from an illustration by Leo Lionni for *Frederick* by Leo Lionni. Copyright © 1967 by Leo Lionni. By permission of Pantheon Books, a division of Random House, Inc.

D Adapted from an illustration by Jack Kent for *The Fat Cat* by Jack Kent. Copyright © 1971 by Jack Kent. By permission of Parents' Magazine Press.

E Adapted from an illustration by Patricia Hutchins for *Rosie's Walk* by Patricia Hutchins. Copyright © 1968 by Patricia Hutchins. By permission of Macmillan Publishing Co., Inc.

Figure 42. Book character patterns

Popcorn

Greene, Ellin. *Princess Rosetta and the Popcorn Man* from *The Pot of Gold* by Mary E. Wilkins; il. by Trina Schart Hyman. Lothrop, 1971.

Preston, Edna. *Pop Corn and Ma Goodness;* il. by Robert A. Parker. Viking, 1969.

Sandburg, Carl. "Huckabuck Family and How They Raised Popcorn in Nebraska" in *The Sandburg Treasury;* il. by Paul Bacon. Harcourt, 1970.

Wilder, Laura Ingalls. "Happy Winter Days" in *By the Shores of Silver Lake;* il. by Garth Williams. Harper, 1953.

Doughnuts

McCloskey, Robert. "The Doughnuts" in *Homer Price;* il. by author. Viking, 1943.

Stamaty, Mark. *Who Needs Donuts?* Dial, 1973.

Gingerbread

Galdone, Paul. *The Gingerbread Boy;* il. by author. Seabury, 1975.

Van Woerkom, Dorothy. *The Queen Who Couldn't Bake Gingerbread;* il. by Paul Galdone. Knopf, 1975.

Recipe for gingerbread people

You need: ¼ cup butter
½ cup sugar (white or brown)
½ cup dark molasses
3½ cups flour, sifted
1 teaspoon baking soda
½ teaspoon cinnamon
1 teaspoon ginger
½ teaspoon salt
5 tablespoons water (about)
Raisins

How to: Cream butter and sugar together. Add the molasses. Sift the flour, baking soda, and spices together and add to the creamed mixture, a little at a time. Water may be added as mixture gets too thick to handle. Use your hands to mix the dough. Chill dough about half an hour for easier handling. Roll dough to any desired thickness on buttered baking pan and cut out two gingerbread people with patterns you've made or bought. Decorate with raisins. Bake at 350° for 8 to 10 minutes, depending on thickness. Cool. Decorate with icing. (There are also commercial gingerbread cookie mixes on the market for quicker cookie making.)

Icing:

Combine ¼ cup confectioners (powdered) sugar with a few drops of water. Stir to make a paste. A drop or two of food coloring can be added. Use a pastry tube or toothpick to decorate your gingerbread people.

Book Cookies (recipe elsewhere in this chapter)

Hoban, Lillian. *Arthur's Christmas Cookies;* il. by author. Harper, 1972.

Pudding

Kunhardt, Dorothy. *Pudding Is Nice;* il. by author. The Bookstore Press (Lenox, MA), 1975.

Jelly Beans

Hoban, Lillian. *The Sugar Snow Spring;* il. by author. Harper, 1973.

Lemon Meringue Pie

Parish, Peggy. *Amelia Bedelia;* il. by Fritz Siebel. Harper, 1963.

Stone Candy

Brown, Marcia. *Stone Soup;* il. by author. Scribner, 1947.

Steig, William. *Sylvester and the Magic Pebble;* il. by author. Windmill, 1969.

Apples and Applesauce

Hogrogian, Nonny. *Apples;* il. by author. Macmillan, 1972.

Scheer, Julian. *Rain Makes Applesauce;* il. by Marvin Bileck. Holiday, 1964.

Spaghetti

De Paola, Tomie. *Strega Nona;* il. by author. Prentice-Hall, 1975.

Joslin, Sesyle. *What Do You Say, Dear?;* il. by Maurice Sendak. Young Scott, 1958.

Rey, H. A. *Curious George Takes a Job;* il. by author. Houghton, 1947.

Raspberry Tarts

Thurber, James. *Many Moons;* il. by Louis Slobodkin. Harcourt, 1943.

Cheese and Toasted Cheese Sandwiches

Blaine, Marge. *The Terrible Thing that Happened at Our House;* il. by John C. Wallner. Parents, 1975.

Garrison, Christian. *Flim and Flam & the Big Cheese;* il. by Diane Goode. Bradbury, 1976.

Lemonade

Asch, Frank. *Good Lemonade;* il. by Marie Zimmerman. Watts, 1976.

Bread and Jam

Hoban, Russell. *Bread and Jam for Frances;* il. by Lillian Hoban. Harper, 1964.

Lord, John Vernon. *The Giant Jam Sandwich;* verses by Janet Burroway; stories and pictures by author. Houghton, 1973.

Singer, Isaac Bashevis. "The First Shlemiel" in *Zlateh the Goat;* tr. by the author and Elizabeth Shub; il. by Maurice Sendak. Harper, 1966.

Lima Beans

Viorst, Judith. *Alexander and the Terrible, Horrible, No Good, Very Bad Day;* il. by Ray Cruz. Atheneum, 1972.

Fruit Basket

Zolotow, Charlotte. *Mr. Rabbit and the Lovely Present;* il. by Maurice Sendak. Harper, 1962.

Tomato Sandwiches

Fitzhugh, Louise. *Harriet, the Spy;* il. by author. Harper, 1964.

At Teatime

Burningham, John. *Mr. Gumpy's Outing;* il. by author. Holt, 1970.

Dodgson, Charles L. "The Mad Tea Party" in *Alice's Adventures in Wonderland,* by Lewis Carroll (pseud.); il. by Arthur Rackham. Doubleday, 1907.

Travers, Pamela L. "Laughing Gas" from *Mary Poppins;* il. by Mary Shepard. Reynal and Hitchcock, 1934.

Chocolate Turtles

Blume, Judy. "Dribble" in *Tales of a Fourth Grade Nothing*; il. by Roy Doty. Dutton, 1972.

Recipe for chocolate turtles

You need: 1½ cups flour
⅟₄ teaspoon baking soda
⅟₄ teaspoon salt
½ cup butter
½ cup packed brown sugar
1 egg
1 egg yolk (reserve white)
½ teaspoon vanilla
Pecan halves

How to: Sift flour, baking soda, and salt together. Cream butter and sugar and blend into flour. Add egg and egg yolk and vanilla. Make dough into balls. Arrange pecan halves in groups of three on greased baking sheet to resemble head and legs of a turtle. Dip bottom of each ball into egg white and press into nuts. Bake at 350° for 10 to 12 minutes. Frost with chocolate frosting.

Chocolate frosting:

You need: 6 oz. package semisweet chocolate chips
Pinch of salt
½ cup sour cream
½ teaspoon vanilla

How to: Melt chocolate in double boiler. Add salt and sour cream. Add vanilla.

Rice

Towle, Faith M. *The Magic Cooking Pot; A Folktale of India*; il. by author. Houghton, 1975.

Sausage

Perrault, Charles. "The Ridiculous Wishes" in *Perrault's Fairy Tales*; tr. by Sasha Moorsom; il. by Landa Crommelynck. Doubleday, 1972.

Peanut Butter Sandwiches

Cleary, Beverly. *The Mouse and the Motorcycle*; il. by Louis Darling. Morrow, 1965.

Home Canned Fruit

Keller, Gottfried. "Hungry Hans" in *Best Book of Read Aloud Stories*; ed. by Pauline Rush Evans; il. by Adolph Le Moult and George Wilde. Doubleday, 1966.

Homemade Jelly

Newell, Hope. "How She Kept Herself Cheerful" in *The Little Old Woman Who Used Her Head and Other Stories*; il. by Margaret Ruse and Anne Merriman Peck. Nelson, 1973.

Walnuts

Babbitt, Natalie. "Nuts" in *The Devil's Storybook*; il. by author. Farrar, 1974.

Honey

Milne, A. A. *Winnie the Pooh*; il. by E. H. Shepard. Dutton, 1926.

Christmas Dinner

"The Cratchits' Christmas Dinner" excerpted in *Tell It Again; Great Tales from Around the World*; ed. by Margaret Hodges; il. by Joan Berg. Dial, 1963. Or in Dickens, Charles. *A Christmas Carol* (Harper, 1844).

Wilder, Laura Ingalls. "Christmas" in *Little House in the Big Woods;* il. by Garth Williams. Harper, 1953.

Gourmet Cooking

"The Most Magnificent Cook of All" in *It's Time For Storyhour*, ed. by Elizabeth Hough Sechrist and Janette Woolsey; il. by Elsie Jane McCorkell. Macrae Smith, 1964.

Ungerer, Tomi. *Zeralda's Ogre;* il. by author. Harper, 1967.

Pumpkin Pie

"The Pumpkin Giant" in *The Lost Half-Hour*, ed. by Eulalie Steinmetz Ross; il. by Enrico Arno. Harcourt, 1963.

Wilder, Laura Ingalls. "Wonderful Machine" in *Little House in the Big Woods;* il. by Garth Williams. Harper, 1953.

Poetry Suggests Food Too

Bananas

BANANAS AND CREAM

Bananas and cream.
Bananas and cream,
All we could say was
Bananas and cream.

We couldn't say fruit,
We wouldn't say cow,
We didn't say sugar—
We don't say it now.

Bananas and cream,
Bananas and cream,
All we could shout was
Bananas and cream.

We didn't say why,
We didn't say how;
We forgot it was fruit,
We forgot the old cow;
We never said sugar,
We only said WOW!

Bananas and cream,
Bananas and cream;
All that we want is
Bananas and cream!

We didn't say dish,
We didn't say spoon;
We said not tomorrow,
But NOW and HOW SOON.

Bananas and cream,
Bananas and cream?
We yelled for bananas
Bananas and scream!

—From *Every Time I Climb a Tree* by David McCord. Little, Brown and Co., 1967. Copyright © 1961, 1962 by David McCord. Used with permission.

Make Some Banana Spread
You need: 1 banana
1 tablespoon honey
1 teaspoon lemon juice
2 teaspoons sugar

How to: Mash banana and sugar. Add lemon juice and honey. Spread on a biscuit and enjoy.

Ice Cream

EIGHTEEN FLAVORS

Eighteen luscious, scrumptious flavors—
Chocolate, lime and cherry,
Coffee, pumpkin, fudge-banana
Caramel cream and boysenberry.
Rocky road and toasted almond,
Butterscotch, vanilla dip,
Butter brickle, apple ripple,
Coconut and mocha chip,
Brandy peach and lemon custard,
Each scoop lovely, smooth and round,
Tallest ice-cream cone in town,
Lying there (sniff) on the ground.

—"Eighteen Flavors" from *Where the Sidewalk Ends* by **Shel Silverstein**.
Copyright © 1974 by **Shel Silverstein**.
Reprinted by permission of Harper & Row, Publishers, Inc.

Strawberry Ice Cream

I LIKED GROWING

I liked growing.
That was nice.
The leaves were soft
The sun was hot.
I was warm and red and round
Then someone dropped me in a pot.

Being a strawberry isn't all pleasing.
This morning they put me in ice cream.
I'm freezing.

—"I Liked Growing" from *Any Me I Want To Be* by **Karla Kuskin**.
Copyright © 1972 by **Karla Kuskin**.
Reprinted by permission of Harper & Row, Publishers, Inc.

Make Your Own Strawberry Ice Cream
You need: 1 10-oz. pkg. of sliced
frozen strawberries
1 cup sugar
1 pint commercial sour
cream

How to: Defrost berries. Add sugar and sour cream. Stir mixture well and put in refrigerator tray to freeze. To prevent ice crystals from forming, stir at 25-minute intervals three times. Now forget it until you need it at booktime.

Peanut Butter

PEANUT BUTTER

"Peanut butter, considered as a spread . . ."
"How else could you consider it, my friend?"
"Well, by the spoonful; or, if sick in bed,
   By licking it from the index finger's end."

—From *Away and Ago: Rhymes of the Never Was and Always Is* by David McCord.
Little, 1975. Used with permission.

Make Some Peanut Butter

Shell a cup of peanuts. Remove inner skin. Grind in a blender until desired consistency. Vegetable oil, preferably peanut oil, may be added for a smoother spread.

Happy book programs and bon appetit!

25 / Creative Dramatics

The most active and in some ways the most satisfying type of participation program can be a series involving creative dramatics. In this activity the audience spontaneously acts out the stories they have heard. A creative dramatics series is not to be confused with a class in drama since it is not expected to result in a polished performance. Rather it explores the methods and emotions of self-expression.

Plan to spend at least five sessions on this activity so that both you, the leader, and the group can fully benefit from these explorations into informal drama. You will be telling stories and reciting poems as possible subjects for pantomime and improvisation, so this is also a time to enjoy literature. If you are interested in formal theater as an art form and you think your group might be too, you could plan to spend some time discussing the history and forms of drama. This might be a good time to plan a field trip to a play in your community.

Many professionals consider creative dramatics merely as an exercise in learning to think logically, understand feelings and emotions, carry out directions, and work with others. It seems to me, however, that such a series could accomplish much more. Learning to use your imagination, to express yourself in language and movement, and just learning to play creatively are worthwhile activities in themselves.

Starting at the End

Everyone has their own idea of how best to introduce children to creative dramatics. In my reading I've found that most experts would agree that the method I recommend, although it has always worked well for me, is starting backwards. My only word of caution is that this seems to work better with children, who are naturally more spontaneous and creative, than with adults who seem afraid to express themselves for fear of ridicule. It also works better if the individuals know each other. My plan of programming for creative dramatics is to skip the preliminaries and plunge directly into playmaking. When the children have fully explored the creation and acting out of a story then we go back to the beginning and more slowly experiment with the component parts of characterization and acting.

Acting Out a Story

In this first phase of contact with your group, let the group take as much responsibility as possible for the making and implementing of decisions. If the group is made up of those who have been listening to stories you can simply say "Choose one of the stories that we've heard this term and put on a play." If the group is young, or doesn't know any stories or needs more direction, begin by telling a story. Next let the children discuss

The characters in the story:

How many
Physical characteristics
Personality: kind, gentle, evil, mean
Emotional changes: e.g., the prince desires the princess, is afraid to fight the dragon, is brave, is happy to win the princess.

The settings of the story: time and place

How much time elapses
How many scene changes are there
What would each of the settings look like, e.g., the prince's home, the dragon's cave, the princess's room, the castle hall.

The action of the story: think through the story to find out what actually takes place.

Keep this preliminary discussion to a minimum at this first session. The play's the thing and you will want to get on with it. Next cast the play. In this first session I always try to let the children decide who will play which role. If this does not work, assign parts. It is true that everyone should get a chance to be a player, but not necessarily at the same session. Those who had lead parts one week can have walk-on parts the next time. Don't forget that people can play inanimate objects as well as animals or humans. After all, the stones in *Stone Soup* are leading characters. Don't feel that everyone in the group must have a part, either. The players will need stage hands and a director. Those that are not acting will become the audience, as important a role as those performing the story.

Reread or retell the story one more time to refresh the group's memory, and if they seem unsure of the order of events these may be jotted down on the chalkboard. Adult groups I've worked with always assure me that they are familiar with *Little Red Riding Hood* until they find themselves in the middle of the forest; then they can never remember what happens next.

Now let the players decide how they will put on the story. Set a time limit for preparation, and then on with the show. I don't discuss anything after the "play." Usually everyone has had a wonderful time, feeling the first triumph of self-expression and I don't want to dampen their enthusiasm with criticism, no matter how constructive.

Continue at the Beginning

The Senses

The next several sessions should involve a more serious and methodical consideration of the senses and emotions. An awareness of the way in which our five senses work helps to establish a clear basis from which to project these senses to an audience. Most of the information that we receive comes through our eyes and secondarily through our ears. The senses of touch, taste, and smell can be developed further to make a child more aware of himself and the world around him. Prepare several experiments to demonstrate the operation of the five senses. Don't try to cover too much ground in a single session.

Taste

Taste test. Bring a variety of tastables to the group. Let each child taste each individual thing and record on a piece of paper what he or she was eating. It is important that the children don't get a visual clue or even a textural clue before tasting. You'll need help to administer this test. Use the children who've already taken the test to help with the others. Put a blindfold on each child and place a dab of each of the foods in turn on each tongue. Find foods that give a variety of tastes. Here are a few that are easy to handle and usually readily available:

> Ketchup
> Butter
> Peanut butter
> Salt ⎱
> White sugar ⎰ Same consistency—opposite taste
> Brown sugar
> Canned fruit
> Toothpaste
> Honey
> Shredded coconut
> Molasses
> Syrup.

Discuss, that is try to orally describe, the taste of each food substance and others you remember. Explore as many adjectives that relate to sensations and taste as you can: sweet, sour, crunchy, slippery, bitter, mild, sticky, salty, curdled, tangy, spicy, hot.

As a group prepare and eat invisible foodstuffs: mashed potatoes, an artichoke, a carrot, an ice cream cone, a steak, spaghetti. Try it once with no observation, then a second time asking such questions as: Do you eat that with your fingers? Will you need a fork and knife? What does it taste like? Show us how it tastes. The participants often over-react to get the taste across. Point out that in actual everyday eating a mild reaction to taste is more acceptable.

Now plan a pretend menu and, as a group, enjoy an imaginary dinner party, combining silent actions with conversations reacting to the food served. Try to make your menus varied with different tastes. Make it a potluck supper. Each child brings something to the party and in pantomime tastes his or her offering and describes to the group the way the food tastes. Is feeling or touching a part of taste?

Smell

The sense of smell is the least developed of our senses, yet in many animals it is the most highly developed. Discuss with your group the need for a sense of smell in humans and animals.

Smell test. Choose a variety of smells for the group to identify. Each item should be in its own container. Empty, small plastic containers are available at the drugstore, or an egg carton with slots cut in the top will work. You may need an assistant for this activity, since you do not want to give the group any visual clues to the ingredients. These will make a good start and are readily available:

Vinegar	Spices: curry, mustard, cinnamon, and cloves
Calamine lotion	Cocoa
Talcum powder	A carnation or some other flower
Coffee	Turpentine.
Mouth wash	

Often a particular smell will bring back memories of a forgotten occasion. Discuss some of these odors: burning leaves might remind you of fall, baking bread of Thanksgiving dinner, the smell of coffee of Sunday breakfast, the smell of ether of the time you had your tonsils removed. Caramel corn might remind you of the circus.

Book publishers and advertising agencies are now experimenting with the use of smell. Small scented squares are pasted onto the printed page. Unfortunately, as yet books rely on this as gimmickery rather than art, but it does make us aware of the use of our nose. *Detective Arthur on the Scent* by May J. Fulton (Golden Pr., 1971) is an example of such a book.

Touch

Most people relate touch to hands, and yet we actually use our whole bodies to touch. The development of this tactile sense varies greatly within a group.

Touch test. Put various objects into a bag and let the children feel the objects, naming and describing each. Use a:

Flashlight battery	Marble
Paper clip	Penny
Safety pin (closed, of course)	Toy car
Lipstick case	Sandpaper
Cardboard shapes (circle, square, diamond, rectangle, hexagon).	

Fabric board. Collect different samples of fabrics and attach them to a board. Let the group feel the difference in texture and discuss the adjectives that describe each example: soft, rough, smooth, stiff, pliable, spongy, silky, rigid, patterned. Use:

Fur	Grosgrain	Lace	Wool
Velvet	Vinyl	Plastic	Polyester.
Silk	Corduroy	Satin	

Discuss the use of touch in:

Baer, Edith. *The Wonder of Hands;* photos. by Tana Hoban. Parents, 1970.

Kunhardt, Dorothy. *Pat the Bunny;* il. by author. Simon and Schuster, 1940.

Newberry, Clare Turley. *The Kitten's ABC;* il. by author. Harper, 1965.

Witte, Patricia, and Evans, Eva K. *Touch Me Book;* il. by Harlow Rockwell. Capitol, 1961.

Feel and show. Collect a number of objects. Actually run your hands over and around each one. Choose some members of your audience to do this too. What determines the feel of an object? Its texture? An object's size and shape are also important. Put the object out of sight, then examine the same object through touch in your imagination. Then have each participant describe what he or she has handled.

Sound

While I was driving with my young daughter through a rain storm, she observed that it was raining but she couldn't hear the rain. We stopped by the side of the road and I turned off the motor. Now we could hear the rain and some birds. We listened for other sounds and heard a boy shouting, a dog barking. When the car was restarted we noticed that the windshield wipers, the motor, and the radio all helped to drown out the sound of the rain. Both of us learned that the world is full of sounds that we often ignore.

Sound test. In this exercise everyone in the group shuts their eyes and listens while you make a variety of sounds. Include:

Shake beads in a bottle
Shuffle a deck of cards
Click a ball point pen
Open and close a zipper
Tear transparent or masking tape from dispenser
Cut with scissors
Shift coins from hand to hand
Wrinkle paper
Rattle seeds in a package.

Ask your listeners to guess what is making each sound and have them describe it.

Sound vs. speech. The use of gibberish in an exercise is usually considered to be of more benefit to the advanced student, but I find that beginning students enjoy and are capable of experimenting with sounds. The idea is to use sounds but not words to get a point across. These may be singing rhythms or gibberish. The rhythm and intonation of speech should tell the audience what the character is trying to get across. Try these individually:

Give an enthusiastic speech supporting a favorite cause
Speak on the telephone angrily, sweetly, or questioningly.

Select two people and ask them to use only sounds, no words to:

Have an argument
Teach a concept.

Sound observation. Have the group sit quietly on the floor. Close your eyes. Consciously listen to the sounds outside the room. Now listen to the sounds in the room. Now eliminate from your consciousness all external sounds and listen to the sounds of your own body. As I write this, if I concentrate I can hear my daughter practicing the piano and giggling upstairs, and a bird making occasional remarks outside the window. In the room where I'm working I can now hear the buzz of the fluorescent light and the drip of the sink behind me. I'll probably have to switch working areas now that I realize how noisy it is in here!

The following children's books explore sound:

Brown, Margaret Wise. *The Noisy Book.* Harper, 1939. *Country Noisy Book;* il. by Leonard Weisgard. W. R. Scott, 1940. *Indoor Noisy Book;* il. by Leonard Weisgard. Harper, 1942. *The Quiet Noisy Book;* il. by Leonard Weisgard. Harper, 1950. *The Seashore Noisy Book;* il. by Leonard Weisgard. Harper, 1941. *The Summer Noisy Book;* il. by Leonard Weisgard. Harper, 1951. *Winter Noisy Book;* il. by Charles Shaw. Harper, 1947.

Shulevitz, Uri. *Oh, What a Noise;* text adapted by Elizabeth Shub from *A Big Noise* by William Brighty Runds; il. by author (Shulevitz). Macmillan, 1971.

Spier, Peter. *Gobble, Growl, Grunt.* Doubleday, 1971.

Thomson, Ross. *A Noisy Book,* by Ross (pseud.); il. by author. Scroll Pr., 1972.

Sight

Although sight is the most developed of the senses some people "see" better than others, in an artistic sense. Try to develop the art of seeing. Looking through a pinhole can help you do this.

Imagine what you would see if you were an ant in a cornfield. What would you see? If you were a giant in the same cornfield how would you see things differently? Take a piece of cardboard. Make a tiny hole in it with a fine pin. Now walk around indoors or outdoors and look at the world through the tiny pinhole. Do you see things differently? How?

Object test

Place a number of objects on a tray:

Fork	Toy truck
Whistle	Feather
Penny	Banana
Sock	Cup
Pliers	Watch.

Pass the tray around. Let each person look at it for 30 seconds. Cover the tray. How many objects on the tray can each list? The same exercise can be conducted with a collection of photographs or pictures cut from magazines.

Observation Test

Select someone to leave the room. Have the other participants list what the absent person is wearing. Next, choose something that everyone in the group has passed so many times they no longer really see it: the statue in front of the school, the motto above the library door, or the like. Have all the participants write down its description. Read some of these to the group and discuss the need to develop the habit of observing.

These books are visual games:

Agostinelli, Maria. *I Know Something You Don't Know;* il. by author. Watts, 1970.

Carroll, Ruth. *Where's the Bunny?;* il. by author. Oxford, 1950.

Hoban, Tana. *Look Again!;* photos. by author. Macmillan, 1971.

Scheffer, Victor B. *The Seeing Eye;* photos. by author. Scribner, 1971.

Ungerer, Tomi. *Snail, Where Are You?;* il. by author. Harper, 1962.

Zacharias, Thomas. *But Where is the Green Parrot?;* il. by Wanda Zacharias. Delacorte, 1968.

These books explore color:

Carle, Eric. *I See a Song;* il. by author. Crowell, 1973.

Duvoisin, Roger. *The House of Four Seasons;* il. by author. Lothrop, 1956.

Haskins, Ilma. *Color Seems;* il. by author. Vanguard, 1973.

Lionni, Leo. *Little Blue and Little Yellow;* il. by author. McDowell, 1959.

O'Neill, Mary. *Hailstones and Halibut Bones;* il. by Leonard Weisgard. Doubleday, 1961. (16mm color film available from Sterling Educational Films, 241 E. 34th, New York, NY 10016)

Reiss, John J. *Colors;* il. by author. Bradbury Pr., 1969.

Rossetti, Christina. *What Is Pink?;* il. by José Aruego. Macmillan, 1971.

Tison, Annette, and Taylor, Talus. *The Adventures of the Three Colors;* il. by authors. World, 1971.

Wolff, Robert J. *Feeling Blue;* il. by author. Scribner, 1968. Also *Seeing Red;* il. by author. Scribner, 1968.

These books explore color and composition:

Mante, Harald. *Color Design in Photography;* tr. by E. F. Linssen; photos. by author. Van Nostrand, 1972.

———— *Photo Design: Picture Composition in Black and White Photography;* tr. by E. F. Linssen; photos. by author. Van Nostrand, 1971.

Moore, Janet Gaylord. *The Many Ways of Seeing: An Introduction to the Pleasures of Art;* il. with art reproductions. World, 1968.

Pantomine

The next exercises you should attempt with your group are pantomime. In these exercises use body movements and facial expressions without words to express actions and emotions.

Pass an object. Sit in a circle. Pass a "hot potato" or a "precious wine glass." Then pick someone to decide on an imaginary object to pass. The last person tells what it was that was being passed. Let the children enjoy themselves, but caution them to pay attention. Don't be too critical until they've had some experience.

Action pantomimes:

Fly a kite	Walk a tightrope
Catch a fish	Row a boat
Pick a delicate blossom	Play the piano
Pull a stubborn weed	Push a stalled car
Pick a flower with thorns	Lift a heavy tray
Walk a dog	Make a snowman.

Action exercises. Now stand in a semicircle with room for each child to move around. Try some of these exercises as a group, individually or with a partner.

Grow from a seed to a flower
Melt slowly like an iceberg in the sun
Wave goodbye to your best friend
Wave goodbye to someone you dislike but are polite to
A wooden soldier picks a flower
A small child picks a flower
Open an imaginary door
Take a shower
Look in a mirror (your partner mirrors your actions)
Read a sad book
Climb a ladder
Blow up a balloon
Ride a horse
Explore a cave
Play a game of tennis.

Longer pantomime exercises

Watch a sports event on television
Watch a sports event in a crowded stadium
Wait in a dentist's office with a painful tooth
Eat spaghetti at a formal dinner party
Ride a carousel
Drink a glass of liquor and walk down the street
Be a fish enjoying a frolic in the ocean
Be a snowflake falling on a flower
Be the wind blowing over a tree
Be a cat stalking a bird.

Write the following ideas on cards. Let each child pick a card and act out the activity described while the group has to guess what the performer is doing.

Open a:

Package of seeds	Umbrella	Jar of glue
Can of paint	Letter	Box of stationery.
Safe	Chinese fortune cookie	
Bottle of catsup	Sewing kit	

You are:

Happy	Tired	Excited
Sad	Cold	Sleepy.
Hungry	Hot	
Worried	Thirsty	

You are a:

Rabbit	Squirrel	Chicken
Cat	Bird	Elephant.
Tiger	Fish	
Monkey	Horse	

You are a:

Hairdresser	Dressmaker
Musician	Painter
Cook	Dancer
Librarian	Shoemaker.

Doing these exercises to music adds a dimension to pantomime. Try using a phonograph, or, if you are lucky enough to have a piano and a talented pianist to accompany you, all the better. Do the exercises both with and without music.

Animal Bag

Assemble a variety of wooden animals, or cut an assortment of animal shapes from posterboard, or use animal crackers for this activity. Place the animals in a bag or box. Each child picks an animal from the bag and acts out in pantomime the animal's movements. To add a dimension of literature to this activity, let each child search in the library for a book or poem that represents their animal.

Charades

My father worked for the United Nations, and my parents were constantly entertaining government officials from foreign countries. Occasionally after a dinner party they would play charades, and this was my first introduction to the brilliance of nonverbal theater. Divide the group into two teams. Each group separately makes a list of short phrases: enough for each player on the opposite team. Decide in advance if you will use movies, book, song or play titles, proverbs, or historical events. Write each charade on a slip of paper. Each player in turn is given a phrase his or her teammates must figure out as the charade is acted. He or she may work on the whole phrase, single words, or even syllables. The way the game was played in my home was that each person was given a chance on both teams: no winners, no losers. If you wish, however, you may time each team, the one with the lowest total time winning. The game involves everyone: guessing a team-mate's charade and acting one out.

Of course it's more fun for the members of each group to work out their own hand signals to indicate common words and phrases, but there are some obvious symbols such as:

Sounds like: pull earlobe or cup ear
Longer word: pull two hands apart
Shorter word: chop one hand against opposite palm
Small word: (and, on, a, the, to) show thumb and forefinger close together
The whole phrase: show a circle with your arms
Antonyms: hold hands together and turn hands over
Synonyms: make circle motion towards you
He: point to boy
She: point to girl
I: point to eye
Start over: motion with hands like umpire calling baseball "safe"

Improvisation

Improvisation adds speech to creative drama, but it is not scripted speech. Read a story and let the children act it out. Try not to direct the play too much, and if possible let the children choose their parts and set up the action.

Try these exercises in expressing one's thoughts orally. Give the children a chance to collect their thoughts before they begin and don't let them talk for too long. Have them describe what it feels like:

To be an ant in a department store
Not to be asked to a birthday party
To win a championship auto race
To fail the spelling test.

Next, without using their hands or body, have the children describe how to:

Make a bed
Ride a bicycle
Play pin the tail on the donkey
Jump rope
Get into a sleeping bag.

Then try more advanced problems in expressing oral thought. Have each:

Describe a member of his or her family, good points and bad
Impress someone with the need for a stoplight across from the school
Argue in front of the United Nations for funds for one's favorite cause
Confess to mother that he or she broke her favorite vase.

The following are useful as group activities:

Scene: In a department store bargain basement
Characters: A maid, her employer
Situation: The mistress is embarrassed at meeting her maid at the bargain counter. The maid, an expert at sales, teaches her mistress how to select a bargain.

Scene: Living room
Characters: Two friends
Situation: The friend has come to visit. The hostess is newly engaged, with a new ring; she wants her friend to notice the ring without actually telling her about it.

Scene: Living room
Characters: Father, Mother, children
Situation: Family conference to discuss summer vacation.

Scene: Veterinarian's office
Characters: Various people and their pets (eccentric old lady, young boy, etc.)
Situation: Each person describes his or her pet's problem to an attendant.

Scene: A meeting hall
Characters: Principal, teachers, trustees, parents, students, reporters
Situation: Choose a problem and have a meeting.

Little Red Riding Hood: Mother, grandmother, Little Red Riding Hood, wolf, hunter (bed, forest).

Audience

Impress your listeners that their role is every bit as important as the players. A performer relies totally on the response of the audience and they have an obligation to show their emotions, to laugh when it's funny, and cry when it's sad. My husband and I attended a formal dance at which there was entertainment that we particularly enjoyed. The performers were having a difficult time acting over the general social buzz in the back of the room. When they were finished they thanked "the table over there" for their attention. The table they indicated was ours. We felt like we were very special. All we had done was show our enjoyment outwardly, and the performers had reacted favorably.

Evaluation

In creative dramatics, it is traditional to learn by "talking about it." The members of the group evaluate each other. This makes for a different kind of growth: thinking about what you see; articulating your thoughts; and being constructive in your comments rather than destructive. As a leader you have a responsibility to see that comments really contribute to the group's understanding.

Prop Box and Costume Box

It is not necessary to have costumes and props. You can imagine almost any object, but it is fun to dress up. Collecting props and making scenery are sometimes more intriguing than acting. Collect old clothes for your costume box. Accessories such as hats, costume jewelry, and shoes are particularly useful. Props can be almost anything. Containers such as baskets (Little Red Riding Hood), pails (Jack and Jill) always come in handy. If you are going to act out fairy tales you'll probably enjoy a crown or two, a magic wand, and maybe a jeweled box. Household objects—brooms, dishes and silverware—are often needed. Building blocks can be made to represent almost anything if you just will them to be something. Four large boxes 3 feet by 4 feet, painted in bright colors, can be used for large pieces: a bed, table, chairs or even a mountain. Depending on the amount of time that you have to spend with creative dramatics, you might want to plan one session making props for the prop box or designing costumes, for these are creative pursuits in their own right.

Books to Use for Creative Dramatics

Almost any story will work as an activity for creative dramatics. Here are some favorites. I've chosen mostly picture books because they can be read in one sitting. Experiment with showing the pictures as you read the story and not showing them at all. Most of the stories will cover a wide age grouping, and even young adults will enjoy acting out these simple tales.

Many of the stories in the bibliographies at the end of chapter 5 and in chapter 19 will be useful in creative dramatics as well.

Aiken, Joan. *The Wolves of Willoughby Chase;* il. by Pat Marriott. Doubleday, 1963. A full-length book gives an opportunity for melodrama.

Asbjørnsen, Peter C., and Moe, Jorgen E. *The Three Billy Goats Gruff.* Harcourt, 1957. A popular traditional tale suitable for young children to act out.

Baylor, Byrd. *Everybody Needs a Rock;* il. by Peter Parnall. Scribner, 1974. How to find and cherish a friend. The Rock has a good part.

Berson, Harold. *Henry Possum;* il. by author. Crown, 1973. A little possum is saved by playing the flute and learning how to feign death.

Brown, Marcia. *Once a Mouse;* il. by author. Scribner, 1947. This story is based on a fable. The cast to dramatize this consists mostly of animals.

Burns, Marilyn. *The Book of Think (or How to Solve a Problem Twice Your Size);* il. by Martha Weston. Little, 1976. Good book to begin discussions about understanding one's self. Discusses logic, tunnel vision, and general problem-solving.

Carew, Jan. *The Third Gift;* il. by Leo and Diane Dillon. Little, 1974. This beautiful African tale might be performed best with a combination narrator and actors.

Castle, Sue. *Face Talk, Hand Talk, Body Talk;* photos. by Frances McLaughlin-Gill. Doubleday, 1977. "A gesture is worth a thousand words" clearly illustrated with black-and-white photographs.

Cunningham, Julia. *Burnish Me Bright;* il. by Don Freeman. Pantheon, 1970. A mute makes friends with a famous mime. This is a longer book, but it has excellent dramatic possibilities.

Daugherty, James. *Andy and the Lion;* il. by author. Viking, 1938. Two major characters, but lots of minor ones and plenty of action make this story a good choice for dramatics.

Domanska, Janina. *The Turnip;* il. by author. Macmillan, 1969. A "tug of war" is the most exciting part of this story.

Elkin, Benjamin. *How the Tsar Drinks Tea;* il. by Anita Lobel. Parents, 1971. A peasant and the Tsar turn out to do things the same way. The people in the Tsar's court give an opportunity for young players to act many types.

———— *The Wisest Man in the World;* il. by Anita Lobel. Parents, 1968. The Queen of Sheba and King Solomon match wits. A major character in this story is a honeybee.

Flack, Marjorie. *Angus and the Ducks;* il. by author. Doubleday, 1930. For three animal characters. Lots of action.

Geisel, Theodor Seuss. *The 500 Hats of Bartholomew Cubbins,* by Dr. Seuss (pseud.); il. by author. Vanguard, 1938. Bartholomew has a dreadful time removing his hat to honor the king.

Great Children's Stories: The Classic Volland Edition; il. by Frederick Richardson. Hubbard/Rand, 1972. Classic tales include "The Old Woman and Her Pig" and "Chicken Licken."

Grimm Brothers. *Hans in Luck;* il. by Felix Hoffmann. Oxford, 1975. Hans reaches home empty-handed after trading with animals and people.

Haviland, Virginia, comp. *The Fairy Tale Treasury;* il. by Raymond Briggs. Coward, 1972. Familiar folktales and fairy tales, mostly for preschoolers.

Langstaff, John. *Saint George and the Dragon;* il. by David Gentleman. Atheneum, 1973. A mummer's play with acting script, music, and stage directions.

Lionni, Leo. *Frederick;* il. by author. Pantheon, 1967. A mouse teaches his friends the worth of words. All the players are mice. The action of working is good exercise. Best done with a narrator.

McCloskey, Robert. *Blueberries For Sal;* il. by author. Viking, 1966. A mother bear and her cub, a human mother and her child in a good mix-up.

Merriam, Eve, reteller. *Epaminondas;* il. by Trina Schart Hyman. Follett, 1968. Epaminondas can't seem to follow directions.

Morrison, Sean. *Is That a Happy Hippopotamus?;* il. by Aliki Brandenburg. Crowell, 1966. A loose story line and an opportunity to imitate animals.

Myers, Bernice. *Not This Bear!* il. by author. Four Winds, 1968. Bears mistake a little boy for their cousin. Good action.

Raskin, Ellen. *Nothing Ever Happens on My Block;* il. by author. Atheneum, 1966. A young boy complains of boredom while fascinating events occur all around him.

Sendak, Maurice. *Where the Wild Things Are;* il. by author. Harper. 1963. Children enjoy cavorting in "the wild rumpus" as wild things.

Seuss, Dr. *see* Geisel, Theodor Seuss.

Oxenbury, Helen. *Pig Tale;* il. by author. Morrow, 1973. Two pigs learn that their life is the good life after all.

Teal, Valentine. *The Little Woman Wanted Noise;* il. by Robert Lawson. Rand, 1943. Lots of animals all create a loud rumpus. A large or small cast.

Turkle, Brinton. *Deep in the Forest;* il. by author. Dutton, 1976. One of many wordless picture books being published. Look, then act out in pantomime or with dialogue. This one is a variant of "The Three Bears."

Ungerer, Tomi. *The Beast of Monsieur Racine;* il. by author. Farrar, 1971. This story should be done in costume so that the identity of the Beast can remain hidden until the end.

Viorst, Judith. *Alexander and the Terrible, Horrible, No Good, Very Bad Day;* il. by Ray Cruz. Atheneum, 1972. Everything goes wrong in just one day.

Wildsmith, Brian. *The Rich Man and the Shoemaker;* based on a fable by La Fontaine; il. by author. Watts, 1965. This is just one of La Fontaine's fables illustrated by Wildsmith that is simple yet fun to perform.

Zemach, Harve. *Duffy and the Devil: A Cornish Tale;* il. by Margot Zemach. Farrar, 1973.

——— *A Penny A Look;* il. by Margot Zemach. Farrar, 1971. Just two of the funny books by the Zemachs that are filled with interesting characters to imitate.

Zolotow, Charlotte. *William's Doll;* il. by William Pène Du Bois. Harcourt, 1972. A little boy is ridiculed until his grandma understands.

And don't forget Grimm's fairy tales, Russian fairy tales, and such fantasy as *The Peterkin Papers* by Lucretia P. Hale (Osgood, 1880).

References

The books that follow are for children but should also give adults good ideas for creative dramatics:

Baylor, Byrd. *Sometimes I Dance Mountains;* photos. by Bill Sears; il. by Ken Longtemps. Scribner, 1973. Photographs of a young girl dancing her feelings.

Carr, Rachel. *Be a Frog, a Bird, or a Tree;* photos. by Edward Kimball, Jr.; il. by Don Hedin. Doubleday, 1973. Creative yoga exercises for children. Photographs of children in action make this an excellent guide to creative movement.

Marceau, Marcel. *The Story of Bip;* il. by author. Harper, 1976. The famous French mime writes and illustrates a fantasy featuring his best-known character. A look into the whimsical mind of an artist.

Mendoza, George. *The Marcel Marceau Alphabet Book;* il. with photos. by Milton H. Greene. Doubleday, 1970. A famous mime acts out the letters of the alphabet in black-and-white photographs.

Adult References

Elementary English, January 1974 (vol. 51) issue, is devoted to creative dramatics (now continued as *Language Arts*).

Crosscup, Richard. *Children and Dramatics.* Scribner, 1966. Mostly theory, some practical examples.

DeMille, Richard. *Put Your Mother on the Ceiling: Children's Imagination Games.* Viking, 1973. Ways to stimulate children's creativity through "imagination games."

Ehrlich, Harriet, ed. *Creative Dramatics Handbook;* il. with photos. Office of Curriculum and Instruction, The School District of Philadelphia, 1971. Distributed by NCTE, 1111 Kenyon Road, Urbana, IL 61801. #08970. An absolute must for anyone seriously and practically interested in creative dramatics.

Elkind, Samuel. *Improvisation Handbook.* Scott, Foresman, 1976. Theater games and scenes to perform.

Howard, Vernon. *The Complete Book of Children's Theater;* il. by Doug Anderson and others. Doubleday, 1969. Practical hints and ideas for adults directing children.

Priestly, John B. *The Wonderful World of the Theater.* Doubleday, 1969. A short introduction to the history of theater. Many illustrations.

Spolin, Viola. *Improvisation for the Theater; A Handbook of Teaching and Directing Techniques.* Northwestern Univ. Pr., 1963. A technical and highly sophisticated treatment of improvisation.

Index

DATE DUE

OCT 23 '79	OCT 8 '79		
NOV 10 '79 BEC 10 '79	OCT 15 '79		
BEC 10 '79	NOV 30 '79		
GAYLORD			PRINTED IN U.S.A.